# BRIDGING FEAR and PEACE:
## From Bullying to Doing Justice

by

**Gerald J. Middents**

Copyright© Gerald J. Middents, all rights reserved

**BRIDGING FEAR and PEACE: From Bullying to Doing Justice**
by Gerald J. Middents

Copyright © Gerald J. Middents, all rights reserved

Pages: x + 278

Printed at:
Manipal Press Ltd.
Manipal – 576 104, Karnataka, India
Phone : 91-820-2571151

ISBN 13: 978-0-9799680-0-6
US $16.95

# Table of Contents

|  | Page |
|---|---|
| Title Page | i |
| Table of Contents | ii |
| Foreword by Professor M. D. Nalapat | iii |
| Acknowledgements | v |
| Introduction | vii |
|     Chapter One: Fearing Freedom, Suicide, Chaos & Control | 1 |
| **Part I: Understanding Violence and War** | 24 |
|     Chapter Two: Making Enemies and Empires | 25 |
|     Chapter Three: Winning Without War | 47 |
|     Chapter Four: Whining or Boasting | 70 |
| **Part II: Managing Conflict** | 96 |
|     Chapter Five: Resisting, Sabotaging and Placating | 97 |
|     Chapter Six: Manipulating with Passive Aggression | 113 |
|     Chapter Seven: Proactively Managing Conflict | 131 |
| **Part III: Resolving Conflict** | 150 |
|     Chapter Eight: Reframing Transformation | 151 |
|     Chapter Nine: Navigating a Course | 166 |
|     Chapter Ten: Collaborating to Resolve Conflicts | 184 |
| **Part IV: Sustaining Peace by doing Justice** | 200 |
|     Chapter Eleven: Re-Marriage of Peace and Justice | 201 |
|     Chapter Twelve: The Long, Rough Road to Peace | 221 |
|     Chapter Thirteen: Challenges in Building Peace | 237 |
|     Chapter Fourteen: Shaping Tomorrow Together | 254 |
| **Epilogue:** Bridging to Future Generations | 273 |

# Foreword

Professor Gerald Middents exemplifies the "Internationalist Nationalist", the individual who- while appreciative of national traditions - has the mindset needed to seamlessly integrate into the varied cultures that together make up the Warp and Woof of human society.

Today, in place of a "Vertical" view of society, that grades different peoples in the form of a descending order of worth, the world is coming around to the saner system of a "Horizontal" view, that acknowledges the inherent equality between the different components of the human race.

Each of us needs to internalize this truth in our behaviour and attitudes, and this become part of a world where "mind barriers" do not separate human from human. Such a process would be immensely strengthened by Professor Middents' important work, which in its approach and texture, operationalizes just such a "Weltanschauung."

Why should we see Conflict as "natural" rather than Peace? Why should Hate and not Love be the emotion that evokes no surprise when witnessed? The reality is that Peace and Love are the natural states. Acceptance that this is indeed so lies at the core of Professor Middents' analysis, one which will of value to the practitioner of Peace as well as to all individuals who play a productive role in today's interdependent world. The ability to navigate seamlessly between cultures is mandatory for success in such a world, and this gift would be enhanced by the reading of this book.

The UNESCO Peace Chair at MAHE takes pride in releasing this work, the product of a mind that has, through learning as well as by experience, understood and absorbed the best in cultures, traditions and ways of life worldwide.

**M. D. Nalapat**
Professor of Geopolitics & UNESCO Peace Chair
Manipal Academy of Higher Education

# Acknowledgements

Why are fear and violence so captivating while the causes of peace and justice grab sparse attention in media headlines, publications, and global affairs? Why is war profitable while peace and justice command few resources? In a recent review [i] of psychological literature, colleagues discovered over 10,000 references to aggression and violence, but only 118 references to nonviolence, pacifism and nonaggression. This imbalance of 85 to 1 reflects human fascination with violence, and prompts my invitation for readers to join together in building bridges between fear and peace.

This book grows out of decades of teaching, public service, global traveling and international consulting. Controversial writings also influence my ideas and responses including internationally acclaimed authors from India. Amartya Sen, the 1998 Nobel prize winner in economics, sees the necessity of re-uniting economics and ethics. Arundhati Roy, the young internationally acclaimed author, penetrates into the unfortunate separation of peace and justice in both family and international affairs.

Helpful colleagues edited a seminal anthology <u>Peace</u>, <u>Conflict</u> and <u>Violence</u>: <u>Peace</u> <u>for</u> <u>the</u> <u>21</u>st <u>Century</u>[ii] along with the excellent publications by David Barash. Samuel Huntington's provocative thesis prompted serious reflection about the potential clash of civilizations. Talbott and Chanda edited a series of essays concerned with globalization published after the attacks on September 11, 2001. Alan Geyer, Charles Kupchan, Lee Harris and Benjamin Barber continue to challenge my thinking with their stimulating ideas.

Visionary organizations directly influenced this book. The United Nations Educational, Social and Cultural Organization, UNESCO, endowed a Peace Chair at Manipal Academy of Higher Education in India. This major international university composed of 53 colleges and related institutions in four countries, invited me to fill their Peace Chair in 2001. Dr. Glenn Christo, Director of Development at Manipal, encouraged publication of this book in a series for this Peace Chair. Professor M. D. Nalapat now fills this Peace Chair while serving as Director of the School of Geopolitics newly developed at Manipal University. He graciously consented to write the Foreword for this book.

For 33 years, I was privileged to teach psychology, counsel students, and direct inter-disciplinary programs on Contemporary Policy Studies at Austin College. This pioneering institution supported my global educational travels to the former Soviet Union, China, Japan, Yugoslavia, India, Nepal, Mexico, Egypt, Ghana, Sweden, Poland and Switzerland. A rare transforming experience occurred at Union Christian College affiliated with Mahatma Gandhi University in Kerala, India. Professor Thomas John invited me to teach and consult in 1998 to form the curriculum for a graduate program in Behavioral Medicine and Clinical Psychology.

The Rotary Foundation provided two University Teachers Grants for teaching in India. The foresight of the Rotary Foundation merits recognition for educational scholarships, health initiatives, plus vision to foster global understanding and peace. The new Rotary Peace Scholars program is particularly noteworthy as a bold experiment in conflict resolution supporting 350 students for graduate degrees at seven International Peace and Conflict Resolution Centers on five continents. Moreover, as a representative of Rotarians from Middle America, I expanded my global awareness during onsite visits to India and Vietnam in 2004.

The Social Science Division of the University of Texas at Dallas invited me to teach my favorite interdisciplinary courses including "Law and Psychology," "Health Care Policy," and "Violence, Conflict and Peace." This later course was completely revamped while teaching and lecturing in India in the weeks just before 9/11/01.[iii] I am grateful to colleagues at the University of Texas at Dallas, Austin College and Manipal University who provided valuable feedback: Dr. Jack Carlson, Dr. Lloyd J. Dumas, and Dr. Tom Nuckols, Professor M. D. Nalapat plus others who read drafts and listened to lectures on these topics. Moreover, I am thankful to Joellyn Quinn and Don Donnelly for invaluable editing services and advice in writing.

Non-governmental organizations gave encouragement in peace, social ethics and justice concerns. Four religious denominations provided spiritual nurture and ethical foundations for writing this book. Most prominently is the Presbyterian Church, USA in which I have served as a minister for over 40 years. This denomination encouraged me to bridge science and religion in my doctoral studies with a major fellowship. Twice my wife and I have been commissioned as Volunteers in Mission to serve in India. Additional encouragement has come through the Church of South India, plus Lutheran and *Mar Thoma* Churches.

The most personal support has come from my immediate family as steady anchors in reality for me. They courageously provide their energy and encouragement. My daughter, who is a social gerentologist, her husband and two beautiful daughters keep encouraging messages flowing. My son is a judge who daily addresses problems of domestic violence, crime, truancy and delinquency while serving as Justice of the Peace.

My wife, Carolann, has bravely traveled to India on four occasions. As an administrator in non-profit Texas League of Credit Unions, she nurtures the family while wisely keeping finances together. She is an inspiration who is ever ready to help me sharpen my ideas. I will never forget her encouraging words when I was troubled by difficult decisions about personal risks and financial feasibility as volunteers when she confidently stated: "Jerry, I think we can do it."

These persons, colleagues and organizations plus other team members contribute vital stimulation, attention, finances, hospitality, and encouragement in this creative process. I deeply appreciate how they help to advance my passion for sustainable peace and global justice.

**Gerald J. Middents**
May, 2004

## Endnotes

[i] Mayton D., et.al., (2002) "The Measurement of Nonviolence: A Review," <u>Peace and Conflict: Journal of Peace Psychology,</u> Volume 8, Number 4, 2002.

[ii] Christie D., et. al., (2001) <u>Peace, Conflict, and Violence: Peace Psychology for the 21st Century,</u> Uppers Saddle River, New Jersey: Prentice-Hall.

[iii] In India, the dates are listed by reversing the day and month as 11/9/01 rather than 9/11/01.

# Introduction

The on-going crises in violence, war and abuse compel me to address these challenges both internationally and domestically. How can we break out of the "crisis-to-crisis" cycle that happens within families and globally between nations? These patterns of domestic violence are more prevalent in many cultures than typically acknowledged. Vulnerable spouses, innocent children, fragile elderly and even the unborn are the victims of direct violence and structural oppression that perpetrate domestic abuse and neglect. International war, ethnic and media violence desensitizes people to violence and killings.

Each day, innumerable children die as victims of war, abuse, starvation and neglect. Dictators recruit children and youth as soldiers to kill enemies. Suicide bombers are motivated to sacrifice in the name of revenge, ideologies and religion. Tens of millions of females are missing in cultures that devalue their gender according to researchers documenting this evidence.[iv] In 2002, International Security[v] reported over 40,000,000 females missing in China, over 37,000,000 in India, 3,500,000 in Bangladesh and 3,300,000 in Pakistan. The figures may reach over 100,000,000 females missing worldwide.[vi]

Weapons of mass destruction (WMD) are possessed by nations and terrorists threatening the security of global humanity and the natural environment. Criminal violence makes schools unsafe for learning and education while cities and communities are ravaged by an atmosphere of violence. Media portrays violence so vividly that the puerile appetites of viewers are seductively drawn to violence in the normal course of daily living. Entertainment including films, sports, and viewing audiences are caught up in the whirlwind portraying angry rage.

Lucrative economic interests are attracted to the profits generated by violence and conflict. Besides the media industry that encircles violence like vultures, there are even more profitable industries. At an international level are the "military-industrial complex," homeland security measures, and professional experts on high tech weapons. Domestically, there are profitable businesses in the "prison industry," "the personal handgun industry," "security services industry," the legitimate and underground protective services, armored vehicles, plus legal defense attorneys. All of these in pursuit of their legitimate purposes can be carried away by exploitative measures to discover enemies and victims. Writers, film producers, researchers and even educators like myself may be drawn to this "market" because the social, legal, constitutional and psychological issues all coalesce into raging torrents of moral issues.

This book presents strategies for sustaining just peace as alternatives to violence. Unfortunately, when peace and justice are separated, aggressive people take control with coercive force. In attempting to re-unite peace and justice, this book applies to parallel dynamics of international war and domestic family violence. Both of these domains are closely related in their causes and dynamics, yet the tactics in family and international violence are obviously different in important respects. The challenging alternatives involve facing, managing, and resolving conflicts. Sustaining peace together with justice is a daunting goal in order to counter these powerful forces of aggressive control and violent war.

## Endnotes

[iv] Sen, Amartya, (2001) "Many Faces of Gender Inequality," Frontline, 9 November, 2001; Wiseman P., "China Thrown Off Balance as Boys Outnumber Girls, USA Today, June 19, 2002; "The Genocide Factor," PBS-TV, April 11, 2002.

[v] Lewis A., (June 19, 2002), "Missing Women," USA Today, reports estimates of deaths due to preferences for male children that results in abortion of female fetuses, infant neglect or killing by parents.

[vi] Kristof N., (August 16, 2002), "Bush vs. Women," The New York Times.

# Chapter One

# Fearing Freedom, Suicide, Chaos and Control

"OK – Now We'll Try It Your Way !"[1]

Inscription on the tombstone of a control freak's last words:

**The only things we have to fear is fear itself... nameless, unreasoning, unjustified terror which paralyzes needed efforts to convert retreat into advance.**[2]

President Franklin Delano Roosevelt

Contradictions are occurring in the many arenas of violence in international and domestic affairs. Freedom is openly advocated by people in democratic nations while controlling people is covertly practiced in human relations and building empires. Most civilized cultures and disciplined professions have repeatedly expressed warnings about restricting freedoms so that suicide and chaos are controlled. Nevertheless, even in this 21st century, people in power continue to restrain many freedoms for fear that other nations and people are irresponsible in exercising their choices. The director of risk communications at the Harvard Center for Risk Analysis reports that people are more afraid when they lack control.[3] Fear is greater when risks are new while the more people are aware of risks, the more afraid they are likely to be. Dreadful fears are manipulated by terrorists and opponents alike into endless spirals of domestic and global horror.[4]

When people are free to interact socially, their initial dynamics vary widely. Two strategies quickly become apparent in their psychosocial interactions. Initial conversations may be lubricated with friendly politeness fitting for civil first encounters. On the other hand, these initial impressions may be cautiously defensive due to the uncertain strangeness of new exchanges. Even abrasive hostility might also be expressed in testy, confusing confrontations.

As psychosocial interactions occur, people frequently discover areas of mutual interests that advance friendly relationships. However, incompatible values and goals can clash into stressful conflicts. When people from modern nations interact, they are usually realistic that frictions frequently occur in competitive international relations. Awareness of intercultural tensions helps people have more realistic expectations during exchanges. People who interact across cultures are also well advised to anticipate conflicts that inevitably occur between competing interests and values. If unruly friction is dreaded, careful preparation may improve possibilities for more constructive responses.

Nevertheless, as well intended as these advisories may be, there are two divergent approaches that people often make in interpersonal, domestic and international relationships. One strategy involves the dynamics of denying that there are differences. Denial frequently occurs within families and in international conflicts. The second strategy involves attempting to control the people who are involved in these unpredictable threats. Both denial and control require further analysis in order to appreciate these differences and deficiencies in coping with serious conflicts.

**Denying vs. Controlling Conflict:**

Denial has both constructive and negative features in dealing with conflict. If denial did not have constructive outcomes at times, it would not be repeated as a plausible response to stress. An illustration can clarify how denial is an effective response to powerfully stressful conflicts. When unexpected deaths occur, survivors often initially deny this tragic news. The heartbreaking report cannot be immediately accepted thereby protecting the survivors from the painful reality of the loved one's death. Unexpected deaths are denied for an unpredictable time while the tragedy is gradually assimilated into awareness. This pain may be so overwhelming that the defense of psychological denial may persist indefinitely accompanied by erratic consequences of unresolved grief.

Why is denial used as a protective defense in the face of stress? A brief psychological explanation in Figure 1-1 depicts persistent cycles of denial encountered in both domestic and international violence. Starting at the top of the figure, conflict that is painfully disagreeable threatens to encroach upon preferred perceptions of reality. Paradoxically, fear provides both distressful negative and essential positive functions about threats. On a positive side, recognizing fear and pain permits living organisms to survive because they signal dangerous threats of violence to survival.[5] Negatively, survival reactions attempt to avoid, reduce or deny painful experience. The threat to confident self-images can result in emotional discomfort and cognitive dissonance due to stark contrasts between important ideals and harsh realities.

An example combines both family abuse and international violence of soldiers trained in special combat forces.[6] Their rigorous military training to fight enemies simultaneously trains them to deny their own vulnerability for being killed and the possibly of discord in their family. In their brave self-image as competent soldiers, they are not supposed to have personal fears of death or domestic problems. However, the fact is that some soldiers abuse family members whom they cannot control. Cases of murdering their own family members and committing suicide[7] themselves dramatically illustrate problems compounded from denying personal conflicts. Soldiers are conditioned by their training to face threatening military confrontations of combat, but they may be unable to deal with their own domestic family problems. Soldiers who crave control and who feel anxious about losing control have contributed to the rate of increase of domestic violence in the past decade.[8] Denial mechanisms protect them from facing the threatening reality of their own death, but they are not protected from family conflicts considered to be unacceptable personal problems in military training. Military leaders are also reluctant to acknowledge the incidence of rape of soldiers by their comrades due to denial mechanisms that these problems exist.[9]

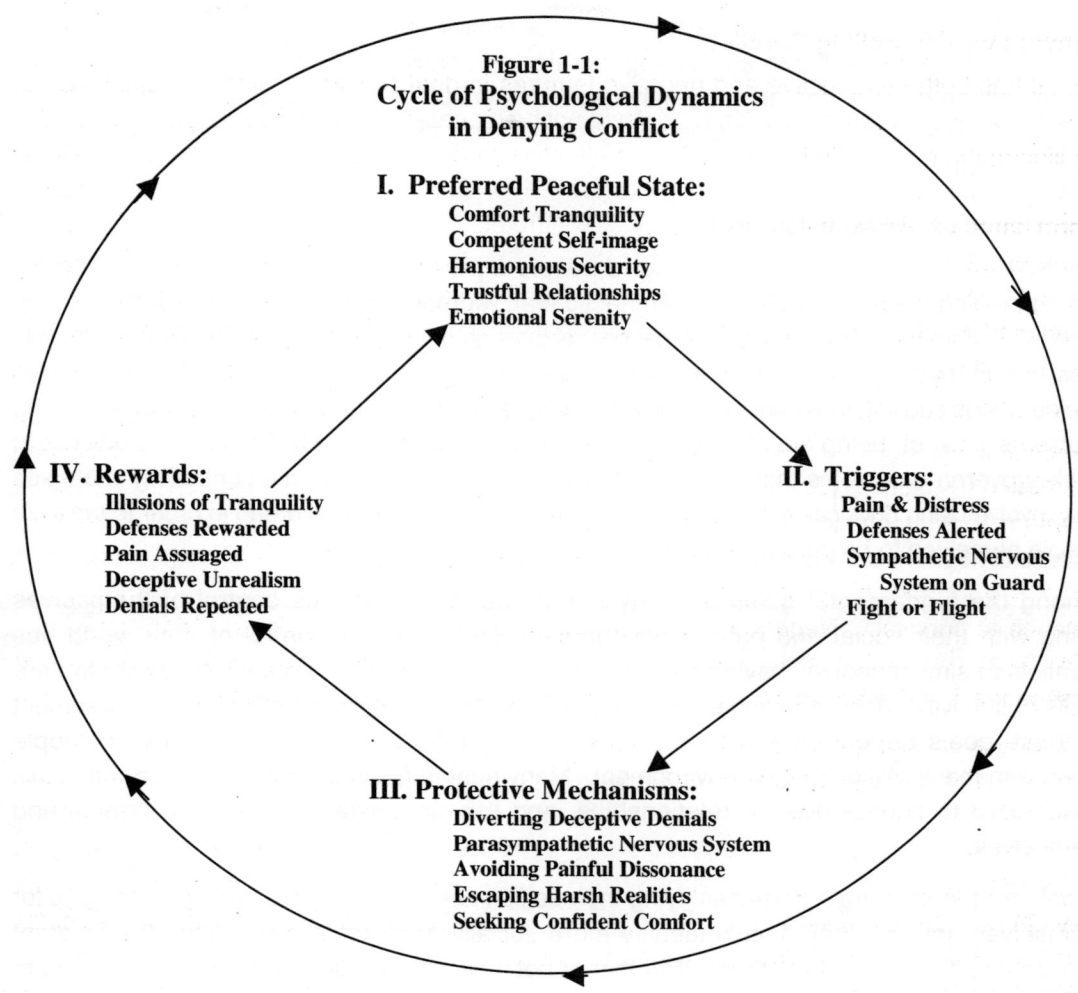

**Figure 1-1:
Cycle of Psychological Dynamics
in Denying Conflict**

**I. Preferred Peaceful State:**
 Comfort Tranquility
 Competent Self-image
 Harmonious Security
 Trustful Relationships
 Emotional Serenity

**II. Triggers:**
 Pain & Distress
 Defenses Alerted
 Sympathetic Nervous
 System on Guard
 Fight or Flight

**III. Protective Mechanisms:**
 Diverting Deceptive Denials
 Parasympathetic Nervous System
 Avoiding Painful Dissonance
 Escaping Harsh Realities
 Seeking Confident Comfort

**IV. Rewards:**
 Illusions of Tranquility
 Defenses Rewarded
 Pain Assuaged
 Deceptive Unrealism
 Denials Repeated

The dynamics on the bottom of Figure 1-1 provide the deceptive protection that is preferred to facing conflicts. These defensive measures may be almost completely unconscious or only partially filtered into awareness since people vary widely in expressing denial processes. Moreover, cultures vary widely about how to cope with real threats to their existence. There is a natural propensity to divert attention away from threats in order to avoid painful conflicts. Ignoring reality can be safer than dealing with it directly since tragedies are highly incongruent with one's preferred self-perception. On an international scale, nations try to keep their homeland safe built upon secure cultural values to make citizens feel safely protected. People want to feel that they are in control of themselves and their destiny. Consequently, suicidal terrorists may manifest similar dynamics in a single desperate protest to control their own life and death.[10]

Except for suicide protests, why are these psycho-dynamics of control repeated by other persons? The left side of Figure 1-1 identifies powerful pay-offs for the chronic denier. Denying conflict temporarily restores an illusion of tranquility, control and peaceful serenity. Individuals and societies attempt to function in an illusory world that denies the intrusion of threatening dangers. Diversionary tactics protect people by helping them to avoid making difficult changes in their behaviors that they try to avoid. These deceptive strategies work effectively because avoiding pain is preferable to addressing threatening conflicts. Because the denial "pays off" with reduction of pain, it is an extremely useful protection in their thought processes. Denial works in their perception of reducing pain so it will likely be repeated when facing dangerous conflicts again.[11]

**Importance of Being in Control:**

Psychological denial may temporarily give people a personal impression of being in control. But controlling conflict is a very different tactic than repressing cognitive processes operating internally in the brain. Rather than internal control through denial, an externalizing strategy forcibly tries to control people who are perceived to be causing the conflicts. People naturally try to decide who is causing threatening conflicts. Consequently, they want to control the people causing problems. Fear of "being out of control" is enormously disconcerting to families and officials in public governmental roles that they react quickly to regain control. These controlling strategies may involve using physical violence, war, punishment, or psychological dread in order to terrorize people perceived to be producing conflicts.

Among the fundamental goals of many human beings is zealous control of themselves along with their social and natural environment. This need for control of their world has parallels to simultaneously having self-control in all circumstances. Parallel to self-control are goals of surviving, achieving and seeking superior confidence in relationships. Accomplishment of these goals depends upon how extensively controls can be exerted on other people along with manipulation of their environment. Many human goals can be subsumed within this basic need to control events, relationships, and the circumstances in which people find themselves.

People frequently refrain from identifying their selfish need to control as an important goal for themselves. Instead they openly identify more socially acceptable motivations than blatant egocentric efforts to control others. Whether or not they are consciously aware of their need to control others, their actions and relationships soon demonstrate selfish values for manipulating important behaviors and outcomes. People may actually deceive both themselves and others by concealing their need for control. However, hidden agendas quickly become evident in human relationships, professional roles and political activities.

Human activities are expressed within public and private organizations. This book focuses upon two social institutions namely the family unit in which people relate intimately, and the family of nations that collectively relate internationally. There are obviously similarities and differences in comparing family and international organizations. Throughout human history, families and nations have been traditionally governed by authority figures. In families, this authoritative role is typically expressed by parental control of family members. Matriarchal leadership exists in a few societies, but the most prevailing pattern has been patriarchal control. Leadership is likewise typically exercised in nations through hierarchical power and autocratic control that traditionally has been patriarchal.

Both families and nations engage in decision-making to manage resources at their disposal. Families and nations experience conflicts when decisions are made and implemented that challenge their need for certainty and control. Both families and nations can resort to command, control and violent coercion in order to deal with these unresolved conflicts. Physical and psychological abuse may be used to discipline and control members of the family. Nations typically use violence to control unacceptable dissent and criminal behavior. Moreover, nations may resort to war along with external coercive threats.

People have used verbal and nonverbal communication to influence, persuade and control other people. Below the human level, animals astutely use non-verbal communication to control the behavior of other animals. Mating rituals and aggressive behaviors are communicated non-verbally to other animals. Human beings have additional competencies with verbal languages in order to influence people around them. Family members interpret the words and actions of family members based upon their long experience of living together. In contrast, nations may not have the same capability of understanding the verbal messages, non-verbal actions or the awesome silences of other nations with difference cultural values. Historically, the rise of modern totalitarianism under Hitler and Stalin was in a large part developed by their clever use of manipulative communications.

High technologies in print, broadcast and informational services are now available. Transmission of information and propaganda occurs through rapid forms of global communication. Promotional campaigns are used to create markets, influence the public and control the consumption behaviors of people. Communication skills using mass media and information technology powerfully influence the behavior of people globally. Political candidates utilize polls and media to understand and impact the voting behaviors of citizens. These methods are exploited not only in developed nations, but also in developing cultures that I observed during five extended visits in Asia. Around the world, public opinion is vulnerable to attractive appeals. It is essential to analyze where and how these controls are exercised to advance the arguments that are being developed in this book.

**Family, Cultural, Religious & Social Control:**

People build the social institutions of their culture over many centuries. In order to build a culture, careful planning and extensive controls are necessary to create, finance, govern, and preserve these social foundations. Unique cultural artifacts of the languages, arts, music, literature, education and technology are constructed through careful design, control of resources, and transmission of values to future generations. Consequently, civilizations vigilantly protect their irreplaceable treasures.

Families are obviously very crucial social institutions for human propagation and survival. Cultural traditions provide a framework of meaningful identity for citizens of that culture. Essential for social existence are gender identity, political leadership for governance, workers for economic production, plus creative advancements and preservation of cultures. Throughout human history, people have imposed beliefs on chaos in social relations, and order upon ambiguity in their natural environment. Religions inherently help humanity cope with threatening fears about human and natural disasters that have been considered out of human control.

Without predictable order in the society, anarchy threatens to destroy the treasured components of a functioning culture. However, fear of diseases, wars, crimes, natural disasters, homicides and suicides threaten the viability of many societies. Reports of violence worldwide in 2000 estimate[12] 1,659,000 deaths including 815,000 suicides, 520,000 homicides, 310,000 war-related deaths in addition to even more accidents and natural causes of death. The same annual report estimates worldwide deaths of 2,940,000 from AIDS, 1,660,000 from tuberculosis, and 1,080,000 from malaria. Recent reports state that malaria is on the increase in parts of the world.[13] At least 700,000 children die from malaria in Africa annually while millions spend several months a year ill from this disease thereby crippling African economies as does HIV-AIDS and tuberculosis.

Families have greater opportunity to form and flourish in the security of a carefully protected environment. Nations flourish when solid social institutions provide predictable futures and dependable heritages for citizens. However, most families in the world exist in conditions that threaten their existence daily. Estimates of needless deaths of children in the world are even further devastating. The World Health Organization[14] released estimates in early 2002 with estimates that some 150,000,000 children suffer from malnutrition with four times that number living in impoverished conditions.[15] In India, data from the World Bank Poverty Update estimated 350,000,000 people living below the poverty line.[16] Worldwide, as many as 1.2 billion people try to survive on less than $1 per day. Preventable diseases claim 11,000,000 lives of children annually according to these reports.

Family violence occurs in societies around the world even though reliable statistics are elusive. Only rough estimates are possible in some governments because domestic violence may be either denied or not considered a criminal offense. It is estimated that 130,000,000 girls in the world have undergone genital mutilation, that one to two million girls and women are annually trafficked into prostitution, and that 60 per cent of children who are kept out of school are female.[17] There are reports of helpless young women immolating themselves to desperately escape family violence in Afghanistan frequently precipitated by a domineering mother-in-law and her family.[18] "Kerosene" fires are not uncommon for young wives in South Asia. Even in more developed nations, there are wide discrepancies in enforcing criminal laws about family violence. Comparisons among countries are difficult because of problems with different statistical records about domestic violence. Box 1-1 provides statistics for the United States reported by the University of Pennsylvania's Center for the Treatment and Study of Anxiety.

Desperate measures are taken in families in order to exert forcible control over selected members of the family in America and other cultures. Men are the most frequent perpetrators of domestic violence and abuse. When dominating persons control their families, they frequently resort to violent force. Their need for control is a common trigger for men who may even kill their spouse and children as confirmed by people who work with victims of domestic abuse.[19] When these abusers sense that they are losing control, they repeat measures that have previously worked to regain control that involve using violent and abusive approaches. Not only do injuries result, but deaths often occur.

> **Box 1-1: Domestic Violence in the United States[20]**
>
> - One of four men use violence against a partner.
> - Women report an average of 572,102 violent acts at the hands of an intimate partner, compared with 48,983 reports by men.
> - 21% to 61% of battered women have also been sexually abused by partners.
> - 31% to 60% of battered women are diagnosed with post-traumatic stress disorder (PTSD).
> - In emergency settings, 24% of women seen for any reason have been battered; up to 35% of those with injuries have been battered.
> - Between 1967 and 1973, 39,000 United States soldiers were killed in Vietnam. During the same period, 21,000 women and children were killed in their own homes in the United States.
>
> SOURCE: Center for the Treatment and Study of Anxiety, University of Pennsylvania School of Medicine, Philadelphia PA, USA.

Authoritarian beliefs are frequently used to justify violent measures in the family, within cultures and between nations. Many wars are rationalized through religious ideologies even though religions purport to inherently hold beliefs about ultimate values of transcendence, peace, love, morals and justice. Nevertheless, religion can be used to perpetrate horrendously destructive actions. Sources of ultimate authority are frequently invoked to justify the use of violent war. Islam, Judaism, and Christianity respectively have sacred books accredited with divine authority namely the Quran, the Torah, and the Bible. These sources prescribe not only the guidelines for beliefs and conduct, but also propositional principles for governance, conflicting worldviews, identification of the sources of evil, and dogmatic indoctrination of adherents. Hindus are guided by the complex sources contained in the Bhagavad-Gita.

Other religions may also have sacred Scriptures that likewise are revered for ritual, tradition, philosophy, law, poetry, myths, art and song. These sources provide guidance for adherents in areas of morals, behavior, plus promises of after life, rewards and punishments. World religions advocate unity, truth, morals plus exhortations to love God and other human beings. Most religions seek to provide standards for justice, ethics and social conduct. Rather than justifying division and strife, there are major themes of unifying truth, understanding divinity and questing for harmony in human relationships and political governance. Additional guidelines are specifically provided for mating, sexuality, marriage, rituals, dress, family relationships, parental responsibilities, child rearing and provisions for inheritance.

Self-control is typically advocated with guidelines for ethical behavior in these religious traditions. Authoritative sources prescribe guidance in community control and human conduct. Adherents may be expected to surrender their individual will to the Will of God, Allah and Jehovah as an expression of obedience and commitment. Control of inappropriate behaviors along with guidelines for commendable actions is central in most religions of the world. Harmonious relationships are typically advocated in order to restrain human propensities to misconduct, greed, sin and selfishness. Many traditions advocate sanctions that human willfulness needs to be constrained in order to control freedom and the uncertainty of chaotic disorder.

Socializing children in responsible citizenship is fundamental in the family, religious training, and most directly in schooling and educational institutions. Without education and schooling, few people function effectively in modern societies with its complex technologies. One of the hallmarks of a classroom is an environment conducive for optimal learning. Expert knowledge and skill development happens optimally in a "controlled educational environment" rather than chaotic conditions. Effective teachers cultivate professional competencies in providing fair discipline of their students in their classes. On the other hand, creative learning may take place in less structured environments with fewer strict controls. The integration of both creative and critical thinking is jointly assimilated within higher levels of consciousness that is beyond lower primates. At the same time, the negative impact of aggressive bullying needs to be controlled in order to protect victims and provide an optimal learning atmosphere.

As a tool for social control, education provides extremely important roles for humanizing students while socializing them into responsible roles of their culture. Schools also have gate-keeping roles in modern societies. Educational institutions provide basic quality control of their graduates through evaluating student performance, assigning grades for achievement, awarding diplomas, certificates and degrees. These credentialing roles provide essential services that recognize academic accomplishments, readiness for employment, and responsible functioning as citizens in society.

Education possesses both positive influences and negative controls in societies through formal and informal schooling. Negative influences will be further analyzed in Part I that is concerned with "Understanding Violence, Aggression and War." Positive influences will be later emphasized in Part III, "Resolving Conflict," and Part IV, "Sustaining Peace and Justice." These chapters also examine the contributions of religion and education for addressing violent conflicts on the road toward building justice and peace. In this first chapter, however, the focus is primarily on the extensive nature of control exerted by most religions, cultures, and educational practices around the world and also in the next section by governments.

**Governmental Control:**

Governments exercise authority through both very constructive influences, but also devastating coercion. Consider the different primary methods utilized to gain control in many fields of endeavor for the positive benefits of society. Politicians in government employ a variety of means to exercise positive control of their people. The provisions of economic, legal, security, and social justice are major responsibilities of governments. Political leaders have many pervasive measures to exercise powerful control. Political leaders naturally may be very astute in using polished skills of persuasion, popular appeals, campaign promises and news releases. Extensive methods are available for gaining control of major populations with mass media at the ready disposal of government leaders. State controlled media are forceful tools in wartime and peacetime. Propaganda and political promises provide powerful appeals for votes from citizens through private media that is market-driven or governmentally controlled.

Leaders of governments possess institutionalized control mechanisms that they can also exercise. Authority to propose laws and justice systems enormously widens their scope for controlling human behavior. Lawmakers typically have delegated responsibilities to manage governmental budgets, policies and resources. Taxation is among the most powerful instruments available to leaders of government to extend control domestically and internationally. Not only are taxes a powerful tool, but manipulations and reductions of taxes are extensively utilized to gain control of votes. Along with formulating legislation, enforcing laws and extending pardons comes the regular exercise of administrative law and regulatory guidelines. Chartering corporations and other institutions broadly extends governmental reach into global economic and political power.

Legislative powers of governmental officials provide vast impact on both the domestic and international activities of a nation. Shaping the priorities of a nation with capital, plus enabling legislation and regulations provides far-reaching consequences. These are delegated to governmental leaders through traditions, policies and constitutions. Possessing delegated power and exercising power exerts extensive controls in a society. Consequently, the balance of power among legislative, executive and judicial branches has become essential for "controlling" governments in addition to voting in elections.

One of the basic institutions of government is the justice system that legally controls the behavior of citizens in the public arena. Without a strong justice system, human pathologies of crime and violence are likely to break out. A reliable justice system provides law enforcement when violations occur, investigations of relevant facts, provisions for fair trials, plus fitting sentences and punishment for convicted violators. Such a society can function equitably because the control of law and order prevails.

Quality justice systems are essential in providing legal and social justice. Interpretations of traditional codes, acceptable social behavior and guidance for the conduct of citizens are all needed. Without the constraints, sanctions and effective controls, societies are vulnerable to chaotic disorder, uncontrolled anarchy and aggressive violence. Protection of civil and human rights becomes the hallmark of a just society. A weak justice system threatens the viability of family life, national activities and international order. Consistent enforcement of laws and legal contracts are critical for human affairs, business and economic activity to thrive. When laws are equitably enforced, both families and nations can prosper and flourish.

On a blatant side, aggressive political leaders may exert unparalleled control in commanding military forces. They possess delegated power to use coercion, budgets, force and military threats in defensive and aggressive actions. Invasions and police actions are at their disposals while global humanity may exist at their mercy. They may give deliberate warnings of possible attacks or the use of threatening weapons. Weapons of mass destruction in the arsenals of a number of nations are at the disposal of political leadership. These weapons controlled by government leaders and non-state terrorists provide devastating global threats. Dread of these weapons vividly identifies the staggering consequences of possessing such devastating weapons. This quote from the rationale of President George W. Bush expresses fear of the suicidal nature of these weapons of mass destruction as he contemplated engaging in war in Iraq. These claims have since been repeatedly questioned for veracity:

> In this century, when evil men plot chemical, biological and nuclear terror, a policy of appeasement could bring destruction of a kind never before seem on this earth. Terrorists and terrorist states do not reveal these threats with fair notice in formal declarations. And responding to such enemies only after they have struck first is not self-defense. It is suicide. The security of the world requires disarming Saddam Hussein now.[21]

Authority to declare war is the most ominous power possessed by government leaders. When war is declared, the headlines and media coverage ominously dominates international, economic and domestic affairs. Hostile enemies can unconsciously have suicidal intentions for engaging in violent war with weapons of mass destruction. Such international violence potentially threatens soldiers and civilians alike plus the existence of whole civilizations, the natural environment and humanity. Sanger astutely provides an analysis of Bush's address recognizing the unfathomable ambivalence concerning suicide. Sanger boiled down Bush's rationale for war with Iraq in a succinct statement:

> In an age of unseen enemies who make no formal declarations of war, waiting to act after America's foes 'have struck first is not self-defense, it is suicide.'[22]

This analysis provides the stark reality of facing extinction as an ominous fear and as a debatable rationale for engaging in war that has unpredictable consequences for humanity. Osama bin Laden utilizes suicidal bombers to deliver attacks by terrorists that instill tragic losses and fearful anxiety in plots against the United States. He exploits suicidal people as a delivery system that high technology cannot effectively fight.[23] He has invented a missile delivery system in the young, educated young people guided by their own brain. There is evidence that the Muslim suicide bombers are often educated above reasonable employment levels as a number have graduate degrees from high-status families.[24] They are also motivated to sacrifice material and emotional comforts, and to travel long distances for which they pay their own way. Psychologists have identified the "copycat" phenomenon that prompts people to imitate violent actions valued by a culture as highlighted in media. Nuclear weapons including "dirty bombs" now circulating on the black market could become the next stage of terrorist for suicidal terrorists to covertly deliver to many targets in the world.

Suicides can be motivated by a sense of both reward and relief in contemporary conflicts. Reward is a positive reinforcement that can come in the form of religious promises of paradise plus direct compensation to families. Saddam Hussein provided monetary compensation to the families of suicide bombers from Palestine who detonated bombs that killed Israeli victims along with themselves. Such religious martyrdom also has a powerful motivation of relief from painful humiliation in carrying out their suicidal missions of destruction. Suicide relieves a sense of deliverance from personal hopelessness, meaninglessness and subjective pain. When people are ready to convert themselves into human bombs, using airplanes, cars, cell-phones, fertilizer, or tennis shoes they have a weapon that is undeterrable, undetectable, and nearly inexhaustible.[25]

Collective suicide and genocide are international deliberations similar to anxieties that individuals entertain in their own bewilderment about existence. While persons consider suicide as an individual option, humanity is now faced with the collective reality of massive suicide because weapons of mass destruction are in the hands of government leaders and non-governmental terrorists. Fear of collective suicide now parallels alarm of suicide contemplated by individuals so that domestic and international concerns become increasingly analogous. Psychologists[26] recognize that considering suicide may be a normal response to hopeless situations faced by Palestinians, Israelis and other groups motivated by ideologies and religions.[27] The cycles of violence in the Middle East in a climate of unpredictable terrorist attacks has devastating impact on the mental health on people in these communities. These citizens along with soldiers experience the long-term effects of post-traumatic stress syndromes and other mental health problems.

Ambivalence about the nature of suicide is reflected in wide variance among cultures and governments concerning the legality of suicide and the status of euthanasia for assisted suicide. Countries in Europe including the Netherlands, Belgium and Switzerland have euthanasia laws with humane provisions to assist suicides of terminally ill persons. Controlling their own death with dignity challenges many cultural values. "Suicide Tourists" travel to Switzerland for assistance in dying thereby evoking mixed reactions from the Swiss.[28] Internal self-control has traditionally been considered highly desirable for individuals to be in charge of their own destiny. On the other hand, social relationships need the constraints and external controls of effective justice systems. Governments reflect differing cultural values in their legal provisions concerning war fatalities, suicide, executions, abortion, birth and population control.

The decisions of political leaders to engage in war result in unnatural deaths of untold civilians who are killed, displaced or die due to devastation wrought by wars. Historically, from 1900-1987, documented evidence[29] reports 169,000,000 civilian deaths related to war is three times the fatalities of military soldiers during the same period including two World Wars. In the past decade, Africa has had its own devastating wars. Africa alone continues to have major civil wars and wars between nations that have not been accurately tallied. In 2000, there are reports of approximately 310,000 war fatalities occurring around the world[30] plus only rough estimates of the multi-millions of civilian casualties that resulted from these wars. National leaders can instigate wars that result in an enormous number of fatalities and chaotic consequences in international affairs.

Control by military power is a humanly devised method of imposing the will of governments on other people by deploying soldiers, weapons, and strategies of warfare. Authoritarian dictators retain control of military power for themselves alone. Democratic constitutions typically place the military under the command of the national leader. Naturally, control of military power offers innumerable conflicts in controlling devastating weapons. *Coups* have frequently occurred when military leaders depose civilian leadership or when national emergencies are declared. The capacity of military forces to fight devastating wars clearly challenges peacekeeping to create order.

Military conscription is a method of equipping armies with trained and disciplined soldiers. Extensive military forces require major resources of a nation for weapons systems, equipment, training, transportation, supplies and logistics. To what extent are soldiers exercising their own freedom or to what degree are soldiers under the control of powerful leaders? The exercise of human autonomy varies in free democratic nations in contrast with totalitarian nations. Yet soldiers are subject to similar control by leaders to whom they are expected to give unquestioned allegiance. Even impoverished nations may expend enormous resources on their military capabilities that become status symbols for controlling both known and unknown threats. The quest for security is almost an insatiable need for power by many political leaders of nations and weapons industries in international markets.

**Scientific Control:**

The objectives of science involve the search for control through different methods that contrast with controls by society, family, religion or government. Science seeks to discover verifiable truths of how the natural order functions with predictable laws. Scientific methodologies are designed to carefully:

- **Observe natural phenomena,**
- **Formulate testable hypotheses,**
- **Collect empirical data to test these hypotheses,**
- **Replicate the tests by independent researchers,**
- **Interpret objectively findings and results.**

Conducting carefully designed experiments is the premier method of determining cause-effect relationships between variables in nature and society. Deliberate efforts are made to control independent, extraneous and confounding variables in scientific research. In a tightly controlled research design, empirical data are quantified to measure the impact on dependent variables. When experiments are carefully replicated, empirical data provide testable scientific conclusions based upon reliable research and validated theories.

The four goals of scientific theory and research are to describe, explain, predict and control natural phenomenon. Natural and physical sciences pursue all four of these goals. Social scientists tend to have reservations about the fourth goal of controlling human behavior. Controversies about the ethics of controlling human behavior prompt hesitation in pursuing this goal. In contrast, physicists, chemists and biologists actively pursue all four goals of theory building based upon scientific methods for discovering laws of nature. Social scientists in sociology, psychology, economics, political science and anthropology have understandable reservations about whether the goal of control is ethically appropriate for scientists to advocate. The dialogue between Carl Rogers and B.F. Skinner, Control of Human Behavior,[31] is a classic contribution to this debate. Rogers, a humanistic psychologist and Skinner, a behaviorist, both provide helpful insights into the issue of freedom and control.

The key point in this brief analysis is that careful control of variables in scientific experiments is a primary feature of this powerful method for discovering truth about natural phenomena. Consequently, scientific discovery of truth involves conducting carefully controlled experiments. Tightly controlled experiments establish cause-effect relationships that are extremely important for understanding creation so that natural and social behaviors are more predictable and consequently less chaotic.

The Manhatten Project during World War II to develop the Atomic Bomb is a classic case of how scientific research is used by political leaders for military weapons. Regardless of how careful controls are used in experimental methods, political powers often make crucial decisions for the utilization of scientific discoveries. When the crucial first test called "Trinity" was conducted in 1945 at White Sands in New Mexico, uncontrollable risks were reluctantly recognized rather than denied. Dr. Robert Oppenheimer, Director of this project at Los Alamos, estimated that the chances of igniting the global atmosphere were three in one million.[32] As a renowned physicist observing the first atomic tests, Oppenheimer consciously cited the Hindu Scriptures, Bhagavad-Gita, at the time of this atomic bomb test:

> I have become death, the shatterer of worlds;
> Waiting that hour that ripens to their doom.[33]

Along with nuclear physics, controls through economics, sociology, psychology, business, policy analysis and political science are singled out because of their wide impact on family and international issues. Economics attempts to use quantitative data to develop scientific explanations for the distribution of natural resources, capital, and human energy. Microeconomics develops models for understanding monetary policy, price, competition and market of supply and demand. Macroeconomics has broader concerns using mathematical models that address the aggregates of global resources, international commerce, concepts of capital investments and global capital formation. Businesses apply these economic concepts to management and ownership of resources, international capital, market distributions, regulations of commerce, and human resource development. Political science in conjunction with economics are combined in the domain called political economy. Social psychology has innumerable finding relevant to understanding domestic and international affairs.

Inherent in economics, business and political science are concerns about controlling behaviors and markets both in domestic and international affairs. There are major concerns about providing predictable forecasts that might otherwise be chaotic conditions of human activity, the environment, natural resources and possible disasters. Political science, economics, sociology and psychology and business management are understandably also major concerns of national leaders and family members. Major conflicts arise over disputes about finances, budgets, and globalization as these impact both families and nations. Government leaders establish priorities when there are conflicts between military and domestic expenditures for human services. Consequently, there are major concerns about capacities to control political economics that influence the well - being of families and the health of nations.

Political science, policy analysis, economics and business do not have precise theories for prediction and control of human behavior. The presuppositions of economics assume that human beings make rational decisions as they attempt to optimize their choices if they have accurate information available. It does not take a social psychologist to point out that people are influenced by a whole array of presumptions and considerations in making decisions in addition to rationality. Moreover, it does not take an expert in information sciences to point out that people have access to limited information that has varying degrees of veracity. Experimental scientific research is less available in methodologies of economics and policy analysis. Consequently, limits in decision-making, in scientific methodologies of experimentation, along with the variance in rational human behavior need further consideration in future chapters that deal with balancing freedoms and regulations.

Control is also inherent in the application of science to medical, psychological and mental health services. Major health concerns involves controlling diseases plus preventing accidents and tragic deaths. In medical science, bioethical guidelines attempt to address the complex decisions about health care, quality of life and its termination. With rapid advances in biochemical technologies and organ transplantation plus the developments in the production of organs and tissues, these options require careful control and distribution. Global control of devastating diseases by preventive and treatment methods is another notorious international concern in public health care particularly in the diseases of polio, small pox, HIV-AIDS, tuberculosis, malaria, SARS, and Asean flu.

Typically control of patients is usually a secondary factor in healing and health care. Nevertheless, beyond curing physical maladies, an important component in healing processes involve helping to re-engage the patient into their social community. Different cultures recognize healers whose functions include helping sick, deformed and mentally ill people to psychosocially re-enter their community. Patients experience alienation in their relationships resulting in isolation and ostracism. In high-tech medicine there is a need to help people re-enter their social relationships particularly in cases of mental illness, deformities and disabilities.

As modern science and technology advance, there are additional issues concerning who is included and who is excluded. With new knowledge about genetic contributions to diseases, major decisions are confronted in health care. Genetic analyses attempt to predict probabilities of defective outcomes of embryos even before conception. Both highly expert professionals and informed parents have decisions to make as they project outcomes. Moreover, with technology to determine gender and manipulate genes, difficult decisions confront parents, professionals and whole societies. Preference in many cultures for male children has far-reaching consequences in the world today particularly in Asian cultures. Aggressive violence, wars, and conflicts are impacted by gender preferences encouraged by cultural values. For example, women and children become victims of civil strife and international wars at higher levels than soldiers who are predominantly males. Masculine dominated cultures are more prone to aggression than feminine cultures. Both family and international conflicts arise out of these preferential decisions.

Rationing and triage are often not explicitly discussed as methods to control the distribution of health care services. Yet every culture has limits on the health care resources that society can be provided to its people. In market-controlled economies, the "ability to pay" rations health care for patients. Obviously, rationing controls access to health care services, products, pharmaceuticals and technology. Patients seek control of their lives for the security of their health. Professionals exercise control in providing their expert services. Governments, insurance and health industry businesses make critical decisions that control their markets and finances of health care. Regulations are designed to control various aspects of health care delivery in societies that effectively ration health resources and control triage decisions.

To this point, the positive and negative nature of control has been analyzed in family settings, cultural practices, scientific methods and governmental influence. Now attention needs to the similarities and differences how families and national leaders exercise freedoms and apply controls.

**Comparing Family & National Leaders in Control:**
For several decades, while teaching courses about domestic and international violence, I was challenged to keep abreast of emerging research and knowledge. Initially, I developed social policy courses primarily concerned with child abuse and neglect. Soon the focus broadened to domestic violence perpetrated by any family members on children, spouses and elders in which careful analysis of family problems, plus state and national policies were addressed.

Subsequently in the 1980's, another focus developed on a global scale with threats of nuclear war and international terrorism including needs for arms control, disarmament and international peace. The similarities in the threatening dynamics of holding hostages in international terrorism contrasted to domestic violence readily became apparent. This parallel compared the victims and the perpetrators in domestic and international violence evident in the 21$^{st}$ century. Holding and terrorizing hostages provided even greater evidence of similarities.

Family abusers terrorize their families with physical violence and psychological threats to control family hostages analogous to international terrorists' control of global hostages. Victims of domestic violence and international violence both are controlled through threats, anxieties and fears. Victims and hostages feel continuously stalked by the need of perpetrators to exercise total control over their victims. Abusive heads of families, terrorists groups, bullies, violent gangs, and aggressive nations are possessed by similar needs to have power over the destiny of their targets. The scope differs largely in the sheer number of hostages held and terrorized. Domestic abusers see their family as their primary realm of influence whereas international terrorists see major regions of the world as their scope of control.

Whole cultures can be held hostage by international terrorists just as family members are the hostages of terrorizing husband-fathers. These observations over the past twenty years were astoundingly confirmed by the report of Lakshmy Parameswaran, President of Daya, Inc., a family counselor specializing in family and date violence and sexual assault issues. She observed after September 11, 2001, that victims of family violence were doubly traumatized by the televised reports of the destruction of the World Trade Center Towers in New York City. Box 1-2 provides a dramatic account that illustrates the close connection between family violence and terroristic attacks in which major populations are held hostage:[34] Parallel fears are found among people in war torn, hostile violence including consultations I have had with health professionals in the Israeli-Palestinian conflicts.

---

**Box 1-2: Rita's Double Trauma**

Rita (not her real name), a survivor of domestic violence stated: "It is difficult for me to share my true feelings with the outside world because I'd be called crazy. I actually saw on TV the second plane approaching the World Trade Towers in New York City...people screaming and finally I saw with my own eyes this plane hitting the tower (on 9/11)."

"Unfortunately, I was in my bedroom at the same spot where my husband...had made this brutal attack on my life two years ago. The psychological impact of watching another act of violence from the same spot where violence was inflicted on me was so horrible that I started screaming...I actually visualized ...(my husband) in the cockpit of that plane flying it through the building."

She continued in disbelief, "I think family violence is in fact an act of terrorism inflicted by one member of the family on other members....Unfortunately, most of the victims of this sort of terrorism do not die. Nevertheless, they smolder in the wreckage with no hope for rescue."

The double trauma experienced by Rita in this domestic case study represents what many people go through in international acts of physical and psychological terrorism. Both family members and entire cultures are traumatized by terroristic attacks that in effect hold them in constant fear. Both family members and whole cultures feel as if they are actually being held as hostages by their attackers. In effect, both perpetrators of terroristic violence and family abusers try to control their victims as hostages with psychological fear and constant apprehension.

Means of control differ between domestic and international violence. International violence usually involves possessing massive military forces with major budgets. Possessors of nuclear weapons can hold major populations and even the whole world hostage. However, international terrorists also use low cost methods of intimidating target populations. They can induce fear in major populations through less powerful means due to their relative weakness in facing powerful nations. They may take hostages, use bombs, biological weapons or even biochemical means. In the September 11, 2001 attacks, airplanes were hijacked and crashed into the towers of the World Trade Center and the Pentagon. Similarly, domestic terror is done on a much smaller scale. Family victims are terrorized by their abusers like hostages held by international terrorists.

Boulding[35] made the perceptive observation, long before the attacks on the World Trade Center in New York, that there are two basic types of conflicts to be resolved. One he called "associative" and the other "dissociative" conflicts. The associative conflicts involve domestic and family relations in which people typically are living together or attempting to reconcile. These include family conflicts and civil conflicts and wars within a country. The disturbing fallout among family members and friends of a suicide by a loved one dramatizes the powerful effects of associative conflicts. In contrast, dissociative conflicts involve more impersonal living apart instead of together. Perpetrators usually have no personal knowledge of their victims who are rather impersonal categories of enemies. Nations in conflict exist separately and impersonally, but are in need of a settlement to preclude international war. Box 1-3 provides concrete explanations why control is a pre-occupation of both family and national leaders.

**Box 1-3: Means of Control**

Who's in control? Who has the control? Here are examples of how control is exerted by perpetrators who wield control in these domains:

Government:
- Life and death control through death sentences and pardons.
- Authority to declare war.
- Authorize conscription for military draft.
- Laws, regulations, taxes, and legislation.
- Dictators and tyrants seek total control of their subjects.

Domestically:
- The "TV Control" provides a technological image of the person who dominates the channels and volume.
- Educators develop techniques to control a classroom using discipline.
- Artists express control of the paintbrush, or the musical instrument, or the dance steps, or the written word, as medium of artistic expression.
- People who possess guns wield control with this symbol of authority to threaten injury and death.
- Family members may influence each other's behavior as control freaks.

Culturally:
- Corporate CEO's exert control over employees, budgets, and decisions.
- In religion, control can be manipulated as power over believers and adversaries.
- Legal codes in law are used to control people or weapons.
- 'Out-of-Control" people upset social groups.
- In sports, controlling the game is a strategy for winning.
- Economic policies control distribution of resources and markets.

Internationally:
- "Line of Control" (LOC) is literally the boundary separating India-Pakistani in their conflict over Kashmir and Jammu.
- Violence is repeatedly employed in the attacks and counter-attacks between Palestinians and Israelis in desperation to control each other.
- United Nations attempt to control conflicts through negotiations, mediation, resolutions and sanctions.
- Arms Control and Disarmament are concerned with the proliferation of weapons of mass destruction.
- Iraq is an occupational challenge to Iraqi and United States governments in controlling people.

This analysis of Boulding parallels the dual concerns of this book. The domestic family conflicts are associative in nature. The international conflicts involve dissociative conflicts among anonymous people living separately. Many of the dynamics discussed in later chapters of conflict management and conflict resolution are parallel whether within the family or whether the conflict is international among countries or sub-national terrorists. In the age of rapid communication and globalization, there is an increasing overlap between associative and dissociative conflicts. International and domestic violence is increasingly fused with detached globalization rather than interpersonal interactions. Coercive threats are expressed by both national leaders in the world as well as by the controlling parent who threatens force to regain control. Naturally world leaders have many more resources at their command than a typical father whose powerful control of members of the family is threatened.

Control is a very powerful concept in domestic abuse. Perpetrators of family violence often manipulate their spouse and children with terroristic manipulations that effect control. "Control freaks" make life miserable for people around them by wanting their way in controlling everyone all the time. Internationally, military violence uses weapons for annihilating, intimidating and controlling people. Obsessed dictatorial leaders are possessed by grandiose illusions of ruling the whole world.

The need for control is inherent in ordering the uncertain, chaotic environment in which people live. They are threatened by the unpredictability of chaotic disorder. Consequently, human beings deliberately try to make their world as orderly and predictable as possible. People inherently try to control themselves plus their own destiny. This self-control is then extended to controlling other people and their environment. Some people actually become preoccupied with ordering the threatening uncertainties around them. They may compensate for this insecurity by over-controlling other people. While it is healthy to develop self-regulation, intensive need for orderly control can become an obsession in interpersonal relationships. This obsession may become pathological control of other people by dominating them, and by expanding their need for control in their family and community. Others exercise control in their nation and further into the world such as veto power on the Security Council of the United Nations.

People with needs to control intuitively sense when they are losing control. In Figure 1-2, this loss of control is explained on the right hand side. They may instantaneously experience painful emotions associated with losing control. They may have their leadership and superiority questioned when disorder occurs among people and circumstances around them. They feel threatened emotionally and cognitively with an ominous sense of inferiority compared to their normal sense of being "in charge." Instead of being able to predict what will happen next, these threatened persons may automatically use violence to regain control. Often the action that leaders take is coercive in nature if not violent in order to restore their sense of power over the chaotic disorder. Their subjective perceptions may even be more important than an objective assessment of the real situation by independent observers.

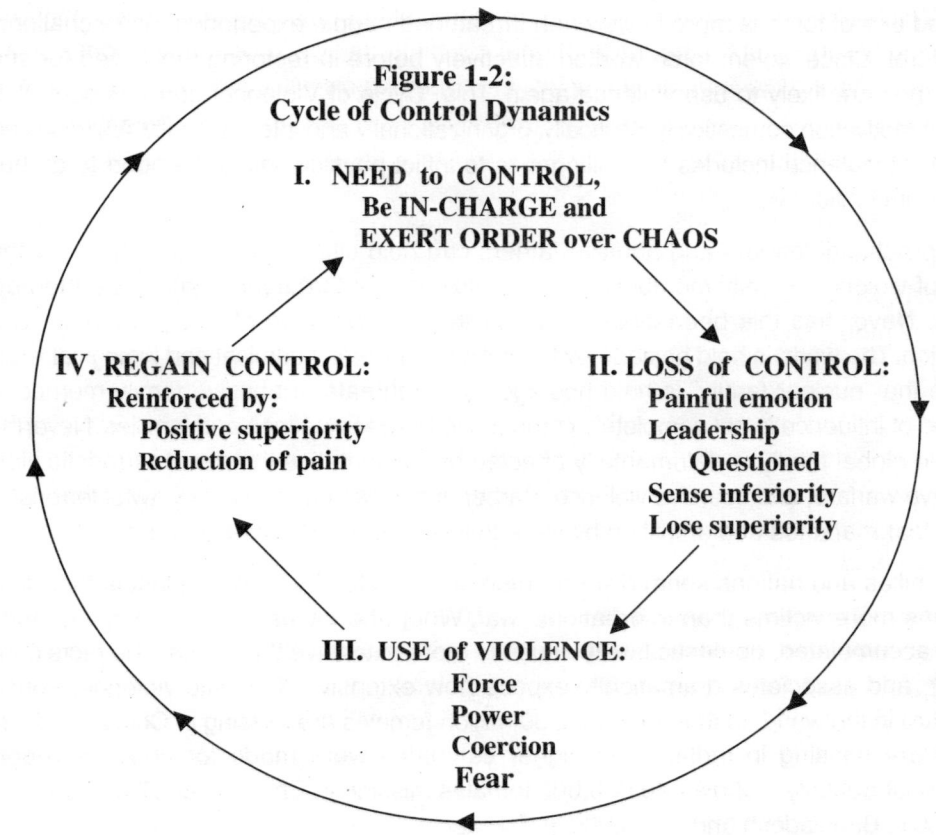

If using violent force is successful in restoring predictable order, then there is a very rewarding reinforcement to repeat violent action. Violence is thus rewarded with the dual impact of both positive and negative reinforcement. The positive reinforcement is the consequence of their use of force to regain control. They feel a reassuring sense of superiority in relation to people who threaten them. They attempt to control events, the circumstances and the surrounding environment. They experience another powerful reward in a reverse way from feeling threatened with painful inferiority. When control is restored, they are also negatively reinforced with the reduction of painful insecurity that previously accentuated feeling inferior when chaotic disorder prevails. Using an analogy of wartime leaders, they had been painfully losing the battle, but with the use of violent force they regain control in order to prevail.

People regain their sense of superiority by using violent force according to the paradigm in psychology of social learning. Bandura[36] provides the term "efficacy" to describe the need of persons to sense that they are competent to handle a challenging situation with confidence. He sees control primarily in terms of personal self-efficacy with further expressions in efficacious organizational and collective functioning. According to Bandura, striving for control permeates almost everything people do because control provides innumerable personal and social benefits. A person's sense of wellbeing and their image as a leader are exercised in self-control. Along with reassuring their need for control, the use of aggression and violent force is primarily socially learned in Bandura's research.

Repeated use of force is more likely when threatened people experience future challenges to their control. Since violent force worked effectively before in restoring their need for superior control, they are likely to use violence again. This "Cycle of Violence" conveys control as the dominant motivation domestically, politically, organizationally and internationally. A simple, working definition of violence includes the willingness to inflict physical injury intended to do harm or cause death in victims.

Both international leaders and abusive fathers can hold citizens or families hostage through threats of violence. Family members and the citizens of a threatened nation are thereby held hostage. Never has this been clearer than in the consideration of using weapons of mass destruction. The world is held hostage by the threat of nuclear, chemical and biological weapons. Likewise the "nuclear family" is held hostage by the threats of abusive family members. The full scope of influence is not completely comparable between nations and families. Nevertheless, the whole global family is detrimentally affected by authoritative threats of terroristic violence, destructive warfare, and coercive violence. Barber analyzes "fear instilled by awful terrorist deeds but also fear marketed and amplified by the administration's responses to terror."[37]

While families and nations seem disproportionate in scale, the alarming fact is that domestic abuse has more victims than international war. When the casualties are compiled and body count is accumulated, domestic family abuse is more extensive than wars. The facts compiled by Sen[38] and associates dramatically expose how extensive domestic violence, abuse and neglect are in the world. In their research, 30 million females are missing in China and 27 million females are missing in India. Even higher estimates were made for 2002, in reports by International Security[39] of over 40,000,000 females missing in China, over 37,000,000 in India, 3,500,000 in Bangladesh and 3,300,000 in Pakistan.

Other nations also contribute to the horrendous nature of domestic violence. The more primitive level of domestic violence not only parallels, but it greatly exceeds international violence. In addition to gender violence, domestic abuse includes:

➢ Hostile anger toward others and self.
➢ Vengeful scapegoating.
➢ Coercive use of force to gain control and compliance.
➢ Structural economic and social oppression.
➢ Psychological threats and intimidations.
➢ Destructive physical abuse and assaults.
➢ Sexual abuse, rape and harassment.
➢ Infliction of pain, maiming and torturing.
➢ Malicious neglect.
➢ Killing and murdering.

Consequently, while war is widely abhorred by most people around the world, an equivalent level of abhorrence is in order for all quietly perpetrated domestic abuse and neglect "behind closed doors." Both national leaders and family leaders have been caught up in cycles of violence. Once the momentum of these cycles occurs, it is difficult to intervene with non-violent and more peaceful means. There is a tendency to deny that such violence and abuse actually occurs. Another response is to over-simplify the conflicts into the dichotomies of "us vs. them," "good vs. evil," and "right vs. wrong" so readily prevalent in fundamentalist religious thinking. Non-violent alternatives are all too often perceived as loss of control or weak approaches.

Family and national leaders are faced repeatedly with challenges to their leadership. Both family and national leaders have found that the use of violent force can quickly restore their authority and control. The dynamics of this learning model are dramatically examined in an analysis of the crises in the Middle East entitled "Chaos vs. Control."[40] Moreover, the War in Iraq exemplifies many of these dynamics of international violence. These case studies will be analyzed in future chapters. From previous experience in regaining control when faced with a crisis, leaders are more likely to resort to using violent force to restore order since use of violence worked for them successfully in the past. When they are faced with another challenge to their authority, they are more likely to use violent force again.

**Recap & Overview:**

Why is control extensively exercised? The threatening intimidation of chaotic disorder, the uncertainty of unmanageable freedom, the disturbing effects of suicide, and the adversity of painful conflicts are primary motivations that impel people to exercise control. The key point of this chapter is to understand why people need to control themselves and control other people in their social relationships, their natural environments and international conflicts. People develop an essential need to exercise domination when they experience domestic and international conflicts. For internal control, they may repress conflicts with protective defenses of denial and distortion. For external control of perceived enemies, they resort to violent force against others including warfare between nations and acts of terrorism.

The struggle between either denying conflict or attempting to control conflict violently is analyzed next in the three chapters of Part I. Applications to both domestic family violence and international conflict are addressed in tandem. Part II provides approaches that involve consciously managing issues constructively rather than controlling conflict violently or denying that conflict exists in reality. In Part III, more advanced strategies are elaborated under the rubric of "Resolving Conflict." Both managing conflict and resolving conflict are seen as strategies that address structural violence of economic and social injustice.

Part IV provides strategies for sustaining peace with constructive justice in the final four chapters. Re-uniting positive peace with justice is the purpose of this book. These enduring strategies go beyond the limitations of unrealistically denying conflict or controlling conflict violently. A significant purpose of this book provides thorough understanding for building bridges between fear and sustainable peace.

## Endnotes

[1] Miller W., (2002),"Non Sequitur," Universal Press Syndicate, www.ucomics.com

[2] President Franklin Delano Roosevelt of the United States in the middle of the Great Depression, 1933.

[3] Ropeik D., (Oct. 28-Nov. 3, 2002) "Fear Factor," The Washington Post National Weekly Edition; co-author (2202) of RISK: A Practical Guide for Deciding What's Really Safe and What's Really Dangerous in the World Around You, Houghton Mifflin.

[4] Barber B., (2003) <u>Fear's Empire: War, Terrorism, and Democracy,</u> W.W. Norton & Company, Ltd. Barber states that "...fear's empire produces an empire of fear inimical to both liberty and security." Barber also sees that in America "...both national parties and leading opinion elites have supported the idea that fear can only be defeated by fearsomeness." page 18.

[5] De Becker G., (1997) <u>The Gift of Fear: Survival Signals that Protect Us from Violence,</u> Little, Brown Books.

[6] Shay J., (2002) <u>Odysseus in America: Combat Trauma and the Trials of Homecoming,</u> New York: Scribner Book Company.

[7] Incidents of suicide among American soldiers in Iraq has recently been reported in 2004 by Assistant Secretary of Defense, Dr. William Winkenwerder: http://www.msnbc.msncom/id/3956787/
These reports have been withheld from the public as reported by T.T. Gegx, (Feb. 21, 2004) "Where's The Army's Suicide Report?" <u>Newsweek;</u> also see P. Beaumont's article (Jan. 25, 2004), "Stress epidemic strikes American forces in Iraq," <u>The Observer.</u>

[8] Butterfield F., (July 29, 2002), "Wife Killings at Ft. Bragg Reflect Growing Problem in Military," <u>The New York Times</u>; plus findings of Christine Hansen's research at the Miles Foundation reported in Gegax, T & Barry J., "Death in the Military," <u>Newsweek,</u> August 5, 2002.

[9] Schmitt E., (Feb. 24, 2004) "Rapes Reported by Servicewomen in the Persian Gulf and Elsewhere," <u>New York Times.</u>

[10] While not an expert in suicidal behavior, the author has successfully treated 90-100 patients who considered suicide prior to and during psychotherapy.

[11] Both negative and positive reinforcement are B.F. Skinner's concepts for explaining how behaviors are conditioned in operant conditioning and research.

[12] Stolberg S., (October 3, 2002), "War, Murder and Suicide: A Year's Toll is 1.6 Million," from the World Health Organization reported in <u>The New York Times.</u>

[13] Editorial (Jan. 22, 2004), "Malaria on the Rise," <u>New York Times.</u>

[14] Olson E., (March 13, 2002.) "U.N. Says Millions of Children Die Needlessly," <u>The New York Times.</u>

[15] Crossette B., "U.N. Official Urges Food Aid for the Poor as a Priority," reporting figures from the United Nations Food and Agricultural Organization prepared by Jacques Diouf that 815,000,000 people go to sleep hungry including 200,000,000 children.

[16] Dube S., (1998) <u>Words Like Freedom,</u> New Delhi, India: Harper Collins, Centre for Monitoring the Indian Economy reported by <u>Business Line,</u> June 4, 1999, reported by Arundhati Roy, (2001) "The Greater Common Good" <u>The Algebra of Infinite Justice,</u> New Delhi, India: Viking Press, Penquin Books.

[17] Kristof N. (August 16, 2002), "Bush vs. Women," <u>The New York Times.</u>

[18] Gall C., (March 8, 2004), "For More Afghan Women, Immolation is Escape," <u>New York Times.</u>

[19] Duke B., (August 5, 2002), Former Director of CARE Center, a shelter and advocacy group for battered women, Associated Press, <u>Dallas Morning News,</u> "Slain Army Wives Wanted to Leave Marriages".

[20] Bauer E., "Trying to Prevent Domestic Violence," <u>DFW Health Monthly,</u> June, 2002

[21] Bush G. W., (March 17, 2003) Address of the President of the United States that provided a 48 hour ultimatum to Saddam Hussein.

[22] Sanger D., (March 18, 2003) "Bush's Doctrine for War," <u>The New York Times.</u>

[23] Friedman T., (2002) <u>Longitudes and Attitudes: Exploring the World After September 11,</u> New York: Farrar, Straus Giroux.

[24] Atran S., (May 5, 2003) "Who Wants to be a Martyr?" <u>The New York Times.</u>

[25] Friedman T., (Jan. 9, 2004) "The War of Ideas," <u>International Herald Tribune.</u>

[26] Tawahina A., (October 2002) "Normal Responses to Abnormal Situations," and Gal R., "Psychology Gives Solace to a Nation in Distress," <u>Monitor on Psychology.</u>

[27] The Jonestown collective suicides of over 750 men, women and children in South America in 1978 is an example of the extinction of an extremist Christian cult led by its leader, Jim Jones.

[28] Langley A. (Feb. 6, 2003), " 'Suicide Tourists' Go to the Swiss for Help in Dying," The New York Times.
[29] PBS-TV Documentary, April 11, 2002, "The Genocide Factor: The Human Tragedy."
[30] Stolberg S., (October 3, 2002 ), "War, Murder and Suicide: A Year's Toll is 1.6 Million," from the World Health Organization reported in The New York Times.
[31] Rogers C. and Skinner B.F., (1975) Control of Human Behavior, Jeffrey Norton Publisher.
[32] Sherwin M., (1975) A World Destroyed: The Atomic Bomb and the Grand Alliance, New York: Alfred A. Knopf Publishers, plus Prince P., "Oppenheimer," British Broadcasting Corporation.
[33] Swami Nikkilananda, (1944) translated from Sanskrit, New York: Ramarishana-Vivekananda Center.
[34] Parameswaran L., (2002,) "Confronting Violence," Texas Psychologist, Fall, also published in the Houston Chronicle, October 22, 2001.
[35] Boulding K., (1978) Stable Peace, Austin: University of Texas Press.
[36] Bandura Albert, (1997) Self-Efficacy: The Exercise of Control, W.H. Freedman and Company.
[37] Barber, op.cit.
[38] Sen Amartya, (2001) "Many Faces of Gender Inequality," Frontline, 9 November, 2001.
[39] Lewis A., (June 19, 2002), "Missing Women," USA Today, reports estimates of deaths due to preferences for male children that results in abortion of female fetuses, infant neglect or killing by parents.
[40] Slevin P., (May 20-26, 2002), "The Ship of State's Unsteady Course," The Washington Post National Weekly Edition.

# Part I:
# UNDERSTANDING VIOLENCE AND WAR

Persons demoralized by war and violence longingly ask "when are we ever going to learn to live together peacefully?" In contrast, aggressive persons may be eager to engage in the next fight or war. Both the discouraged and aggressive parties entertain images that feed upon their inability to discover alternatives to violent war or unrealistic peace. Part I is concerned with the importance of early steps in creative problem solving. A major challenge in problem solving involves identifying the symptoms and the causes of conflicts. Without in-depth recognition of conflict, there is little hope for constructively addressing the problems peacefully.

Part I focuses on violent approaches to conflict. Addressing violent approaches may seem a long ways from sustainable peace. There are well-considered reasons for dealing with violence directly including the realization that for peace to be sustainable and just, its enemies must be faced. Peace cannot be understood in depth unless its polar opposite of fearful violence is comprehended.

Chapter Two confronts the dynamics of anger, plus the fear of failure the leads to war and destructive activities both domestically and internationally. Structural violence of economic injustice and social oppression are identified for being as insidious as direct violence. Domestic family violence and international conflict are addressed in tandem. The parallels between domestic and international hostage-takers are compared. An explanation is provided for using the term terroristic violence rather than terrorism. Both conscious scapegoating and unconscious projection are analyzed.

Chapter Three deals with stalemates that frequently thwart movement toward resolving tensions. These delaying tactics are essential in order to grasp both domestic family conflicts as well as international tensions. The role of media is addressed in family and international violence. Perpetuating conflict into cycles of violence is connected to the difficulties in letting go of an enemy.

Chapter Four introduces the necessity for taking ownership of unresolved differences between disputing parties. By claiming responsibilities, conflicts advance beyond the blame games that often occur in families or between countries. The crucial step of identifying key issues involved in disagreements is then addressed. Until a problem is definitively identified, there is little hope for moving forward toward a lasting resolution. The dynamics of enemy-making are also addressed in order to realize the major challenges involved in establishing durable peace.

## Chapter Two

# Making Enemies and Empires

**Since wars begin in the minds of men,
it is in the minds of men that the
defense of peace must be constructed.**

Preamble of the UNESCO Constitution

Why is conflict so prevalent in international and domestic relations? Our human obsession with needing to control other people in human and international relationships is a major contributor to violence. Chapter One analyzed the propensity to dominate other people in domestic violence. On an international scale, obsessions to control natural resources and accumulated national wealth become major contributors to violent confrontations and wars. In the pursuit of control, aggressive political leaders seek to build empires while domestic controllers can also become imperial. In quests of domination, peace and justice are separated so that neither can be effectively sustained.

Violent conflicts occur daily in global hotspots with casualties from bombings, terroristic retaliations, civil wars and vicious threats of violent revenge. News reports daily flash scenes of bloody war in tension-filled regions of the world. Headlines are filled with accounts of violence, hatred, malicious injuries and killings. Examples are outlined in the selected "Headlines about Violence" in Box 2-1.

Domestically, many families face conflict both within the home as well as in their community. Tense communication heightens into intimidating threats among family members. Women disproportionately share the twin burdens of violence and inequality throughout the world. In communities, schools ferment with tensions, cliques, gangs, and rivalries. The reports of "Peace Officers" in police departments and school systems reflect that communities are in turmoil, families are fighting, and vicious people are being arrested for assaults.

---

**Box 2-1: Headlines about Violence**

- ❏ **DOMESTIC VIOLENCE:**
  - ➢ **Father kills Daughters as revenge on Ex-wife**
  - ➢ **Mother drowns her five children**
  - ➢ **Former employee kills nine co-workers**
  - ➢ **Two youth gun down classmates & teachers**
  - ➢ **Lovers end lives in dual suicide**
  - ➢ **Serial killer paralyzes Washington area**
  - ➢ **Religious conflicts inflame tragic violence**
- ❏ **INTERNATIONAL VIOLENCE:**
  - ➢ **Thousands killed in world trade center**
  - ➢ **Suicide bomber kills dozens in westbank**
  - ➢ **Leader voices fear of failure**[1]
  - ➢ **Gujarat erupts in India's religious violence**
  - ➢ **60,000 casualties in Kashmir/Jammu**
  - ➢ **Hundreds of corpses found in Iraq**
  - ➢ **Attack on Baghdad kills civilians**
  - ➢ **Millions die in sub-saharan Africa**

It is difficult to predict how people will respond when they are confronted with intense conflict and fighting. Deniers go to extreme measures to distort reality by not acknowledging that problems exist. This passive approach involves withdrawing from the threatening world by denying that the threat exists. They may yearn for the comfortable inner tranquility of blissful serenity. On the other hand, aggressive people fight back against predators with hateful vengeance by attempting to control their threatening environment with manipulation and violent force. These polar extremes are expressed in the following continuum:

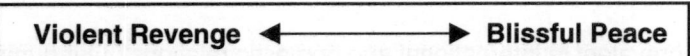

These opposite human responses rapidly dominate people's emotional feelings, their cognitive thinking, and their physical actions. Whether they engage in either bitter fighting or hope for serene peace, basic physical, social and psychological needs, people hope to regain control of threats, themselves, and the world in which they live. Similarly, international leaders want sovereign control of their citizens, their national boundaries as well as threatening adversaries. Parents want control of their children and their homes. Families and national leaders want predictable control over chaotic disorder.

People often rebound between the polar extremes of violence and peace. They may have limited capacity to tolerate the difficult middle battleground of managing tense conflicts. When their problem solving skills are limited, people bounce between the two extremes of either violent revenge or blissful, inner peace. They need alternatives to these polar extremes that will be the core of the last half of this book. Consequently, creative problem solving skills are needed that develop constructive responses to these conflicts.

Empirical observation about animal behavior demonstrates their propensity to react to threats with either the response of fight or flight. Behavioral scientists have discovered many cases in which violent conflict rips people apart so that they react by either fighting or fleeing. International threats and interpersonal fears dominate the lives of many persons around the world. Family strife, divorce and separations become a battleground for a number of fractured intimate relationships that psychologically result in depression, anxiety and panic. The victims of violent abuse and war are overwhelmed with turbulent emotions and bruised bodies. International conflict typically inflicts violence upon both military casualties and collateral civilian victims.

In 2001, I was invited to fill a Peace Chair at Manipal Academy of Higher Education in India. To meet this challenge, I built upon nine previous international experiences. I was intrigued with how conflict is handled in India compared with other cultures. Indians reflect fluctuating patterns between preoccupations with terrifying war and the polar opposite of blissful peace. Idealized hope for a serene existence is not only expressed in Hinduism but also in other world religions. In both Hinduism and Buddhism, *karma* is generated by a person's actions that perpetuate transmigration into their next existence. In contrast, Muslim writers[2] are critical of this *karmic* type of intrinsically valued blissful peace that politically tends to identify with the *status quo* rather than challenge it. Khan contrasts intrinsically "privileged peace" that fails to confront injustice with approaches of instrumental peace that expresses concerns for human rights, freedom and justice.

Detached serenity is likewise critically analyzed by a Buddhist monk, Thich Nhat Hanh, in his book entitled <u>Creating True Peace</u>.[3] From his viewpoint as a Vietnamese, blissful peace is more a state of being and personal existence in contrast with proactive peace that is concerned with social action and duty. He submits breathing practices a person can learn for ending violence in yourself, your family, your community, and the world. Many western perspectives have parallel patterns with eastern thought. Although western views are often more proactive and scientific, there are also major themes of benign neglect and passive acceptance of violence in western cultures. Pseudo-religious determinism can sedate people into an attitude of fatalistic inaction.

In much of Western psychotherapy, major emphasis is given to treating symptoms of stress with little attention to the causal factors that produce the stressful fears. Peace and flagrant injustices are readily separated by fascination with spiritual bliss that fails to probe the social problems that contribute to mental stress, physical symptoms and social disorders. Such treatment in health care assumes that by healing the symptoms of persons, they can return to society to cope effectively with pathological environments that are exacerbating their health problems. Escape into spirituality appears to be disconnected from the causes of oppression, poverty, abuse, violence and neglect.[4]

On the surface, the connections of mind-body are psychologically related to the issue of violent revenge vs. blissful peace. It is possible to advocate similarities between a tranquil mind and blissful peace akin to the physical body and forceful violence. There is a tendency in eastern cultures to assume that the mind controls the body. On the other hand, there are western inclinations that view the body as dominant over the mind. Simplified connections of mind-body are more suggestive than conclusive that blissful peace can dominate violence. More empirical evidence is needed. The complex connections between mind-body add to difficulties in establishing direct cause-effect relationships.

While divergent beliefs persist about the interaction between the mind and the body, the pursuit of sustainable and just peace is even more complicated. The interest of people in practicing yoga in western cultures reflects more their interest in exercise than in grasping the complexities of the yoga traditions of India and the Far East. Moreover, the over-simplified retreat to ethereal states of mind may be a diversion from the tough challenges of delving deeply into conflicting issues of social and economic injustice.

The problems faced by people in South Asia concern many people around the world. There is also a noticeable tendency by people to limit their own personal preoccupations about conflicts that divert them from deadly violence and neglect. Uncomfortable experiences quickly tear them away from troubling conflict toward an inner state of mind based upon peaceful meditation and personal calmness. There is limited tolerance in facing unpleasant causes of bloody violence and idealized, inner serenity. There is a noticeable tendency to skip over this vast middle ground where the difficult problems of typical conflicts and injustice transpire. Disturbing human experiences are frequently avoided such as bitter revenge, hateful anger and aggression. Internal feelings of envy, hatred, jealousy, and impatience are also not constructively addressed.

When these uncomfortable experiences of violent tension and conflict arise, psychic numbing[5] soon desensitizes people along with hardening their negative emotions. Two likely responses follow after exposure to bludgeoning violence: One involves longing for inner serenity and blissful peace. The other response involves over-reacting with vicious rage, retaliation, and revenge. When the first response prevails, this sense of blissful peace is sought at a price. The quick leap to idealized tranquility neglects thorough analyses for understanding the causes of the brutal structural violence and oppressive injustice. Peace is quickly sought, but is often temporary. The unresolved conflicts fester repeatedly without proactively addressing the deeper factors that cause these highly volatile problems. Serenity in the face of conflict can be similar to masking an inappropriate smile in the face of depressing tragedy.

This unfortunate separation between peace and justice becomes apparent in hotspots around the world. In both domestic abuse and in international violence, there is a flagrant disconnect between peace and justice. In the brutality of family abuse, violent men resort to controlling vulnerable family members by means of coercive force. Abusive men usually control their families with violence to "enforce peace" rather than providing fair treatment.

Throughout history, nations have resorted to violent war in order to dominate other nations instead of pursuing nonviolent alternatives. Dominating powers frequently impose their control through military force rather than negotiating differences. Violent wars have been used to control other nations rather than to create peace through just means for settling disputes. Peace and justice are flagrantly disconnected in domestic and international arenas. The need to re-unite peace and justice is another theme of this book so that violent force does not continue to be the leading strategies.

**What feeds violent conflict?**

In order to cope with the challenges of living together in a global culture, it is essential to understand internal and external causes of human conflict. At this time in human knowledge, it is impossible to definitively identify all the causal factors of violent conflicts. Vollmann tries in his seven volumes on his understanding of violence from multi-disciplinary perspectives.[6] Nevertheless, there are limits in understanding the sociobiology, etiology, history, political injustice, inhumanity and cultural pathology of war and violence. However, it is possible to identify a number of environmental and innate contributors that are experienced by people in most cultures.

The brain recognizes physiological and emotional disturbances that are detected by the central nervous system of the body that attempts to maintain balance and homeostasis for survival of the organism. Imbalances are quickly recognized by the brain in order to automatically restore biological equilibrium. Stressors are addressed by adaptive neurology and physiological functioning described by the pioneering researchers including of Selye[7] and more recent scientists. In addition, the senses provide awareness of the immediate environment so that we have input visually and auditorially, but also through touch, smell, taste and related sensory mechanisms.

Social psychology, humanities and social sciences provide awareness of cultures, individuals, and the natural environment. Along with interior feedback from the central nervous system, human beings process awareness of comfort and danger in their exterior environment. Threats are quickly processed into protective responses of flight or fight depending whether a friend or an enemy is perceived. Survival is a basic response of living organisms. However, as a psychologist, policy analyst and pastoral counselor, these concerns are frequently encountered in the course of professional consultations. When people panic with crises, they are primarily motivated by fears of failure and loss of control. Clinically, these fears are encountered in the deepest needs of human despair, struggles and conflict.

In ordinary exchanges, pain and suffering are not part of typical personal conversations. However, these fears quickly surface in professional clinical consultations with leaders facing crises of decision-making, and with persons in the throes of devastating crises. Persons facing personal, professional and leadership catastrophes unload fears and anxieties that test literally their human capacities to cope and survive. Box 2-2 identifies fears that motivate people in avoiding the ominous threat of failure as a responsible person.

| **Box 2-2: Fear of Failure** |
|---|
| Fear is an enormously powerful motivator for protective actions and unconscious ego defenses both for people and threatened societies. Psychological, social and physical dread include:<br>• **Fear of annihilation:**<br>　o **Death that terminates volitional choices.**<br>　o **Fatal injuries and terminal illnesses without known cures.**<br>　o **Non-being that terminates social existence.**<br>• **Health failure:**<br>　o **Loss of mental faculties and leadership capacities.**<br>　o **Unbearable pain and suffering without available relief.**<br>　o **Living longer than financial resources can support.**<br>　o **One's body is considered physiological machine.**<br>• **Social Isolation:**<br>　o **Dying alone without family, friends, caregivers or support.**<br>　o **Inability to communicate while consciously aware.**[8]<br>　o **Irreversible vegetative state while brain-dead.**<br>　o **Phobic anxieties and panic attacks that paralyze behavior.**<br>• **Impoverishment:**<br>　o **Starvation of body, mind and spirit.**<br>　o **Natural or human disaster.**<br>　o **Inability to afford essentials for economic survival.**<br>• **Loss of dignity as a person and society:**<br>　o **Dehumanized to less than meaningful personhood.**<br>　o **Inability to suffer and die with dignity.**<br>　o **Servitude to merciless tyrant.**<br>　o **Family tormented with guilt, pain, expenses or death.**<br>• **Humiliating embarrassment:**<br>　o **Attacks of credibility, humanity, self-respect and character.**<br>　o **Shamed and considered unworthy of love and trust.**<br>　o **Undeserved punishment and inhumane torture.**<br>　o **Denial of personal rights, volitional mind & transcendent soul.**<br>• **Eternal damnation:**<br>　o **Judged as irredeemable without opportunity for appeal.**<br>　o **Oppressive condemnation and endless torment.** |

There are constructive aspects of anxiety, pain and fear that should be recognized. These unpleasant experiences do have a survival function for living creatures.[9] Pain is a signal that there is a physical or emotional state that needs attention parallel to a fever signaling that the body is ill. Without pain, an animal or human might not survive. Fear of danger is likewise a warning that needs attention in order to avoid injury or life threats.

Fear can be motivating to take constructive action just as pain and fever serves as an advisory to seek healing in order to cope with conflicts that are inherent in being alive.[10] When free-floating anxiety can be connected to specific causes, then people and collective groups can identify what they specifically fear in order to marshal their problem-solving strategies more effectively toward corrective actions. These manageable degrees of pain, anxiety and fear can motivate positive responses. However, overwhelming levels of dreadful fear can paralyze into immobile states of traumatic panic.[11]

Both emotionally and linguistically, the word "conflict" itself can create negative reaction disturbing in many people. Mental discord occurs for persons when they are confronted with such emotionally triggered concepts such as problem or mathematics. Other persons may experience cognitive dissonance when a thorny conflict is identified. These apprehensions occur very rapidly when people are personally invested in the outcome of the dilemma. Leaders of large cultural societies and groups face their human limits while troubled by their personal capacities to cope. Creative persons are particularly sensitive to these issues. It has been a personal privilege and social responsibility of mine to counsel with persons who have faced major dilemmas in their professional and personal lives. Helping people discover valuable alternatives has been a major facet of my clinical, public policy and pastoral focus.[12]

If given a choice, many people are more comfortable in dealing with alternative terminology for crisis, conflict and problem. For example, negative memories of vulnerability can emotionally upset persons attempting to pass tests or solve mathematical problems. Sensitive conflicts are triggered about a previously painful trauma that initially gave persons a protective barrier against the threat of another negative reaction. Conflicts have a tendency to multiply if they are not quickly addressed. Damaging conflicts can perpetuate bad memories, negative emotions, and inadequate problem solving strategies.

Labeling a dilemma as a game, puzzle or a challenge can help some people cope more constructively in countering negative reactions. These positive terms can subjectively help people overcome resistance in dealing with conflict that have tender emotional scars. Since it helps to incorporate a parallel synonym for conflict or problem, further exploration can be productive. But all of these linguistic adjustments may be artificial protections that avoid the serious nature of brutal violence even though there are autocrats who consider war as a game. A more tolerable approach involves exploratory issues about troubling challenges in international relations. The following questions can ease people into addressing aggression, vengeful retaliation, and violent war.
- Why do justice and peace become separated?
- Why do people resort to violent rage, revenge and retaliation?
- How do stereotypes contribute to racial, sexual, socio-economic, religious and political strife?
- Why is superiority over people sought rather than their well-being?
- How do acquisitive needs and consumption contribute to violence?

On a social level, there are numerous reasons that human beings feel insecure. Fear triggers powerful human motivations that include being threatened with death, shame, injury and survival. Since many people can be obsessed with controlling others, there is also a painful fear of losing control of people whom they feel should be subservient. Fortifying one's control becomes a powerful factor in domestic and international reactions to fear. Imminent insecurity can readily result in using force in order to restore basic security.

While consideration has been given in previous paragraphs to negative motivation of fears and phobias, fortunately positive motivations are equally as powerful. Many of the needs identified in Box 2-3 are found in most cultures and may be universal. They also counter balance the fears previously discussed. These positive human needs can be given more extensive understanding since they are not exhaustive.

| Box 2-3: Sources of Human Needs[13] |
|---|
| **Physiological Needs:** Basic needs for food, air, water, housing and shelter, protection from premature death and preventable accidents. |
| **Safety and Security Needs:** Protection from natural disasters, predators, loss of family, home, resources, and environment. |
| **Social Needs:** Interpersonally belonging to a social group in meaningful, trusting relationships in family, marriage and community. |
| **Needs for Love and Self Esteem:** Capacity for self-respect, appreciation, integrity, acceptance, significance, fulfillment and recognition. |
| **Needs to Self-Actualize:** Quest to know, to grow and to develop creative potentials, personal capacities and human accomplishments. |
| **Meta Needs:** Pursuit of self-transcendence, universal connectedness, hope, harmony, meaning, truth, unity, wholeness, beauty, justice & peace. |

When the needs identified in Box 2-3 are applied to international relations, questions expand about how do:
- Hierarchical governing organizations inherently create conflict?
- Quests for homeland security polarize international conflict?
- Boundaries and ideologies provoke jealous antagonisms?
- Dichotomies of "friend-foe," and "enemy-ally" contribute to wars?
- Weapons endanger both owners and adversaries?
- Differences seen as deficiencies contribute to inter-cultural tensions?

Basic psychobiology identifies the need of living organisms for both homeostasis and heterostasis. Homeostasis seeks balanced equilibrium so that whenever an organism is biologically imbalanced the organism automatically attempts to restore itself to stability. Heterostasis is the opposite tendency for living organisms to seek stimulation through change within tolerable limits. When an organism's survival is threatened, its sympathetic nervous system is activated to defend itself. When the threat subsides, the parasympathetic nervous system regulates the organism in order to return to equilibrium. Parallel forces analogously occur when social threat triggers distress. In order to restore peaceful stability, coping skills attempt to reduce stressful imbalances. As a corollary, organisms seek stimulation in their environment by taking risky changes that can be tolerably managed. These counter-balancing forces provide biological explanations for conflict as organisms seek both stability and change. Extensive research in genetics raises provocative questions about:

- Psycho-biological explanations of violent conflicts.
- Socio-biological accounts about interactions of learned and innate factors in violent aggression.
- Gender differences that influence patriarchy and matriarchy.
- Culture conditions concerning predators and prey.
- Contributions of brain functions to internal and external conflicts. [14]

Biological explanations are very attractive since recent genome studies emphasize genetic factors in explaining aggression. Another reason is the ready-made attractiveness of medical and biochemical explanations for parents excusing their children's aggression. For example, prescribed medications or even illicit drugs are frequently used to account for violent behaviors. If aggression can be genetically determined and biochemically explained, societies readily conclude that they do not teach aggressive violence to offspring. Parents can then reduce their guilt about directly contributing to aggression because genetic explanations presumably can be blamed. As a consequence, less is attributed to social conditioning, parenting practices and environmental influences.

Each of the questions identified above merits intensive examination because issues about the causes of aggression directly apply to understanding international and domestic violence. Naturally attempts to address all of these challenges are overly ambitious. The inter-disciplinary fields of the social sciences, policy analysis and applied social ethics are given primary attention in this investigation. This book is designed to examine conflicting strategies in order to move from violent conflicts to strategies of peace that are sustainable domestically and internationally. Further attention will be given to psychosocial and public policy factors that contribute to violent conflict in future chapters.

**Posturing by national governments:**

Formal relations between national governments are largely guided by traditional protocol among government leaders rather than between citizens from countries. While official diplomatic relations are very crucial, citizens' diplomacy becomes more powerful in our globalized world today. Alongside official government relations, other relationships among nations occur at multiple levels including people-to-people exchanges, business and commercial relations, and informal relationships of non-governmental organizations (NGOs). In addition, there are the global communications developed by information technology of worldwide television, radio, arts, sports, the internet, e-mail, telephone, chat rooms, plus professional and literary publications.

In international relations the problems of intentional and unintentional misperceptions are rampant. Relationships restricted to official inter-governmental communications are subject to frequent misinterpretations even when deliberate efforts are made to carefully design formal communications. Image-making for media coverage, national posturing and propaganda dominate the agenda of official communications. With the frequent change in leadership and ambassadors, it is unusual in international relations if the official decision-makers have personally met for more than brief periods.

A "crisis management" mentality has been powerfully facilitated by "hotlines" critical in avoiding war. Management of minor crises is often neglected as evident by misperceptions and manipulation intelligence sources. How many national leaders have confidence in accurately deciphering the messages of antagonistic nations? How accurate is media coverage of international conflicts? Persons who have inter-cultural experiences realize how inaccuracies aggravate tense misunderstandings by both the leadership and citizens of nations.

Media give impressions that leaders of national governments are interested in peaceful co-existence, but simultaneously immense military expenditures are made to prepare for war. These expenditures, in the name of national security, are made to protect the homeland and advance global control. Many national leaders are prone to invoke the enemy for a variety of reasons. These tactics include the lust for more power, plus the insidious quest for coercive control, and additionally to divert from internal problems. Threats of external enemies become particularly appealing when the domestic affairs of a nation are impervious to solution. Subsequent build up of the military-industrial complex adds immeasurably to global tensions and wars.

Military threats are often inflated during election campaigns by aspiring leaders who may exaggerate the danger of enemies. Leaders do not want to appear weak to their constituencies. Consequently, displays of military power enhance the leader's influence, power and control. One of the temptations of international leaders who are inclined to military action is threatening a pre-emptive strike against a perceived enemy. Political leaders often "invoke the enemy" as one function of enemy-making that enhances the leaders power and control over his citizens. The author identifies six menacing functions that enemies serve in previous publications:[15]

- ➢ Political function that provides a leader with power and control.
- ➢ Psychological function to identify the superior "us" vs. inferior "them."
- ➢ Sociological function for fostering national cohesive support.
- ➢ Economic function for gaining territory, resources and profit.
- ➢ Religious function for polarizing the "good" vs. "evil."
- ➢ Media function for providing headlines from conflict and violent war.

Harris provides additional insights about how enemies are originate in his recent philosophical-historical analysis about responses to the terrorist attach of 9/11/2001 entitled <u>Civilization and Its Enemies: The Next Stage of History.</u>[16] He offers three theories for explaining the roots of enemies:

- ➢ The greedy as a rational actor who seeks his economic advantage and prepares to use force to obtain economic gain.
- ➢ The oppressed enemy who struggles for the recognition of his equal status by those who refuse to grant this to him.
- ➢ The overbearing enemy who seeks to force others to recognize his superior status.

While a preemptive strike as a military tactic has been employed on a number of occasions in military history, a recent rationale has been reformulated. National leaders with military capabilities at their command are tempted to rationalize a defensive pre-emptive strike in order to prevent war. In this dangerous line of reasoning, presuppositions are used to validate a pre-emptive strike against a presumed enemy. The concepts of self-defense and preventive war add to complex military strategies that try to bolster the necessity of an aggressive, pre-emptive strike. The need of political leaders to control any threat can be readily used to contrive the necessity for national security. Unpredictable consequences for utilizing this tactic exemplify the aggressive approach illustrated in initiating the war in Iraq. As a consequence, deep fissures have developed between the United States, its allies and the rest of the world.[17] Buruma cites historical conflicts feeding the conflict in Iraq because many Arab Muslims consider it a war unleashed by Zionists and Crusaders.[18]

Another reason why military options are quickly considered involves avoidance behavior by national leaders. Fear is motivated by harm avoidance that is a powerful genetically based facet of human personality.[19] A related basic need of human beings is avoiding inferiority that makes people quickly panic and vulnerable. People unconsciously fear problems they do not know how to solve. Often these threatening problems are about insidious social and economic injustices that feed structural violence. These very difficult problems may arise internationally or domestically within their own borders. The real enemy may be injustice, poverty, violations of human rights, structural violence or colonial wars of independence.

Because long-standing injustices are too thorny to address politically, dealing with an imagined or actual military threat has double appeal. Supposed external threats not only give powerful control to leaders, but they also avoid the pain of appearing weak in the face of difficult domestic problems. In order to avoid touchy internal conflicts, an external conflict has inherent appeal for a leader to engage in order to appear strong. A contrived scapegoat becomes a powerful diversion when domestic problems are threatening the authority of political leaders.

There are natural tendencies to avoid working through structures that have less heroic appeal. Informal conflict management efforts are very cumbersome processes that call for negotiation, legislation and enmeshed decision-making processes. Powerful leaders may feel embarrassed if they give attention to leaders of lesser powers. Peace summits rarely have a dramatic break through except for photo opportunities. Leaders do not want to be present in the same room with despised enemies. The Israeli and Palestinian leaders who negotiated at Camp David with Presidents Carter and Clinton were hardly enthusiastic about being in the same room.

Superpowers are reluctant to involve the cumbersome deliberations of the United Nations. This international forum diffuses a number of international tensions, but rarely provides flashy outcomes for leaders of antagonistic nations. Since the United Nations relies primarily on non-violent measures such as peacekeeping and negotiations, it has limited appeal to strong-minded leaders who would rather posture dramatically before the world stage and their own citizens. Box 2-4 describes national propensities to pursue their own self-interests and national agendas.

> **Box 2-4: My Way or Else**
>
> "My Way or Else" briefly expresses the theme of many leaders who insist on their way. This is the approach of authoritarian leaders from ancient history to the modern era. In recent centuries, notorious leaders who insisted on their way include Napoleon, Hitler, Stalin, and Mao. They emerge as leaders after considerable turmoil, anarchy and unrest to provide a way to address grievances held by the people who respond to violent solutions.
>
> Leaders become obsessed with the power that they gain for their own purposes. They deliver a sense of cultural identity plus an image of deliverance from disorder. Most people have little realization that the power of these leaders systematically is dominated by military enforcement and possible expansion.
>
> In political psychology, power seduces people into both control and acquiescence. Violence terrorizes people caught up into a frenzy of nationalistic empire building. Leaders centralize power so that they can gain control and authority over people wanting to be delivered from fear. Leaders limit freedom of press, religion, movement and civil rights to a major degree. Security and harm avoidance take precedence over liberty and human rights. Through insidious conformity to authority and obedience to orders, people find themselves trapped in regimes that control them. They lose control to authoritarian controllers.

There is an immense amount of posturing and veiled threats conveyed by deploying military expeditions, naval positioning, and impressive media coverage of weapons. The volatility of confrontations between Israeli and Palestinian armed forces and terroristic violence is a tinderbox that explodes with unpredictable frequency. The posturing between India and Pakistan over Kashmir/Jammu is another example of dangerously fragile international relations. The use of military force by the United States and other nations in Asia, Africa and Central America illustrates the forcefully violent interventions of the past half-century.

International hotspots represent the volatility of actual military confrontations. When nations reduce their alternatives to only peaceful relations or violent war, the likelihood of violent force heightens. Self-declared rulers and rebels can also express violence in dreadfully malicious ways including terrorists who perpetrate violence against targeted enemies and symbolic targets. Accelerating levels of threats of extreme violence include neglect, abuse and violence. There are also threats of lawless chaotic anarchy in family and nations plus unconscious projections of hostility onto enemies. Passive aggression divorces peace and justice with either terroristic or indirect violence. Dangerous weapons of mass destruction can lead to an arms race along with declarations of pre-emptive and second-strike capabilities.

Why do nations threaten to go to war? Often international leaders are trapped in the mentality of war by their limitations in seriously considering alternatives. Moerk[20] psychologically analyzes factors leading to wars in which the United States has engaged in the past century. In order to make war appear unavoidable, leaders have relied heavily upon "scripting war-entry." One theme repeatedly scripted is that an attack automatically requires a much larger, violent reprisal than the attack, thereby justifying the initiation of warfare. Another theme involved the steeply declining resistance of Congress and the population to presidential manipulation along with a steep learning curve in accepting the script of predominance by presidents in war-initiation. Both President Lyndon Johnson and President George W. Bush have been severely questioned about their decisions to engage in wars in Vietnam and Iraq respectively.

Hegemony has been practiced by nations throughout history. There are five reasons that hegemonists endorse as they try to build empires as elaborated by Daalder and Lindsay in their book <u>America Unbound:</u>[21]

- The world is dangerous in the Hobbesian view that life is brutal, hard, and short, rather than Kant's perpetual peace that advanced world citizenship centuries ago.
- Self-interested nation-states are the key actors in world politics. National interest is the prime consideration in forming policies.
- Power matters in both possessing it and using it whether political, military, scientific technology or economic muscle.
- Multilateral agreements and institutions are neither essential nor necessary in developing foreign policy.
- Exceptional great powers are unique in self-perception and that of other nations. This view holds that special "exceptionalism" drives policy.

Non-violence rarely filtered into policy alternatives by autocrats and national power structures who advance hegemony in international affairs. The image of the strong leader, a militaristic "caudillo," is unfortunately prevalent not only in South America but also around the world. While there may be many peace-talkers among national leaders, rarely have there been peacemakers and peace-builders. By most definitions, the "powerful leader" has official power to command ominous military forces that evoke fear. However, less frequently have leaders carefully considered the numerous alternatives for nonviolent peace-building and international justice.

**How Religions Contribute to Violence:**

It It is possibly ironic and even disrespectful to suspect that religions contribute to aggressive violence. After all, peace is purportedly an important goal sought by world religions. In fact, peace is considered the quality living condition God desires for humanity in most religions. However, in seeking ideal peace, religious people ironically engage in violent practices and militaristic tactics that contribute to hellish wars. Religious posturing incorporated into autocratic posturing are volatile ingredients of sanctimonious crusading.

There are basic reasons why many religions are misused in contributing to violence. The first reason involves neglecting social justice that addresses structural violence found in many societies. Even pacifist religions lack significant involvements that penetrate deeply into problems of injustice. Religion has many active roles in the lives of people, but there are also neglectful sins of omission. These oversights systematically contribute to structural violence gradually over time as explained in Box 2-5.

> **Box 2-5: Structural Violence**
>
> **Structural violence refers to social structures that embody injustice, violation of human rights, unjustified economic disparities and blatant oppression. Structural violence includes slavery, caste discrimination, sexism, racism, genocide, ethnic cleansing, killing females, and holocausts. Atrocities foster exploitation and poverty as major forms of structural violence that kill many more people than violent wars.**
>
> **For example, each year millions of children die needlessly from starvation and malnutrition according to a report of the World Health Organization even though sufficient food is produced globally to feed them.[22] Almost 11 million children die of preventable diseases including diarrhea, malaria, measles, pneumonia, H.I.V. / AIDS and malnutrition. This report also stated that 600 million children attempt to survive in impoverished socio-economic conditions.**

In order to understand the complicity of world religions in structural violence, it is important to recognize both what religions profess and also what religions do not condemn in structural injustice. These oversights leave immense moral vacuums resulting in feeble measures that are far too little and too late. On an active level, religion is used as a pretext in lusting for power by perpetrators of domestic and international violence. Religious authorities can provide self-righteous validation for adherents who affirm the religious sources that are quoted.

For example, apartheid and slavery were justified by quotations from biblical sources and sacred scriptures. Patriarchy is justified by many religions for subordinating women and children to the domination of male authority. Self-righteous political, economic and social ideologies frequently cite religious sources in fortifying viewpoints that include domestic abuse. Religion can be exploited as a commodity tailored for bolstering almost any ideology that human beings can conjure up. Religion is vulnerable to distortions in justifying the methods of people using domestic control and international violence.

World religions have not consistently addressed gaping injustices of structural violence. Instead, world religions have perniciously often called for "Peace, Peace" when sustainable peace is not possible because flagrant injustices are expediently overlooked. Slavery, castes, poverty, war and other forms of oppressive structures are called God's Will when the "voices of social conscience" are silent. Negligence results when ineffectiveness and inaction silence religious people and institutions. In the inception of a number of religions, the prophetic voice of many religions was proclaimed with strong condemnations of unjust practices in immoral societies. In these desperate situations, reluctant prophets eventually are compelled to speak out on behalf of truth and justice. Historical evidence can be found in the prophetic condemnations in Jewish, Christian, and Muslim religions. Mohammed addressed the chaotic disorder of tribal violence in Arabia in his day. Confucianism likewise arose as the ethical voices of young men reacted to the chaotic immorality of their time.

The prophetic voice involves the ominous dual responsibilities of "disturbing the comfortable" while also "comforting the disturbed." "Troubled Prophets" are reluctant to speak because their condemning message upsets their audience as prophets convey judgment and condemnation of unjust social practices. As a consequence of disturbing the power structures, few challenging prophets survive. Many are rejected if not martyred as seen in the case of Jesus, Gandhi, and M. L. King Jr. Their messages become unbearable to the prevailing power structures that fear exposure to moral truths. In contemporary times, liberation theologies have challenged the *status quo* of powerful economic, political and religious practices. A number of the voices such as Bishop Oscar Romero in Central America have been assassinated. Many others are imprisoned in an attempt to quiet them as in the case of Nelson Mandela in South Africa.

The priestly ceremonial functions plus the pastoral roles of religion frequently fail to be balanced with the difficult prophetic role. The pastor and priest "comfort the disturbed." The message of peace, tranquility, and forgiveness are readily emphasized in comforting people facing distress. When people are fearful, anxious, and grieved, the one-sided message of "peace, comfort and tranquility" is often over-emphasized while neglecting the difficult tasks of restoring justice. Agitating prophetic voices "disturb the comfortable." As a consequence, reforming prophets are often denounced, muted or ostracized. Imprisonment is another hallmark of prophets while some suffer martyrdom. Religious views that challenge the power structure are typically condemned both by the secular leaders and religious institutions. History is replete with death sentences by these established powers that are later condemned by history. The recurrent conflicts between science and religion involve a number of dramatic cases that reveal that even where religion is wrong, religious authorities used violent power to condemn, imprison, and even execute.

In addition to neglecting justice, there are other reasons religions contribute to violent aggression. In the rush to provide simplistic answers to very complex problems, religion readily provides authoritative answers that may be irrelevant for addressing the conflict. Many religions have reduced complicated issues into "either-or" dichotomies. The most obvious are the dichotomies of "good vs. evil," "faithful vs. reprobates," and even "heaven or hell." Many world religions also play upon the images of "light and darkness," with very vivid descriptions of who are the children of light and who are the children of darkness. Ultra rational thinkers can very quickly force exclusivist thinking upon complicated problem. Most religions also advance worldviews of the specially "chosen" believing and obedient faithful. Jesus can be quoted on the one hand that "he who is not with me is against me." Mohammed also recorded harsh words for the non-believer. A Muslim cleric in Spain has recently been jailed for advice on how to beat wives.[23] On the other hand, there are additional balancing citations with messages of inclusion, love and tolerance.

Extremist thinking becomes radicalized into exclusive camps. In India, extremists known as "ultras" can exclude others by citing remote traditions, historical assertions, or ancient scriptures claiming geographic sites. In Palestinian-Israeli disputes, religious claims to land are resurrected by both sides. Exclusivist tendencies separate the faithful into protected forts for like-minded, compliant people. Strangers are seen as dislocated aliens who are disenfranchised. Throughout human history, authoritarian leaders quickly interpret who are the chosen, faithful believers and who are disobedient outsiders. Kimball identifies five indicators in his book that signal <u>When Religion Becomes Evil:</u>

- Claims of Absolute Truth.
- Blind Obedience.
- Establishing an "Ideal" Time.
- The End Justifies the Means.
- Declaring Holy War.

No single indicator by itself identifies how fundamentalistic religion becomes dangerous. However, combinations of these factors signal increasing probabilities that religions that possess all of these ingredients are more likely to become evil. People who are attracted to these types of religions are vulnerable to imbalanced worldviews that lead to violence.

Young people can be lured into militant religious causes particularly in Europe and the United States according to Karatnycky.[24] Young Muslims in the diasporas of Islamic and Arab nations are vulnerable to fundamentalist messages. According to these sources, young men are not "sleepers" planted within Europe years in advance by the appeals of Osama bin Laden. Instead they are minted right in the West where they emigrate as searching young men. From my own extended observations with multi-cultural groups in India in 2001, a number of highly educated, young Muslims identify with the rhetoric of Osama bin Laden.

According to Karatnycky, for many young Muslims, "Islamism is the new universal revolutionary creed, and bin Laden is Sheikh Guevara." Bin Laden is also compared to the charisma of Carlos the Jackal, the notorious figure in Central and South America of a few decades ago. These recruiting dynamics are parallel to recent developments except that information technology of the twenty-first century multiplies their capacity to organize and deploy on a global scale.

The powerful appeal of terroristic cells in the 1970's and 1980's has historical validity in understanding their attractions to cultic appeals. Karatnycky argues that these persons were attracted to charismatic leaders of America's Weather Underground, Germany's Baader-Meinhof Gang, Italy's Red Brigade and Japan's Red Army Faction that I had previously researched. As transplants in strange environments with their frustrations and humiliation, these young people are university educated converts to neo-totalitarian ideologies. Box 2-6 describes the parallels between recruitment techniques used by military, religious cults, terrorists, and criminal gangs.

### Box 2-6: Authoritarian Recruitment Techniques

Religious cults and militant groups notoriously recruit people who are vulnerable to the appeals of simplistic worldviews. My research in social psychology on the authoritarian leadership styles and membership recruiting found amazing parallels among religious cults, terroristic cells, military recruiters and militantly criminal gangs. While teaching courses on "Cults and Religious Freedom," I educated thousands of college students on the characteristics of persuasive communication used by tyrannical authority figures. Cult leaders, terroristic organizations and charismatic leaders have more observable similarities than differences.

Recruits for religious cults tend to be naively idealistic and intelligent young people seeking a clearer identity for themselves. They seek exciting adventures for channeling their personal energy and their inherent capacities for making commitments. Clinical experience helped me discover that many recruits are confused young people who frequently experience stresses when they discover that the real world is very threatening, insecure and complex. Their choices produce fearful anxiety that intimidates their basic human need for security. They are in limbo between leaving their families of origin and securely establishing their own family. In this frustration, they are vulnerable to the message of simplistic worldviews and ideologies that have easy answers rather than complex questions.

Young people can be frustrated in translating their idealism into concrete action. They want quick gratification, clear explanations, and compelling causes to invest their youthful lives. They are readily attracted to powerful personalities with whom they identify for investing in "a righteous cause," or an ideology, or a ready-made identity. Frustrated young people are eager to escape the distress of mature adulthood, financial responsibilities or testing at career entry gates such as difficult exams. They are confused by the competing ideologies and complicated theories in the market place of ideas. Their enthusiasm and energy can be readily recruited, quickly diverted by "catch phrases" or easy promises of important roles. Direct observation of powerfully charismatic leaders discovers that young people are particularly vulnerable to the exploitation by deceptively attractive promises that are spoken by recruiters exactly when youth are vulnerable.

These young people can be indoctrinated into fundamentalist religious or philosophical cults, political ideologies or socio-economic causes, military service or patriotic organizations. Manipulative practices can be employed to attract young people into radical viewpoints or criminal activities that sound appealing to their desire for adventure and personal direction. Charismatic leaders in America, Japan, India, China and other cultures recruit members for offshoots of world religions, radically militant, counter-culture or cultic groups.

Gullible young people can be exploited by powerful personalities to give up their earthly possessions, devote their lives, and even be willing to sacrifice their lives for the cause. If these dynamics seem implausible to the reader, several suggestions are offered. In talking with members of radicals-anonymous, former cult members and cult leaders, I have discovered that they tell stories of their innocent gullibility to ideologies they thought were sincerely promoted by charismatic leaders with religious-sounding worldviews vaguely familiar to them from childhood. They found themselves surprisingly vulnerable to being quickly recruited, innocently used and exploited.

Dislocated from the traditional structure of Islamic cultures into the unrestrained freedom and open practices of the West, it is understandable that frustrated young people are attracted to radical worldviews promoted by Muslim Wahabbis in Saudi Arabia. Memorized religious literature from early childhood in traditional Muslim schools called Madrasas can pre-condition bewildered youth who experience stress and disappointing uncertainty in adapting to strange cultures. Untempered idealism may accentuate their desperate search for meaning and purpose in life. A cultic, militant or terroristic ideology can have powerful appeals psychologically, emotionally, intellectually and religiously at such a formative life juncture. Radical Muslim groups have become more vocal in various parts of the world including Southeast Asia and Indonesia.[27] Muslims leaders suggest that religious counseling is needed to find out why young people turn to terror groups and misunderstand *jihad*.[28]

A few empirical studies investigate the reasoning employed when young people are frustrated in employment and opportunity in their society. Khan and Smith conducted research with Pakistani in Karachi about the conflicts of individualists in collectivist cultures. Research indicates that when there is a lack of fit between individual personality and collectivist culture, feelings of oppression result that leads to either leaving the culture or changing it. They found empirical data in Karachi to support the hypothesis they tested that this lack of fit may explain the motivation to change circumstances through political protest and violent behavior. Parallel findings suggest that the notion of "mujahideen" resonates with warriordom, power, social status and recognition. Consequently, violent activism may facilitate discovering personal meaning in cultures that has both psychological and material benefits for the individual.[29]

When radical interpreters couch an ideology into terminology that sounds even half way religious, frustrated young people easily resonate to such messages. The critical judgment of young people to be maturely reflective can easily be placed on the shelf for the glory of religiously conditioned recognition. Eager, rebellious youth can become disciples of whatever cause captivates their youthful readiness in making unreflective commitments. With their physical, psychological and sexual appetites wetted, young people may be vulnerable to "fulfill their great moment in history," "the challenge of a lifetime," and "the cause to save the world." A rush to become involved can lead to their "willingness to sacrifice everything." This approach is inconsistent with teachings of the *Quran* that there is no compulsion in religion.[25]

Friedman agrees with Karatnycky's assessment that is also consistent with my own observations from teaching in India and the United States:

> "….the real challenge of the West is to understand what is happening not just in Iraq or Saudi Arabia, but also in its own backyard, in the chemical reaction between Western societies and their own mosques and Muslim diasporas. That's where the killer pilots were conceived, and that's where they must be tracked – but in a way that respects the fact that 99.9 percent of the Muslims in Europe and America are good citizens, not militants."[26]

Why are many causes formulated with the malleable youth? Chronological age is not the primary criteria for evaluating a worthwhile cause. Why are many recruits educated with college background and frequently recruited at the most frustrating times in their educational experience? With the research and documentation of studies in social psychology, the plausibility of religious radicalism is more readily fathomed. In addition, the results of Milgram's[30] experiments in militant obedience and conformity demonstrate how mature people can be influenced by authoritarian and scientific causes. The well-known "Stockholm Syndrome"[31] also provides case studies of how criminals and hostages can influence each other.

In the marketplace of ideas, religions and worldviews, there is a lucrative market for recruiting enthusiastic members for untested causes. Elegance and simplicity has even more appeal in modern times because of the anxiety inherently related to the stress involved in complicated life choices. The appeal of television and radio evangelism provides further examples of religious appeals to people who respond to simplistic answers to complex issues in media cultures. Freedom provided in many cultures offers an equivalent market for recruits who are primed and ready for "Escape From Freedom" explained by Fromm.[32] These fears are existentially associated with the freedoms analyzed throughout this book. Moreover, people in developing cultures who see the disparities between local poverty and glamorous societies of luxury are particularly vulnerable to radical ideologies that may be unsubstantiated.

The appeal of radical militancy and religious fundamentalism is more powerful than realized by many comfortably complacent people or people hostile to religion. It is not only happening in special locales. Radical ideologies have been known to abscond with Jewish, Christian, Islamic, Hinduism, other Asian, African, and American religions in forming groups that advocate extremely violent approaches. The far right in Christianity in America is likewise vulnerable to polarizing with cultures that fundamentalist Christian views do not accept or tolerate. Crusading violence is considered one of the most destructive forms of violence.

Hindu fundamentalists are drawn to ultra strategies evolving in India. Fundamentalism in Judaism has equivalent patterns of ideologies and actions to justify polarized views. Religious languages of militant radicals and fundamentalist ideologies have kidnapped particular off-shoots of these world religions for their own need for powerful influence and authoritative control. Traditionally religious people too easily are apathetic, reluctant or even sympathetic to the familiar sounding language and concepts used in marketing these extremist ideologies. As a result, humanity around the globe is subject to violent aggressiveness and war-like mentalities of these crusading religious warriors. These radical groups can claim to be at war with other cultures and against people with whom their ideas have polarized them as adversaries.

**Unilateral actions & monologues:**

When Americans interact with persons from other cultures, we tend to display our limited capacities for listening skills. Instead we have a propensity to make barbed observations, offer opinionated perspectives, and give ethnocentric speeches for other people to hear. When people from these other countries try to engage in dialogue, Americans may attempt to correct them, lose interest or easily become diverted into other involvements. Sometimes Americans escape from engaging in dialogue by simply leaving the scene of prolonged discussions or promising dialogues. Of course, people from other cultures as well as Americans also engage in similar unilateral pronouncements.

Why do people engage in monologues rather than to exchange viewpoints in dialogues? One-sided communications readily breed antagonistic conflicts that could otherwise be mutually beneficial interaction. In monological communication, limited perspectives are expressed while contrary viewpoints may be completely disregarded. For examples, speakers are considered authoritative experts; political leaders make pronouncements; writers as authors make assertions; marketers promote services and products. One-way information technology and traditional lecture halls encourage these monologues. Television, movies, and videos also are monological with programs that foster passive viewing of largely pre-digested content. Traditional religious structures have pulpits for one-way communication to passive listeners. It takes an exceptionally gifted speaker to create a sense of dialogue with listeners.

Why are these physical arrangements constructed? The economics of reaching large audiences is one pragmatic reason. Other sociological and technical reasons highlight how monologues dominate communication that provide for little exchange or expression of conflicts. Parents typically utilize "The Lecture" in order to exhort children. Children quickly learn to placate their parent's harangues. They may tune out while appearing submissive and obedient. Pronouncements that offensively warn often result in the judgmental feeling that they have set things straight. On the contrary, one of the most effective ways to undo the aggression of a powerful authority figure is to placate them. This technique that all teenagers have learned involves listening, giving a compliant appearance, and then doing very little to actually comply. Domestically, estranged spouses battle in divorce court over disposition of personal property, real estate, and investments that are major controversies. Even more important are contests over the custody of children who become the focus of dramatic human struggles about the quality of parenting, living standards, and life styles.

Inherently, people and civilizations prize their homelands and culture while highly valuing possessions that they have accumulated and protected. People have financial interests that they protect important to their security. These property interests in many civilized societies are protected with the force of law, legal contracts and documents of title. These financial possessions and treasured resources readily become vested interests both on a personal and national level. Threats to these possessions plus protection of these economic interests provoke major efforts for providing security to people and their resources. Threats to these special interests can result in hazards to personal and national security. Citizens and governments expect the lives of people and possessions to be protected from vulnerable attacks to their homelands as well as investments abroad.

People on every continent of the earth have experienced battles over possessions and power rivalries that have persisted over decades and centuries. Major World Wars have been fought with enormous losses to the nations involved. European nations have had notorious wars that continue among sub-cultures in the Balkans. The United States has been engaged in wars in different parts of the globe including unilateral actions. Other countries of North and South America have seen frequent civil wars while people in Africa and Asia have countries and cultures with ongoing strife and war over extended periods of history. Oil interests continue to feed major regional conflicts as potential world wars particularly in the gulf region of the Middle East. Writers in the Vietnam News criticize the unilateral actions of the United States in efforts to impose democracy in Afghanistan and Iraq.[33]

Another difficult hotspot remains unresolved between India and Pakistan. The border disputes between India-Pakistan in Kashmir and Jammu has persisted over 50 years. Repeated outbreaks of violent war have occurred with over 60,000 casualties. Both sides seem almost impervious to resolving this problem. At times, both sides seem to hold onto this violent conflict in order to advance their own interests and identities. Questions arise as why both sides persist in this conflict. To what degree has the leadership on both sides used the Kashmir disputes as a diversion from even more difficult internal problems? To what degree has the leadership retained power by projecting hostile motivations to the leaders of the other country?

The long-standing conflict since the middle of the 20th century between Palestinians and Israelis has been a focal concern of the rest of the world. Both sides claim historical rights to the land and resources in dispute. Both sides claim religious justification for their assertions as a basis to occupy this highly disputed land. Hostility and antagonism is justified by claims and counter claims of ancestral precedence in arguments that have persistently evaded resolution. Repeated attacks and wars have been fought interrupted only by temporary stalemate of hostilities. Resentments have festered to further fuel the demands and counter-demands so that verbal, terroristic and military battles continue to be fought.

Both Palestinians and Israelis appeal to the broader world audience for sympathy and support. The roles of the bully and the victim are difficult to distinguish. Harris also uses the terms the "bluffer" and the "bully" in determining who is willing to risks death in making claims.[34] At different times, both sides claim the role of victim as exchanges continue in this violent cosmic drama. The bully becomes the victim and the victim becomes the bully in appeals for recognition, rectitude and righteous indignation. Neither the peoples of both cultures, their own leaders, nor world leaders have discovered common ground to resolve their differences. Consequently, violent outbursts have erupted in a volatile tinderbox that could further ensnare broader constituencies into a global conflict far beyond this geographical region. Each side holds onto rigid positions of self-interests that have consistently been seen as unacceptable to other viewpoints. The broader perspectives of mutual interests have been explored primarily with sweeping diatribes but with unrealistic expressions for lasting peace. Instead of working out a just peace, hostile antagonisms over many decades continue to fuel this imbroglio.

## What future for posterity with violence?

Historical evidence would suggest that domestic and international violence may persist in some destructive forms into the future. There is no assurance that if the authoritarian excesses of patriarchy and matriarchy are addressed that violence will be eliminated or reduced. On the other hand, the future of humanity will be belligerently impaired if violence and war continue. The negative fear of failure, loss of control, and positive humanitarian needs are powerful motivators for both violent and peaceful activities. There is clearly a need to challenge the validity of violent war for addressing international conflicts and settling domestic differences.

The prospects of humanity are severely threatened by violent actions that could irreversibly destroy future development of human beings plus the whole natural environment. The horrendous levels of violence of the wars and conflicts cast doubts on the potential for sustainable development grounded in justice into the future. The generations of the past one hundred years have witnessed unprecedented growth by most cultural measures. Over the same period, humanity also invented the most devastating threats ever created that literally threaten the future of life on this planet. The production of biological weapons, chemical weapons, nuclear weapons plus the exorbitant consumption of irreplaceable natural resources stand as threats to life as currently known. Both humanity's genetic pool and the natural environment are dependent on ominous human decisions.

Are human beings designed to control other people by inventing methods of destructive violence? Are the gifts of human creativity, genes and intelligence destined for annihilation, slavery, war, terror and destructive violence? The current generations possess both the gifts and time to influence the future of humanity. Posterity is dependent on the decisions of contemporary people individually, socially, biologically and internationally. Posterity cannot exist with continued acceleration of current levels of violence. Hopefully humanity possesses a cosmological future in which peace and justice are reunited.

## Endnotes

[1] Stated by President George W. Bush in interview by Russert on NBC-TV, Feb. 8, 2004.

[2] Khan M., (2002) "Peace, Justice and Change in Islam," paper presented at the Second Regional Conference on the "Role of Religion in Promoting World Peace," Association of Muslim Social Scientists, Dallas, TX, September 28, 2002.

[3] Tich Nahat Hanh, (2003) Creating True Peace: Ending Violence in Yourself, Your Family, Your Commuity, and the World, Simon and Schuster. Plus his book : (1985) Being Peace, Berkeley CA: Parallax Press.

[4] Well over half of the professional articles in professional publications in psychology, medicine, psychiatry, physical and mental health focus on treatment for symptoms rather than etiological factors that cause or aggravate the stresses that patient's experience.

[5] Lifton R., (March 26, 1982) "What Can The Academic Disciplines Contribute...Psychology in Addressing the Issues of Nuclear War, Conference Address in Washington, D.C.

[6] Vollmann, William T. (2003), Rising Up and Rising Down, San Francisco: McSweeney's Books.

[7] Selye H., (1976) The Stress of Life, McGraw-Hill Book Company.

[8] Dow D., (Feb. 7, 2004) "End of Life Decision-Making and Public Policy: Reflections on the Terri Schiavo Case," University of Texas at Dallas, Bioethics & Public Policy Symposium.

[9] De Becker G., (1997) The Gift of Fear, Little, Broan and Company.

[10] Hiltner S., (1963), "The Constructive Aspects of Anxiety," New York: Abingdon Press.

[11] Middents G., (1970) "The Relationship of Anxiety and Creativity," Journal of Religion and Health," Vol. 9, No. 3.

[12] Professional ethics about confidentiality prohibits revealing personal identities and case studies.

[13] Adapted from Maslow A., (1993) The Further Reaches of Human Nature, Penquin Books.

[14] Newberg A., D'Aquili E. and Rause V., (2001) Why God Won't Go Away, New York: Ballatine Books.

[15] Middents G., (2001) Crisis in Violence and Peace, Manipal, India: Manipal Press.

[16] Harris L. (2003), Civilization and Its Enemies: The Next Stage of History, New York: Free Press.

[17] Schmemann S. (Jan. 1, 2004), "The Only Superbad Power," The New York Times, identifies seven recent books that analyze recent chasms between the United States and other nations.

[18] Buruma I. (March 17, 2004), "Killing Iraq With Kindness," The New York Times.

[19] Cloninger C. R. (2004), Feeling Good: The Source of Well-Being, Oxford University Press.

[20] Moerk E. (Nov. 3, 2002), "Scripting War-Entry to Makes It Appear Unavoidable," Peace and Conflict: Journal of Peace Psychology, Volume 8, Number 3.

[21] Daalder I. and Lindsay J. (2003), American Unbound: The Bush Revolution in Foreign Policy, Washington, D.C.: Brookings Institute Press.

[22] Olson E. (March 13, 2002), "U.N. Says Millions of Children Die Needlessly," The New York Times.

[23] Article from Associated Press (Jan. 16, 2004), "Cleric Jailed for book on violence," The Straits Times, Singapore.

[24] Friedman T. (Jan. 28, 2002), "The Two Domes of Belgium," New York Times; Sciolino E., & Butler D. (December 9, 2002), "Europeans Fear That the Threat From Radical Islamists is Increasing," The New York Times.

[25] Quran Al-Baqarah, JUZ –3, Section 34, 2:256-257, Muhammad Farooq-I-Azam Malik, *Al-Qur'an:* The Guidance for Mankind, The Institute of Islamic Knowledge, 1997.

[26] Friedman, op.cit.

[27] Rekhi Shefali, (Jan. 16, 2004) "Radical Muslim Groups Getting More Vocal," The Straits Times Singapore.

[28] Yusof, Helmi (Jan. 16, 2004) "Address misconceptions of Islam" The Straits Times., Singapore.

[29] Khan N. and Smith P., (2003) "Profiling the Politically Violent in Pakistan: Self-Construals and Values," Peace and Conflict: Journal of Peace Psychology, Vol. 9, No. 3.

[30] Milgram S., (1983) Obedience to Authority, Harper Torchbooks.

[31] Havard J., (1987) Stockholm Syndrome, Charmwood Publications.

[32] Fromm E., (1994) Escape From Freedom, Henry Holt and Company.

[33] Collett-White M. (Jan. 12, 2004), "Afghan elections under a cloud," Viet Nam News, Vol. XIV, Number 4455.

[34] Harris L., op.cit.

# Chapter Three

# Winning Without War

> "War is organized industrial slaughter."
> Chris Hedges[1]

A small but significant movement toward peace involves stepping back from violent war and devastating rage. When hostile parties are at the verge of violence, they simplify their contests into either winning or losing. When the only alternatives are to win or to lose, a tempting conclusion is that the enemy must be dehumanized and then possibly annihilated. It is dismaying to discover how this mentality pervades human cultures with few exceptions. Losing is usually not considered an acceptable option for participants. In some cultures, being killed can be more honorable than surviving or taken prisoner. Fanatical soldiers are trained to fight to the death or commit suicide. Ideological indoctrination of their culture may honor sacrificial death or suicide for a righteous cause. Cultures that value death before dishonor may even express disdain for a combatant who quits fighting.

Suicide bombings and attacks have been practiced in various cultures that promise rewards in paradise for those who sacrifice themselves while killing others. In a militant interpretation of *Islamic Jihad,* advocates of suicide missions destroy themselves and their victims with violent deaths. The Israeli-Palestinian conflicts have seen violence perpetuated usually by Muslim young men and women who are given assurance of an honorable after-life in paradise. Cohen makes the observation that suicide bombers are not killing just themselves and others, but they are killing the very humanity of their own people.[2] Box 3-1 provides a characterization that expresses the tragic irony of enemies who challenge the possibilities of peaceful coexistence.

---
**Box 3-1: The Scorpion and The Frog**

A scorpion wanting to cross the Jordan River, asked a frog to carry him on his back. The frog refused, claiming that the scorpion would sting him. The scorpion explained of course he would not since this would mean the scorpion's death as well.

Seeing the logic, the frog agreed. But halfway across the river, the scorpion could restrain himself no longer and stung the frog. With his dying breath, as both he and the scorpion began to slip under the waves, the frog croaked out, "Why?" The scorpion explained, "Because this is the Middle East."[3]

---

Among the most flagrant have been the dreadful attacks perpetrated in New York City on September 11, 2001, Madrid on March 11, 2004, plus numerous suicide bombings in Iraq, Afghanistan and the Israeli-Palestinian conflicts. Young people apparently from Islamic cultures hijacked planes and passengers crashing them into the World Trade Centers, the Pentagon, and a field in Pennsylvania. In Madrid, commuter trains were blown up with carefully planted explosives. The Middle East attacks also exemplify the actions of persons so committed to ideological beliefs about perceived enemies that they are willing to kill innocent victims. Both symbolic and innocent targets are destroyed in desperate attempts by terrorists to send dramatic messages to the world.

Historically there have been parallel suicidal attacks perpetrated in desperation against powerful enemies. The willingness of over 5000 Japanese kamikaze pilots to sacrifice their lives in attacking enemy ships in World War II illustrates values that a desperate culture imbued in its young men.[4] In the middle of the 20th century, Algerian freedom fighters willingly carried death-inflicting bombs to drive out the French colonialists. In Vietnam, Buddhist monks practiced self-immolation in their desperate protests about war, violence and injustice as pacifists who do not directly injure other victims. They, too, thought that they were winning without war.

Religious ideology and super-patriotism are the alleged reasons that motivate these types of sacrificial martyrdom. Often young people claim that these deadly actions generate out of commitment to religious values. The history of religious wars provides evidence that intensely held beliefs and ideologies motivate human beings to carry out self-destructive acts and perpetuate deadly violence against others. Devotion to an authoritative divinity expresses adherents' heroic dedication to their religion and society. Patriotism provides further explanations to sacrifice for one's nation.

From an initiator's perspective, the success of their cause is so powerful that these persons commit themselves to self-destruction with hopes that their action will advance their beliefs. Their ideology indoctrinates them that the cause is more important than their personal survival or the target victims. When either winning or survival is threatened, these alternative actions are frantically pursued. Violently terminating life may be considered more acceptable as an alternative of losing.

**Why does Winning have Compelling Appeal ?**

To true believers, anything less than defeat and destruction of their enemies is devalued as secondary considerations. Obsessed fundamentalists and super patriots often hold similar views to true believers in these regards. Hedges states that war is organized industrial slaughter in his book <u>War is a Force That Gives Us Meaning</u>.[5] He claims that war has been part of humanity that will probably continue until we are snuffed out by our own foolishness. This mentality of victory in order to find meaning widely appeals to people captured in the hubris of victory— winning is not everything, winning is the only thing. This zero-sum game in war is competitively structured so that someone wins and others lose so that victors win at the cost of the losers.

Competitive sports have appeal on multiple levels. Testing one's strength and skills motivates participants to achieve at high levels of performance. This intense desire to win easily becomes the prime motivation for athletes obsessed to achieve victory. National cultures can place similar external pressure for winning as clearly displayed in the excesses of Olympic competition despite its high ideal. But there are careful safeguards that govern organized athletics. Rules regulate participants in what is acceptable behavior in sports. These rules have been agreed upon by a consensus of people officially involved in organizing these activities. Referees and umpires enforce established rules with warnings and penalties. Fair play in competition is the hallmark of winning athletes who achieve recognition in the spirit of sportsmanship.

There are sports that have become exceedingly violent in different periods of history. The gruesome Roman entertainment of violent fighting by gladiators had certain basic rules governing the deadly events. Later in history, dueling was practiced to uphold honor. Personal honor was at stake in dueling, but it also was governed by strict rules that were carefully applied. Dueling obviously had a winner and loser with the outcome of death or near fatal injury to the loser. Within the past two hundred years, more civil practices were adopted as modern cultures slowly arrived at a consensus that dueling is unacceptably violent and inhumane.

The dichotomy of a winner and a loser has wide appeal. It continues to attract ultra nationalism and fundamentalist ideologies with extremely violent consequences. Many true believers make clear distinctions between winners and losers with a sense of triumphal glee by militant radicals and their constituents. Militant Muslims believe that martyrs will go to heaven where faithful winners will be eternally rewarded, and the losers will go to hell to be eternally punished.[6]

To hold the power of life and death over people is an ultimate control that obsesses authoritarian figures. They search for unquestioned authority in order to hold threats over subjects, enemies and victims. Their power to make threats of violent destruction has diabolical appeal to persons obsessed with controlling others. Governments historically have power to declare war against other nations. Terrorists assume a sub-state authority in criminally attacking targets in war-like executions. Traditionally, the ultimate power of legal execution has been lodged in the authority of the state. In more chaotic times, executions may be carried out by vigilantes who take the law into their own hands.

Not only does this obsession for control appeal to enemies contending in international violence, it also arises in inflicting domestic violence. The abusive parent holds their family as hostages with fierce violence that has life and death consequences. The horrendous killing by parents of their own children has shocked people beyond belief who ordinarily attribute nurturing love to parents. In 1999, the latest year in which statistics were available in the United States,[7] 607 children under the age of five were killed by their own parents. Many of these parents apparently suffered from mental illnesses and related derangements. Equally horrendous are children killing parents plus spouses killing their mates as indications of horrific domestic violence in families.

Domestic violence raises its ugly face in many cultures of the world. On a trip to Southeast Asia, media from Singapore report spouse violence. Zainol entitled an article "Why she killed the 'Soulmate' she loved."[8] While this grandmother saved her husband from a life of poverty, he beat her and spent her money on liquor. One day she snapped in this roller coaster relationship and killed him. Another report from Singapore described a woman who had been abused for three hours in a tiff over $5 by a man who was a neighbor even though people on his street had complained previously to police about his abusive behavior.[9] These incidences are multiplied innumerable times in most cultures.

The simplistic thinking of ideological autocrats is also expressed in terrible atrocities perpetrated by authoritarian figures. Their intoxication with power separates people into categories of the ruler and those who are ruled. History is replete with terrifying rulers who ruled over their subjects with threats of life and death. Powerless subjects become victims of imprisonment, torture and death at the whims of a ruler obsessed with evil destruction. Hitler, Mao, Stalin and Hussein were dictators who accumulated political power over their victims. The intoxicating evil of the fanatical "isms" has haunted even civilized people. Fascism, Communism, Nazism, terrorism, Maoism, Stalinism, Baathism, and colonialism have resulted in millions of violent deaths and oppressive injustice for untold victims.

There are people who believe that violence and war are biologically determined through inherited genes. However, there are reputable scientists[10] who have discovered persuasive data supporting the conclusion that social conditioning is the primary contributor in learning violent aggression. These are very important issues needing careful investigation. These empirical issues need further research in order to formulate public policy based upon scientific findings. At times in modern history, scientific discoveries have prematurely reduced very complex behavior to over-simplified explanations accrediting violent aggression to either innate genes or environmental factors. The interaction of inherited genes and social conditioning is best considered as a very complex mixture that does not readily lend itself to favorite, simplistic explanations.

## Is Winning the only Acceptable Option ?

For the sake of argument, consider the alternatives other than winning at the expense of an adversary. What are other options to winning by means of war and violence? Small steps that back away from the brink of violent warfare can help humanity move from the simplistic notions restricted to either winning war or losing peace. There are numerous intermediate steps that can alleviate humanity from becoming entrapped. In order to discover approaches other than violent war, the following options are plausible for parties who are able to tolerate ambiguous complexity in human and international relations.

- **Interrupting Destructive Attacks**

A "cease fire" is a plausible intervention in order to stop hostilities. It provides a cooling off period for warring adversaries to temper the infliction of fatal casualties and further injuries. The cessation of killings in the civil war in Bosnia provides an example parallel to a "time out" in domestic hostilities. Both sides agree to provide breathing room so that more lives are saved and fewer injuries are sustained. Cease-fire is neither a solution nor a stable condition of peace. However, cooling off periods provide time for rational nonviolent approaches to be considered rather than killing each other.

India and Pakistan have repeated "cease fire" in the tense stand offs involved in the long-term conflicts in Kashmir/Jammu that has resulted in over 60,000 deaths. Neither the Pakistanis nor the Indians have arrived at a permanent peace although during the winter of 2004 renewed negotiations occurred that are continuing. There is some reason to suspect that the leaders of both countries symbiotically stay in power because of the threat of their enemy on the other side.

Similar types of explanations in the Israeli-Palestinian violence have been made. In this type of international analysis, the Israeli and Palestinian leaders need and almost select their adversary. In recent administrations, Prime Minister Sharon needs President Arafat although cooling off periods have not been sustained. If these leaders did not have an enemy with whom to contend, they might have to create such an enemy in order to remain in power.

Former United States Senator George Mitchell[11] has been involved in several difficult negotiation processes in prolonged violent conflicts. These include the violent conflict in Northern Ireland, and the violent conflicts between the Israelis and Palestinians. Mitchell identified two steps that are essential facets in peace negotiations: one is the end of violence, and secondly, a cooling off period. These steps apply to both domestic and international violence. Ending violence is sometimes confused with a state of peace when the same leadership and policies continue. Ending violence is only a temporary truce in ongoing imbroglios that persist with numerous violent interruptions over decades. Negotiations for enduring peace must proceed toward more constructive steps than a temporary truce interspersed between violent episodes.

Usually we think of a cease fire as a measure taken to cool down a hot, violent war. There are parallels in family violence that can be just as devastating in a family that has war going on inside their home. Box 3-2 provides an illustration that represents the chaotic conditions of a large number of violently abusive families in the United States.

---

**Box 3-2: Domestic Violence Interrupted[12]**

**A couple with a small infant, a girl five and a boy seven, became embroiled in destructive violence. Child Protective Services intervened with an investigation when neighbors reported violence in this family. Social workers took action to rescue the three children from further violence. This government agency then searched for a family that could provide foster parenting to these children. A family decided to become a foster family for the five-year-old girl and seven-year-old boy. This foster mother (since deceased) had her own school in which she created self-directed learning centers that she had developed. Her philosophy and practice in teaching provided attention to both the social and cognitive development of four, five and six year old children.**

**The seven-year-old boy who was slender and wiry had been physically and emotionally abused. This young boy and his father had been shot at by the mother when they were trying to escape from one of her angry rampages. Other information came in fragmented pieces from the young boy and girl. Naturally, the boy was much more cautious in relationships with new people. He had frightening nightmares, enuresis (bed wetting) and also walked in his sleep at night. This boy would be found by the foster parents to be wandering around the house in an altered state of consciousness.**

**At least in foster care, there was a ceasefire in this family. The boy was protected from further death threats from the weapon his mother had used previously. These children were under the guardianship of Child Protective Services supervised by a wise District Judge. These children continued in foster family care for six months before being awarded custody to their father. While they went through several additional adjustments in childhood, eventually they became responsible adults. Fortunately, the time spent in foster care provided a "time out" that led to further constructive development.**

---

- **Calculated Hidden Oppression**

Structural violence is characterized by oppressive social injustice that differs from direct violence that is usually fierce and immediate. Oppression is deceptively tolerated and socially condoned in order to appear peaceful. Structural violence is also more long term rather than using quick force. Box 3-3 provides Gandhi's perspective about "Seven Blunders" of injustice that describe the oppression of structural violence. Gandhi discovered these ideas when he lived in South Africa as a young lawyer in his early career. Later he observed this oppression when he returned to India for the last part of his remarkable life as a pioneer of nonviolence. Gandhi identified the concept of "passive violence" which is perpetuated and compounded by the structures of oppressive societies. He described these blunders to his grandson, Arun, who was born in South Africa and spent time with his grandfather as a teenager.

---

**Box 3-3: Seven Blunders**[13]

IN 1947 BEFORE HIS ASSASSINATION, GANDHI GAVE HIS GRANDSON, ARUN, A TALISMAN LISTING SEVEN BLUNDERS OF PASSIVE VIOLENCE THAT BEGET MORE VIOLENCE:
1. WEALTH WITHOUT WORK
2. PLEASURE WITHOUT CONSCIENCE.
3. KNOWLEDGE WITHOUT CHARACTER.
4. COMMERCE WITHOUT MORALITY.
5. SCIENCE WITHOUT HUMANITY.
6. WORSHIP WITHOUT SACRIFICE.
7. POLITICS WITHOUT PRINCIPLES.

GANDHI BELIEVED THAT OBVIOUS, ACTIVE AND PHYSICAL VIOLENCE IS FUELED BY THIS PASSIVE, STRUCTURAL VIOLENCE.

---

This oppressive violence is more invisible than obviously visible assaults of victims with violent weapons. Victims of structural violence may not even be aware themselves of their oppressive conditions. They may live with insidious deprivations so long that they may not be consciously aware that they are victims slowly dying through starvation, malnourishment and benign neglect. People who have lived in impoverished conditions for generations may not realize that they are living in poverty as defined by their society. For example, people in impoverished counties of the United States denied that they were living in poverty when the government announced their condition.[14] They knew they were poor, but that was the economic circumstances they had always known. They did not like to be informed that they were living in poverty. Nevertheless, when they found out the benefits of being in poverty, they quickly adapted to their new status. They could even justify their acceptance with Biblical quotations "to be content with what you have," or "the poor will always be among you."

In America, the Agriculture Department reports that many people have to decide between paying their rent and feeding their children.[15] Similar conditions occur in India where schedules of different communal groups are promised social benefits. Impoverished people around the world may likewise fatalistically accept their deprivations while not personally having awareness of their deprived conditions.

However, information technology and instant communication increases many people's awareness of inequitable disparities between the privileged wealthy and the impoverished poor. Awareness of their relative conditions can be very disruptive in larger societies and countries. When people have high expectations for improving their socio-economic-political conditions, different dynamics develop. Gurr and Graham[16] have developed a theory based upon empirical research identifying conditions that precede riots and violent rebellion. Their inverted "J" curve is diagrammed in Figure 3-1 that provides a visual representation correlating peoples' expectations of satisfaction and the actual experience of meeting those expectations over time. This inverted "J" curve visually depicts dynamics when rebellions, riots and revolutions are likely to occur. According to this theory, if people expect that their conditions will improve, they are conscious of relative disparities that threaten fulfillment of expected improvements. In contrast, people with low expectations are not as likely to engage in riots and revolutions.

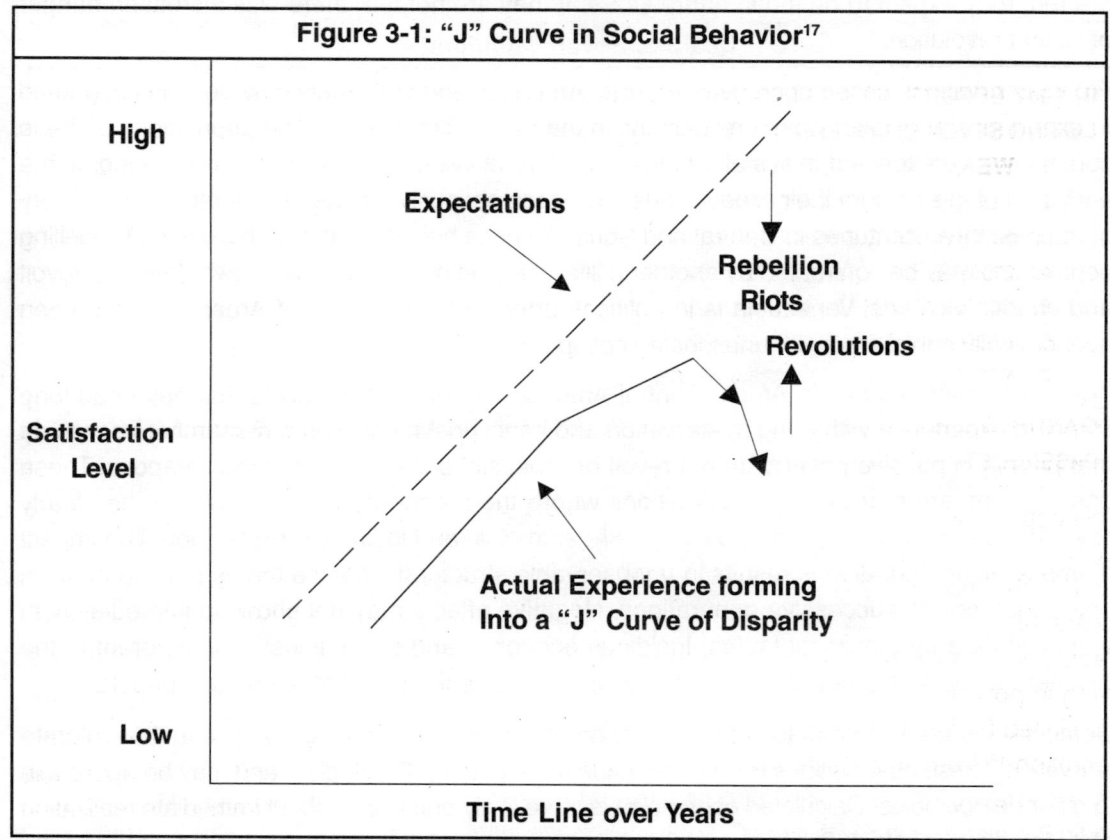

Figure 3-1: "J" Curve in Social Behavior[17]

People with high expectations only tolerate limited frustration of their hopes and aspirations. They tolerate temporary setbacks if they have reasonable expectations that there will be a recovery in their foreseeable future. However, when conditions become hopeless, people with high expectations become increasingly testy and hostile with discontent.

Nehru, the renowned statesman of India's independence, intuitively understood this J curve in his leadership of India when millions were starving in the middle of the twentieth century. At that time, India could not produce enough food and grain to feed its burgeoning population. Nehru entered into negotiations to procure wheat from the United States agricultural surpluses. However, the U.S. State Department did not permit more than a one-year contract at a time. Nehru wanted a long-term agreement that would assure food for his starving millions. He hoped for a dependable 20-year agreement or at least a 10-year assurance of dependable supply of food. Nehru was very perceptive about unrest and violent revolution during famines in India. He told United States' grain negotiators that if he could not have a dependable long-term agreement to buy wheat, he did not want to enter into a short-term, one-year arrangement.[18] He knew that if he could only feed his people for one year, their expectations would naturally build up to be fed in future years. He astutely predicted that if he could not count on grain to feed his starving people the second, third, fourth and future years, India would be better off if the starving people were never adequately fed in the first place. Without food, there would likely be food riots and violent revolts rather than passive acceptance of poverty and malnourishment. Once people are fed, they expect to be fed in future years. If they are not fed, there was increased danger of violent revolution.

From observations based upon news reports, Argentina and Venezuela may be a nation primed to experience additional violent revolutions in the twenty-first century. The populations of these countries have expected to live at a higher standard of living than they are experiencing. In the early part of this century their expectations have been seriously threatened. Moreover, the history of the past three centuries in Central and South America heightens the probability that rebelling populations may be confronted by another military regime seeking to quiet down domestic revolt and chaotic violence. Venezuela is in political turmoil. Many citizens of Argentina have been economically confronted with unexpected collapse into poverty.

There are other cultures in Africa, Central America and around the world that have had long standing experience with hunger, starvation and impoverishment. Some researchers conclude that people in passive poverty do not revolt or rebel since they cannot afford weapons. These observations are made of open conditions where the preconditions for revolt can be clearly seen. Internal rebellion is more invisible, self-destructive and indirect in expression. The impact of impoverished conditions results in unobservable structural violence that is passed on from one generation to successive generations. Negative effects may not show up immediately in empirical data for statistical tables. Insidious economic and social injustice is inherent in the long-term effects of structural violence seen in inhumane treatment of oppressed people.

Democracies are known to tolerate poverty among its populations, but rarely can they tolerate starvation. These observations have been made among analysts in India[19] and may be applicable to other democracies. Calculated oppression is more likely practiced without immediate realization of its insidious neglect. Such oppression has long-term negative impact upon a society. How do people die? Some die quickly from violent weapons. Others die slowly from neglect and malnourishment. The consequences in the long term are similar, but the measures accounting for deaths and reactions to impoverishment are different. Sen makes the observation that no famine has ever taken place in a functioning democracy.[20] A recent issue has been raised in India whether democracy averts famine.[21] Sen changed the way economists think about welfare economics, measuring poverty and collective decision-making. He has also pioneered the use of economic tools to highlight gender inequality.

Irrespective of the quickness of dying, violence has devastating effects not only for the immediate victims, but also the residue of hopelessness that is seen more in the despairing eyes of the victims who experience slow, agonizing deaths. In India, Roy claims that globalization is killing people in order to save them according to her analysis in "Confronting Empire."[22] She claims that impoverished farmers are committing suicide by consuming pesticides. Unfortunately, these claims have been verified in recent years with over 20,000 suicides among Indian farmers who face debts they cannot tolerate. The working poor who struggle to keep body and soul together experience a very impaired quality of life. Health care, nutrition, housing and education can only be experienced to a limited degree. Roy observes that the massive populations are many, while empires are few. She concludes that empires need the masses more than the masses need them.

Disparities become obvious between the privileged and unprivileged. The need for a living wage is a noble goal that Jim Lawson learned when he was studying nonviolent approaches developed by Gandhi in India. Gandhi's concepts were later used by Lawson for training young people in a civil rights academy in the United States in Nashville. Lawson continues to fight for a living wage for people in the Los Angeles area in his efforts to seek economic justice for the working poor.[23]

- **Proportional Retaliation – An Eye for an Eye**

In ancient cultures, disproportional retaliation was often practiced in tribal wars. If only one or few warriors were killed by an adversary, primitive revenge called for slaughtering many times more of the enemy tribe. In fact, a revengeful tribe retaliated by attempting to completely annihilate the tribe that attacked them including noncombatants such as women and children. In the face of such magnitudes of slaughter, the glaring lack of proportionality was called into question as cultures become more humane. Pragmatic self-interests of survival prompted neighboring tribes to civilize barbaric retaliation of massive annihilation of their enemy.

Suppose massive retaliation were practiced to its logical conclusion. Out of self-preservation, perceptive leaders realize that their whole population could be wiped out, killed or taken into exile with such disproportional retaliation. The leader, if he survived at all, would have a very small kingdom to govern if he had any kingdom at all. Consequently, the concept of proportional retaliation slowly emerged among the more civilized cultures. Proportional retaliation became the mark of a more civilized culture, in contrast to the barbaric revenge of primitive retaliation that hatefully slaughtered many of the hated enemy. Appropriate revenge more humanely evolved as "a tooth for a tooth, and an eye for an eye."

Monotheism, the worship of one God, also emerged among religions such as Judaism and later by Christianity and Islam. Monotheism prompted the awareness that one Universal God would also be the God of other people in different localities. Moreover, at a higher level, how could a religious culture advocate expressions of humaneness such as "love of self and neighbor," if an adversary's tribe were annihilated in revengeful hatred? As monotheism evolved, concepts of universal peace and justice emerged in social ethics. Both Jesus and Gandhi recognized the negative consequences of revengeful retaliation in their teachings and the need to "love your enemies."

An eye for an eye still guides many people today where conflict arises. In fact, there is a phenomenon known now as instrumental justice that is self-serving.[24] Rather than relying upon a government to impart justice on behalf of society, in self-serving justice private citizens impute what they considered appropriate level of retaliation for an offense perpetrated against them. Vigilantes act outside justice systems in using instrumental violence to decide who is to be punished or executed without trials. Under vigilantism, an offended party takes out revenge privately upon the supposed perpetrator and those around. Gang killings, mafias, and terroristic revenge are often expressions of this type of retaliation through means of instrumental violence outside constitutional law.

With nuclear weapons increasingly available, reconsideration of proportional retaliation is needed. Weapons of mass destruction (WMD) have ominous danger for massive populations. The vigilante motif remains powerful in the revengeful thinking of many civilized people, belligerent terrorists and governments. Vigilantism is not restricted to deranged rebel groups or the traditional tactics of the mafia. The availability of WMDs to unaccountable bandits and anarchists add heightened dimensions of ferocity to indiscriminant attacks from little known sources.

There still remains a major problem with proportional retaliation. It can result in a cycle of violence, retaliation, counter-revenge, and counter retaliation until theoretically everyone is dead except one last violent survivor. These cycles need to be interrupted if civilized humanity is to enjoy any peaceful future particularly given the massive destructiveness of modern weapons. Revenge is an enemy of civilization.

- **Limited Force Necessary to Restrain Violence**

Berkowitz produced an intriguing pamphlet for public education designed to curb the use of handguns in the United States. The pamphlet had an intriguing title – "When the Trigger Pulls the Finger."[25] Instead of the finger pulling the trigger, he warns how the trigger seductively attracts the pointer's finger. With reference to guns and rifles, he points out how the trigger of the weapon seemingly possesses the strange power that influences the finger to pull the trigger. His main thesis dramatically suggests that whenever weapons are present in a situation, the probability of violence heightens. A confrontation between persons in which a weapon is present increases the likelihood that the weapon will be used for violent purposes. The presence of guns or rifles intensifies the likelihood that the trigger would find a desperately itchy finger.

The converse is also true. Whenever weapons are absent, the likelihood of violence decreases. This finding is counter-intuitive to advocates of weapons who see weapons as a means of protection and security. However, the evidence from weapons in the home supports the conclusion that when a weapon is available, it increases the probability of violence and injury to someone in the family. The logic is straightforward. The owner of the weapon is likely to heighten a confrontation into an unpredictable encounter and dangerous injury to the weapon's owner. Battling parties quickly resort to weapons to injure an intruder. Even the children of the owner and their friends are more likely to be unintentionally injured by the presence of a weapon. Accidents with guns are notoriously frequent in the home when children discover weapons. Unfortunately, children find almost everything in the house, including carefully concealed guns. There are major reasons to question whether weapons actually provide protection to a family. It can be argued with empirical evidence, that the presence of weapons in the home increases the eventual likelihood of violent injury to an innocent victim.

Weapons pose an even greater danger in the larger community. The introduction of nuclear weapons into the arsenals of nuclear powers raises parallel global issues. The world has been held hostage since 1945 when the first atomic weapons were developed and quickly utilized in

World War II against Japanese cities of Hiroshima and Nagasaki. The availability of these weapons has increased the possibility of massive destruction, nuclear contamination and extensive annihilation. Geyer[26] labeled these destructive weapons as the means for ultimate terrorism. The very presence of these weapons is accompanied by the terrifying realizations that unintended accidents will likely occur. Nuclear war and accidents wreak such devastation that it can cancel the civilized past, plus negate a livable future for much of humanity.

The end of the Cold War reduced military tensions between the two super powers. Both super powers possessed enormous arsenals of nuclear missiles that could end life as we know it. In this arms race, the United States and the Soviet Union each had tens of thousands of these weapons for tactical and strategic purposes. Both presumably have made major efforts to control these weapons, but the danger of accidents continues to exist. In recent agreements to reduce nuclear weapons, the United States and Russia have dismantled but not destroyed thousands of weapons. The older nuclear weapons become, the greater the probability of unintended nuclear accidents. Moreover, the likelihood of procurement and intentional use of these weapons by deranged terrorists directly increases the risks that these weapons are available to anarchists.

When the Cold War ended in the 1990's, there was a sense of relief in global tensions. There was hope for a peace dividend when neither side would continue to invest in weapons of annihilation. However, the end of this war was not a victory for either super power in its long-term effects. Trillions of dollars had been spent with humanity held as hostage in nuclear threats and counter threats. The end of the Cold War was not an occasion for triumph, but rather an occasion of very temporary relief. It was not an occasion to announce a victory over a vanquished contender, but rather a pause or a time out to carefully manage these exceedingly dangerous arsenals. Nuclear proliferation continues with fewer constraints and controls. There is evidence that the danger of these weapons continues to be ominous for humanity as fewer careful precautions are being practiced by the possessors of these weapons.[27]

Military expenditures continue to increase with projections that the United States will spend as much in 2002 on defense as the other 191 nations of the world combined.[28] This proliferation of weapons increases the danger of violent wars. The probability that anarchists can obtain portable weapons has increased dramatically in recent years with the capacities to deliver them to targets around the world. Nuclear, biological and chemical weapons are increasingly available as commodities for a price in secretive black markets. In the hands of unaccountable terrorists and fiercely hostile people, these weapons could magnify the vulnerability of major populations of global humanity. Schell[29] has made a challenging case that humanity has the "gift of time" to deal responsibly with these weapons of unfathomable destruction.

- **No Pre-Emptive, Nuclear First-Strike Policy**

In contrast to the strategy of pre-emptive first strike, there has been extensive strategic analysis given by nuclear powers to a "No Pre-emptive, Nuclear First Strike" military policy. Nations that possess nuclear weapons take different positions about whether they will use these weapons either offensively or defensively. Nations that are trying to acquire nuclear weapons have not announced how they would use these them. Most of the nuclear powers have made official policy declarations of no first strike for purposes of a military offensive. North Korea is one exception. With a declared policy of no first strike, massive retaliation would be reserved as an option if first attacked by an enemy. Within this declared policy is the deliberate intention of not using nuclear weapons offensively in an initial attack. As military strategists have discovered, an announced policy of no first-strike should necessarily be taken with cautious trust.

What a pledge of no pre-emptive first strike suggests is a challenge to the viability of warfare in which nuclear weapons would be deliberately deployed and launched. This policy then becomes a calculated stand-off in which people assume that no responsible nation would dare to consider the offensive use of these weapons. Barber makes astute assessments of policies that include pre-emptive and preventive war. He bases has analysis on solid historical studies in international relations plus an informed grasp of ethical systems respected in western democracies. In applying military strategies to Iraq and North Korea, Barber sees that when preventive war is applied to these nations, it rapidly melts down into something like a special case of deterrence. Consequently, he sees containment and deterrence more suited to these nations.[30] Moreover, he also sites Lindberg's claim that pre-emption can be seen as "the violent reestablishment of the terms of deterrence."[31]

International law has been more forgiving of "pre-emptive war" against a country about to begin a strike of its own than it is of "preventive war" against a country that may pose a possible threat to another country in the future.[32] At this point, the capability to deliver nuclear weapons is important to realistically bring into this discussion. Various delivery systems of intercontinental missiles and tactical missiles have been developed, tested, produced and placed in strategic locations. Nuclear weapons can now be miniaturized for ready concealment and transporting.

The most ominous war machine to date is the American Trident class of nuclear powered submarines with a devastating capability of delivering nuclear weapons. Concealed in the secret depths of oceans, these ominous war machines function with stealthy surprise. Each Trident submarine has the capability of carrying 24 missiles that can be covertly launched from under the surface of oceans around the world. If deployed to its maximum with Multiple Independently-targeted Re-entry Vehicles (MIRV) warheads each containing each ten nuclear missiles, the total capability theoretically amounts to being able to launch a total of 240 independently-targeted warheads. Strategically located, these Trident submarines are the most ominous war machines ever invented in human history.

Haunting historical records have shown that whenever a type of weapon has been invented, it has been developed and eventually used. The unthinkable scope of devastation that nuclear and biochemical weapons could deliver makes a secure future understandably difficult to comprehend. Throughout history, human beings have demonstrated inordinate capacities for destruction. Humanity has also deluded itself with assumptions that the unthinkable would never happen. National leaders, terroristic criminals and leaders of families are susceptible to possessing these optimistic delusions. Unfortunately some of these people have control of dangerous weapons associated with their delusional thinking. Psychological delusions are extremely dangerous. Consequently, the next section is frightening to contemplate.

- **BULLY or HERO?**

Bully and heroic figure are terms that can be applied to both individual and collective actions by groups and nations. Bullying and heroic actions refer to international conflicts, terroristic crimes, and domestic violence, as well as school violence, workplace and criminal violence.

Aggressively violent people can display similarities with either a bully or a heroic figure.

Bullies and heroic figures may use similar aggressive behavior in subduing their opponent through physical violence and psychological intimidation. However, bullies chose a victim against whom to display their aggression and terrorizing fear. In contrast, typically heroic figures do not directly select their adversary. Rather a crisis arises within their society that a hero or heroine is called upon to address. Heroic figures may not directly decide who the external threat is, but rather they may be thrust into the challenge in order to heroically defend their people. A bully usually selects his or her victim so that the bully can prevail without undue risks. On the other hand heroic figures may be required to risk their lives against an adversary who is a threatening danger to their culture. They do not have assurance that they will survive the challenging ordeal as they attempt to save their people from the ominous adversary.

Victims have their own unique characteristics that are noticeably different from the cultural norm. Victims may possess a peculiar deficiency so that they are distinctive targets for a bully. Moreover, victims can be of at least two types:

- One kind has a provocative verbal style that may irritate a bully into aggressive verbal and physical action. When provocation is part of the interaction, it may be more difficult at times to determine who is the bully or who is the victim.
- A second type of victim is one who is basically passive in social relationships in such a way that makes them an easy target on which a bully picks to vent his or her hostility.

Bullies generally know how to act with disarming innocence as if they were provoked into the aggression by the victim. From psychological analysis, these enticing bullies winsomely appeal to an audience for sympathy. They respond to group pressure to act out the fantasies of bystanders by the means of projective identification. This weakness is further compounded by the narcissism of the bully who fears the injury of humiliation so they compensate while performing violence against a victim before this audience of bystanders.[33]

| Box 3-4: <u>**BULLIES**</u> or <u>**HEROIC**</u> <u>**FIGURES?**</u> ||
|---|---|
| **Heroic Figures** | **Bullies** |
| TARGET an ENEMY | TARGET a VICTIM |
| USE NECESSARY FORCE | USE DRAMATIC VIOLENCE |
| MOTIVATED by a NOBLE CAUSE | MOTIVATED by SELF-AGGRANDIZEMENT |
| RISK THEIR LIVES | ENCOUNTER FEW RISKS |
| JOURNEY WHEREVER NECESSARY | SELECT PLACE, TIME, & AUDIENCE |
| RECOGNIZED by Their SOCIETY after HEROIC FEATS | WATCHED by LIVE AUDIENCE & BYSTANDERS |

It should be noted that bullies and heroic figures can be either males or females. Both bullies and heroic figures are motivated by different reasons to engage in aggression. Both have different opponents and victims, have bystander audiences, and are recognized in different ways by their cultures.

As Box 3-4 outlines, bullies have bystander audiences to recognize their aggression. In fact, they may need special attention in order to bolster their inherent needs for unfulfilled recognition. When a bully is fueled by hostile perceptions of a victim, the bully typically chooses when, how and where to attack. Simultaneously, the bully tries to select what bystander audience will be spectators of their prowess. In both international conflict and domestic violence, the grandiose bully may envision themselves as playing upon the stage of a world drama. There are also two types of bystander audiences:

- One can be called "puppet bystanders" who unknowingly become accomplices in the violent action.
- Another type may be "helpful bystanders" who might even attempt to rescue the victim.

Members of the surrounding community, whether local or international, are often the participating audience before whom the bully performs. In contrast, a hero or heroine may have no immediate bystander audience to observe their heroic feats. Instead they are recognized after they survive their heroic test, if in fact, they do endure. They are tested to the limits of their fortitude not knowing whether they will survive the dangerous challenges. In contrast, bullies are rarely endangered since they avoid retaliation once they sense that they might not prevail in such a manner that would glorify their self-image. Barber considers deterrence as practiced by the Superpowers in the Cold War to be an aggressive form of "active deterrence" that others see as bullying.[34]

How can a local or global neighborhood reduce the violent threat of terroristic bullies against victims? Obviously interventions by parents and society are critical for reducing the incidence of terrifying bullies. Harris suggests that violence by young people can be reduced when societies convince young men to invest their energy and aggression into employment, family responsibilities and constructive outlets.[35] These socially acceptable involvements are known psychologically as sublimation of aggression into activities that contribute to the benefits of the social order. Freud pioneered understanding this psychological dynamic. When young men do not have challenging opportunities, meaningful roles, and satisfying involvements, they are more readily subject to expressing their energy into aggressive and sexual behavior to the detriment of domestic safety and international security. Economies that frustrate young men and women without employment or significant roles directly contribute to the danger of victims within the family and internationally.

Bully nations and heroic nations can be contrasted on similar bases. When there are endangering threats, heroic nations may rise to the threatening challenge often not knowing whether they will be able to overcome the enemy. On the other hand, bully nations carefully select their victims so that they will have a favorable audience before whom to perform their military prowess. Another nation may become a victim by provoking actions by confrontational threats. Nevertheless, bully nations usually pick the time, place and occasion to initiate one-sided military actions that are most likely to defeat their victim. Italy's invasion of Ethiopia in pre-World War II is an example. Some analysts see similar behavior in the invasion of Iraq by the United States and allies.

Nations rarely receive adulation from other nations who may perceive that the aggressive military action is a pretense to defend the rest of the world against a presumably dangerous enemy.

The tyrant's motto is "Let them hate as long as they fear."[36] By comparison, heroic nations are appreciated, recognized and respected for taking great risks to defeat a threatening enemy who had to be defeated on their own terms in order to make the world safer. In the case of bully behavior by a nation or group, observing nations who are audiences rarely respect bullying behavior by an aggressive nation. In fact, the broader global audience may actually develop sympathy for the victims expressly stated to me by people in India and Vietnam.

The conflicts that have persisted in the Israeli-Palestinian violence illustrate many of these bully-victim dynamics. While Israel may appear to many people to be a bully nation acting as a surrogate of America, it is also difficult to assess whether Palestinians are exclusively victims.[37] There are times when the actions of the Palestinians display bullying behavior that provokes Israel to retaliate. Israel frequently interprets that they are the victims of Palestinian aggression in this mutually defiant violence. Who is provoking whom is difficult to determine. This is not unusual because bullies can easily convince an audience that they are responding as victims themselves.

There are parallels in other conflict situations. The Wars on Terrorism and Iraq provoke anti-American sentiment among some traditional allies and certainly among people from other unaligned nations who see the United States as the bully.[38] In another international scene, it is difficult to assess who is the bully and who is the victim in the India-Pakistani conflict in Kashmir/Jammu. Both display different characteristics at various times from other perspectives. Either India or Pakistan can act like an innocently unprovoking victim and at other times may appear to be the deviously conniving bully.

Likewise, in the microcosm of domestic violence, one family member may appear on the surface to be instigating bully behavior. Deeper analysis may even discover that the so-called victim can actually have cunningly provoked violence against themselves. Some even enable incest with children in their family. At times the victim may have insidiously been the instigating bully in the violent exchange that ensues. The attacks and counterattacks between spouses can make it very hard to decipher who started the violence and who is defending themselves. When one of the spouses kills the other, police and juries may have difficulties in deciding who is the innocent victim and who is the guilty party.

## Deterrence Threatening Mutually Assured Destruction

The assumptions under girding the theories of deterrence have been explored by some of the most intelligent minds in the world. The advent of nuclear weapons challenged the traditional concepts of a "just war" that had been developed by Augustine and others philosophers in the Middle Ages of the Western World. Mutually Assured Destruction is the intellectually conceived strategy behind the equally ominous acronym called MAD. Military strategists, philosophers, theologians, policy analysts and innumerable scientists have developed both theoretical scenarios that try to anticipate many of the possible permutations conceivable in wartime theory. MAD as developed in the Cold War resulted in another example of "winning without nuclear war" from a historical perspective. Such an analysis does not directly take into account the human, social and economic resources consumed in waging MAD during the Cold War.

The technical arguments explaining the rationale of MAD are available in a number of unclassified sources. On an elementary level, MAD deters any possessor of nuclear weapons from ever using them in an offensive attack. The strategy behind the theory is that the opponent who is attacked by nuclear weapons would also possess second-strike capability for protection. Second-strike retaliation would irreparably devastate the provocative attacker. MAD has been strategically designed to counteract anyone who possesses nuclear weapons from seriously considering the use of a first-strike with nuclear weapons.

MAD is a rational approach designed to avoid nuclear war. It assumes that the leaders of the targeted adversary can be expected to act totally rational while having their very existence threatened with overwhelming annihilation. These assumptions need critical examination for its own rationality and presuppositions. Can human beings who have their survival threatened also hope that other defenseless human beings can make predictably rational decisions in response? Barber considers both deterrent and preemptive war doctrine rest on assumptions of perfect human rationality.[39] His analysis provides incisive analyses of historical, psychological, political, and ethical limitations that question these assumptions of total rationality on the part of both sides. He concludes that preventive war and democracy as simply self-contradictory.

The Cuban missile crisis in 1962 illustrates an awesome confrontation between two superpowers in which self-preservation prevailed. It is uncertain whether other scenarios will have similar outcomes. Deterrence strategies fall far short of identifying the underlying causes for the hostilities. In addition, these analyses do not penetrate problems about the limits of human beings in their rational thinking when provoked with annihilation. Yet, these military strategies such as no first strike, pre-emptive action, and MAD are viable alternatives to outright nuclear warfare and other direct military violence. Indirect structural violence is likely to accompany these hardened military measures that should not be ends in themselves. Rather this analysis submits that these military strategies are transitional steps in order to gradually move away from nuclear weapons to less violent means of managing conflicts and threatening differences.

Other weapons of mass destruction (WMD) in their present biochemical forms may be intermediate levels of threat between conventional and nuclear weapons. These biological and chemical weapons of mass destruction provoke comparable psychological and physical threats between adversaries provided by nuclear weapons for mutually assured destruction (MAD). Terrorizing bullies whether they are nations, sub-state anarchists or individuals can potentially hold cultures hostage as well as specific target populations.

While it may seem that international violence is the primary focus, a number of parallel tactics are found in domestic violence. For example, abusive threats and abusive language may be less vilifying than direct physical violence. Nevertheless, poisonous words can psychologically damage another person's self-respect while simultaneously destroying family relationships. Sometimes provocative words can be tuned-out or ignored, whereas physical injuries typically cannot be denied or overlooked. Target audiences might withstand verbal harangues, but there may be no constructive movement toward resolving the menacing crises.

The threat of retaliation at least gives an option for avoiding an ominous domestic confrontation or battle that has no possible winners. Intimidating propaganda that involves slighting the truth is considered less violent than bloody injuries. Authoritatively lording over a family member may be temporarily better than direct physical blows. A cease-fire has an equivalent in domestic violence of locking up the weapons such as handguns, knives, whips and cigarette burns. Force that is less than deadly can also be intermediate methods short of ending lives. Strangulation is a frequent experience in which the aggressor repeatedly chokes a victim in domestic violence. A significant number of female victims have been strangled just short of death due to asphyxiation.[40]

An abusive father or husband psychologically holds his family as hostages in constant fear comparable to the same terrorizing way that kidnappers hold their hostages. The hostages held by the terrifying hostage-takers have the equivalent effects as a raging father or husband who threatens his vulnerable family. If he comes home under the influence of alcohol or drugs, the family advisedly goes on full alert to defend themselves against unpredictable taunts, threats, and torture. Ordinary controls located in the prefrontal lobes of the brain are dis-inhibited when alcohol and drugs are ingested. Victims of domestic abuse can be equally as terrified of their intimate attackers like populations are fearful of terrorists who are intoxicated with the power derived from weapons of mass destruction.

Small steps provide limited alternatives between the extremes of winning and losing, in many cases life and death. Helping a perpetrator of violence understand that there are alternatives to violence can be a life-saving measure. The family can hopefully win without war or at least survive with wounds. Alternatives also expand over-simplistic thinking that there is no other choice but the options of abuse or tranquility in the home, or only war or peace between nations.

- **Power of Media and Language**

The roles of media in modern times have become increasingly significant. While used only to a modest degree in most domestic family conflicts, the various methods of media are a major weapon in the arsenal of modern nations. Occasionally in high profile divorce cases that are contested with acrimony, the public press engages in slanted reports about the grimy episodes concerning the parties involved. This coverage of celebrities involves attempts to attract attention by both agents and lawyers for their respective clients. Media find these stories attractive for marketing to their readers' about notorious divorce or sordid assault cases. Images of the intimate enemy often have inflammatory impact upon the citizens of both the protagonist and their opponent.

With information technology, much of the world can be constantly targeted with images of truth, propaganda and sensationalism. As proponents of media are influenced by profit or control, there is even more need for evaluating reliable comprehensiveness of news coverage particularly when it is employed for entertainment purposes. Private ownership has influenced developments in news coverage in recent decades particularly as a fewer large corporations broaden their control of broadcast and print media seeking to maximize profits. Public interests are not always well served by solely private ownership of commercial media.[41]

In war, one of the first casualties is truth. Broadcast, print and internet media are controlled for maximum effect with the contradictory purposes of informing, persuading, inspiring and even misleading adherents and opponents alike. The most positive claims are frequently disseminated to gain allies for fighting the declared enemy. The correct images and conventional wisdom are continuously emphasized. Citizens of the opposing side are demoralized with dissimulation and innuendo. If censorship can be managed, the messages are limited, distorted or even deviously designed during war.

The Project for Excellence in Journalism[42] reveals these trends in reporting global conflicts. Their study found that when fewer sources of information are consulted in news reports, the more likely the news programs are filled with opinion and speculation. Less than 10 percent of the coverage of the conduct of the "War on Terrorism" offered significant dissent or different views. Straight reporting of the war had dropped from 75 percent factual reporting in mid-September, 2001, to 63 percent by two months later. Only 30 percent of Americans rated media's performance as excellent in mid-November, 2001, down from 56 percent two months earlier. Kovach and Rosenstiel accredited this decline to the realization that the stories became much more complex as the war proceeded. Moreover, the Pentagon in the United States had imposed the most stringent restrictions on the press in American history according to this analysis. They also suggested that the more the government restricts press coverage, the less the public is likely to sustain support of a war effort.

Kovack and Rosenstiel also claimed that factual reporting was harder to sustain in this war. Cable networks substituted opinionated talk for factual reporting. Local newspapers pulled reporters off the stories according to this broader study. At the same time, the press's performance began to decline even while the press was overwhelmingly supporting the government execution of the war. The researchers concluded that many citizens intuitively know that the best and most reliable work of the press "comes when it is providing independent information."[43] Another international journalist ironically decries that the sword can be mightier than the pen – especially if you have a lot of swords.[44] But how can the pen be mightier than the sword? Words and language can have immense power when composed by an aggressive craftsman of words. Invoking the enemy is a frequent focus of opposing leaders. Language can shape facets of reality in the thinking and attitudes of audiences. Careful psychological and political messages can be carefully carved out and projected with maximum influence. Moreover, the manner in which messages are delivered provides clues about nuances and meanings that may be interpreted by the astute observer of non-verbal communication and international posturing. Penning soft words in serious causes of peace and justice provides greater promise in reducing the hard military destruction that ruins environments and slays both soldiers and civilians as collateral damage.

My travel in the Soviet Union during the Cold War provided a firsthand experience in comparing my own records of observations in assessing incidences as a social scientist compared with very inaccurate media coverage of identical events. Even the most prestigious media in the United States misled Americans about events that I observed firsthand in Moscow. One newspaper editor who published my reports actually wondered if his secondhand sources were reporting on the same events that I described in his newspaper based upon personal observations. He decided to print both accounts side by side for readers to evaluate. Other professionals discovered similar inaccuracies by prominent broadcast and print media that disillusioned them while confirming my own observations. Box 3-5 provides another example of the need for evaluating both verbal and nonverbal media messages.

> **Box 3-5: Nonverbal Messages Within Verbal Media**
>
> A personal experiences in 1984 helped me understand the positive and negative roles that media has in interpreting developments in international relations. On a trip to the Soviet Union, I was part of an entourage of about 260 citizens of the United States and Canada. In our second visit to the Kremlin in Moscow, we were involved in exchanges with experts in Soviet Foreign Policy and International Relations.
>
> One official representing the perspectives of the Soviet Union was Gennadi Gerisamov, editor of the Moscow News. In the course of this meeting, questions and responses were the dominant format for this exchange. When I identified my research on the psychology of enemy-making and peacemaking, Gerisamov immediately took special interest directing his photographer to take photographs. The next day in June 1984, my photograph appeared on the front page of the Moscow News as a spokesman for this group of Americans.
>
> Later when Gorbachev became Prime Minister of the Soviet Union, he appointed Gerisamov as his media spokesman for Foreign Affairs. American television featured him frequently in news broadcast. He was not only well informed as a journalist for global affairs, but he was also very fluent in analyzing developments in the United States. In 1986, it was particularly interesting to hear not only his comments on national television, but also to watch his nonverbal behavior. His behavior was very transparent in a live broadcast of a summit between President Reagan and Prime Minister Gorbachev. Gerisamov's nonverbal demeanor suddenly came on full alert when he heard President Reagan make a surprising statement about nuclear arms control negotiations. Gerisamov quickly interpreted this announcement as a break-through development.
>
> The statement was concerned with a spontaneous remark President Reagan made about radically reducing the number of nuclear weapons to a level that could be destabilizing in the Cold War. Gerisamov was obviously startled and pleased with this development. His nonverbal behavior was an additional clue that an unexpected break-through was being placed on the negotiating table.

The presence of leaders and their comments can have immeasurable impact upon the world during international tensions. A few poignant words can have overwhelming impact upon an adversary's responses including widespread international reactions. These timely comments have immense power. Embellishment of coverage results from selecting data that affirm preconceived viewpoint or opinionated ideologies. At the same time, it is always important to note what is omitted in the communication and not stated in reports. Carefully noticing biased omissions requires extensive background in international affairs in order to sense what is missing, left out or serious partiality. In tense negotiations, the missing elements that are intentionally omitted may have major impact on the next phase of either friendly or hostile interactions.

Obviously words may wield powerful influence analogous to swords or weapons. In pursuing just peace, nonviolent words and non-verbal communication may be the most crucial methods for establishing peaceful relations. International exchanges fortunately help human beings communicate with each other. Words can have powerful influence on the nature of both domestic family relations and international affairs. Well-chosen words employed for peaceful purposes are essential for negotiations. Words can be utilized both constructively as well as destructively in intimate and international relations.

Advanced skills in linguistic communication may eventually become even more important than advancement in offensive weapons and defensive measures. The writings of a professional colleague[45] provide resources that are used extensively in international workshops and cross-cultural training. His work is constructively reducing domestic and international violence on several continents with room for addressing problems of structural violence and injustice.

- **Deliberate Listening**

One-way communication does not guarantee mutual understanding. Listening is an important ingredient to cognitively understanding messages along with perceiving how messages are delivered emotionally. It is surprising how few people develop skills in carefully listening with attentiveness, accuracy and precision. In effective communication, people listen to others expecting this courtesy will be reciprocated. Hopefully all participants will possess skills in listening to substance, format, emotions, nuances and tone of messages.

Dialogue and multi-logues are much more promising than monologues. Listening becomes even more vital for mutually accurate exchanges. Being accessible to each other is crucial both physically and psychologically. Many marriages and family disputes could be avoided if both parties consistently practiced listening skills. Time invested in talking over minor concerns can have immense consequences when major concerns need careful attention. Unfortunately, many marriages are ruined by one-way monologues that block out the ability to truly hear the other partner. When couples are not personally available to each other, the success and satisfaction of a marriage diminishes rapidly.

In international relations, careful arrangements are essential for leaders to communicate about foreign policy. If one of the parties is not willing to engage in talks, there is only limited possibility that negotiations can ever take place. Pontificating pronouncements quickly reach insufferable limits in delicate negotiations. Honest brokers can help provide the setting and hospitality in peace talks and negotiated agreements. World leaders need to pay careful attention to the pre-summit, summit, and post-summit meetings. The most competent world leaders inherently demonstrate polished capacities to engage in meaningful exchanges. Former President Jimmie Carter is an example of a global leader who listens carefully to facilitate conflict resolution now recognized with a Nobel Peace Prize. Another Nobel Peace Prize has been given to the Secretary-General of the United Nations, Kofi Annan, who also demonstrates capacities listen while engaging in very difficult international negotiations.

The effectiveness of world leaders is obviously impaired when they have not cultivated equal capacities to negotiate with both allies and adversaries. Adversaries present the greatest challenges for all parties involved. The secure well-being and peace of humanity are at stake as global representatives meet or fail to communicate. Magnanimous symbolic gestures are essential operational skills of great national and world leaders. When these qualities are rare, problems of conflict and violence burgeon without peaceful resolution.

In stalemates between disputing parties, there are times when the two sides have little or no capacity to enter into any meeting for joint discussion of mutual concerns. The term "soft peace hand-wringing" is a gesture that expresses an alternative when all other considerations fail. Fretful worrying may actually have constructive impact upon the hand-wringing party or even on the party that may temporarily be unavailable. At least there may be the connotation conveyed of concern about what is not transpiring constructively. Being noticeably upset is obviously less destructive for international leaders to become violently hostile. In domestic affairs, family members may convey frantic despair more dramatically in fretting. International leaders have not always demonstrated sensitivity to the negative impact they had when they are unavailable to address grave global tensions.

On some occasions, all one can do is to wait patiently until there is readiness by at least two of the parties to come together. There are subtle ways of letting another party know that the other party would be receptive to having an invitation extended for a joint meeting. The example of Pope John Paul illustrates an effort in dealing with the tensions of the Cold War. Pope John Paul very diplomatically let it be known through proper protocol that he would be interested in personally visiting the Soviet Union. Moreover, he transparently indicated that he would be ready to accept an invitation to come to Moscow if the Soviet officials would be so magnanimous as to invite him. The Soviet officials fretted endlessly over this possibility, but took the initiative to extend such an invitation. Nevertheless, the Pope's readiness to accept an invitation plus his willing availability as a revered world leader was an important gesture in global relations. His firm but soft words turned away wrath.[46] His initiative prompted the Soviets to take account of this world religious figure. Eventually, Pope John Paul influenced the peaceful breakthrough in Cold Ward hostilities.

It is increasingly apparent that the intransigence of the leaders of the Israelis and Palestinians is a boiling global volcano. There have been repeated major efforts to bring the leadership of these antagonists together by a variety of concerned global leaders. Both sides have repeatedly foiled a variety of efforts for a negotiated agreement that would be nonviolent. Each side seems to have blunt and ingenious maneuvers to undo the approaches of their archenemy. Both conveniently exchange the role of bully and victim for their own interests. Both have tacit backing of world leaders with vested interests so that direct analyses of these conflicts become even more Byzantine in nature. The United States has aligned itself with Israel and the leaders of Arab states have supported Palestinian causes. The leaders seem to retain their position by repeatedly demonstrating their respective capacities to frustrate their external opposition while retaining their internal support from their own people. This one-sided obstinacy is only paralleled by the obduracy of the other side.

The Pakistani-Indian fault line also has rarely produced interaction between leaders that has been effectively sustained. The games that are played are often protective of each side's self-image along with their unwillingness to take the risk of rejection. One ploy articulated in December 2001, was that one side would not extend an invitation to the other leader. The reason given was that they did not want the other side to have the privilege of rejecting an invitation. At such a convoluted standup, a credible third party might be an honest broker for hosting a meeting of these disputing parties. Where indeed are these trusted third parties? The world needs people who can function in these roles for addressing the resolution of conflicts by engaging in negotiations that can preclude open hostilities and war. Fortunately, by 2004 after patient but attentive listening, the leaders of India and Pakistan have entered into direct peace negotiations.

While these negotiations took place, M.D. Nalapat, Director of the School of Geopolitics at Manipal University, personally shared his observations with our delegation of American Rotarians in New Delhi for humanitarian projects. As an astute observer of Asian, European and American affairs, he noted a serious omission in the approaches of "Viceroy Bremer," the American representative, overseeing the transition in power in Iraq. Nalapat observed that "Viceroy Bremer" to that date had not personally met with the almost 600 tribal leaders in Iraq who hold traditional residual power in Iraq.[47] Serious doubts can be raised when officials are not consulting or at least listening to powerful leaders in an occupied country.

In difficult interpersonal relations, making oneself available is an important step that comes as a critical step for bringing hostile people together. Risking vulnerability is inherent in dealing with nasty opponents particularly when they are dangerously violent enemies. The testy process of courting each other is a skill essential in the progression toward sharing, relating and exchanging viewpoints. Effective leaders astutely talk with their adversaries. There is even greater importance in talking with enemies than talking with friends. "Dancing with the devil" is an apt phrase to convey the risks involved in interacting with an adversary. However, without a willingness to meet, few peaceful breakthroughs of hostilities can ever occur. Winning without war hopefully can result by taking risks in nonviolent strategies.

**Concluding Comment:**

Winning or losing are not the only criteria to consider by people in conflict, and as nations who are antagonistic toward each other. In fact, the tendency to only value winning has stalemated many mating partnerships and numerous international alliances. Win-win strategies inherently involve searching for mutual interests that at times involve risking compromise. This chapter questions whether winning through violent means is a viable option for nations and families to use in settling their differences.

The possibility of winning without war raises alternatives to violent aggression. It is more important to become directly involved in relating, talking, listening, exchanging, cooperating, and sharing than standing up another party who is waiting to be invited. Without sensitive exchanges with each other, there is little risked and even less accomplished. First, it is necessary to be available. Next to become personally involved to interact with adversaries. While engaging in personal involvement, transforming alternatives to violence can emerge.

## Endnotes

[1] Hedges C., (2002) <u>War Is A Force That Gives Us Meaning,</u> Public Affairs Book.
[2] Cohen R., (Feb. 7, 2002) "Suicide Bombings Transform Image of Palestinians," Washington Post writer published in <u>The Dallas Morning News.</u>
[3] Barash D. (1991) <u>Introduction to Peace Studies,</u> Belmont CA: Wadsworth Publishing Company, page 88.
[4] Hill C., (2002) "Clashing Civilizations or Mad Mullahs: The United States between the Formal and Informal Empire," edited by Strobe Talbott and Nayan Chandra in <u>The Age of Terror,</u> Basic Books.
[5] Hedges, <u>op.cit.</u>
[6] Some religions provide for a temporary intermediate suspension pending final judgment, while others believe in reincarnation.

[7] Patterson K., (Feb. 17, 2002) "From Maternal Instincts to Killer Impulses," Dallas Morning News. Since 2002, a number of dramatic cases involve parents killing their children in the Texas and other states.
[8] Zainol Vivi, (Jan. 10, 2004) "Why She Killed the 'Soulmate' She Loved," The Strait Times.
[9] Kin, Chong Chee, (Jan. 10, 2004) "Everitt Road Man Charged in Neighborhood Spat," The Strait Times.
[10] Berkowitz L., (1991) Aggression: Its Causes, Consequences and Control, McGraw-Hill Book Company; Goldstein A., and Segall M., (1983) Aggression in Global Perspectives, Pergamon Press; Adams D. et.al., (1986) see the conclusion of the The Seville Statement on Violence and War, cited in Barash D., (1991) Introduction to Peace Studies, Wadsworth Publishing Company.
[11] Mitchell G., (March 9, 2002) NBC-TV News.
[12] The author and his family provided the foster care for these two children who located me two decades later. They wanted to introduce me to their own families and expressing gratitude to my family for providing them with temporary protection and care during their own childhood.
[13] Gandhi Arun, Grandson of Mohandas Gandhi, in a personal communication in 1997.
[14] Weisman J., (Dec. 23. 2002 to Jan. 25, 2003) in a series "How Poor is Poor?" The Washington Post National Weekly Edition.
[15] Glickman D., (Feb. 16, 2004) "Hunger should be an election issue," Dallas Morning News.
[16] Gurr T. & Graham H., (1979) Violence in America, Beverly Hills, CA: Sage Publications.
[17] Ibid.
[18] Middents M., (1970) personal communication based upon professional world trade grain negotiations as a Corporate Executive in International Grain Negotiations conducted for Cargill, Inc.
[19] Sen A. and Dreze J., (1996) India: Economic Development and Social Opportunities, Oxford University Press.
[20] Sen A. (1999) Democracy as Freedom, Anchor Books.
[21] Massing M., (March 3, 2003) "Does Democracy Avert Famine?" The New York Times.
[22] Roy Arundhati, (Feb. 3, 2003), "Confronting Empire," Medical Consulting Group.
[23] Lawson J., (2000) The concept of a living wage were communicated in workshops in Feb. 2000, at Southern Methodist University and the Dallas Peace Center.
[24] Barash D., (2001) editor, Understanding Violence. Boston, MA: Allyn and Bacon
[25] Berkowitz L., "When the Trigger Pulls the Finger," American Psychological Association.
[26] Geyer A., "Ultimate Terrorism," Churches Center for Theology and Public Policy, Washington, D.C.
[27] Dumas L. J., (1999) Lethal Arrogance: Human Fallibility and Dangerous Technologies, St. Martins Press.
[28] Zakaria F., (March 24, 2003) "The Arrogant Empire: Part Two – The Age of Generosity," Newsweek.
[29] Schell J., (1998) The Gift of Time: The Case for Abolishing Nuclear Weapons, Owl Paperback Books.
[30] Barber B., (2003) Fear's Empire: War, Terrorism, and Democracy, New York: W.W. Norton and Company.
[31] Lindberg T., (Feb. 3, 2003), "Deterrence and Prevention," Weekly Standard.
[32] Op-Ed Editorial, (Jan. 28, 2004), "Bush Backs Away from His Claims About Iraq War," The New York Times.
[33] Harris L., (2003), Civilization and Its Enemies: The Next Stage of History, New York: Free Press. Harris provides an incisive analysis based upon historical and philosophical western perspectives into the narcissistic needs of the bully and "bluffer" behavior. He also see the dynamics of the victor- vanquished in international history. His provocative assertions and propositions need further testing with behavioral research and empirical data in order to verify his philosophical claims.
[34] Barber, op.cit.
[35] Harris L., (2003) Civilization and Its Enemies: The Next Stage of History, New York: Free Press.
[36] Daalder I., and Lindsay J., (2003) America Unbound: The Bush Revolution in Foreign Policy, Washington, D.C.: The Brookings Institution Press.
[37] Kaiser R., (Feb. 17-23, 2003), "A Special Closeness: The Bush Administration Embraces Sharon's Likud Government," The Washington Post National Weekly Edition.
[38] Ibid.
[39] Barber, op.cit.
[40] Walker S., (2001) lecture on "Domestic Violence," at University of Texas at Dallas.
[41] Barton S., (2002) American Television News: The Public Interests and the Media Market Place, Sharpe, M.E. Incorporated.
[42] Kovack B., and Rosenstiel R., (Jan. 29, 2002) "In Wartime the People Want the Facts," The New York Times.
[43] Ibid.
[44] Zakaria Fareed, (June 3, 2002) "Europe: Make Peace With War," Newsweek.
[45] Rosenberg M., (1999) Nonviolent Communications: A Language of Compassion, Keep Coming Book Company.
[46] Proverbs 15:1, (1991) Life Application Study Bible, Tyndale House Publishers, Inc.
[47] Personal consultation with M.D. Nalapat, an Editor of The Times of India, New Delhi, January 8, 2004.

## Chapter Four

# Whining or Boasting

> You won this time, – BUT WE'LL
> GET YOU NEXT TIME!
>
> Why Don't We Learn That
> We Don't Learn?" [1]

Diamond [2] made insightful observations about the War on Terrorism. He analyzed the folly involved in assuming that war is won to correct its causes only to find out that the basic causes were not remedied. Structural violence, social injustices, regional disputes and economic oppression are often inadequately analyzed prior to resorting to the violence. Consequently, war becomes the prelude to further conflict and terrorism. Failure to understand causes of problems leads to subsequent international and domestic conflicts. Critics increasingly suggest that Americans and British insufficiently understand the causes of terrorists attacks before launching into the War on Terrorism.[3] When structural violence is not addressed, victims warn about "getting even the next time."

In his book on Guns, Germs, and Steel: The Fates of Human Societies, Diamond[4] states how governments insufficiently addressed challenges of wide spread injustice involving structural violence. Developed nations like the United States neglect the fragile global environment and inadequately treat ominous global public health problems. Economic globalization ravages agricultural production in poor developing nations. Another example occurs in public health care. Diamond identifies malaria as the world's leading infectious disease with 400 million new cases per year while pointing out that the United States spends less on malaria research than the cost of a few days of war in Afghanistan. Moreover, mal-distribution of food results in poor nutrition, starvation and numerous preventable diseases. Instead of proactively addressing problems of diseases, over-riding social and economic injustice, or violations of human rights and population issues, negligent nations react with belated crises management of symptoms without remedies for causal factors.

In interpersonal family violence, there are often defiant threats made – "wait until the next time." Behind this humiliating resentment of losers is a clear threat of future violence. Unresolved cycles of violence grow out of seething differences and oppressive injustice to more vicious confrontations. There is immense difference between games with careful rules and cyclical violence that is not guided by rules or mutual respect. Even efforts to civilize marital strife, called fighting fair, have little constructive effect in reducing repeated violence among family members. Time out can temporarily foster more rational thought to counter angry rage. However, calling time out inherently assumes that the fight will continue after a momentary interruption of violent action.

The title of this chapter suggests that whining is a reaction to loss or negligence. Many people know how to complain very well, but only reflective whiners have insight why they are humiliated. Therapists suggest careful reflection to correct ineffective chronic complaining about physical and psychological problems. In marriage, when wives complain, it is often called "nagging." When husbands do it, we call it "rationalizing." When athletes gripe, we call it "sour grapes." When nations whine, it is about humiliation and oppressive neglect.

During extended periods in India, I have been amazed to read perceptive writers criticizing their own countrymen about whining that never ends. These columnists have critical insights supported with convincing data. In essence, these gutsy Indian writers repeatedly criticize Indians to get beyond whining in order to solve their own problems. When a prophet analyzes the faults of his own people, negative reaction might be expected from readers. Instead there is frequent feedback in print media of India agreeing with pointed criticisms about commiserating. People of India do not have a monopoly on whining. Most people around the world openly complain. Some whine passively by letting it fester into sore boils. From a psychological viewpoint, whining functions as a humiliating need for sympathetic attention or a cry for help. Inadequate problem-solving skills result in complaining, scapegoating, and projecting onto others. Narcissism perpetuates blaming others and outright denying that arrests mature development of coping skills.

Policy analysts enumerate parallel reasons why citizens and elected representatives engage in unproductive complaining. Whining has multiple roots such as diversion from intractable problems, or a campaign strategy to attack the opposition party, or a deliberate unwillingness to face hard realities. Commiserating is also a stalling tactic in budget crunching, an unwillingness to promote controversial legislation, or a refusal to use political capital for designing alternative solutions.

Elected figures encounter a suicidal challenge in facing social problems in public policy. They fear committing political suicide if they identify problems for which they do not already have a solution. If elected officials identify problems they cannot solve, they have set themselves up for defeat by a challenger. Another reason people whine is the difficult challenge of thoroughly analyzing causes of problems before offering solutions. There is a tendency to recommend popular but ineffective solutions. Pet answers are applied irrespective of whether they adequately address the problem or compound problems further. For a carpenter with a hammer, every problem becomes a nail to pound. Unfortunately some surgeons and politicians have analogous solutions. Surgeons recommend surgery, while political leaders recommend appointing a commission. Diagnosing causal factors involves very complex processes that are easily avoided when there are conflicts of interests. In-depth problem solving involves identifying known causes plus carefully defining complicated issues. Such analyses require thorough research, theory building, and data-gathering.

There are also erroneous assumptions that today's answers continue to fit future problems. Military tactics are frequently outdated especially when the strategies from the last war are repeated. Using war as a solution to address terrorism illustrates employing available but outdated military force to address puzzling tactics of non-state based terrorists. Many military strategists and civilian engineers discover that the half-life of their ready-made answers is less than 18 months. In effect, only half of their current answers will be sufficient within two years to address problems they typically encounter. Half of their current answers will be obsolete due to the acceleration of improved technology and advancements in knowledge. Consequently, this chapter provides well-defined processes in solving problems in contrast to hoping for silver bullets.

**BEYOND WHINING: Creative Problem-Solving Methods:**

Procrastination pervades human behavior when people are faced with complicated problems. Who has not stalled hoping that problems will disappear? Anxious hand-wringing gives precious time for slow-growing cancerous to metastasize.

| Box 4-1: Symptoms or Causes? |
|---|
| The dilemma of limited analysis is illustrated by an incident during my first weeks in India where I had been invited to fill the Peace Chair at Manipal University. The attacks of September 11, 2001 occurred just two weeks after I arrived. My hosts observed the International Day of Peace on September 19$^{th}$ by arranging for eleven colleges to send representatives to a campus-wide convocation. |
| Each college selected a delegate to address the theme "Shaping a Better World." These representatives were from two Medical Colleges, two Dental Colleges, the Manipal Institute of Technology, the Pharmacy School, the Nursing School, the School of Allied Health Sciences, the School of Hotel Administration, and the Manipal Institute of Communications. Naturally, scientific methods dominate the educational approaches in this large university. |
| My response was made after listening to and analyzing these eleven presentations while I used problem-solving methods of policy analysis. While I was pleased with their passion for peace, I was not surprised by their recommendations for formulating a better world. Understandably eight of the eleven stated their favorite answers without analyzing causes global problems. Three presenters provided remarkable analysis of structural violence including political factors, economic conditions, and social injustices. They used diagnostic problem-solving and scientific analyses while eight needed to analyze the problems with greater depth. |

Treating the obvious symptoms distracts from addressing deeper causal contributors that fester into structural violence and injustice. Box 4-1 provides an explicit illustration from India.

Before jumping to answers and solutions, it is essential to take difficult steps in problem identification and problem definition prior to arriving at solutions that may lead to recommendations. Otherwise quick solutions with superficial remedies are pasted over hidden wounds and inadequately analyzed problems. It is like plastering band-aids over a cancerous tumor because that is the only available treatment for a life-threatening disease. Key steps in solving violent conflicts include the following basic approaches in clinical diagnosis and policy analysis:

- **Identifying Problems Based on Empirical Data:**

Consider how a health professional clinically examines a sick patient. Clinicians make numerous observations when they examine a patient. Thereafter, more data are gathered with clinical observations, personal background, medical case history, interviews, and technical tests leading to a tentative diagnosis. When the patient's problems are complex, further research is necessary. Professional's skills in differential diagnosis are essential plus analysis of causal factors from scientific methodologies. These competencies require professional education, training, and clinical experience in observing symptoms, conditions, etiology and treatment options. Additional test data may be needed to verify an initial diagnosis.

"Geopolitical clinicians" face even greater complexities in assessing global pathologies in international conflicts. In the post-Cold War era, nations are searching for how to cope with regional conflicts, one dominant superpower, and economic stresses of digital globalization. Global tensions are modern symptoms that reflect the need for better treatment strategies for managing and resolving conflicts. The metaphor of tectonic "fault lines" from which earthquakes erupt has been used to analyze the challenges encountered in the post-Cold-War era since the United States has emerged the dominant superpower. Provocative prognoses stimulate thinking by international experts in predicting future conflicts. One of the most perceptive analysis is Huntington's clash between civilizations[5] briefly described in Box 4-2. These clashes would be roughly analogous to shifting tectonic plates called fault lines that geologically describe the plates of the earth's surface that may lead to the eventual eruption of earthquakes.

It is not unusual that there are disagreements about Huntington's controversial thesis. People misunderstand the potential for cultural collisions. Intensively held cultural beliefs particularly those rooted in religion often preclude appraisals of colliding consequences. In major conflicts, there are ominous threats of cultural violence. For example, the tensions between India-Pakistan over Kashmir and Jammu involve serious conflicts in which over 60,000 casualties have occurred in the last 50 years. Beyond battles at the "Line of Control", in the state of Gujarat alone there has been major religious violence in early 2002 when over 1000 people were killed by hostile clashes between Hindus and Muslims.

---

### Box 4-2: Huntington's Hypothesis

**Huntington's hypothesis entitled "The Clash of Civilizations,"[7] attempts to explain the potential of international conflicts in the post-Cold War period. In the for search world order, Huntington suggests that future wars will not likely occur between nation-states, but rather between traditional civilizations. These clashes would hypothetically occur where frictions between these civilizations abrasively rub against each other thereby producing unresolved conflicts and wars.**

**Huntington submits his thesis that with only one super power in the world, civilizations with different religious heritages will experience clashes with each other. He hypothesizes that these clashes could occur between Islamic and Chinese civilizations; between Christendom and Islamic civilizations; and between Hindu and Islamic civilizations.**

**In his 1996 publication,[3] Huntington is concerned with the West's insistence on its universal mission. Imperialism is the necessary logical consequence of universalism. According to Huntington, Western intervention in the affairs of other civilizations can be the single most disastrous source of instability and potential global conflict. Western society is dangerous to the world because it could lead to major inter-civilizational war that could lead to the defeat of the West in Huntington's view.**

**Critics of Huntington's thesis stimulate policy analysts to assess evidence that tests this hypothesis. Whether one agrees or disagrees with Huntington's thesis, it serves as a very provocative conceptualization of global conflicts after the Cold War.**

Smock[8] identifies three limits in Huntington's thesis: 1) How much does religion actually shape cultures and politics in various parts of the world? 2) Within religions there are enormous differences that include extremists, fanatics and what are called "ultras" in India; 3) So-called civilizations have had violent conflicts right within their religious traditions such as the war between Islamic Iran and Iraq, plus the conflicts within the Christian traditions in Northern Ireland.

Violent clashes do not happen only between civilizations or religious cultures. On the smaller scale of domestic violence, there are frequent clashes that occur within families in many different cultures. Religious tensions often foment into collisions that threaten the very fabric of family cohesion. Strongly held religious views contribute a great deal of conflict between people when beliefs clash. For example, disputes about how to nurture children occur between when parents collide over battles in cross-faith families and also mates from within the same tradition. Religious and political ideologies also fuel domestic and international crises.

Policy researchers in international relations from India, other Asian countries, Europe and the United States are intrigued by Huntington's thesis. Journalists have mixed reactions to his ominous view of possible violent clashes. Halberstam,[9] indicates concern about the confrontation between the leader of the Western Christian democracy and Saddam Hussein in Iraq with its long-standing Islamic traditions. He sees the hatred of the West as a dangerous conflict that has precipitous risks of an unpredictable war with serious implications in its aftermath for occupation forces and civilians.

"Fault lines" as a metaphor stimulate additional diagnoses of global conflicts in the post Cold War era with one dominant superpower. These perspectives include:

- Kennedy's "The West vs. the Rest."[10] This diagnosis provides insights into the global tensions that confront humanity may quickly label conflicts between western and other nations. On some ways, this approach over-simplifies conflicts into East-West economic and political tensions. However, Daalder and Lindsay see this fault line increasing recently between the United States and the rest of the world in their 2003 book, America Unbound: The Bush Revolution in Foreign Policy.

- Kaplan's sees fault lines between the prosperous North vs. impoverished South.[11] These contrasts are also known as the rifts between the "Rich and the Poor." Kennedy and Kaplan together consider the disparities between nations of the North and South as fault lines in pending global conflicts.[4] These conflicts are more complicated than dividing the world into two major sectors of developing and developed nations. Praful Bidwai, an editor of the Hindustan Time of India in early 2004, reports increasing inequalities between North and South. He sees as tripling of disparities over the past half century with one-third of North prospering, another third having no future, and the middle third hovering in between with great uncertainty.

- Fukuyama contrasts democratic vs. non-democratic societies.[12] His analysis identifies a modern conflict between democratic nations and those dominated by autocratic dictators. Paul Lipitz, a Professor at an Israeli university in a lecture on January 28, 2004, suggests that once you try to impose democracy upon another nation, you lose it.

- Friedman sees major chasms between the fast digital world vs. slow globalization.[13] His later analysis identifies modern consequences of high technology that are influencing globalization for better or for worse. Friedman also sees another generational fault line between the younger generation and the old generation plus zippies succeeding yuppies.

- Nye provides a perceptive analysis that examines the fault line between nations with "Soft and Hard" strategies. Hard approaches involve the readiness to use major weapons of war to settle disputed differences. Soft approaches involve the use of diplomacy, negotiations, treaties, sanctions, inspections and mediation.

- Kupchan notices the different strategies in dealing with a single super power, currently the United States(19). He provides historical accounts that suggest other nations deal with one super power by various strategies like surrounding and containing with concerted efforts by smaller nations. Typical counter-balances to the United States in the future could come from the European Union, while others see China emerging as a balancing force.

**Noticing Obscurities:**

An essential skill of a professional problem-solver involves noticing gaps of what is not readily apparent from surface observations. Seeing obscurities may initially seem contradictory so further explanation follows. What is observable is usually obvious even to non-scientists who may not have the necessary analytical skills to identify unclear phenomenon. A professional analyst tries to dissect what is observable while perceptively noticing missing elements. From theory, experience and research, the investigator notes what is dysfunctional. For examples:

- A child therapist draws upon theories and research of child psychology in order to notice what is underdeveloped cognitively, physically, emotionally, educationally, intellectually and socially in a child's behavior.

- A budget analyst quickly notes what a financial statement obscures, omits or erroneously reports.

Likewise, policy analysts are challenged to perceptively note missing factors, gaps, and obscure elements in dysfunctional intercultural systems. Taleb in his book, <u>Fooled by Randomness</u> raises the Black Swan predicament: "Why Don't We Learn That We Don't Learn?" Human beings have a phenomenal blind spot in not seeing what they do not expect or want to see. But, seeing what is not expected or obvious can empower people who confront baffling problems. With astute observational and analytical skills, people can move beyond whining about their frustrating problems. This analytical work is similar to investigating a complex criminal case. First, the relevant facts must be explained before an indictment can be developed into criminal charges of homicidal violence. Then appropriate procedures of legal justice can take corrective action. In a similar manner, people can move toward constructive alternatives when they have developed deeper understanding about causes of structural violence. Critical investigative clues and creative processes include noticing obscure causes that can then lead to better remedies.

In both domestic and international violence, it is helpful to have professional methods and theoretical models for better visions to replace the persistent conflict that has historically happened. Useful theories can suggest sequential steps or missing links in order to progress toward solutions. There is usually tension between the dysfunctional situation and possible improvements. When missing factors between violence and just peace are explicitly identified, it is possible to make initial diagnoses of the problems. For example, in a family where a female teenager is the victim of incestuous abuse by her father, family members may not realize that incest is a criminal act. The mother may be unconsciously encouraging incestuous behavior. In such denial, until the mother becomes aware that she is an enabler of this pathology, the family may not stop such incestuous behavior. Criminal charges confronting the father with is unacceptable behavior may also be necessary to end this sexual abuse that has been covertly hidden in the family.

In complicated cross-cultural studies, researchers need to be cautious when comparing developed and developing cultures. Modern technology may not be affordable in developing cultures with limited resources. Insensitive contrasts between modern and less developed practices can result in serious clashes in cultural values and relationships. It is preferable to discern what are differences rather than arrogantly labeling them as deficiencies, a term that implies cultural superiority and inferiority. There are more effective approaches in observing the distinctive characteristics of various cultures. An example involves comparisons on economic variables. Rather than comparing countries on per capita income, it can be more accurate to use "purchasing power parity" called "PPP" in comparative economics. Per capita income in India is less than $450 per year compared to over $30,000 in a number of developed countries. Per capita income has limited relevance in understanding the quality of life. Purchasing power parity (PPP) compares the relative ability of people to procure essentials such as housing, food, health care, education, clothing, and social services.

The positive concept of "the mutual benefit of differences" fosters a sense of respecting diverse cultural practices. Just as there are benefits from biological diversity in nature, socially there are also enriching benefits from cultural diversity as well as conflicts. Cultures enrich each other when both obvious and obscure differences are valued rather than disparaged. People are naturally conditioned by their own ethnocentric values based upon the ingrained worldviews of their native culture. From narrow ethnocentric perspectives, differences in cultural practices may not be appreciated. Nevertheless, by broadening perspectives of different worldviews, diverse cultural practices can foster mutual respect and enrichment.

---

- **Defining Problems:**

According to many scientists, defining the problems is more than half the solution. Problems of violence need to be defined in depth by digging beyond symptoms to analyzing causes often embedded in conflicting issues. Without thorough attention to thorough definition, solutions may erroneously be addressed to a wrongly defined problem. Solutions applied to an inadequately defined crisis actually can further complicate the original predicament. For example, treating a person with an erroneous diagnosis permits the hidden disease to advance while the patient suffers. Similar errors arise in international policy analysis. Has there ever been a malpractice suit brought against national leaders for misdiagnosing international conflicts? In a democracy such leaders may be belatedly voted out of office in the next election. However, societies continue to suffer when political leaders erroneously diagnose and define either domestic or international problems.

Citizens have difficulties in defining complex international and domestic difficulties. Governmental leaders should be expected to skillfully cope with much greater complexities than citizens. However, policy groups are subject to errors in biased analyses of grave problems. Janis helped policy analysts understand the dire consequences that occur when policy decision-making groups become subject to the social-psychological pathology of "group think" in dealing with difficult conflicts.[14] Most national leaders have been insidiously misguided by the powerful dynamics of "group think" unconsciously provided by loyal cabinet members and special advisors of powerful leaders. Both the Clinton and Bush Administrations illustrated narrowed intelligence perspectives in the revelation reported in the "C.I.A. Was Given Data on Hijacker Long Before 9/11."[5] Group think obviously happened in the Bush Administration in its approach to terrorism, the War in Iraq, and to many domestic problems in American policies. This inexperienced administration suffers from inadequate analysis of intelligence data and international complications in dealing with the challenges of the Middle East and terrorism.

The inadequate methods of intelligence gathering have not yet reached the scientific level of medical practice. In medical diagnosis, pathologists eventually determine whether a clinical diagnosis was accurate. In political decisions, policy analysts and historians eventually provide feedback, but typically such discoveries are far too late for voters to become aware of erroneous domestic strategies and international policies instigated by hastily formulated decisions by administrations.

In scientific problem-solving, the definition of the predicament is crucial for developing the best alternative solutions. Much time, effort, analytical skills, integrative theory and thorough research are needed to apply professional competencies in policy analysis. When crises threaten the survival of humanity, it behooves citizens to expect to rely on the best problem-solvers that humanity can produce in making these ominous decisions. Competent leaders elected by responsible citizens are essential to formulate solutions for international challenges in structural violence. Malpractice suits are not available for recourse against political leaders. The rulings of international tribunals long after tragic atrocities will never restore the loss of human lives because wrong decisions were made about war, policies and ideologies. Punishment of violent leaders can leave social justice bitterly short-changed. Consequently, people who can accurately define problems are indispensable in developing effective policy decision-making.

Detecting an actual or a contrived enemy is crucial in accurately defining problems. There is a tempting pattern for traditional leaders to prematurely invoke an enemy as the evildoer rather than wrestling with complicated but manageable conflicts. Invoking an awesome enemy dramatically invites a leader aspiring to be a hero who is cloaked with an aura of a false messiah. Polarizing the conflict into "us vs. them" can also divert attention from the causal factors that ultimately contribute to the crisis in the first place. Heroically demonizing a real or an imagined enemy can deceptively over-simplify the problems. It is not wise to declare war as the only alternative in confronting a designated enemy. Once the world is polarized into enemy camps, reconciliation is very difficult to achieve.

The past century has been cluttered with world and regional wars. *Realpolitik* was a strategy to achieve peace by establishing a balance of power among nations. Both major world wars had clearly defined enemies with only rare confusion about who the actual opponents. In World War I, the consensus of the Western allies was that Germany was the enemy. In World War II there were the Axis Powers against the Allies. In the Cold War, the two superpowers dominated the international arena with the status of super powers engaged in a cosmic struggle.

In subsequent wars, enemies have been more difficult to define. Containment wars were fought designating communism as the diabolical enemy. The Vietnam War is called the American War by Vietnamese as revealed during my trip there in 2004. Confusion existed about who the enemy was and why the designated opponent was being fought. The humiliation of the unresolved American War in Vietnam provided pause in the roles of superpowers in Asia. Again in the 1980's, America supported the Afghan effort against a common enemy, the Soviet Union. Was withdrawal from Afghanistan by the United States appropriate when the Soviets withdrew? With withdrawal, billions of dollars of weapons were left for the Taliban Mujahadeen. Was that an effective way to resolve the problem? To what extent was a power vacuum left in Afghanistan that attracted contentious tribes to war against each other? Is there validity to the accusation of some that the United States contributed to the problems that continue to fester in Afghanistan including the Al Queda?

In the 1991 Gulf War, an immediate target enemy was clearly defined but not eliminated. Iraq and its leader, Saddam Hussein, were driven out of Kuwait but not destroyed. Demonizing Iraq was dramatized while attempting to contain this nation with sanctions. Only partial resolution was achieved because the problem was very narrowly defined. To what degree was Hussein a symptom of bigger problems rather than a primary cause of terrorism? Was the Gulf War a solution or a quick operation that avoided the cancer festering in the polarized international relations in the Gulf region and the Middle East for the over fifty years? It is appropriate to raise pointed questions in order to penetrate further into causal factors that more accurately define contemporary international problems. How adequately is the War on Terrorism defined to accurately comprehend the nature of this global crisis? What objectives are achievable? Which enemies are ignored such as structural violence left to grow and metastasize? Whose global interests are actually protected by capturing Hussein? What power vacuums are created that feed oppression, injustice and belligerent unrest?

The proverbial cart is placed in front of the horse when favorite solutions are determined before problems are defined. When aggressive leaders favor military approaches, problems may be purposely defined to fit these ready-made solutions. War solutions may be in search of targets that are identified as the problem. The decision by the United States to invade Iraq in 2003 may be a case of using the strategies of war as a solution without adequately defining the problems presented by non-state based terrorism. There is evidence that the Bush administration did not fully understand the intricate problems before deciding to engage in war. It became more obvious when the challenge of occupying Iraq and transferring power to its citizens is bungled with inadequate planning.

In the downside of "group think," advisers frequently isolate policymakers thereby dangerously narrowing their focus on international and domestic issues. Additional problems are interpreted to fit existing military resources rather discovering innovative strategies that more precisely address the problems. These policy distortions are particularly troubling when novel challenges emerge from obscure sources. For example, structural violence is difficult to analyze because its causes are hidden under layers of cultural practices. Decision-makers in international and domestic quandaries quickly resort to traditional violent responses of war instead of developing nonviolent measures to address conflicts that result from economic, political and social injustice. Kristof traces similar over-reactions for secrecy by the Soviet Union in 1981 that nearly led to a nuclear confrontation between the superpowers during the Cold War. He also sees parallel intelligence secrecy in the Bush[6] administration about decisions to engage in war with Iraq.

On a family level, polarized members can unknowingly provide plots for television dramas of court cases. Polarized relatives rarely move ahead toward reconciliation. Miraculous steps are needed to repair broken trust among estranged family members. Domestic and international violence, while vastly different in scale, have very obvious similarities. These similarities become apparent in diagnosing the problems plus demonizing announced enemies even while pursuing self-interests that break into open warfare. Starting a battle or war is simpler than resolving problems with lasting solutions. Quick remarriage after divorce parallels how nations seek other partners and enemies in war. Unresolved problems of previous battles carry over into the next intimate relationship or perpetuate problems into the next war between nations.

## IDENTIFYING ISSUES in CONFLICT:

After systematically defining problems, it is important to clearly analyze key issues that need to be comprehended before solutions are formulated. From intercultural perspectives, we are always limited by our own ethnocentric experiences. The processes of identifying key issues provide further understanding of domestic violence and international wars.

## POLITICAL ISSUES:

- ***UNILATERALISM vs. MULTI-LATERALISM***

Wars demonstrate contrasts in how nations take unilateral, multi-lateral or no action. The War of Iraq was undertaken by the United States with fewer allies than the Gulf War a decade earlier. Since the end of the Cold War, the United States has been searching for whether its foreign policies will be unilateral, multi-lateral or isolation. Other nations have reason to wonder how this remaining superpower will define its role in the world.

Gaddis[15] suggests that in post-Cold War transitions the United States has led NATO without listening. This has caused resistance even among nations who are otherwise predisposed to follow American initiatives. Gaddis also sees America as overbearing, self-indulgent, and insensitive to the interests of others. He suggests that the United States neglects cultivating power relationships in the world. While America often acts unilaterally in international relations, there are major challenges in developing multilateral relations. America has not yet discovered its role as a responsible superpower. Consequently, strategies of encirclement may be employed by other nations to cope with unilateral American foreign policies.

On a domestic level, unilateral approaches are widely practiced in family affairs. Many patriarchal fathers act unilaterally in relating to their families by exercising possessive control over all family members. Such authoritarian approaches rule over family members who understandably react with both respect and fear. While decision-making may be efficient, authoritarian rule fails to democratically interact with family members. Patriarchy has severe limits in cooperative collaboration. In contrast, multi-lateral approaches attempt to share power and decision-making in order to respect personal differences in family dynamics.

Long-standing patterns of authoritarian rule have been perpetuated from family patterns, tribal traditions, plus leadership styles in nation states and corporations. Few institutions in modern society are predominantly democratic. The Chief Executive Officer (CEO) prevails in private corporations, public organizations and families. Unilateral decision-making often comes from the top-down rather rising up from the bottom by sharing leadership with teamwork. Until families and organizations practice greater democratic decision-making, there are limited possibilities for contending with unilateral approaches. Similar to small nations, family members may find value in the strategy of encircling aggressive patriarchal males like smaller nations collaborate to encircle a superpower. Harassed families and nations can find that multi-lateral coalitions are effective for coping with unilateral actions by autocrats.

- **RULE by LAW or AUTOCRATS ?**

There are vivid contrasts between nations that are ruled by laws that are legislated from constitutional bases in contrast with nations controlled by authoritarian rulers. Rule by law finds expression in democratically and theocratically governed nations that have independent justice systems, elected legislatures and executive leadership. At the other extreme, when dictators rule without other branches of government that balance the ruler, the less stable rule by fiat is a clear contrast with rule by law.

Succession of leadership can be unpredictable when constitutional laws do not make explicit provisions for how leadership in transition takes office. The consent of the governed is an essential feature of democratic nations. Even authoritarian rulers often do not endure without acquiescence by the governed. Sovereigns need to acknowledge the consensus of their citizens. As democratic institutions become more prevalent around the world, unstable dictatorships will decline. In international affairs, nations ruled by autocratic leaders exemplify specific problems for other nations. Without powerful institutions of credible international law, relations between nations are understandably tenuous. Conflicts may be accented with unpredictable succession in leadership. Lawlessness may bring chaotic conditions within such nations. Examples are found in developments in the lack of stability in Pakistan and Latin America.

Rule by law or humans also is evident in family and domestic conflicts. Patriarchs may typically rule with capricious authority over family members who are beholden to an authority figure or their successor. When there is a need for succession of authority, selection of the next leader may be spelled out in cultural tradition. However, usually problems occur when a powerful figurehead dies without clear patterns of succession. There may be informal struggles for control of the family affairs. Family members can be subject to unpredictable dangers from rivals. Family members who were previously governed by the old authoritarian head of the family may be mistreated by successors, exiled, imprisoned or even killed.

The world scene is challenged by unevenness in applying the rule by law in democratic nations. In theocratic societies the interpretations of religious codes may range from predictable consistency to revised interpretations to chaos. New interpretations of religious laws present unpredictable latitude about internal and external relations among nations. When radical interpreters impose their views upon others without the safeguards of public accountability, there are limited constraints for the public to exercise. Accountability is a feature of rule by law whereas rule by human beings provides grave potential for abuse of power, violent conflicts, and lapses in continuity. If peace and justice are in the hands of human beings rather than institutions of law, there are serious dangers to the security of nations and domestic families.

- **NATIONALISM vs. GLOBALISM**

Diverse worldviews are also found in this problematical issue concerned with factions called nation-states. Compartmentalized nations are prime examples of political structures that both guide and divide the human family. Narrow nationalism can become as divisive as intolerant religions. If a particular nation becomes an "idol of ultimate concern" by its citizens, nationalism can become a religion in itself. Mutually exclusive loyalties can arise. How can a person be a global citizen and at the same time be patriotic to a particular country? Dual citizenships occur among nations with reciprocal agreements. Experiments like the European Union are attempting to balance inherent conflicts in national allegiance. Human identities are transforming from narrow identities to more unified views by global citizens. In these processes, identity crises arise due to the conflicts between nationalism and globalism.

Globalization has become a contentious issue again as it has been in earlier periods of history. Now the strategies of globalization are technological as well as primarily economics, cultural, and geopolitical. Information technology has accelerated the global interactions that affect most of people around the world. In recent decades, there have been increasing efforts for transnational businesses to become the dominant voices of global markets. The last four American administrations have promoted economic expansion in the world. Mark Clark, executive director of the U.S. Chamber of Commerce, states that "the business of U.S. foreign policy in the 1990's *was* business." A number of multinational businesses have tried to implement economic hegemony in making American nationalism the agenda for the rest of the world.

Several illustrations indicate how former government officials have migrated to powerful corporations with global interests in oil, energy, health care, and military weapons. An example of a complex transnational business is the Carlisle Group. Former top executive branch Americans have become directly involved in international weapons business. Oil interest and energy technologies are also important components of the Carlisle Group. Former government officials capitalize on their powerful positions to become wealthier in a practice of reshuffling into the private sector and back into federal government or lobbying. With dual roles in public and private roles, they continue to exert influence in governmental deregulation that favors their private business interests in the use of national resources. Those who recycle into governmental roles enmesh their influential connections both within the nation and into the dual power structures of economic globalization and international relations.

Insiders from Washington have also left the government with knowledge about the huge loopholes in the health care industry. Since the 1980's, former government insiders have exploited provisions of Medicare and Medicaid to purchase public hospitals and develop privatized hospitals for profit. Mental health services in the United States were ravaged when enterprising promoters preyed upon vulnerable patients and health professionals. These entrepreneurs continue to have economic interests in international health businesses including pharmaceuticals and health insurance. When lawsuits are finally settled, the business strategy has been to sell off unprofitable holdings and use insider advantage in another vulnerable market such as rehabilitation services.

In recent years, one of the most dramatic cases of privatization on a global scale in the energy industries has been the Enron scandal. Unethical accounting practices with concurrence by Arthur Anderson consultants have been conducted both on a domestic and international scale by Enron executives. Eron's Dabhol Plant in India is one illustration of privatizing an international public industry that backfired for both Enron and India. Enron's debacle illustrates how top-level executives recycled from government positions into private business and back again into powerful government roles that influence favorable policies affecting major defense and energy industries.

Pedaling influence and power around the world is not unique to Americans but are found in Europe, Asia and South America as well. These ambitious agendas have historically happened among ambitious people who are politically powerful and profit oriented. They find transnational corporations as the vehicles to develop enormous wealth. When an opponent in a foreign nation exploits their political influence, it is called corruption. When private corporations pursue these strategies, it is more likely to be labeled as creating market that advance free trade. A whole new vocabulary has emerged such as "marketing warfare," "guerrilla marketing," and "predatory marketing." Capturing a share of the market has been the strategy of sales forces when an alluring Enron executive gained favorable contracts with Indian officials.

In another market, who would ever think that the basic ingredients for weapons of mass destruction would be for sale? When there is not an openly legitimate market in operation, a black market can be created. Who would be so desperate or so financially enterprising as to buy and sell these weapons, or enriched plutonium, or secrets about how to implode a nuclear weapon? Would nuclear scientists ever entertain ambitions for monetary reward, wealth and power? Would the leadership of threatened nations consider solving their budget problems by covertly selling ingredients of nuclear and mass-destruction weapons? When such questions are posed, the conflicting issues of narrow nationalistic interests vs. global concerns needs vigilant attention by governments, citizens and media. The case of Pakistan's leading nuclear scientist, Dr. Abdul Qadeer Khan, selling nuclear supplies and secret research to Iran, Libya, and North Korea is just one example of nuclear proliferation for profit. Entrepreneurs around the world engage in legal, illegal and questionable practices. Sustainable peace and justice are constantly threatened when narrow allegiance serves the interests of the power hungry over the well being of humanity. These unresolved conflicts of blackmail and injustice feed international tensions that contribute to violent wars.

**CULTURAL ISSUES:**

- ***EXCLUSION vs. INCLUSION***

Most religious and political organizations discover how people are included and excluded in social relationships. Exclusion vs. inclusion concerns the nature of world religions that anyone finds difficult to address objectively. Realizing that this is a controversial issue, this analysis is approached cautiously because religion is at the crux of many global concerns and conflicts.

Moreover, cavalier attitudes about religion may miss the point while extreme approaches can seriously compound the risks of conflict.

Jewish, Islamic and Christian traditions make claims to exclusive authority to truth with distinctive revelations from Divinity. Yet all three traditions have widely diverse interpretations of their authoritative sources. Consequently, generalizations can be immediately challenged by divergent views about these religious traditions. These problems concern diverse understandings in hermeneutics, science and logic. Hermeneutics involve applying historic interpretations of authoritative texts to the contemporary contexts of changing conditions. Hermeneutical problems present diverse complications in interpreting who is included and excluded based upon religious positions and cultural contexts.

Islamic and Christian traditions can collide in their respective worldviews especially in strategies to proselyte new adherents. Collisions in these practices not only affect each other, but may also involve testy relations with other religions and the non-religious. If these conflicting practices did not provide enough problems, there are serious misunderstandings, lack of accurate awareness, and even misinformation that compounds attempts to engage in constructive dialogue. Respectful exchanges that encourage mutual understanding among adherents of religious traditions are essential for the future peace of humanity. Nalapat sees a need for India, Israel and the United States to provide a "level playing field" for all communities within their borders. As an editor of The Times of India, he suggests that through the practice of inclusivist moderation, the menace of Wahabbism-Khomeinism can be countered in the world. As the Professor of Geopolitics at Manipal Academy of Higher Education, Nalapat reports his ideas in the Bharat Rakshak Monitor (2003). He recommends that cultures fight "Fire with Water", "Intolerance with Inclusivism," and "Etremeism with Moderation."

All world religions and philosophies possess distinctive worldviews that influence practices of tolerance and exclusion. While there are strengths and limitations in each world religions, there are also conflicts in their social and political practices. Traditionally, Hindu religion is inclusively tolerant, but violence has erupted in recent decades among Hindus, Muslims, Jews, Jains, Sikhs, Bahais, Buddhists and Christians. These awesome tensions present serious implications in global relations for living together as neighbors. At the same time, many religions compete with each other for uncompromising allegiance from adherents. Naturally, conflicts arise that threaten the peaceful coexistence of humanity when exclusive claims are exercised without balanced respect and tolerance.

Human beings have long practiced dynamics of excluding out-groups who do not share the same traditions, socio-economic class, racial identity, religious beliefs, or political views. Inclusion is stereotypically extended to blood relatives who are like-minded with similar characteristics, compatible values and shared values. The family or tribe has typically been an in-group with a few exceptions of the black sheep or the crazy in-law. Families protect their interests so that solidarity provides a safe-haven from external threats. Family members seek mutual protection that minimizes conflict but risk intimate relations that can become abusive. Smothering families may become incestuous controllers of secrets kept within the tribal group.

Exclusion and inclusion dynamics also operate on an international level. Allies in a strong coalition barricade themselves into a fortress of like-minded nations who are threatened by a common enemy. These alliances are more *ad hoc* and typically are not as strong as blood ties in a family. Consequently, alliances among nations may only last as long as there are shared interests against shared enemies. Political and religious ideologies can readily be mixed to justify whatever position seems expedient. Strange bedfellows frequently develop alliances into political coalitions only to be broken when the threat is no longer shared. If nations were required to go through the processes of divorce like estranged couples have to do, there might be fewer international alliances. The role of non-aligned nations is a puzzling mystery to nations that are highly committed to a particular political or religious orientation. The contemporary world has obvious examples of the impact of divergent religious views upon international coalitions.

The polarity of insiders vs. outsiders necessitates careful management both on domestic and international levels. The dominant alpha male in domestic and international courtships often struts in searching of receptive females. "Masculine nations" with a controlling father image may court or snub "feminine" nations with a nurturing mother image with surprising dynamics. Mother Russia has been penetrated during historic wars in self-defense. Colonial powers have roamed the sea for liaisons at many ports of the world. Mother India displays uncertainty about its contemporary place in international affairs.

The conflicts in exclusion and inclusion have tremendously powerful implications for families and nations. World religions paradoxically are both divisive and integrative in their pursuits of peace. All religions intentionally advocate peace as a goal for humanity. At the same time, religions have conflicting differences in realizing how to live peacefully together. Discovering common interests provides one of the greatest challenges of the modern age when cultures interact daily. Respecting religious heritages while appreciating their unique contributions holds promising hope of peace building. It is crucial that unresolved disagreements become the modern-day occasion for greater respect rather than the ominous alternative of additional violent conflicts. One of the great challenges of this century involves constructive religious dialogues for the sake of global humanity.

- *GOOD vs. EVIL*

Theologians and militant leaders of religions have a propensity to dichotomize the world into good vs. evil. International leaders also exploit this simplified polarization. Manichaeism is the traditional term for dividing the world into the dualism of good and evil. These ideas developed in Zoroastrianism in Persia as well as Greek philosophical thinking. In ancient times the intangible spirit was considered good and the material world was considered evil. Many cultures dramatize variations of these struggles in their cultural mythology, religions and political ideologies.

These influences continue in religious conflicts between the forces of light and the forces of darkness. Psychoanalytic perspectives consider the conflicts between good and evil as a cosmic drama between the battling archetypes of heroic figures and personifications of evil. The medieval myth of St. George slaying the dragon is known in many cultures of the world that have their own versions of similar cosmic battles. Hindu religions have gods of creation, destruction, prosperity, pleasure and happiness. Heroic figures become possessed with an archetypal destiny to save their culture threatened by forces of evil symbolized in enemies who engage in battles of life and death.

In the twentieth century, the World Wars can be analyzed by western interpreters as struggles to the death between the Allied forces for good and the Axis forces of evil. During the Cold War, the former Soviet Union traditionally considered the West to be decadent, evil and materialistic. In turn, anti-communist thinking in the West projected similar images onto the Communist Bloc. In the 1980's, President Reagan pronounced the Soviet Union to be an evil empire. This mutual antagonism fed Cold War projections that attributed evil to each other while considering themselves to be sanctimoniously good and right.

President George W. Bush repeatedly uses dualistic thinking to declare Iran, Iraq and North Korea as the axis of evil. Naturally this polarization appeals to some Americans, but it does not resonate consistently with other people and nations. A number of cultures consider America and much of the West as decadent infidels inferring that evil materialism motivates western cultures that polarize the world into cosmic struggles. These over-simplified analyses rarely contribute to mutual understanding or nonviolent peace. Rather such polarized analysis adds to the conflict between the leadership of governments. Each tries to generate antagonism toward an enemy that its leaders invoke as dangerously threatening. These statements aggravate anti-American sentiments in the world that build on resentments psychologically generated by dependency and enemy relations.

Even in domestic relations, the labels of good and bad are often used to describe certain vulnerable members of the family. The member nominated as "good" displays the qualities highly valued by self-appointed designators of morals. Families also have equivalent labels for the bad member who may be called evil when their behavior becomes notoriously outrageous. Dependency relationships inherently generate anger and resentment between family members who often are co-dependent. There is a propensity to discredit behavior that negatively challenges family values. Family therapists have learned to make careful assessments in their diagnoses when the most outspoken members of the family designate others as the problem. The capacity to dichotomize the family into the good ones and bad persons is problematic in family therapy. Symbiotic relations are compounded further with emotional dynamics of positive joy and angry hostility.

- **INDIVIDUALISM vs. COLLECTIVISM**

One of the most challenging issues in intercultural relations involves conflicts that arise from the excesses of unbridled individualism in contrast to protective collectivism. Rampant individualism is expressed in selfish greed and national interests. It is also expressed in major symptom of global conflicts that contributes to strife and war. In the animal world, some animals take care of themselves without becoming a predator or victim. Insofar as human beings share animal qualities, can we assume that civil human beings will satisfy their own instinctive appetites without interfering with the rights of others? Unfortunately, egoism tries to satiate basic appetites for power, greed and domination at the expense of other people.

Unrestrained individualism can prey upon vulnerable victims unless both predator and prey control these needs for the benefit of humanity. The rights of other people are violated when competition is the primary motivation for self-preservation. Family abusers express their egotistical need for dominant control that exalts their own authority. Narcissistic abusers act violently when their individual needs are threatened. They may further justify their actions with religious and cultural traditions that sanction their abuse of dependents.

In contrast to individualism, collectivism can stifle creative innovation, personal growth, and bold entrepreneurship. Collective strategies search to gain control with powerful authority that includes dangerous appetites to devour entire societies and natural resources. Atrocities committed by the Japanese, Chinese and former Soviets reveal the devastation wrought upon oppressed human victims and the natural environment. Pol Pot devastated his own Cambodian citizens with tragic consequences resulting from the atrocities of extreme collectivism.

When cultures impose their values upon other cultures, basic conflicts of values are encountered. Political leaders naturally value the qualities emphasized by their ethnocentric traditions. However, these same political leaders would be affronted if another nation's leader imposed their values upon them. The issue of individual and collective rights is replete with clashes of Eastern and Western Cultures when aggressive values of conquering empires that have imposed their values upon defeated culture. For example, the Balkan states were formed to be a buffer between Christianity and Islam with deep cultural conflicts leading to internal civil wars over many centuries.

The destruction of war is evident in Afghanistan from bombing and chaotic violence. What has happened to women and children in these authoritarian cultures? In collective cultures, the personal worth respecting human personality has only had dismally poor attention. In a number of nations, human appetites prevail for dominating control. Capacities to balance the excesses of both individual and collective bodies remain a critical issue for addressing conflict of interests, violence and peace. These problems are found in domestic family violence, women's rights, and international conflicts.

- ***SECULARIZATION vs. DE-SECULARIZATION***

The issue of secularization vs. de-secularization can be difficult to appreciate. Western societies have been largely secular since the Enlightenment of the eighteenth century with glaring exceptions. Defining the realms of sacred religion and the secular state is more easily declared than practiced. In America, separation of church and state was derived from constitutional provisions. The First Amendment of the United States Constitution includes counter-balancing provisions that there shall be no "establishment of religion" alongside of protections for "the free exercise thereof." Most democratic constitutions provide for the freedom of religion subjected to varying interpretations that provide degrees of tolerance for diverse religious practices.

Historically in international affairs there have been different models of a sacred theocracy dominated by religion, and a secular state in which religion does not have a prominent role in governance. There are powerful issues re-emerging about whether there should be a sacred or secular state in a number of nations. Western democracies have primarily established secular societies in recent centuries without a dominating religion. While there have been Hindu kingdoms in the past, Nepal is now the only nation with such a monarchy. This monarch is balanced by constitutional constraints including a Parliament according to the Nepalese governmental advisor, Rishikesh Shaha, who conveyed this information in personal conversations in Kathmandu in

1995. The royal family even with the assassinations of a number of its members in 2001 has continued to hold the throne.

Other major cultures have different relationships between the realms of religion and the state. Longstanding practices of tolerance by different religions may prevail during peaceful times of economic prosperity. Intolerance can abruptly change a peaceful atmosphere into violent strife. There are major segments of humanity where religion and state are embraced as one unified realm. A number of the Muslim cultures are governed in accordance with *Sharia* derived from traditional Islamic law. However, not all predominantly Muslim cultures have a theocratic state. A secular society is not completely compatible with theocratic perspectives. Consequently, the prevalence, if not dominance, of religious law and tradition govern the society in stricter Islamic states. In these societies, religious leaders have major influence upon social and political practices. There may be little tolerance for other religious ideologies that are not subservient to the prevailing interpretations of religious leaders who expect that the state is subordinate to traditional Islamic law. In India, for example, Muslims have separate laws that govern their marital and family affairs distinctive from but condoned by the national government of India.

Strong reactions may occur with any attempts to de-secularize Islamic states. Islamic *Sharia* takes priority over the institution of the state by not explicitly providing for the existence of a state. Traditional Islamic governance is based on the *umma*, the community of believers, which supposedly knows no boundaries other than the religion itself. The Islamic political tradition stresses a seamless unity of faith and power, a concept that is incompatible with Western ideas of statehood.[16] Countries that have been governed by *Sharia* include Iran and until recently another adaptation of the Taliban in Afghanistan. Hill reports that of the twenty-one countries in the League of Arab states, few seem comfortable with their own statehood except as a means of providing a veil of international legitimacy to their own version of power politics[16].

Some states that were previously secular are experiencing internal pressure to become theocratic. These developments have been occurring among radical Islamic movements in Egypt, Iran, Bangladesh and Indonesia. In addition, Arab cultures are undergoing transitions on this issue of secular vs. sacred states known as theocracies. Influential religious leaders provide interpretations from earlier historical sources of authority. Lewis[17] accredited the historian Josephus with coining the term theocracy during the early Roman Empire when Caesar was considered divine. Earlier in Hebrew history there had been theodicies where monarchs were purportedly selected by *Yahweh* and anointed by prophets. Later in the Muslim tradition, *Allah* became the supreme sovereign of Islamic culture, and the Caliph was his vice-regent or his shadow on earth.

Efforts to de-secularize states have encountered major conflicts within their boundaries. Huntington[18] identified efforts of de-secularization in some traditional cultures since the Cold War that could contribute to clashes between civilizations. While this issue has been traditionally laden with conflict, major struggles persist in sacred theocracies and secular states. Political analysts and historians have identified this issue for the inherent conflicts that may happen internally within these nations and internationally among clashing nations. While militant leaders may offer simplistic solutions, careful attention is needed to understand the religious conflicts that are emerging in the contemporary world.

The American slogan, separation of church and state, is one approach in addressing these difficult issues about the relationship of religion and government. With pluralistic religions, the church is one among a variety of images of temples, mosques, sacred sites, religious shrines, and other religious institutions. An Islamic state under religious law, *Sharia,* is one model among others for the role of religion and government in political life. Mutual respect and profound understanding are essential for wrestling with the conflicts present in this issue of the secular state and the sacred theocracy.

Variations of democracy are being practiced in an increasing number of countries in recent decades. Some 120 of the almost 200 countries in the world today now have democratic governments according to Kupchan.[19] There are substantial reasons to believe that there will be inherent conflicts between the secular and the sacred in many cultures in the future. Many academics, international leaders, researchers, professionals and business leaders are neither well informed nor comfortable with these issues. The potential for conflict and violent wars requires careful attention by leaders and citizens to issues involved in secularization and de-secularization.

- **VALUES vs. INTERESTS**

Values are integral to religious perspectives. While religions have political and economic interests, religion has more affinity for ethics and moral values including justice and peace. National governments and organizations tend to have interests and markets. Both religions and secular organizations have vision and mission statements. The statements of religion embody the metaphysical while the secular organizations have more tangible interests.

Political leaders appeal for the support of their citizens to remain popular or powerful. Some political leaders readily encourage a confluence of religious values and national interests. Both religion and secular institutions in a culture share statements about values and character since both function within the same society. Enculturation develops so gradually that many citizens are not consciously aware of how their personal values are conditioned by traditional ideals. For example, western cultures obviously value freedom and equality without recognizing inherent problems. If both freedom and equality are pursued to their fullest extent, there are conflicts when both are maximized. Freedom moves toward diminished equality while equality inherently moves toward reducing individual freedom. Yet western cultures continue to simultaneously advance both values of freedom and equality while collective cultures advocate conforming obedience.

Nations naturally have political interests that are inherently related to the cultural values of that nation. However, values and interests are not the same. Values are more intangibly conceptual whereas interests tend to be more tangible. Values are more theoretical whereas interests are expressed in specific national policies. Major conflicts arise when values and interests are intermingled as if they are the identical.

Current conflicts in international relations demonstrate the basic lack of clarity in differentiating cultural values and national interests. Unfortunately the two are confused in international conflicts. It behooves national leaders to clearly distinguish and understand both. Gaddis[20] shows how the United States has been inconsistent in advocating human rights and justice while confusing these values with economic interests of free markets and globalization. These conflicts lead into the next section that focuses on economic issues.

**ECONOMICS ISSUES:**

- **PRIVATE vs. PUBLIC OWNERSHIP**

This issue has many variations in the developing and industrialized economies about ownership of institutions, businesses, enterprises and organizations. In public ownership, the government owns the means of production, distribution and exchange while employing people to provide goods and services. Nationalizing an economic sector is a strategy in socialistic economies when governmental ownership prevails. In capitalistic economies, ownership is held by private citizens and chartered entities that hold the enterprises that employ people to operate them.

Publicly held organizations have been privatized in a number of countries of the world. Now selected utilities, public services, and some prisons are being run by privately own business enterprises. Education is often divided into public and private education. Security services vary widely including transitions back and forth from private security to public security. Since the hijacking of airline planes that were then crashed into the World Trade Center and the Pentagon, personnel in airport security are now federal employees in the United States. Law and order varies widely in developing nations so that extortion, corruption and bribery may be widely practiced. Protective services may demand charges as a widely accepted practice of doing business.

Many aspects of traditional government are now under the influence of special private interests. There is extraordinary influence of public officials by special interests to privatize government sectors. Lobbyists, who are supported by organizations with huge quantities of capital, influence legislation favorable to their economic interests. The Enron debacle is a symptom of the wide reach of corporate interests supporting political candidates in order to buy special access to elected officials. How access differentiates from influential favors is linguistically unclear in actual practice. Moneyed interests certainly have greater access to influence the ingredients of pending legislation and government decisions that serve these special interests.

Pointed questions are appropriate about how many of our elected offices and executive branch officials are in effect offering to privatize governmental functions? Elected officials rely heavily upon private and corporate contributions to finance expensive political campaigns. Even judicial and law enforcement officials are subject to financial support for election expenses in states where judges and sheriffs are elected by popular vote. Appointed regulators who should be theoretically independent of vested financial interests are pressured to compromise their offices. Sometimes this is known as the fox watching the chicken house or even foxes watching other foxes. Some government regulators have co-mingled their interests with private organizations the regulators are entrusted to monitor for protecting public interests.

Three economic sectors have particularly heavy privately funded pressure. One is in the defense industry where corporations in the military-industrial complex have well-funded lobbyists in Washington to cultivate lucrative defense contracts. This military-industrial complex not only employs military personnel, but many civilians are employed in this sector. Military weapons and equipment industries are also heavily reliant on sales to other nations. This market globally amounts to almost a trillion dollar industry per year.[21] While arms merchants boast about the sales of weapons, the tragic downside in fatalities is paralleled by military expenditures that drain economies. The research of Leebaert discovered the economic price of America's victory in the Cold War. He reports that the real cost of military purchases in the four decades after 1948 totaled around ten trillion dollars.[22]

The sale of weapons to impoverished nations also depletes the ability of poor nations to cover essential services for their vulnerable citizens including education, food, justice and health care. Expensive military weapons are readily promoted for very profitable sales to power-hungry authoritarian leaders. These military leaders of developing nations try to make the case that they need to raise their status in the eyes of neighboring nations, their own citizens, and the world. Chief suppliers of military weapons include the United States, South Africa, Israel, Russia, Pakistan, North Korea, Germany, France, and China.

A second area of privatization involves the heavily financed interests in the health care industry. These industries include insurance companies, pharmaceuticals, hospitals, and even health professionals themselves. Having taught health policy courses for three decades, it is evident that vested financial interests influence campaign elections and lobby for favorable legislation. Aggregate expenditures for health care in the United States are over two trillion dollars annually and rising so rapidly it could double in ten years. This figure is roughly twice the entire Gross Domestic Product of India that has a population of over three and one-half times that of the United States.

Yet in America, the needs for patient care actually are given secondary attention by legislatures. Health care is also negatively affected as long as big money interests can persuade legislators, presidents, and governors to protect corporate and financial interests over the consumer. Ill patients are the most vulnerable and least powerful politically. Women and children in particular suffer the brunt involved in mal-distribution of health care services. Expensive hi-tech health care is also pedaled to diseased cultures that also want the latest in costly pharmaceuticals from firms in Germany, Switzerland, United States, India and Canada. Who would ever think of selling poor nations hi-tech equipment, drugs and services? Ask officials trying to equip hospitals in Nepal where I observed American promoters attempt to market hi-tech equipment when low-tech prevention is more cost effective for developing nations. Clean water, sanitation and inoculations are the most cost-effective in these poor cultures. Ask public health officials in Africa who have difficulty trying to procure medications for HIV-AIDS.

The energy industries are the third sector that pressure their own governments and also peddle enormous influence in the affairs of oil and gas producing countries. Every country that has oil and gas reserves has felt the impact of these global energy businesses. There are perceptive analyses of the vital interests of the developed world in the oil and gas fields of Western, Southern and Central Asia. Nations like the United States, European countries, Japan, and India are all heavily reliant on oil from producing countries in the Gulf region of Southwest Asia. Many observers suspect a hidden agenda of developed nations involves the energy resources of the Gulf nations plus the oil-rich regions north of Iraq, Iran, and Afghanistan in Central Asia.

Energy-famished nations can be sold expensive damns for power generation. Markets primed for power needs are made aware of energy sources with privatized power plants. The prime contractors promoting unsubstantiated needs are from Germany, Russia, England, France, Japan and the United States. Enron made an effort in India to privatize water as a commodity so that people, who naively thought water was free, learned that they are consumers of water as a marketable product. What are the public and private sources of large amounts of financial capital for all of these marketable consumer goods? Naturally, commercial banks and venture capitalists are involved. How much is the World Bank and the International Monetary Fund advancing western models that cannot be sustained in developing countries?

Since the end of the Cold War, capitalism is being tried in developing nations with mixed results. Latin American countries of Venezuela and Argentina, Asian countries of India, Indonesia and Turkey, Europeans nations of Poland and Russia, African nations of Egypt and others are all struggling with the effects of free market globalization. The disparities between rich and poor widen. According to Canadian Feed the Children report,[23] the richest 358 people in the world have a net worth equal to the combined annual income of the poorest 2.3 billion. Eichenwald[24] questions whether capitalism can survive the appetites of capitalists themselves? He then claims that ultimately capitalism will almost certainly survive for-profit capitalists if only because survival is the most profitable outcome for all involved.

- **_ENTREPRENUERSHIP vs. REGULATION_**

The world has enviable resources and expansive markets that have attracted economic interests over many centuries. The British East India Company from 1604 was a prime example of mercantilism in South Asia. Humanly-devised corporate structures and non-governmental organizations add parallel tentacles around the entire globe. In contrast to governments that have modicums of direct accountability to their constituencies, private corporations and chartered ventures have only "limited" accountability and liability. This feature of limited liability has contributed to the high-risk adventurism by domestic and transnational businesses. Major international ventures have expanded their global markets. Transnational corporations have flourished under charters that allow them to engage in capital ventures that exceed the gross domestic product of many nations. Most cultures benefit or are victims of irresponsible exploitation that in turn feeds angry resentment festering in the world.

Attempts by governments to monitor corporations have had mixed effectiveness in controlling the excesses of free-market approaches. Countries like India only permit limited investments by external financial investors. Such controls have protected the Indian population while also limiting their own economic development with foreign investment. Efforts at deregulation have had mixed results as seen in the exploits of Enron, Union Carbide, and other global business ventures. Naturally countries have reactions when India's own resources such as energy and water are exploited as marketable commodities. It was not surprising that some of these aggressive businesses evoke fiercely negative reactions before they failed, or withdrew or became bankrupt.

This issue of entrepreneurialism vs. regulation requires careful attention because there are vacillations from one extreme to the other. In economically expansive times, advocates of free trade can run rampant until eventually creating chronic problems. In other periods of tighter regulation, entrepreneurship and innovative exploration are stymied. Both regulation and free enterprise are essential for economic development. The challenge involves managing the attractive upside before the inherent downside of each approach become disastrous. The ideal of self-regulation tends to ignore the human limitations involved in controlling selfish greed and egotistical self-interests. At the same time, human beings have limits for providing wisdom to place boundaries upon each other.

There are other fields besides business where entrepreneurial approaches have been introduced. Entrepreneurial education is an instrumental approach in education to be trained for a specific career field in all cultures. While this approach to education has merits, it is possible to obtain degrees with limited understanding of history, literature, ethics, mathematics, science or art. Religion has also been marketed without a committed sense of vocational calling. Medicine can be pursued for power without a strong commitment to healing. Law can be pursued entrepreneurially in a quest for control rather than justice. Business administration can be primarily pursued to become wealthy rather than to provide better products or services to society. Entrepreneurs are also operating private prisons as the prison industry expands into the criminal justice field. Where instrumental education prevails predominantly motivated by economic interests, vocations to serve public and social needs become secondary considerations.

In the long term, society suffers from short-term economic pressures that exploit human appetites. Box 4-3 describes Argentina that illustrates many of these regulatory problems in political economy.

### Box 4-3: Argentina as a Case Study

There is evidence that the citizens of Argentina have been extensive whining. Argentina illustrates many of the problems analyzed in this chapter. Their complaints turned into violent confrontations and riots that addressed by public officials. According to Rohter,[25] Argentina is paying heavily for their squandered riches. In his analysis, there is evidence of self-complacency along with narcissistic self-love in the culture. Argentina has experienced problems of a deregulated free-market model copied after the United States.

Using literary metaphors, Rohter describes Argentina's problems as a culture that praises Jose' Hernandez's character, "Martin Fierro," who glorified values through its solitary hero, a gaucho cowboy. Their problems are complicated by distrust of this isolated state, wide tax evasion, and murders of political opponents by the military. Argentina harbors few restraints where the judicial branch is independent of the executive branch. Lack of external regulations has left Argentines vulnerable to exploits of enterprising leadership.

Argentina is not the only country that attempts to emulate free market economies. A number of Southeast Asian, Eastern European and Latin American countries are experimenting with free market models balanced with varying public regulations. Based upon travels in Vietnam, it is apparent that the entrepreneurial approaches are thriving in the southern part of the country around Ho Chi Minh City. It is evident, that if Vietnam had not been ravaged with repeated wars in the past century, it would already be one of the economic tigers of the Pacific Rim.

Economic cycles have whipped up the peaks of exhilarating expansions and the depths of depressions. The excesses of egocentric greed and the tragedies of economic failures are extolled in the histories of enterprising political economies. There are indices to externally validate the social benefits of almost any enterprising endeavors. For example, if politicians do not serve the public interests, they may not be re-elected. If teachers do not attract students to educate, they probably will not survive as educators. If farmers do not produce food products, they make limited contributions to human wellbeing. If physicians do not heal, they may not have patients. Unless clergy are called by both God and the people they serve, they may not continue in their religious roles. Eventually the entrepreneurial approach with self-interests needs to contribute to the common good of society. Public regulations are essential to protect humanity from exploiters who need to be monitored. Both enterprising and regulating functions are essential in the long term for balanced economic development as addressed next.

- **DE-REGULATION vs. RE-REGULATION**

Deregulation is a controversial twin of free market competition since Adam Smith offered the dubious religious metaphor of the "Invisible Hand of God" for operating providentially in free markets. Deregulation has had a cyclical history of vacillations countering the excesses of the free market. One assumption underlying the free market involves an optimistic view that the self-interest of human beings will inherently benefit other people. Another assumption is that consumers make rational decisions in their market choices. It is essential to realize that consumers may not benefit since there will be some irrational losers or uninformed people who are difficult to help anyway. Advocates of free markets realize that public regulators have human limitations in formulating and implementing controls supposedly for the public good. Free market tactics can generally function better without the constraints of regulations that are typically designed to protect the public including vulnerable victims.

These contending twins, deregulation advocates and individualistic free marketers, are natural opportunists. When economic and political doors open, these contenders attract both business and government promoters announcing that they "have come to help." Under strategies of deregulation, privatizing the public sector is targeted as fair game. Promoters of the private sector promise to do the business functions better than the inefficient, inconsiderate and heavy-handed government. Consumer appetites are aroused by advertising that potential buyers did not previously have in their awareness. Many products, services and resources are distributed as commodities. They can be packaged, marketed and delivered to consumers by distributors who create the need through promotional advertising. Producers of all types of services and products can be delivered at some price. Such economic globalization can threaten the social fabric, the financial viability and the structural justice in vulnerable cultures around the world.

Who knows all of these secret marketing tactics and free market strategies? Who would suspect that former military and government officials would be attracted to these lucrative positions and markets with their profitable commodities? Energy industries also have market interests. Who would ever think that religion could be pedaled promotionally as a commodity? Who would imagine that religious people would not need to be audited since they are so trustworthy? Charitable and religious organizations are vulnerable to these same dynamics in business marketing. Furthermore, the health care sector also illustrates similar prime vulnerability. Health

Maintenance Organizations and insurance companies have economic conflicts of interests between the care of patients and the profits of these private organizations. In the public sector, public health in a number of countries has compromised the trust it has historically held for the protection of human beings around the world as seen in the spread of SARS, HIV-AIDS, plus contaminations of food, blood, and vaccines.[26]

Is this analysis influenced unduly by cynicism about disillusioned idealism or stark realism? If the reader has uncertainty about how to respond, one is encouraged to dig deeper for better facts than what is provided daily by media owned by private interests for maximizing profits or controlled by government for national interests. The search for truth is never-ending in its quest for understanding complicated issues. Economic self-interests and validated truth are often in direct conflict. Herbert sees a need to watch "The Halliburton Shuffle" as military contracts are conveniently arranged with this contractor that has made major profits in wartime.[27] Democratic societies have even more responsibility than oppressed societies that do not have access to credible sources to challenge the economic power of private and political interests.

Obedience and conformity are commendable character qualities. But how can people discover balanced choices in response to powerful economic influence? Unquestioning obedience and readiness to conform to authoritative powers are not the characteristics of informed citizens in free societies. Wisdom was provided in the aphorism that "power corrupts; absolute power corrupts absolutely."[28] There are many issues that clash economically, politically culturally and religiously. These are conflicts of vested interests that need to be addressed in order for humanity to pursue just and sustainable peace for living together.

**TRANSITIONS toward MANAGING CONFLICTS:**

Human boasting about gains that serve self-interests also result in unresolved conflicts in many domains of living. Historical evidence continues to support the observation that humanity has many internal conflicts as well as external problems. Reinhold Niebuhr provided penetrating insight for these contradictory challenges in his paradoxical aphorism: "Man's capacity for justice makes democracy possible, but man's inclination to injustice makes democracy necessary."[29]

Responses to international and domestic problems vary all the way from whining to retaliation to problem solving. Whining is rarely a constructive response. Violent alternatives are plausible when a dangerous enemy threatens a family or nation. Unless one is a categorical pacifist who will not resort to violence under any circumstances, there are numerous types of violent measures that may be quickly used. Violent retaliation includes options of war, state terrorism, killing, "nuking," destroying, bio-terrorism, invasion, destructive anger, oppressive measures, and other aggression.

Skills in creative problem solving are essential for developing nonviolent alternatives. Steps in problem solving include accurately identifying the problems, carefully defining the problems, thoroughly analyzing the key issues, followed by creatively developing and implementing effective alternatives. Nonviolent approaches are alternatives addressed in the remainder of this book with the next section concerned with managing conflicts.

# Endnotes

[1] Taleb N., (2004), Fooled by Randomness
[2] Diamond J., (1/21-27/02) "Let's Not Think We've Won the War," The Washington Post National Weekly Edition.
[3] Mohammad Mahiathir, (Jan. 25, 2002.) Malaysian Prime Minister's criticism voiced at the 2003 World Economics Forum reported by the Associated Press in the Dallas Morning News.
[4] Diamond J., (2001) Guns, Germs and Steel: The Fates of Human Societies, Highbridge Company.
[5] Huntington S., (1993) "The Clash of Civilizations," Foreign Affairs, Vol. 72, No. 3, Summer 1993.
[7] Ibid.
[3] Huntington S., (1996), The Clash of Civilizations and the Remaking of the World Order, New York: Simon and Schuster.
[8] Smock D., (2002) "Clash of Civilizations or Opportunity for Dialogue," paper presented at the Second Regional Conference on the "Role of Religion in Promoting World Peace," Association of Muslim Social Scientists, Dallas, TX,. September 28, 2002.
[9] Halberstam D. Interview by Ira J. Hadnot, "The Conflicts of a Lifetime," Dallas Morning News, 1/19/03.
[10] Kennedy P., (1994) "Must It Be The Rest Against the West," Atlantic Monthly, Vol 274, No. 6, December, 1994.
[11] Kaplan R., (1994) "The Coming Anarchy," Atlantic Monthly, Vol. 273, No. 2, February, 1994.
Kennedy P., (1993) Preparing for the Twentieth Century, New York: Random House.
Kaplan R., (2000) The Coming Anarchy: Shattering the Dreams of Post Cold War, New York: Random House.
[12] Fukuyama F., (1992) The End of History and the Last Man, New York: Free Press.
[13] Friedman T., (1999) The Lexus and the Olive Tree, New York: Farrar, Straus and Giroux. Friedman also draws upon David Rothhopf for seeing the young-old faultline in Saudi Arabia and the Muslim world as reported in his article "War of Ideas, Part 6," The New York Times, January 25, 2004. Friedman T., (Feb. 22, 2004) "Meet the Zippies," The New York Times, introduces to the United States the term "zippie" as the new Indian generation that is replacing the American yuppies in filling high technology jobs that have been out-sourced by American companies to young, educated people of India.
[14] Janis I., (1982) Groupthink: Psychological Studies of Policy Decisions, Houghton-Mifflin Company. These psycho-social dynamics will be addressed further in later chapters along with corrective solutions.
Intelligence data before 9/11/01 was apparently pre-screened in both the Clinton and Bush Administrations as reported by James Risen and Eric Lichtblau (Feb. 24, 2004) "C.I.A. Was Given Data on Hijacker Long Before 9/11," The New York Times.
[15] Gaddis J. L., (2001) "And Now This: Lessons from the Old Era for the New One," chapter in The Age of Terror: American and the World After September 11, edited by Strobe Talbott and Nayan Chanda, Basic Books.
[16] Hill C., (2202) "A Hurclean Task: The Myth and Reality of Arab Terrorism," in The Age of Terror, edited by Strobe Talbott and Nayan Chanda, Basic Books.
[17] Lewis B., (2002) What Went Wrong? Western Impact and Middle Eastern Response, Oxford University Press.
[18] Huntington, (1993) op.cit.
[19] Kupchan C., (2002) The End of the American Era: U.S. Foreign Policy and the Geopolitics of the Twenty-first Century, New York: Alfred A. Knopf.
[20] Gaddis, op.cit.
[21] Sivard R., (1997) World Military and Social Expenditures, World Priorities, Inc.
[22] Leebaert D., (2001) The Fifty-Year Wound: The True Price of America's Cold War Victory, Little Brown Publishers.
[23] Rothkopf D., "The Failures of Capitalism," The Washington Post Weekly Edition, Jan. 28-Feb. 3, 2002.
[24] Eichenwald K., (June 30, 2002), "Could Capitalism Actually Bring Down Capitalism?" The New York Times.
[25] Rohter L., (February 8, 2002.) "Argentina Paying Heavily for Squandering Blessings," New York Times.
[26] Garrett L., (2000) Betrayal of Trust: The Collapse of Global Public Health, New York: Hyperion.
[27] Herbert B., (Jan. 30, 2004), "The Haliburton Shuffle," The New York Times.
[28] Acton Lord, (1988) Essays in Religion, Poetics and Morality, Liberty Fund, Incorporated.
[29] Niebuhr Reinhold, (1944) The Children of Light and the Children of Darkness, New York: Charles Scribner's Sons.

# Part II:
# MANAGING CONFLICT

Part II is designed to help responsible citizens and public officials deal constructively with conflict and violence. Managing conflicts demands skills and tolerance. There is a need to tolerate the anxious distress of perplexing problems without expecting silver bullets. For realists who struggle with difficult problems, this section offers strategies for coping with domestic and international problems.

Methods are provided in this section for dealing effectively with polarized situations that do not lend themselves toward easy resolution, but rather are so complex that these issues need to be continuously managed. Chapter Five recognizes that cagy players in conflict know how to sabotage constructive remedies. Contenders in domestic relations and officials involved in international conflict will readily recognize the delaying tactics that are discussed. Stonewalling is another tactic used by crafty poker players who try to fake out an opponent. Such procrastinating tactics are not recommended. Instead they are unmasked so that the players of these unproductive games can face delaying and undoing tactics as typical negative strategies.

Chapter Six deals with the dynamics of passive aggression. Stalling tactics are learned by most teenagers and immature leaders in order to thwart the attempts of a power figure to solve problems. Passive aggression is deceptive so that power players might actually believe that they have prevailed. However, this tactic only temporarily defeats forceful power. Momentary truces permit the problem to become further infected with resentments in the quagmire of many domestic disputes and international conflicts. What Went Wrong? is the apt title of Bernard Lewis' new book which provides an historical account of Middle Eastern and Western attempts to deal with both passivity and aggression. "What Went Wrong?" is likewise the question that many couples puzzle about when their relationship irreparably deteriorates into destructive co-existence.

Finally, Chapter Seven is intentionally more proactive in providing methods for coping with difficult issues as well as identifying insoluble polarities. Both domestic issues and international tensions have commonalities that are identified for families in conflict and people concerned with foreign policy. The analysis of issues is not exhaustive. Rather polarized issues are selected that cyclically perpetuate distortions in cultural differences and worldviews.

## Chapter Five

# Resisting, Sabotaging and Placating

> Your freedom is being restricted for
> your own security.
>
> Anonymous

The Patriot Act has become increasingly controversial since it was enacted 2001 in the United States in response to the 9/11 terrorist attacks. Concerns for freedom and security naturally conflict. In order to provide safety, certain freedoms may be constricted. Constraints of freedom depend on what authorities can tolerate in the free expression of speech, migratory movements, economic choices, military conscription and political activities. From the citizens' perspective, concerns arise as to what restrictions of freedoms to tolerate by authorities.

The greater the fear of violence, the more restraints are made on freedoms in both domestic and international affairs. Usually these controls are negatively tolerated for the sake of safety. The difficult issue of freedom vs. security often needs to be balanced with the degree of threat, common sense and constitutional credibility. Because freedom and regulation can be excessive, both necessitate responsible protections. If either reckless freedom or stifling restraints become extreme, unforeseen consequences can generate even greater conflicts.

In domestic settings, coercive measures used typically by an abusive male constrict the movement, language, economic resources, and social behavior of family members. Vulnerable spouses and children quickly recognize the devastating power of an angry husband or father. Children may cower in obeisance with unexpressed resentment as their "degrees of freedom" are capriciously controlled. Should a spouse or a child defy this household authority or not seek permission, dyer consequences can be expected.

"Your freedom is being restricted for your own good" is an aphorism employed by controlling parents and public officials resorting to control of freedoms they sense are justified by dangers to national security. Examples include restrictions in immigration measures and airport security or grounding by parents. When the threats are seen as imminent, limits may be imposed upon other constitutional rights and social practices. For example, people tolerate security inspections at airports as long as they weigh potential benefits over intrusions and delays.

**Passive Aggression:**
One method of dealing with aggression involves placating the source of power. Threatened nations learn how to placate another aggressive nation particularly when there is an obvious power differential. The early stages of World War II demonstrated this placating response in the face of the Axis powers of Germany and Japan. Germany overpowered Poland, the Sudetenland, the Rhineland, the Baltic and Balkan countries, plus France, Denmark and Norway. Japan overran Korea, Vietnam, Manchuria, much of China and Southeast Asia, plus many islands in the Pacific

Ocean. These Axis Powers had overwhelming military forces that they were not hesitant to use brutally. Sabotage, passive aggression and nonviolent resistance were employed during this war by countries that were overrun, exploited and occupied by these vicious aggressors.

Colonial powers eventually come to realize that demanding compliance builds passive resistance and angry resentment against oppressive occupation forces. Festering anger about dependent status is a psychological dynamic known in international and interpersonal relations. Wars of independence by former colonies reveal the seething hostility toward imperial powers in Africa, Asia, North, Central and South America. In international conflicts, passive acquiescence is a survival technique used against powerful nations. The citizens of occupied countries can slowly but systematically undo and demoralize an intrusive power through resistance and sabotage. The citizens of Denmark effectively used subterfuge and sabotage when the powerful German military overran them in World War II. By placating the Nazis, the Danes not only resisted the superior occupying forces. An account of their passive resistance explicitly described the Danish nonviolent strategies that effectively demoralized the Nazis.[1]

Evidence shows that both the Palestinians and Israelis use subterfuge to foil efforts to end violence in the Middle East. There have been numerous peace efforts unsuccessfully initiated by Americans, Norwegians, Egyptians, and Saudi Arabians. Officials of the United Nations have also attempted to promote measures for a peaceful resolution. Major attempts to end violence have been frustrated by repeated accusations made by both Israelis and Palestinians that undo peace in the Middle East.

Developing nations and powerless ethnic minorities resort to passive aggression when uninvited nations try to intimidate them. If a superior power cannot be defeated, alternatives range from compliance, to neutrality, to acquiescence, or finally to captivity. Leaders of the former Soviet Union realized that a number of their satellites were passively awaiting the demise of the Soviet Union. The United States only partially recognizes similar compliance among "nations of the willing" against terrorism. Spain's change of leadership in 2004 indicates just how tentative alliances are when confronting ominous terrorists. Fragile coalitions show reluctance when aggression is threatened or financial aid is curtailed. Passive aggression was also a response of Saddam Hussein to the resolutions of the United Nations concerning inspections of weapons of mass destruction.

Switching from international wars to domestic scenes, the parallel tactics for facing an overpowering aggressor can be seen. Most teenagers learn survival technique in order to cope with powerful parents and other authority figures such as teachers, police, bullies, friends or supervisors. Many of these self-defeating behaviors are portrayed in Box 5-1 on passive aggression that also are manifested in international relations.

> **Box 5-1 : Passive Aggression**
>
> A docu-drama of school and teenage violence in Florida has been described in a book called <u>Bully.</u>[2] This account of manipulative teenagers engaged in criminal violence has been produced into a horrifying movie. Based upon factual information, the book recounts how teenagers undo aggression directed at them, express hostile resentment, and respond violently to their intimate bully.
>
> The families of these teenagers showed frustration about the passive manipulation of their children, and then were shocked into awareness about the violent crimes of their affluent offspring. Dramatic scenes show how parents lacked awareness the shocking capacity that their own deceptive children had to be extremely violent.
>
> This true account revealed the reality of criminal charges, indictments for murder, and dramatic court trials. It ends with harsh punishments of teenagers who were found guilty of conniving to kill their close acquaintance who was also a manipulative bully.

The tactics of passive aggression are readily learned because they are effective in obtaining desired results. When a powerful authority makes demands, it is wise to passively listen, be agreeable, but then not do whatever is demanded. This is one of the most effective survival mechanisms when the authority feels "I told them what to do," while simultaneously preserving his control. The teenager gives the appearance of listening, obeying and yielding to the authorities' power. However, the placating teenager does not take action to comply and neither do overwhelmed employees, subjects, citizens or family members.

A passive aggressive person can even pretend to act completely compliant with the wishes of the aggressor. When the confrontation is over, the powerless figure resorts to passive aggression by not obeying. When the authority figure is out of sight, he may become the target of ridicule blatantly expressed by powerless victims. Less conspicuously, an inexperienced victim may momentarily feel humiliated, develop festering resentment, and minimally comply with orders. During the interim, major portions of the demands are left undone thereby frustrating the authority figure.

Lest there is an impression that passive aggression is undervalued, there are occasions when it is a nonviolent alternative useful for survival. Most people are well advised to learn this technique in power struggles. It is a survival tactic that works except for feeling the revengeful wrath of a frustrated aggressor at a later time. When the odds are low for gaining any satisfaction from coercive manipulators, passive aggression will likely unglue them. Powerless persons can resist aggression with seething resentment, retribution, and even fierce hostility. Many parents who have felt defeated by their children come to these bewildering realizations.

History is replete with accounts of powerful nations that are eventually forced to face the hostile antagonism of oppressed cultures. Defeat can be the result of overweening arrogance or by making uninvited interventions. Passive aggression is primarily reactions to undo unwanted force. It is not proactive. Consequently, passive aggression is not effective when direct positive action is necessary to resolve conflicts. Sheer survival does not assure that the benefits of either durable peace or sustainable justice will result from continued existence.

**Refusing to Communicate:**

The silent treatment reduces many relationships to hostile sulking while living in a constant state of unresolved tension and undeclared war. When communication is primarily in the form of lecture and monologues, family members often co-exist without verbally communicating. "He does all the talking," so "We don't talk anymore." "What's the use, he never listens?" These complaints arise in dysfunctional families with interpersonal conflicts. People give up in when they cannot speak to each other with some degree of civility. Lack of communication is usually a symptom of deeper personal problems. Psychotherapists are occasionally puzzled by an autistic child who once talked, but then becomes non-communicative. This condition bewilders parents because autistic behavior frequently augers up guilt, frustration and depression.

International officials become autistic by refusing to engage in diplomatic communications. Rather than assuming that their silence may mean concurring acquiescence, diplomats often assume that no news is not good news. Moreover, secondary media sources often provide misleading accounts. Assumptions can be influenced by wishful thinking by disputing parties who are unduly optimistic. Presuppositions readily conjure up the worst possible scenario of paranoid people who imagine conspiracies with the worst possible outcomes. Neither of these extreme perceptions is sufficiently adequate for making decisions.

Breaking off relationships has unpredictable consequences. Couples who can no longer communicate preclude further growth in their relationship. Sullen couples can quietly destroy each other by withdrawing from wider social relationships. Internationally, nations can break up sub-cultures into warring, hostile conflict. The fragmentation of North and South Korea illustrates failure in communication in this once unified culture. This fragmentation of long historical tradition has left North Korea with limited contact with the rest of the world while it threatens to develop, market and deploy nuclear weapons.

Conflict management can take a variety of styles with differing degrees of effectiveness. Restoring communications between conflicting parties is a crucial process for managing differences. In addition, Isenhart and Spangle[3] identify four other conflict styles in their helpful resource for managing conflict in both domestic and international tensions. These strategies of accommodation, compromise, competition and collaboration are considered in future chapters concerned with constructive approaches.

**Escape, Avoidance or Walkout:**

Whereas silence is bewildering to people, escape and avoidant behaviors involve understandable omissions. Aggressive people have various reactions when they encounter aggression that differs from war games or athletic contests. Violent people often avoid other aggressive persons unless the encounter heightens into violent confrontations. When aggressive bullies are confronted with equal aggressiveness, the bullies tend to escape from the encounter out of cowardly fear or harm avoidance with concern about their own preoccupation with losing control.

Aggressive parents demonstrate different behavior when confronted by assertive relatives or police. If a young person survives the abuse of aggressive parents, an adult son or daughter may confront the abusive parent who may have never been challenged earlier by their child. It is very difficult to confront an over-powering parent who has had a long history of violent aggression. A belligerent parent also runs the risks of elder abuse from family members later when they themselves are frail and dependent. Violence against the elderly is increasing in western cultures where respect for elders is not a strong cultural tradition.

Anti-social sub-groups that feed on criminal violence are hostile to rival groups, the police and the public. What is called gang behavior in America, or hooligans in Europe, or ratting in India varies widely when they encounter hostility. These gangs honor the self-declared turf of the rival groups. Invading another hostile group's territory without explicit permission may trigger violent reaction. Confrontation is avoided on neutral territory where new members can be recruited and prowess displayed. Violent encounters are often not accidental transgressions of territory. Rather, these encounters are planned to test recruits or carry out revenge. The mentality of gangs ranges from war-room intelligence, to invading drug territory, to revenge for romantic break ups.

Some aggressive executives and professionals also display avoidant and escape behavior when they are confronted with comparable aggression. In turf that they can dominate, these aggressors become overbearing in relations to less powerful subordinates who usually are submissive because of the unequal organizational, political, social or economic power. However, a noticeable pattern occurs when aggressive executives and professionals encounter someone who also displays similar aggressiveness. Many aggressive people typically find excuses to escape from these encounters. They may not show up for subsequent meetings in order to avoid the turf they cannot readily dominate. Cross-cultural patterns of behavior vary widely often influenced by social stereotypes in investigations the author has conducted in India and America.[4]

The near nuclear confrontation between the Soviet Union and the United States in the Cuban Missile Crisis in 1962 illustrates two superpowers backing off to avoid nuclear war. History does not assure that such situations will never arise again between nuclear powers. There is little assurance that rival nations or terrorist groups will carefully manage weapons of mass destruction in their possession. Leaders of nuclear powers and sub-state terrorist groups increasingly confront a bewildering world of chaotic anarchy.

India is puzzled by Pakistan while western nuclear powers are bewildered by North Korea, Iran and Libya. Lack of communications during decision-making in worst-scene scenarios is notoriously disturbing because these threatening circumstances might occur again with unknown nuclear, biological and chemical threats.

A number of nations engage in variations of passive aggressive, escape or avoidant behavior. Evidence of these behaviors can be found in the hostile relationship between India and Pakistan, or in the vengeful relationship between Israelis and Palestinians. Meetings to explore negotiations are readily avoided with convenient excuses or walkouts. Leaders are evasive when they are confronted with challenges from other armed nations. Regular meetings on neutral turf among representatives who have equal status are essential for preventive dialogue rather than fear avoidance and ineffectively contrived meetings.

Terroristic threats heighten the level of uncertainty that disastrous violence might take place without explicit warning. These attacks come with almost complete surprise and unpredictability. This surprise element elevates psychological fears that paralyze vulnerable populations. In war, military leaders use sudden attacks as strategies for surprising an enemy who might resort to evasive tactics in order to survive. Tactics of terrorists heighten tense conflicts because they can unpredictably strike with the very rapid transportation and information technology. Within minutes attacks can be orchestrated almost anywhere on the earth by dangerous aggressors located in remote command and hidden control centers.

**Stand-off Strategies:**

The stand off between the former Soviet Union and the United States dominated international relations in the last half of the twentieth century. Both sides projected the worst of motives onto the other side. This mutual projection of evil hostility diverted enormous resources away from domestic, humanitarian, environmental and global problems. The internal devastation wrought upon people in Eastern Europe, alongside economic demise, and raping of natural resources will require that sector of the world many decades to recover. Cold wars like most hot wars divert enormous talents and waste irreplaceable resources into unproductive military expenditures.

The terms "Soviet Union" and "Communism" became metaphors in the West for the identifying the enemy. One analysis suggests that these metaphorical enemies were real threats that became politically exaggerated in presidential election campaigns in the United States. Barnet[5] claims that the threat of Soviet Communism was a diversion from a more difficult enemy that neither the United States nor the Soviet Union wanted to address. The economic oppression, social injustice and structural violence experienced by impoverished people in developing nations cried out for justice during the Cold War. The two superpowers focused almost exclusively on their rivalry as neither America nor Soviets were committed to addressing structural violence that is extraordinarily difficult to solve. Consequently, unattended problems were ignored out of convenience as well as ignorance about how to solve these problems. It is almost immeasurable how much these superpowers were preoccupied with their own status while neglecting to provide leadership in the regions ravaged with structural injustice. These horrendous problems of violence, starvation, pollution, social injustice and economic disasters continue to fester in Africa, South and Central America, plus many parts of Asia as well in the North America and Europe.

Two other enemies have prolonged their animosity over an equivalent number of decades. What are Israelis and Palestinians avoiding by perpetuating a political stand-off of suicidal dimensions? Does this tension in the Middle East help them and their allies to be diverted away from other pressing international and domestic issues? Why does the United States continue to give one-sided support to Israelis while ignoring the violence they provoke? Why do Arab countries have a tendency to point at the pitiable treatment of the Palestinians while neglecting to address the humiliation of their own people along with structural violence in their own internal affairs and international relations?

A conference on terrorism[6] at Harvard University's Kennedy School of Government provided insights into the causes of the attacks of September 11, 2001 on the Pentagon and the World Trade Centers. Rather than blaming illiteracy, unemployment and poverty as causal factors feeding terroristic violence, three other factors were identified. One intangible factor is the humiliation of the Palestinians in the Middle East. Another factor is the economic isolation of nations that are not part of the World Trade Organization including North Korea, Iran, Iraq, Syria and Saudi Arabia. A third factor identified is the one-sided American foreign policy in the Middle East.

The Cold War mentality perpetuates assumptions and inaccurate perceptions held by many parties of the contemporary conflicts. Nations with conflicts have collective memories based upon ethnocentric perspectives. Impervious viewpoints are augmented by a fortress mentality that sees the outside world as dangerously hostile. Xenophobia is practiced by many cultures. Dysfunctional governments stay in power by perpetuating old hostilities. In domestic affairs around the world, many families live in similar fortresses within their own home. Mutual frustration diverts them from constructively addressing the problems that may not even be recognized from narrow inside perspectives. Instead of peace and tranquility, hostility regerminates from generation to generation. Many people believe that their ethnocentric assumptions are absolute truths. As a consequence they are pre-empted from addressing the deeper issues of structural violence while also violating human rights.

**Regressing to Non-Negotiation:**

Both the Israelis and Palestinians repeatedly regress to an intransigent status perpetuating additional cycles of violence and retaliation. They have difficulty letting go of each other as archenemies. Historical justifications have hung onto resentful hostilities perpetuated into contemporary excuses for prolonging the struggle. Looking back to old animosities has prevailed in their reasoning whenever peaceful accommodations are about to be considered. Fleeting attention is given to shaping a better world when clinging ferociously to past justifications by each side. These regressions may be worse than stalemates since historical conflicts dominate their hostile relations. People seem to forget that they cannot change the past. However, they can change their perceptions of the past in order to alter their views of current circumstances that shape their future.

Divorce proceedings have parallels in regressive behavior. Past hurts, animosities and injuries are conjured up to block the dynamics of resolving present conflicts. Angry husbands and wives play out these processes over prolonged periods of time. Divorce is a process. It can be a very destructive process that threatens to consume the humanity of both parties. When a marriage is over, beating up a dead relationship has no known constructive benefits except to vent hostility. The more venomous the divorce, the more difficult it is for the parties directly involved and their children to move beyond regressive immaturity to future growth and development. Rather than getting on with their lives, many resentful people destroy both themselves and the people they have previously loved.

Young people are very vulnerable in broken love affairs. Their regression to childhood can result not only in emotional tantrums, but also destructive hostility. It is not uncommon for one-sided romances to end up in hatreds that feed teenage violence and revenge. The more fragile the self-image of the offended one, the more likely self-destructive behaviors may ensue with potentially vengeful injury to the other party. Tragic deaths result from abruptly breaking off one-sided love affairs. Unrequited love can also result in self-destructive suicides or immature suicidal threats.

The immature brain of teenagers engenders heightened interpersonal misunderstandings. The limited development of their pre-frontal lobes hinders their capacity in making rational judgments, managing emotional controls and evaluating long-term consequences of their irrational behavior. Many think that they are invincible so many accidents and crimes are attributed to young people. Because they are ready to take risks, young adults are readily attracted to military service and other high hazardous adventures. Unfortunately, many teenagers are channeled into the adult judicial system in the United States particularly to prosecute major felonies including murders. This prompts another question that compares adolescent and adult accountability. Should adults in divorce proceedings not be expected to display appreciably more maturity than teenagers in comparable interpersonal conflicts?

International leaders should be expected to make rational decisions as they evaluate consequences of their actions. Government officials would hopefully promote policies that operate out of national interests. Their responsibilities demand that they use wise judgment in evaluating intelligence data about domestic and international conflicts. Protecting national interests would presumably add to the predictability of their international actions. However, when internal domestic problems occur within a country, national leaders frequently divert attention by energetically engaging in international affairs. Balancing domestic and international concerns can provide bases for predictable behavior. Peace with justice contributes positively to the development of cultures socially, economically, and politically.

While the first half of this chapter focused on immature passive responses to conflict, the following section addresses direct behaviors rather than reactive responses.

### Direct Aggression:

#### *Intimidating Tactics*:

Physical intimidations and verbal "put-downs" are designed to control other people. Experienced manipulators ingeniously find the vulnerable side of someone they want to taunt by using negative comments directly communicated to opponents such as "trash talk." Manipulative trash talkers try to upset the emotional and physical rhythm of an opponent. Psychological innuendo is frequently used to intimidate a contender's mental performance. In family relations, siblings often use intimidation to show their superiority over younger siblings. In destructive relations, spouses can resort to embarrassing accusations and sexual harassment that express emotional and physical domination. In many traditional cultures males dominate the marriage relationship. In more liberated cultures, there are alternatives styles accompanied by frequent confusion about which spouse dominates an equalitarian relationship.

Lawyers have learned to use intimidating tactics for dealing with the opposition's witnesses. Lawyers make a game of degrading an adversary while at the same time advocating forcefully for their own client. Witnesses who have been intimidated in an adversarial system have consulted with me professionally for counsel. Advice is sought particularly when their credentials have been degraded during tough cross-examination. The adversarial legal system assumes that it is fair game to discredit witnesses and their testimony. The ethics of the legal profession encourages strong advocacy for their client with assumptions that eventually the truth is evaluated by a jury or judge.

On an international level, nations frequently attempt to intimidate enemies. Displays of military prowess, highly trained soldiers and latest technologies may be auspiciously displayed. Posturing is part of the game. Avoiding combat is high on the agenda of most military leaders who fear that intimidating hype can quickly lead to unplanned counter attacks that result in disastrous violence. Yet, intimidation is part of the rationale behind MAD – Mutually Assured Destruction. Divorce, war, and terroristic violence are all similar tactics employed in domestic and international relationships. Intimidating people are often very adept at expressing manipulative control of other persons. Such power plays tend to reproduce themselves with repeated attacks. Cycles of violence are perpetuated because of the addictive quality in violent behavior that is effectively reinforced by regaining control.

**Arguing from Rigid Positions:**

Defending a pre-determined position is an active tactic involved in controlling another person's thinking and behavior. How effective are rigid positions in managing or resolving conflicts? It is important to distinguish between positions and interests. Hard liners take a firm stand that can be called a fortress mentality. Dividing sides into good and evil divisively narrows options. Drawing a line in the sand is likewise a tough position that simplifies conflicts that are much more complicated. When disputing parties forcefully declare rigid positions there is little hope for resolving a conflict. Egos become defensively hardened and simultaneously fragile since hard shells crumble quickly when cracked.

Toughness is over-valued by many people who possess rigid personalities in the middle of conflicts. Flexibility has more promising possibilities in shaping human relationships. In negotiating with hostage-takers, fluid positions are essential for optimal outcomes. Most professionals in law enforcement in America learned this important lesson in the past two decades. It is in the interests of law enforcement officials to negotiate in order to value the life of both hostages and their own police forces. More people survive when law enforcement officials engage in negotiations rather than primitive assaults that lead eventually to violent consequences for all sides. More deaths might have been avoided if the FBI had continued to communicate in the Ruby Ridge stand off in Idaho and the Branch Davidian cultic religious compound in Texas.

One of the risks in law enforcement involves losing control in the middle of a puzzling situation that includes the life or death of hostages. Rigidity is not a quality that negotiators should prize when dealing with hostage-takers. To protect their own best interests, law enforcement professionals have learned to develop skills in fluid negotiations along with give and take communication based upon informed sources. Quickly developing trustful relations are highly prized qualities when dealing with unknown hostage-takers. More people survive on both sides when flexible communication is fostered.

Hostages may be taken in either domestic or international violence. An angry, controlling father and husband literally holds his children and spouse hostage. This confinement of women and children by abusive men has many parallels to situations when criminals hold hostages. Abusive men, criminals and terrorists all hold hostages with forceful intimidation and terrorizing fear. Hostage-takers often possess rigid worldviews that are operative when they bargain with hostages. Law enforcers negotiate more effectively when they understand these ideologies that originate from strange worldviews.

**Seeking Unfair Advantages:**

When disputes arise between parties, the strategy of seeking the higher ground is commendable on the surface since it appeals to the basic moral values of a culture. However, there can be a dark side to these pious statements. In domestic conflicts within families, often a pious family member may appear to be the good one standing on higher ground. This self-serving image is frequently an effort to show moral superiority while putting down adversaries. Manipulators often point out the evil, dark side of an adversary. Judges see this technique utilized during custody settlements in crass attempts to curry a favorable ruling for one of the parents. In trials for domestic disputes, balanced judgment is essential on the part of judges and juries. Judges make rulings according to the rules of evidence when one side is unfairly gaining advantage over the other.

In sporting contests, both the offensive strategy and the defensive strategy attempt to seek advantages for their team. In games with standardized rules, fouling an opponent results in a penalty that is carefully scrutinized by the teams as well as the fans. Unfair advantage is almost always labeled as a deliberate effort to gain an undeserved position. In soccer and in most popular sports, fans can be enraged if the official does not quickly blow the whistle on violations that gives one team an unfair advantage. Olympic athletes have been investigated lest they have advantages in their sport that can be derived from dishonest tactics or misuse of forbidden drugs.

In contests as well as in courts, there are rules designed to determine unfair aggression by participants who challenge the integrity of the contest. There are innumerable disputes that are not officiated by an official umpire. Uncontrolled fights and chaotic wars do not have umpires officiating to enforce rules. Seeking advantage is a crafty tactic that military leaders use to become heroes acclaimed by their victorious side. Military tacticians and family abusers learn from mentors, heroic figures, abusive parents and leaders of historically violent cultures.

While trust is one of the key ingredients of a lasting relationship, devious tactics are readily used by manipulative combatants. There is little mystery why police and military personnel themselves have high incidence of violence in their own families. They know how to subdue an enemy, but they unfortunately also carry these aggressive skills into their private life. Families frequently rehabilitate combat veterans while also becoming the victims of violence learned by soldiers. Military veterans cannot automatically unlearn forceful violence when they re-enter civilian life. Veterans have a disproportional share of inner battles that they may turn upon themselves or their loved ones. Shay[7] provides insight into the difficulties that combat veterans experience when domestic conflicts and mental health problems are ignored or misunderstood by the military. Learning to be violent unfortunately contributes to outbursts in societies when wars have been part of their history.

Among nations in conflict, seeking advantages in the name of national security has repeatedly been historically documented. *Realpolitik* strategies favor the crafty military and political leaders who gain powerful advantages in their positions. Business and professional leaders are applauded for their aggressive executive leadership. The targeted victims of crafty Machiavellian approaches look at these maneuvers differently. These strategies have inherently challenged peaceful forums like the United Nations. It has been very difficult for nonviolent organizations to be effective in keeping the peace while trying to reduce strife among sparring nations of the world. When the deceptions of international members are considered, it is an amazing fete what the United Nations has accomplished in settling disputes that promote global peace and justice. Few developed nations seek to advance economic justice unfavorable to their narrow security and interests.

**Protecting Self-Interests:**

The previous section leads right into defending national security. Problems develop into contentious conflicts when the self-interests of one party violate the basic rights and interests of others. This predicament prompts the following pivotal question:[8]

**How can self-interests be ethically expressed without interfering with the rights of other persons?**

Expressing human rights creates a conundrum. Self-interests may adversely interfere with the rights of others. Aggressive behavior is frequently pursued in order to control rivals. Passive approaches leave people vulnerable to the divisive schemes of opponents whether they are in the family and international relations. Violent persons resort to coercive measures that intimidate others into submission if not outright defeat. Aggressive persons use force in order to achieve their own goals.

Manipulative persons are very difficult for both assertive and passive persons to cope with ethically. The aggressor astutely utilizes "one-up-man-ship" in their crafty relationships with vulnerable people. If the victim is naively trusting, the aggressor dominates them. Aggressive people often have difficulty understanding anyone's perspectives but their own advantage. Such aggressive people may be heroically lauded in organizations that reward such competitive interests. Peers and subordinates may be astonished by the recognitions given to unethically deceptive manipulators.

In the lengthy marriages and family relationships, few crafty manipulators can contribute constructively to the health of a growing family. People carry forward into their own marriages the manipulative aggression they learn from parents and other models. Fragile first marriages are now called "starter marriages"[9] in which the couple expects divorce will probably be followed by subsequent marriages. These starter marriages have even higher risks for breeding unsatisfactory relationships. The aggressive dynamics brought into a starter marriage suggests that seeking advantage by protecting self-interests are styles learned from parents.

Partners often carry into their second and third marriages the unresolved conflicts of previous generations without learning to make lasting commitments, supporting each other, or nurturing their children. Even more threatening to children are non-biological mates in the home. Non-biological mates present notoriously greater risks in perpetrating abusive violence against children.

In international relations, national interests dominate every relationship with other countries. As in violent criminal behavior, personal and national narcissism violate the wellbeing of adversaries. According to research,[10] violent criminals are notoriously narcissistic in their own narrow perspectives. Likewise, leadership of nations may predictably display parallel narcissism on a collective scale. There is consistent evidence that Saddam Hussein was plagued with delusions of grandeur and related psychological pathology. Further research is needed on how narcissistic behavior is displayed by leaders who pursue hegemony to advance national interests?

## Gathering Intelligence:

Checking up on a mate is a game for a suspiciously distrustful spouse. In such paranoid investigations, suspicions become the basis for distrust and legal complaint. When relationships in a marriage or family are reduced to intelligence gathering on their mate, the trust level is already seriously impaired. When extended families surround the social environment couples, there are many more observations of tempering violent or neglectful behaviors by relatives. In the era of the isolated, nuclear family, the awareness of abuse behind closed doors is rarely in the awareness of equally isolated neighbors. In modern society, there are few villages in which families know each other face-to-face in order to help raise children in the traditional style, or to extend sanctions that circumscribe unacceptable abuse in families and violence in the community.

In international relations, it is assumed that foreign intelligence is gathered by rival nations. Surprises in the military capability of a potential enemy are considered inexcusable with the availability of modern technology. However, the investigations about the quality of international intelligence in Great Britain and the United States about the threat of Iraq suggests that intelligence gathering and interpretation are subject to wide variations in conclusions. Even with high technology, it is impossible to maintain adequate intelligence about a nation or of technically mobile terrorist groups. The unpredicted targets of recent years have gone far beyond the surprise attacks like Pearl Harbor and the beachheads of World War II. Watching the military preparedness of nations is a conventional intelligence challenge. Accurate intelligence about terrorists' tactics is unpredictably difficult to gather in order to provide protection.

Accountability is lower for dissidents who operate like radical clandestine cells. These nemeses can operate like a cancer on a body without pain or direct awareness to the host. In fact, terrorist groups can operate physically within an open society without detection. While nations try to have public accountability, these cells operate anonymously and secretly. By design, terrorist cells may not have awareness of members in other destructive cells. These stealth operations can occur without public awareness.

This secrecy has come into bold relief in gathering, using and evaluating intelligence in the decision by the Bush Administration to launch a war with Iraq. Richard Goodwin[11] suggests that people are more likely to know what they want to know than what they do not want to know. He provides historical accounts of an eternal principle that "presidents and other decision makers usually get the intelligence they want." These insights illustrate the problems encountered by policy makers caught in "group think." Policy makers readily are insulated by their aides who serve as "mind guards" excluding independent information that may be contrary to their preconceived ideas. In such a protected cocoon, decision makers become isolated from the real world while possessing limited contacts outside their advisers. Another source submits that both Saddam Hussein and the Bush Administration may have been out of touch with reality in decisions prior to the war.[12]

The whole industry of investigative intelligence gathering provides clandestine intrigue. There is never enough reliable intelligence. Terrorists typically instill psychological fear with piecemeal revelations of their intended destruction. Intelligence gathering is an endless task including the surprisingly dramatic excitement of international spies. Secretive operations of terrorists are difficult to penetrate when the playing field is global in scope. Moreover, cyber terrorism is possible without even disclosing important geographical locations.

Intelligence agencies frequently amass data from diverse agents and sources. A number of government agencies in the United States are criticized for the lack of overall analytical competencies in intelligence gathering. There is truth to these accusations, but that is only part of the problem. There are three other capabilities that also need attention besides analytic capabilities:

- Firstly, when gathering data, there is the need for coordination among separate agencies rather than "stove-piping" that prevents them from sharing data about potential threats. Stove-piping is a metaphor about the lack of lateral coordination among agencies who have a pattern of sending the smoking data straight up rather than to exchange with other concerned groups. Intelligence gathering is a very complex responsibility that presents limitations in providing data about the operations of very clever groups that intentionally employ secrecy and surprise as strategies.

- Secondly, even more important is the need for capabilities to integrate massive data into overall intelligence pictures. Conceptual models are necessary to synthesize discrete discoveries into integrated, well-conceived recommendations. Greater attention to comprehensive theory-building is essential along with thorough analysis and coordination among international intelligence agencies. Inter-disciplinary approaches are essential since the field of intelligence gathering has not achieved the precise accuracy of scientific methods.

- Thirdly, is the difficulty in getting the interpreted data into the hands of policy decision makers in a timely manner. In the face of these limitations, policy makers must be expected to have competencies of evaluating intelligence data that are always in short supply. Preoccupation with traditional superpower threats has resulted in neglect of investigating non-state terrorist groups and other covert anarchists.

Since gathering accurate intelligence is very difficult, there are numerous reasons to challenge preemptive strikes against sovereign nations. Preemptive military actions need to be based upon intelligence without reasonable doubt about the threat of imminent danger to the security of a nation. But large quantities of intelligence are limited in value unless synthesized into timely and high quality reports. Moreover, there is a need to gather intelligence on site over extended periods of time. Keegan suggests the continuous need for intelligence that grows out of deep knowledge of cultures and languages that is derived from being embedded in the context of local settings rather than primarily from high tech satellites.[13]

**Making Peace Through Strength:**

This strategy has been pursued repeatedly with mixed success. Peace through overwhelming military strength possesses both positive and negative characteristics in domestic and international conflicts. The Cold War exemplifies this approach in the modern history of superpowers. In addition to a stand-off by the Soviet Union and the United States, their huge military forces frightened potential and real enemies while sapping the resources of civilizations during the Cold War. Eventually the Soviet Union could no longer sustain the expenditures for military weapons that drained its humans and natural resources. Nations are vulnerable to exhausting their resources for military expenditures in order to maintain threatening superiority.

In the 1980's the slogan of "Peace Through Strength" generated the largest nuclear forces ever to occupy the face of the earth. While the military prowess intimidated potential adversaries with commanding respect, such inordinate military force generated resentment among people who were oppressed, trounced and impoverished. Peace by intimidation created criticism about moral priorities when enormous problems in structural violence, poverty and genocide were neglected around the world. Moral conflicts arose about producing military weapons when billions of people suffered from such abject economic and social injustice.

The Cold War strategies of peace through strength have continued to persist into post-cold war years. Paul Kennedy[14] reported that the military budgets of the United States accounted "for over one-third of all the defense expenditures of all 190 countries on our planet." According to Kennedy, in 2000 the Pentagon's military budget was equivalent to the combined defense spending of the next nine largest military powers in the world. By 2002 this increased to an even greater advantage.

Dumas[15] provides penetrating analysis of the overwhelming redundancy of the United States military-industrial complex during the Cold War. He also raises serious concerns for the "overburdened economies" that are weakened with military expenditures for both conventional and technological military systems.[16] Dangers of inflation, unemployment and economic decline are dangerous side effects of economies overburdened with military expenditures that neglect civilian needs.

Questions also arise in an age of terrorist tactics about whether traditional military advantages provide security against non-conventional attacks. The debate in the Congress of United States about the "Crusader" weapon and traditional fighter planes exemplified the problems in exorbitant and possibly out-dated military weapons. These military expenditures have a double edge. Superior military forces may intimidate potential challengers as claimed by advocates of peace through strength. At the same time, the arrogance of military power contributes to profound resentment around the world about collateral structural violence and neglect along with military policies that contribute to revengeful attacks.

Peace through military superiority is vastly different from peace sustained with superior justice. Economic and social justice is much more difficult to accomplish than military victories or forcefully subduing family members. Wars may be won while the peace is lost. Battles were won as in Iraq and Afghanistan, but establishing democratic institutions is much more challenging to implement. Weapons indirectly kill many more people through poverty, oppression and starvation than through war casualties.

Likewise, subduing family members through forceful violence, or embarking on military victories over vulnerable people have both been notoriously short-sighted. Ironically, homeland security contains double meanings in countries concerned about domestic and international protection. Preoccupation with homeland safety may come at the expense of the security of the health, education and technological innovation of nations whereas cooperative relations provide more effective safety in the long run rather than risking revengeful hostility. Investments into human resources become increasingly important in a technological world over traditional military strength. In contrast, efforts to build peace with justice result in establishing greater mutual respect among nations and family members.

The parallels of homeland and military security are obvious in domestic affairs when a controlling parent manages the family budget that neglects overall family needs. Domineering parents set their own priorities that often neglect long-term concerns for health care, nutrition, and education of family members. There are additional factors in securing peace through strength among members of the family that are similar to the oppression in affluent nations. Which will build more lasting relationships – powerful military strength or social justice, healthy citizens and technological superiority? All of these investments are inherently costly since equitable justice also demands sacrifice in the interest of mutuality, harmony and sustainability.

**Competing in Win-Lose Games:**

Proactive approaches in conflict management involve forming competitive relationships in which there is a winner and a loser. The international competition of Olympic games symbolizes a highly structured approach to identifying gold, silver and bronze medal winners. Even losers take pride in the recognition that they were among the finest athletes to achieve recognition in their respective sport. Naturally the rules are carefully formulated in Olympic competition. There are a series of competitive games to determine eventual champions to reduce unfair competition.

Competition also has a double edge since it can be very constructive in producing high quality winners. But competition can also be very destructive when only winners gain recognition and rewards. Observations of Russian citizens reveal a decline in quality of life, lower longevity of men, and unreliable legal justice. Moreover, destructive competition can consume human resources, energy and economic production. Wasteful supplies of marginal goods can sap the natural and human resources of a county. The demise of the Soviet Union is a classic modern case study of investing redundantly into unproductive military expenditures at the expense of the economic strength and human well being of their society. When there is zero-sum competition, losers are victims of rejection, remorse and defeat. They can also be unfairly vilified in societies who disgrace those who do not win high honors. Russian veterans are demoralized and destitute.

War has traditionally rendered the spoils to the victor with dismal demise to the loser. Whole nations have been occupied and dismantled as coherent cultures when they are losers in violent and cold wars. The defeated cultures may cease to exist as viable societies. What will be a prospect for citizens of Iraq, Afghanistan and the republics formed out of the former Yugoslavia? In few cases are victims rehabilitated with degrees of dignity rather than completely eliminated.

Equitable rules are being formulated in global tribunals. War criminals are tried in international courts resulting in acquittal or conviction followed by punishment. There have been notable inconsistencies in international justice. Global justice is still developing about issues of jurisdiction, procedures, effectiveness, and consequences. The noble pursuit of fair and enduring justice needs to be fostered with equitable laws, effective legal procedures, reliable processes, and enforceable decisions.

**Concluding Comments:**

This chapter analyzes marginal strategies for managing conflict short of violence and war. Parallels are made between domestic family conflicts and comparable dynamics in international tensions. The limits of passive aggression are obvious for arriving at lasting peace with justice. The folly of short-term tactics is deceptively manipulative for sustaining just peace.

This chapter lays the predicate for managing conflict in a constructive, fair and nonviolent manner. A series of provocative questions are posed to focus attention about failures in addressing structural violence. The dynamics of manipulative control are analyzed in depth in order to recognize that addiction to coercive control occurs in the cycles of forceful violence in both domestic abuse and international conflict.

The reader is advised to consider this chapter as immature phases for handling conflicts. Before examining more promising constructive approaches for managing conflict in Chapter Seven, it is next necessary to make a transition through Chapter Six. Otherwise, there may be a temptation to leap to "silver bullet" solutions that in effect actually reduce the likelihood that people will struggle with the tough processes of working through conflicts to discover opportunities for nonviolent alternatives. It is important to have patient determination to work toward peace building that effectively addresses horrendous problems of structural violence.

## Endnotes

[1] Ackerman P., et. al. (2000) editors, A Force More Powerful, New York, St. Martins Press.

[2] Schutze J., (1997) Bully: A True Story of High School Revenge, Avon Books has also been produced into a dramatic movie.

[3] Isenhart M. and Spangle M., (2000) Collaborative Approaches for Resolving Conflict, Thousand Oaks, CA, Sage Publications.

[4] Middents G., (2001), The Crisis in Violence and Peace, Manipal Press.

[5] Barnet R., (1972) Roots of War: The Men and Institutions Behind U.S. Foreign Policy, Penguin Books, Inc.

[6] Kristof N., (May 7, 2002) "Behind the Terrrorists," The New York Times.

[7] Shay J., (2002) Odysseus in America: Combat Trauma and the Trials of Homecoming, New York: Scribner Book Company.

[8] These questions are elaborated in a chapter of the author's book in 2001: "Assertively Expressing Human Rights," Crisis in Violence and Peace, Manipal Press.

[9] Paul P., (2002) The Starter Marriage and the Future of Matrimony, Villard Books.

[10] Fishbein D., (2000) (ed) The Science, Treatment and Prevention of Antisocial Behavior, Kingston, N.J.: Civic Research Institute.

[11] Goodwin R., (Feb. 8, 2004), "Making the Facts Fit the Case of War," The New York Times.

[12] Editorial (January 27, 2004), "Mr. Cheney, Meet Mr. Kay" The New York Times.

[13] Keegan J., (2003) Intelligence in War: Knowledge of the Enemy From Napoleon to al-Qaeda, New York: Knopf.

[14] Kennedy P., (2001) "Maintaining American Power: From Injury to Recovery," in The Ages of Terror, edited by Strobe Talbott and Nayan Chandra, Basic Books.

[15] Dumas L. (1999) Lethal Arrogance: Human Fallibility and Dangerous Technologies, St. Martins Press.

[16] Dumas L., (1986) Overburdened Society: Uncovering the Causes of Chronic Unemployment, Inflation and National Decline, Berkeley, CA: University of California Press.

# Chapter Six

# Manipulating with Passive Aggression

**The significant problems we face cannot be solved by the same level of thinking that created them.**

**The world is a dangerous place to live; not because of people who are evil; but because of the people who don't do anything about it.**

Albert Einstein

Human beings inherently avoid painful conflicts in order to optimize comfort and pleasure. The propensity to escape pain is so powerful that it is difficult to cope with the stress of unpleasant conflicts. Fear of violent pain can paralyze action or provide motivation to formulate solutions. Coping with conflicts is one of the hard tasks of life according to the aphorism: "to be alive is to have anxiety and conflict." This book systematically bridges fear and peace in order to transform the threat of violence into nonviolent alternatives for addressing conflicts. The reader is reminded that both family and international violence are being addressed in tandem. The interactive parallels are so intertwined that learning about the dynamics of conflict on both interpersonal and international realms are alternately addressed. People are naturally caught up in passive aggression on both levels. On the micro level of the family relations and the macro level of international relations, people initiate aggressive violence while others counter with a wide range of responses.

## Hiding Agendas:

Who has never advanced their own hidden agendas either seriously or humorously? Human interactions simultaneously involve conscious and unconscious levels of awareness. Hidden agendas are more unconscious. When someone announces that they are completely above board or totally honest, their comments quickly reveal that at times they are unaware of their lack of transparency. Listeners should best be defensiveness because another person's self-proclaimed openness prompts suspicions of manipulative agendas. These cautions may also be necessary when someone implores you with the best of motives with requests to "trust me." A number of scientists question whether pure self-less altruism even exists. Recognizing hidden agendas realizes that motives may be primarily selfish while few are purely altruistic.

The nature of mixed motives provides us with understanding about how parents and children function in families. Children rely on the trustworthiness of their parents. The renown developmental psychologist, Erik Erikson, calls the first developmental task of infancy a conflict between trust vs. mistrust.[1] If a child's experience with parenting figures is predictably dependable, a child develops trust. As trustworthiness prevails, an attitude of hope develops as a favorable outcome when facing fearful threats. By contrast, abused children painfully discover that abusive parents cannot be trusted to provide basic security. When these basic safety needs are not met with regularity, the child develops difficulties trusting people in future adventures.

Political scientists use the term "confidence-building measures" to describe the nature of bilateral working relationships between nations. Trustful confidence does not happen in a vacuum overnight. Both historical and contemporary conditions influence current relations. Since the leadership of nations changes frequently, there are constant needs to confirm confidence-building measures. Otherwise instability results when treaties signed by previous administrations are not honored by successors. Naturally, nations have different relationships than a parent-child relationship. In international relations the more appropriate paradigm would be sibling relationships that may be aggressive or passive depending on the intensity of rivalries. Sibling relationships can be supportively nurturing and destructively competitive.

Propensities for national rivalries make international relations very complex. Most nations have peer relationships except for those who have historically emerged out of a dependent relationship of colonialism. Economic, technological, security and cultural dependency can complicate mature international relations. Like cultures, nations go through stages from birth to adolescence to maturity to old age and eventually to decline and demise. Few nations realize where they are in this terminal framework of development and decline. Many nations perennially act as if they are still young, virtuous, and culturally superior. Collective wisdom is understandably elusive among nations possessed by self-interests parallel to that of narcissistic adolescents.

An adolescent's emotional volatility contributes to a number of expected crises at this stage of development. Passive aggression is an important survival skill for adolescents in coping with powerful authority figures and manipulative peers. National leaders are challenged particularly when their survival is threatened. The fragile leadership of many nations also goes through rough stages of learning. Few international leaders are consistently imbued with wisdom in serving their own interests. Lack of transparency and hidden agendas add to the complicated conflicts for most nations in international and domestic relations. Many citizens in countries of Europe, Asia and South America are expressing their mistrust of the United States with careful wariness in view of developments in Iraq and the Middle East.

High technology can disguise hidden agendas in difficult social relations. National leaders are particularly attracted to the latest developments in military technology. Leaders are influenced by the fears of their citizens in the face of economic pressures, social conflicts and political unrest. As new scientific discoveries emerge, both leaders and citizens crave for quick solutions from technology in weaponry and security devices. Fears motivate people to buy expensive technology that reduces threats, reassures comfort, and provides safety. People want simple solutions to feel secure particularly when their lives are in peril. The search for new technology and life-saving medicines parallels national addictions to military weapons. Box 6-1 describes overly optimistic hopes attached to the media technology.

## Box 6-1: Technological Seduction

High tech is seductively alluring in modern society for solving complex social issues. Racial integration is a challenging social issue that emerged as problems for segregated schools in the United States during the mid twentieth century. Official court orders were imposed upon communities for schools to integrate racially. One approach for racial integration was busing children from one neighborhood to another school. People who resisted such measures sought for technological alternatives during the era of white flight from urban areas to the suburbs. An alluring technology was two-way interactive television to accomplish racial integration of public schools. This technology was just emerging for wider educational application when pilot projects were undertaken without adequate research.

School officials in Dallas, Texas, considered using two-way interactive television to solve racial segregation. Schools with better educational systems would be connected to racially segregated schools by audio and visual television. With two-way interactive television to connect segregated students, both busing and integrated housing could be avoided. According to this optimistic but untested approach toward integration, positive racial attitudes could be effectively fostered.

Ten creative college students created an experimental design to test these assumptions. The experiment included 64 sixth graders engaged in an environmental curriculum, art and educational interaction connected by the two-way interactive television. Control groups were assessed for social interaction, racial attitudes, academic achievement, creative thinking and social behaviors. They invited me to be their advisor for this National Science Foundation Grant.

The outcomes were clearly contrary to what many school and community officials hoped to discover. The children learned academically, but they did not establish positive social interactions or racial attitudes. In fact, a number of the children actually became hostile in behavior toward the technology that was connecting them by two-way interactive television. The research design approximated actual school environments with understandable limitations in which not all variables could be ethically controlled. However, the negative results were clearly established. The research contributed to the findings that this state-of-the-art technology could not effectively achieve educational integration via two-way interactive television.[2]

Domestically, fears preoccupy societies when traditional practices are threatened. Racial relations and ethnic tensions are deeply ingrained as social conflicts in many cultures. Citizens search for painless solutions to deeply entrenched social strife. For example, racial segregation is a problem for public schools, for affordable housing and discrimination in employment. At one point, hi-tech promoters assumed that two-way interactive television could become a major solution for problems of integration. However, there was little research evaluating this optimistic hypothesis that also carried a hidden agenda with it.

High technology helps increase productivity, labor-saving devices, transportation, communications, and improved health care. However, new technical break-throughs can make only limited contributions to managing conflict. Technology can improve weapons and tranquilizing medications, but human beings need to learn how to improve the human relations in domestic and international conflicts. New drugs can neither create trustful parent-child nor credibility in international confidence-building.

**Imposing Models:**

In social learning there are also distinctive patterns in cultures with divergent values. Family traditions provide guidance for parents and children to function responsibly in their culture. Immigrants may clash when they do not respect these cultural values. Religions, moral conduct, mating values[3] and social patterns all have major influences in acceptable behaviors. Imposing models from one culture onto another can contribute to incredible problems in human relationships. These problems confront efforts to introduce structures of democracy in Iraq. Imposing models is perhaps more difficult than blending models. Efforts to blend different traditions require care, patience and mutual understanding. If important cultural values are misunderstood, the potential for difficult conflict is heightened.

While boundaries cultivate self-regulatory competencies in people, few nations tolerate external sanctions. Unilateral actions may be launched by nations who have difficulty perceiving the perspectives of other cultures. The United Nations faces enormous challenges in securing world order. Who else can introduce acceptable procedures for decisions, comprehensive sanctions and directives upon sovereign nations? Consensus about fair justice is struggling to emerge amid many disputes about which systems of jurisprudence will be imposed upon member nations. Major steps toward world order develop slowly with international tribunals for war crimes. Attempts to impose fair procedures of justice recognize limits due to cultural variations in legal jurisprudence. Imposing models from another culture has unworkable procedures that lead to devastating results. Divergent social values, religious practices, historical institutions and unique languages all have distinctive influences on cultures.

The Nuremberg Trials of German military leaders set a precedent in recent years. The Nuremberg Principles advanced the legal doctrine that individuals are criminally liable for crimes defined by international law. Based upon these principles, former Yugoslavian military and political leaders are tried for war crimes against humanity. Sanctions by the powerful democracies have a chilling effect upon some military and civilian dictators. There are still a number of judicial procedures yet to be refined for use by legitimate world courts. A major problem involves enforcing decisions of international courts.[4] The problems involve conflicts with national sovereignty in matters of justice. Nations may insist on latitude in jurisdiction, procedures and sentencing not allowed to their own citizens.

A setback to international jurisprudence was the decision of President George W. Bush to "unsign" the agreement for the International Criminal Court. This independent war-crimes tribunal was endorsed by the Clinton administration, but the Bush administration notified the United Nations that the United States does not intend to seek ratification of the treaty. The rationale for this action by Undersecretary of State Grossman states:

> We believe that the International Criminal Court is built on a flawed foundation. These flaws leave it open for exploitation and politically motivated prosecutions.[5]

Spokespersons for Human Rights Groups react to this decision contending that a high-profile prosecution of U. S. citizens is highly unlikely. There is speculation that the Bush administration is protecting itself from future accusations of war crimes in Iraq and Afghanistan, plus interventions in Vietnam by previous administrations. Counter-arguments state that the United States forfeits a valuable role in a worthy effort of international justice.[6] As a consequence, the United States removes itself from an influential position in the development of this court. These unfortunate actions impair progress in establishing international law.

The struggle toward consensus in international justice remains a noble cause. National sovereignty precludes peaceful settlement of many judicial, social, political and economic disputes. The protective sovereignty of the nation-state model is constrictive for addressing global issues. Just as rule by law is superior to rule by human beings, the rule of international law is likewise superior to the rule of individual nations with special interests. Universal principles of legal jurisprudence, social ethics, and world order are among the greatest challenges of global humanity searching for fair justice and enduring peace.

Problems in developing universal jurisprudence place additional limitations on social relations, global trade and commercial contracts. In economic development, there are needs to establish reliable legal contracts that are enforceable. Problems arise when economic models have unworkable limits in another society. Concerns for the appropriateness of external models are major issues confounding agreements with developing nations such as China, India, Argentina, Venezuela and Russia.

The model of a free-market economy has mixed results for these nations in recent decades. Russia is going through the downside of the so-called "shock treatment" which India and Poland are trying bravely to survive. The free market model advanced by the International Monetary Fund and World Bank is being questioned by how different economies adapt to the erratic gyrations of competition. Imposing external models can result in serious political, economic, social and legal problems that cause instability in national governments.

**Peace-Keeping Complications:**

Peace-keeping is a major challenge for traditional military forces. Defeating a threatening enemy has been a traditional function of military forces. However, military soldiers typically are not trained for occupation on the road to peacekeeping in a defeated culture. The military mind-set, decision-making, and training do not equip soldiers for coping with the disorder inherent in creating a civil society.[7] Occupation forces despise their assignment to maintain law and order. These troops are frequently demoralized in assignments to keep the peace in post-war military efforts. Problems in Afghanistan and Iraq are similar to occupation problems faced in the former Yugoslavia or in Germany and Japan after World War II.

People of defeated countries display an array of problems that soldiers are unprepared to address. Violent insurgency by resisting forces pose dangerous confrontations. Passive aggression in the defeated civilian population counters initiatives to rebuild a demoralized nation because they have many contradictory reactions to victors. These reactions include remorseful hatred, hesitant cooperation and active sabotage. Because troops are untrained in nation-building skills, their occupation role deteriorates downwardly into negative relationships. The occupying soldiers do not want to be there because defeated people develop extremely hostile reactions that reflect resentful attitudes. These negative attitudes fester into disdain and major enmity are reflected in the experience of veterans of the war in Iraq. Demoralizing retaliation is usually experienced by foreign troops who are not welcomed.

With such lack of constructive engagement, there may be doubts that this chapter can provide any insight toward conflict management. However, bridges between violent war and lasting peace are essential for rebuilding institutions and infrastructures of a society trying to nonviolently reinvent itself. When wars end there is a predictable pattern of increases in violence and crime. Personal boundaries of control break down when chaotic turmoil occurs in the aftermath of war. Both the society and the military have been trained to be violent against enemies during wartime. Major rehabilitation is necessary for civilian law and order to be re-built over a prolonged period of time.

On a domestic level, when a family survives the tension of a major battle, there are obstacles to rebuilding a marriage and a tranquil home. Parents may still be seething with resentment let alone the disillusioned children who may be in shock from the abusive battles. The physical scars remain while the hidden emotional trauma is painfully tender. Emotional scars may even be more difficult to heal than obvious physical wounds that can be medically treated. Therapeutic approaches are limited in re-establishing the loving care essential in a family who has been all the way to hell and back.

The authoritarian approaches of an abusively controlling father become a major challenge for an un-reconciled family. Boot camp discipline in the home may make it more of a prisoner-of-war camp for hostages than a safe home. Memories of past abuse cannot be forgotten when nightmares traumatize children and spouses. Horrifying memories beg for fair justice because without fair treatment the future is tenuously troublesome. Abusive families go through battles that approach the severity of combat in war, including guns, torture, wounds and skin burns. Family members feel they are being held against their will as hostages. Research on the consequences of trauma in the cycle of violence by professors at Stanford University School of Medicine[8] is helpful in understanding intergenerational aggression that is maladaptive. This pattern is frequently expressed in the aphorism that "what goes around, comes around."

How can such a family move toward peace while trying to keep some semblance of normalcy? Without community support and professional help, their tasks may seem insurmountable. Since it takes a village to raise a child, it takes the community of nations to rebuild broken countries. Both loving care and financial stability become major challenges to accomplish during this strange peacetime. When they have limited experience with anything but chaos, no wonder their adjustments are similar to military veterans returning to civilian life. As they go through post-traumatic stress syndromes, there may be a real need for social rehabilitation and re-socialization for criminals. During these transition periods, there is persistent fear that the violent abuse will be unpredictably repeated again at any time.

The tense fear that pervades domestic violence needs to be recognized as the tactic of second-strike retaliation. After combat, families and nations have major obstacles to overcome to reach stability. Is it any wonder that after humiliating defeat, people have difficulty focusing on positive goals? When resentful anger is boiling hot, one can easily appreciate that members of a restored family think of retaliation. There are emotional and physical scars in their bodies, spirits and brains that can erupt without apparent provocation.

"Living with the enemy" requires immense adjustments in order to overcome the defenses needed to survive constant fear and chaos. Since abusive families come near to killing each other, who can trust a threatening person who has the characteristics of someone deranged in the house? Who can trust a parent who has previously beaten you as a defenseless child? Who can place faith in a family member who constantly holds life and death decisions over you? No wonder traumatized persons experience difficulty in re-adjusting to their society after war, imprisonment or terrorism. Post Traumatic Stress Syndrome (PSTD) has consequences that are ravaging homes and societies that have been through war, violence and abuse.

Occupying forces have parallel difficulties when occupying a defeated nation. How many times have defeated nations harbored resentments? Look at Germany after the humiliation over the war reparations after World War I. Look at the reprisals that have occurred between Israelis and Palestinians after their wars of 1967 and subsequent conflicts. Repeated humiliations are experienced by Palestinians at the hands of Israelis according to Shipler[9] in his analysis of Arab-Jewish hostilities. My own professional consultations[10] with eight Palestinian mental health professionals provided confirmation of how their people are held in compounds in Gaza and the West Bank. Many of these Palestinians suffer from both physical deprivations and imposed confinement, but they also experience post-traumatic stress from prolonged oppression. There are also persistent resentments that occur between Pakistan and India in their overt wars over Kashmir and Jammu. The hostility of international conflicts is similar to family combat except in magnitude of damage, geographical scale and degrees of intimacy between combatants. There is little reason to doubt that repeated domestic and international violence and neglect contributes to breeding grounds for terrorism.

Hatred generated in military combat can linger for generations as well as between civilians who belong to hostile groups. The conflicts between Islamic cultures and Western cultures have seethed understandably since the Crusades. Major devastation was wrought in the Crusades as well as humiliation. The ethnic wars of the Balkans have torn Yugoslavia into warring factions for centuries. The "balkanization" of many regions and families has been etched deeply within the collective psyche of rivals. The unquestioning patriotism of many veterans of wars to their nation signifies how further military violence is justified and perpetuated. "My country right or wrong" guides many people in their readiness to engage in additional warfare with major military expenditures regardless of international developments.

Second-strike retaliation in modern nuclear tensions has historically had short-term connotations. Being able to retaliate after a first strike is a component of military strategy. Second-strike capabilities require such extensive war fighting resources that the attacked nations can withstand the initial assault with sufficient resilience that it can wage a viable retaliation. Such extensive destruction can be launched with modern weapons of war that the opponent may not feasibly be able to retaliate.

When devastation occurs, a defeated nation may suffer an unrecoverable setback. In the collective memories of warring cultures, revenge is scarred deeply into the cultural psyches of defeated cultures. The Civil War in the United States illustrates how the North humiliated the

South. Historically, victorious forces display an inflated sense of triumph over defeated opponents rather than providing humanitarian concern. Triumphalism continues in the foreign policy of the United States after the end of the Cold War according to assessments by Kupchan.[11]

Another tactic has been almost equally as devastating. After the loss of untold lives in battle plus unaccountable numbers missing in action, nations often withdraw from the battle scene as quickly as possible. Escape involves forgetting pain, cutting losses and the horrifying memories that the scars of war engender. By leaving the battle scene, a vacuum can be created that unsavory groups may relish an opportunity to enter. Afghanistan is an example of a vacuum after 1979 left by the withdrawal of the United States and the former Soviet Union. Weapons left behind fell into the hands of *Al Qaeda* forces.

On the other hand, there are positive patterns that have had more humane results. The Marshall Plan after World War II rehabilitated a number of war-torn nations of Europe. Japan also recovered to become a peaceful and productive culture. South Korea has thrived after the Korean War as well as Vietnam.[12] However, whole pockets of poverty and structural violence continue after wars in Central America, Africa, and North Korea. It is too early to predict what will eventually work out with rehabilitative nation building in Afghanistan and Iraq in the foreseeable future.

**Limiting Empathy:**

Compassionate humanitarian concerns are frequently expressed in times of war and conflict. These concerns are appropriate when devastating atrocities and overt cruelty have been experienced. In contrast to this direct violence that is obvious, hidden oppression is obscure to public examination. Structural violence can be invisible to people who lack first hand awareness of these inhumane conditions. Only incomplete steps may be taken when oppressive conditions are partially suspected. In domestic violence, a number of countries have already established procedures when there is suspicion of child abuse. In the United States, concerned persons can anonymously notify authorities when they suspicion that a child is endangered by abuse and neglect.

In the United States, educational, social service and health professional are required by law to report suspected abuse. If they do not report their awareness of violence, they can actually be liable for criminal negligence. Anonymous reports provide an opportunity for authorities concerned with child abuse and neglect to investigate the reported case firsthand. Careful procedures outline the steps for addressing problems of direct and indirect violence. First, there must be awareness that violence may exist threatening the safety of a child. Secondly, action is essential in order to address the problems with appropriate remedies. Without taking the second step, little effort may be done to protect life and foster human development when corrective action is passively neglected.

In international relations, taking corrective action is even more difficult to accomplish than in domestic violence. Lack of authority to intervene in the internal affairs of a sovereign nation can obviously limit intervention. Respect for national sovereignty often takes precedent over intervening upon another country's integrity. External pressure may be adequate for humane changes, but these sanctions may be inadequate in international violations. The limits of the

United Nations in enforcing direct intervention without the approval of member nations are apparent in volatile situations. Pre-emptive war initiated by the United States exemplifies unforeseen problems in taking action to enforce resolutions that the United Nations approved concerning Iraq.

Humanitarian efforts can simultaneously be very paternalistic as well as compassionate. Benevolent intentions may not be understood as humanely altruistic. Dominating powers can use a rationale contained in the aphorism – " this punishment is really for your own good." The results may vary widely with unpredictable outcomes. Many developing nations are ambivalent about the hidden agendas of humanitarian efforts. In addition, hegemonic interference, missionary memories and cultural insensitivities impact how empathetic assistance is intended and actually perceived.

War-torn regions can be decimated into unlivable conditions. Box 6-2 identifies violence to the environment in which people live on this earth. In the process of identifying domestic and international conflicts, environmental violence that affects the quality of life for human beings needs to be brought into the consciousness. Some of these conditions continue to be found in the devastating aftermath of the War on Terrorism in Afghanistan and Iraq. The global environment is neglected when resources are invested into the costs of military weapons.

---

**Box 6-2: Awareness of Environmental Violence**

**Environmental violence directly influences the well-being of people often without awareness. Since power structures are enmeshed with host ecosystems, it is essential to raise consciousness before empathetic responses can work through these entangling public and private conflicts. Human beings are now at risk with impending danger to the environment:[13]**

- **Potable water is endangered with pollution from chemicals, fertilizers, herbicides, and toxins.**
- **Increasing populations consume resources that are not renewable.**
- **Agricultural land and fisheries are being depleted.**
- **Ecosystems including rain forests, wetlands and coral reefs are threatened without management.**
- **The atmosphere is polluted while ozone and ocean levels rise.**
- **Biological diversity suffers as flora and fauna are endangered.**

**High levels of environmental violence show disrespect for sustaining natural resources. Unsustainable consumption endangers the human posterity in the natural ecology. Appetites for energy need to be managed and new technologies developed. Short-range visions about next quarter's profits, stockholders' dividends, and the next election are crassly narrow timelines in decision-making. Planet Earth has sustained cycles of life and extinction over hundreds of millions of years. Decisions to avert disaster are increasingly crucial to protect humanity in this global ecosystem.**

**Compartmentalizing:**

Nation-states have geographical borders, but compartmental boundaries separate both people and fields of human knowledge. Science and technology increases exponentially with double-edged effects. More and more is known about nature, but there is less and less capacity by human beings to comprehend themselves. This rapid acceleration into distinctive specializations results from analyses into component parts. Medicine illustrates these specializations along with nearly all fields influenced by similar trends. For example, cardiovascular surgeons and brain neurological surgeons have problems understanding the same patient since each professional has highly specialized knowledge about particular organs of a whole person. By analogy, these professionals are similar to ancient people from foreign tribes who did not possess a common language or tradition around which to build working relationships. These problems limit meaningful discourse among people who address closely related issues. Analytical methods that dissect phenomena into components can drive people further into isolation. As a consequence, there are disconnects that result in such a specialized environment.

Specialists are experts who know a great deal about their field but less about the bigger picture. This paradox produces specialized experts while it is the function of social consensus to bind cultures together.[14] Experts are essential, but they may not fathom the interests of lay people whose views are consolidated into political consensus. Both the functions of the expert and the processes of social consensus are needed, but mutual understanding is readily impaired. Interaction in a culture composed of similar people is psychologically more comfortable. As a result, controversial issues inherently produce tense conflicts. In fact, constructive conflicts are avoided in many fields of study. When humanity needs to understand better approaches to conflict, meager attention goes to these remedies.

The difficulty of coordination between agencies in public government came into play during the piecemeal warnings about terrorist attacks on the World Trade Center and parts of the Pentagon on 9/11/01. Critical pieces of intelligence were not integrated by the Federal Bureau of Investigation (FBI) and the Central Intelligence Agency (CIA). Foreign nationals were suspiciously training as pilots at different locations in the United States with unusual interests in specialized facets in flight training that did not involve landing an aircraft. However, inferences were not synthesized into a bigger picture of possible hijackings. The metaphorical term is that "the dots were not connected." There were "blind spots" that happen in security and intelligence gathering. News analysts characterize the counter-terrorism apparatus as "too lumbering, compartmentalized and inattentive to grasp the emerging pattern of threat."[15] Uncoordinated agencies at state, national and international levels can compound detecting contributors to violent wars.

Analytic competencies are essential to address these gaps in intelligence gathering. Equally important are the needs to integrate data into comprehensive strategies so that pieces are holistically synthesized. One of the competencies lacking in modern education and science involves integrative capacities. The quest for specialization leaves serious gaps in unifying knowledge. Box 6-3 provides an example in which a lack of coordination between departments limits envisioning a bigger picture.

> **Box 6-3: When Departments Become Compartments**
>
> **Traditional organizations are rigidly hierarchical. These structures are particularly evident in government, military and large corporate organizations. A comment by a business professional in India provided insight when I asked him about an organization that had invited me as a consultant. He replied: "It's just a bunch of compartments!" I thought he said "departments" but he adamantly emphasized again "No, compartments!"**
>
> **It dawned upon me that "compartments" fit the ultra specialization in organizations. In the United States, the FBI and the CIA experience uncoordinated compartmentalization. Narrowly defined "compartments" are prevalent in government empire-building, educational disciplines, and many business organizations.**

People often feel bombarded with information. One prevalent response to this overload is passive acquiescence by people while they search for zones of comfort. This is a spectator mentality in which people are discouraged from becoming directly involved in conflicts. People develop protective shells because they are already dealing with more than they want to handle. Isolation, denial and indifference are ready-made passive options for isolated non-involvement. With intensive differentiation of special self-interests, responsibilities are carefully delineated. Traditional social castes influence these patterns of behavior. Manageable tasks are carved out that protect a person from overload by retreating into a specialized niche.

Individuals and people in organizations process intelligence data differently. As Heuer identifies, individuals can more readily use intuition, experience and feel for the intelligence in contrast to people in structured organizations where job descriptions spell out distinctive functions, responsibilities, and relationships.[16] Organizational tables carefully define hierarchical levels of management, status, and authority. Efforts are made to spell out unique decision-making procedures not dictated by tradition. Supervisors and workers are carefully boxed into departments, divisions, teams, and projects. On the positive side, these distinctions avoid overlapping and conflicting roles. On the down side, these clear distinctions can be used to avoid involvement that is none of your business. As Garrison Keilor humorously states, freedom may mean not knowing what is going on.[17]

The downside of specialization results in an inability of people within diverse compartments to work together let alone understand each other. Over-specialized people have misunderstandings and inaccurate perceptions. The pseudo-scientific assumptions in intelligence methods have left gaps in penetrating accurately into cause and effect relationships. These tribal compartments become fertile soil for rivalries, protectionism and lack of respect.

With specialized research in science, there is an increasing gap between laboratory research and application to social problems that confront pathology in society. One example is representative in my professional areas of interests. The gap is apparent between research in neuroscience with humans and animals that involve addiction to drugs. Researchers in laboratories isolate themselves from extending applications to public policy for at least three reasons. If they would connect their findings to social problems of drug, alcohol and tobacco addiction, they may jeopardize obtaining further lucrative research grants that challenge the economic interests of lobbyists for addictive substances. A second reason involves the indefensible belief that scientists should refrain from engaging in political issues of social policy. A third reason comes from lack of competencies in addressing policy research that refrains from implementing their findings in prevention of pathology but rather primarily treats the problems reactively rather than proactively.

Interdisciplinary perspectives help correlate specialized pieces that result from over-emphasizing differentiation in scientific analyses. Bridges are needed between investigative methods of the natural and social sciences plus the enlightening perspectives of the humanities including ethics, philosophy, cultures, history, arts and literature. There are grave limitations at this stage of knowledge for understanding the mind of murderers, terrorists, abusers, and bullies in predicting future violence.[18] Integrative capacities require the ability to synthesize obscurities when separate parts are identified. Multi-disciplinary approaches are vitally essential in discovering solutions to problems of crime, gangs, and social pathologies. Peace and justice studies naturally build integrative approaches so that specialized knowledge is creatively synthesized.

**Deadlocking:**

Two global hotspots in the West and the East exemplify diversionary deadlocking. In Northern Ireland, factions are labeled by religious identification with serious limits of surface analysis. The so-called Protestant and Catholic oppositions have had decades of violent conflicts. Socio-economic factors have repeatedly festered into persisting disputes that end in deadlock. British and Americans have attempted to negotiate a peaceful resolution. An effort to seek forgiveness for civilian fatalities has been one positive development in these long-standing disputes. Persistence may facilitate a break through in the inertia of these vicious killings.

The other situation involves the Middle East dispute between Palestinians and Israelis. Both sides have engaged in this violent imbroglio with terroristic violence, suicidal bombings, and counter retaliation. These relentless cycles of violence have seen only brief interruptions of violent hostilities. One analysis suggested that the leaders of both sides need each other in order to stay in power. In fact, inferences made by the former Ambassador Ahsani[19] from Pakistan suggest that the Israeli and Palestinian leaders in effect nominated each other as their opposition without conscious awareness of their need for an enemy. If their opponent were not already in place, they would need to create such an adversary.

The earlier analysis of the functions of enemies suggested that opponents create their own dysfunctional relationship. When they cannot let go of each other, there is a deadlock with mutual animosity. They may be symbiotically engaged in a lethal impasse that will devour both of them. External intervention can result in hostile blame aimed directly back at the naive interveners. Intolerant external sources may also interfere with a peaceful settlement according to Hill[20] who has provided a penetrating analysis of the Middle East deadlock.

The United States Congress, as well as other legislative bodies, frequently deadlocks so that no forward movement occurs. Passive aggression can be expressed in reaction to power plays by the opposition. Breaking through the deadlock may be necessary in order to make constructive progress. However, the inertia of balanced power plays can also result in little or no movement toward constructive legislation.

Obviously a similar plateau can be reached in family relations when no one in a quarreling family will budge. Some families live as perpetual stalemates when neither party in the conflict makes a constructive move or compromising step. Silent hostilities can be feeding the sullen environment until crises jolt them out of a standstill. The destructive effect of such an arrangement may not be seen in the short run. Consequences in future generations may be seen in the longer-term. Mediation may not be effective if all the parties remain dysfunctional in a hostile deadlock.

**Moving toward Improved Strategies:**

**Competing:**

When cooperation and compromise are impossible between disputing parties, competition or disdain between opponents usually persists. A balance of power is then maintained as long as both sides perpetuate their respective positions. These polarities preclude moving forward into collaboration in which all sides take some ownership of the problem. At a competitive stage, opponents make efforts to have their opponent labeled as the source of the problem. Self-reflection is deflected when an opponent is persistently blamed. These dynamics are evident in the stand off between Israelis and Palestinians or the confrontations between Pakistan and India. Box 6-4 provides another example of challenging angry hostility into more constructive alternatives rather than perpetuating old hostilities.

> **Box 6-4: Channeling Anger Into Constructive Action**
>
> In 1990, the Tenth World Congress of the Organization Development Institute held its annual conference in Slovenia, at that time still a republic of the former Yugoslavia. As an international consultant, I presented a paper entitled: "Channeling Anger Into Constructive Action." It was an analysis of social policy issues including constructive steps in problem identification, definition and development of policy solutions.
>
> Our host at the University of Maribor, Vice-Rector Mulej, provided an analysis of the long-standing ethnic conflicts within Yugoslavia. His broad perspectives were very helpful since he had refused to be considered as one of the rotating candidates for the Presidency of Yugoslavia. He shared an observation that the ethnic minorities were extremely difficult to govern in Yugoslavia since there was a tradition called the "cult of disobedience." Professor Mulej was intrigued by my paper for two reasons. First, it provided a model for channeling anger into constructive public policy. Secondly, we were both scheduled to deliver programs later that year at the First International Conference on Work Teams. He provided a provocative keynote address concerned with "When Work Teams Do Not Work."
>
> More important than these conferences has been the two developments that since emerged. Slovenia became an independent nation breaking off from other Yugoslavian republics as civil war broke out in the early 1990's. The second development occurred in Poland where professional members of the Organizational Development Institute were invited to provide consulting services. We provided services for the steel and construction industries as Poland made the transition from a central command economy under communism toward a free market economy.
>
> "Channeling Anger Into Constructive Action" turned out to be very appropriate thesis for Slovenia and Poland. Two invitations were later extended to teach at the University of Warsaw and Lublijana University. However, conditions in Belgrade and Warsaw in the mid 1990's did not permit acceptance of these invitations.

The former nation of Yugoslavia experienced violence among the ethnic groups in the Balkans after the Cold War was concluded nonviolently. Besides Slovenia, the other republics sank into a series of civil wars that perpetuated religious, tribal, historical and ideological rivalries. External intervention has tried to bring these conflicts to manageable level with bad-tempered conditions still persisting.

In domestic relations, courting couples may become contending competitors. When each partner is strongly independent and craftily controlling, competitive resentment emerges. One of the partners comes out of their boxing corner to confront the other in sparring that is the name of this game in its non-destructive stage. Friendly sparring can persist as long as their endurance lasts. But a win-lose contest determines who eventually dominates or concedes. Shear exhaustion of energy and resources may terminate the strife. Divorce proceedings results in a verdict decided by a judge. Rarely can both parties be victorious in a win-lose match.

In fair competition, a set of civil rules might be introduced so that a respectable agreement is fostered. Destructiveness and defeat are then not the goal of the contending opponents. Rather, the goal of winning within the framework of acceptable rules may circumscribe the relationship. With angry couples, mutual respect might provide a degree of civility to foster positive growth. Among hostile nations, there are only limited rules of engagement except by mutual or multilateral agreements. Certain treaties provide for amended changes within the predetermined ground rules. The history of treaties provides limited hope for a longstanding balance of power for fair competition. Instead, treaties have generally been an intermediate stage on the way toward sustainable peace, or as a brief transition until open hostilities break out. A quote from Johann Arnold[21] aptly described the dilemma of treaties:

> In political terms, peace may take the form of trade agreements, compromises, and peace treaties. Such treaties are usually little more than fragile balances of power negotiated in tense settings, and often they plant seeds of new conflict worse than the ones they were designed to resolve. There are many examples, from the Treaty of Versailles, which ended World War I but stoked the nationalism that started World War II, to the Yalta Conference, which ended World War II but fueled tensions that led to the Cold War. Cease-fires provide no guarantee of an end to hatred.

This quote is similar to the cries throughout the history of agreements that treaties supposedly would preclude conflict. Negotiated treaties foster constructive communication, clarify national interests of the parties, and provide face-to-face interactions among international leaders. Some treaties have been overly optimistic in resolving basic differences among conspiring global powers. Consequently, humanity has heard the premature announcement after the signing of treaties expressed in the realistic appraisal: "Peace, peace, when there is no peace."[22]

**Promoting Democratic Processes:**
One of the greatest successes in international relations has been peaceful relations among democratic countries. According to both Barash[23] and Barber,[24] democracies do not tend to engage in war with each other. This claim depends upon definitions of democratic states that leaves it open to challenge. It should be recognized that democratic processes have many interpretations in different nations who consider themselves a democracy.

In the history of the 20th century, when great devastation was experienced, democracies consistently advanced humane governance and relationships. Consequently, an ideal goal involves promoting democratic institutions and governments in future international relationships. Democracies have found the capacities to trust each other and to respect each other's citizens.[25] This peaceful mutuality suggests greater hope for humanity. The European Union is a new experiment that has been created by democratic nations. Democracy has promise for coping with the evil in human beings while at the same time fostering the potential of humanity.

Any form of world order needs to recognize the capacity of democratic practices to promote sustainable peace and irenic justice. Provisions for justice, human rights, deliberate protection of the most vulnerable, and promotion of equal freedoms are all valiant expressions of civility. Accountability by officials in any state protects the citizenry. Abraham Lincoln stated hopefully in midst of the Civil War that such as a democratic union "by the people, of the people, and for the people shall not perish from the earth."

When authoritarian leaders manipulate referendums with only one name on the ballot, or when elections repeatedly fail to have multi-party candidates, the nature of democratic processes are subject to almost complete control by powerful manipulators. The "Human Development Report, 2002" concludes that although a majority of the world's people live in at least nominal democracies, civil and political freedoms may be very limited in many countries. Efforts to foster democratic practices in responding to structural violence against the poor have faltered in nominal democracies.[26]

Special financial interests can have disproportional influence in contrast with the power of individual voters in democracies. According to United Nations report, corporate contributions to elections rose to $1.2 billion in the 2000 election in the United States, and in India 80% of funds for political parties came from large corporations in 1996.[27] These figures increased substantially in the presidential elections of 2004 in the United States.

It is important to recognize that democracy is a fragile form of governance. Participation by the people for their common good is essential to sustain democratic institutions. Unless citizens take direct responsibility to participate directly in a democracy, there is limited hope that it can persist as a viable form of human governance. The endurance of many democratic institutions is threatened by the lack of direct involvement by passive citizens in their civic duties and privileges. Unless citizens actively exercise their voting privilege to hold elected officials accountable, democracy is imperiled. In one generation of careless passivity, a democracy can be a victim due to the neglect of citizens. Likewise, efforts to establish democratic institutions in countries of the Middle East will take many years of responsible citizenship by Iraqis. If citizens do not exercise civic responsibilities, a vacuum results that would likely be filled by power hungry people. Condensing Edmund Burke's[28] apt statement – for evil people to succeed, it is only necessary that good people do nothing.

Moving to domestic considerations, several implications are obvious. There are several types of relationships between husband and wife. One is the patriarchal and another is a matriarchal which are both authoritarian relationships. While authoritarian practices have longevity, there is limited evidence that such one-sided relationships promote opportunities for optimal development and growth in both partners. In authoritarian-subservient relationships, both parties arrest their growth and development. Reports[29] from Afghanistan provide both optimism and pessimism about prospects for women's rights in that country. Cautious optimism has been reported by findings from the Revolutionary Association of Women of Afghanistan about efforts to overcome the devastation inflicted upon women by the Taliban. However, pessimistic views report the return of control by the Northern Alliance and tribal leaders who impose male domination of women.

Equalitarian relationships are much more fragile than authoritarian relationships since equality inherently assumes joint responsibility in decision-making by both parties in the relationship. Partners share responsibilities and duties to be accountable as equal partners. Each partner is legally liable for the debts and obligations of the other. Each partner benefits when one of the partners prospers. Each grows as the other grows while each suffers when one is sick or impaired. Partners have implicit duties to support each other in sickness and in health, in plenty and in want, in joy and in sorrow as long as both shall live.

From decades of experience of marital and pre-marital counseling, it is obvious that mutual respect and sustained support is vital to the health of a marriage relationship. Mutual respect and love is crucial for rearing offspring. Whenever ingredients of trusting mutuality, honor and support are lacking, all family members are impaired. Where trusting mutuality, respect, and forbearance are present, there can be expectations for optimal development, actualization and growth of all the persons to thrive and hopefully pass on to their progeny.

The sanctity of marriage is enriched with the support not only of the couple to each other, but also their families, their friends, the community, the state and the world. Laws and legislation that do not encourage secure marriage and family relationships create landmines in marriage and family. Couples that do not foster each other's well-being can devastate their relationship and also the well-being of their children.

Democratic practices in both the family and the nation are essential to fostering the potential of the people involved. Internationally, democratic institutions have established a track record for peaceful co-existence with other democratically grounded institutions. These peaceful practices provide evidence that democratic processes are preferable for both domestic and international relationships.

**Concluding Comments:**

This chapter is a transition toward constructive management of conflict that identifies noticeable progress on the rough journey toward peace and justice. These intermediate steps may not be sequential, but they are part of the "peace dance" that goes backward as well as forward. These elusive steps include dealing with hidden agendas that can be either negative or positive for international and domestic relations.

Peacekeeping by external forces may be imposed upon conflicting parties whereas democratic processes require lengthy refinement in order to be established. Conflicting parties may develop second-strike capabilities as defensive measures to retaliate against aggression. Self-defense is appropriate for both nations and couples who fall back to retaliation and time-outs in the midst of conflict. Deadlocked negotiations can stymie progress until a break through occurs.

In conflict management, the hope for viable alternatives helps movement in constructive directions. Fair competition may be an intermediate challenge when parties spar to test each other's commitments. This may strengthen or weaken trust and confidence building measures.

Finally, democratic practices have greater promise than often realized. While democracy is a fragile institution, so are marriage and world order. Because democracies avoid engaging in war against each other, there are definite reasons to believe that international and domestic relations have greater potential for peaceful development. Patience is essential in establishing solid democracies and marriages.

# Endnotes

[1] Erikson E., (1993) Childhood and Society, W.W. Norton and Company.
[2] Snider R., and Middents G., (1973) The Effect of Two-Way Interactive Television on the Racial Attitudes of Sixth Grade Students, National Science Foundation Grant for Student Originated Research, Austin College.

[3] Photiades J., Thomas M. and Middents G. (1999) "Preferential Values in Cross-cultural Mates," Discourses: A Journal for Interdisciplinary Studies, Vol. 2, No. 1.

[4] Barash D., (1991) Introduction to Peace Studies, Belmont, CA: Wadsworth Publishing Company.

[5] Quoted in article by Peter Slevin "U.S. no longer backs permanent tribunal," The Washington Post, May 7, 2002.

[6] Ibid.

[7] Priest D., (2003) Waging War and Keeping Peace with America's Military, W.W. Norton & Company.

[8] Steiner H., (March 19, 2004) "From Victim to Perpetrator," lecture at Southwestern Medical School, Grand Rounds in Psychiatry. Additional data available in Steiner H., (2003) The Aggressive System.

[9] Shipler D., (2002) Arab and Jew: Wounded Spirits in a Promised Land, Penguin USA.

[10] Consultations conducted under the auspices of the State Department of the United States in conjunction with the Center for Survivors of Torture, Dallas, Texas, January 21, 2003.

[11] Kupchan C., (2002) The End of the American Era: U.S. Foreign Policy and the Geopolitics of the Twenty-First Century, New York: Alfred Knopf Publishers.

[12] From a visit in January 2004, it was discovered that Vietnamese call it the American War rather than Vietnam War which suggests that Iraqis may likewise label the war in Iraq as an American War.

[13] Moyers B., "Earth on Edge: Bill Moyers Report," PBS-TV Documentary, April 22, 2002.

[14] Wildavsky A., (1979) Speaking the Truth to Power: The Art and Craft of Policy Analysis, Boston: Little, Brown and Company.

[15] Johnston D., Lewis N., and Van Natta D. (May 27, 2002) "F.B.I. Inaction Blurred Picture Before Sept. 11: Agency Was Cautious with Its Terror Data," The New York Times.

[16] Heuer R., (1999) "Psychology of Intelligence Analysis," The Center for the Study of Intelligence.

[17] Keilor G., (Feb. 8, 2004) "Lake Wobegon," National Public Radio.

[18] Monahan J., (1981) Predicting Future Violence, Sage Publications.

[19] Ahsani Syed, (2001), Chairman of the American Islamic Alliance, Southwest, in a personal communication, Central Islamic Mosque, Richardson, Texas.

[20] Hill C., (2001) "A Herculean Task: The Myth and Reality of Arab Terrorism," in The Age of Terror, edited by Strobe Talbott and Nayan Chanda, Basic Books.

[21] Arnold J., (1998) Seeking Peace, Farmington, PA: The Plough Publishing House

[22] Jeremiah 6:14 in the Hebrew Scriptures of the Old Testament.

[23] Barash D., op.cit.

[24] Barber B., (2003), Fear's Empire: War, Terrorism, and Democracy, New York: W.W. Norton & Company.

[25] Harris L., (2004), Civilization and Its Enemies: The Next Stage of History, New York: Free Press.

[26] Crossette B., (July 24, 2002), "U.N. Report Says New Democracies Falter," The New York Times.

[27] Ibid.

[28] Burke E., (2000) Writings and Speeches of Edmund Burke: The Hastings Trial 1789-1794, India, edited by P. Marshall, Oxford University Press.

[29] Benard C., and Schlaffer E., (2002) Veiled Courage: Inside the Afghan Women's Resistance, Broadway Books.

# Chapter Seven
# Proactively Managing Conflict

**Conflicts are unavoidable, necessary and they can even have their benefits in innovation and activity, identity and reflection. But the benefits will depend on our ability to manage conflict, to resolve them fairly, and to prevent their violent destructive manifestations.[1]**

**We're not going to win the war on terrorism; we're going to have to manage it.[2]**

By now, the reader may well be wondering – when will this book address the strategies for managing conflicts? This concern is at the core of many difficult human domestic and international conflicts. The previous six chapters focused on violent war, making enemies, family battling, retaliating, stalling tactics, passively resisting, and manipulatively sabotaging an opponent. These barriers are frequently used as tactics to preclude negotiations from working out difficult problems. They are used because intransigent problems do not have enduring solutions. Consequently, when domestic and international problems cannot be readily solved, they have to be managed very carefully.

The question arises: Are there actually problems that cannot be solved, and if so, what can be done to address these problems? Yes, there are problems that do not have permanent solutions. Examples include the perennial conflicts between the older and younger generations, or between good and evil forces, or the timeless conflicts between men and women. If any reader has durable, lasting solutions to these types of conflicts, they are personally requested to inform the author without delay, and then arrest reading this book. From the author's perspective, there are at least five deceptive approaches to problems that resist enduring solutions:

- Deny that the problem exists;
- Seek temporary, quick relief;
- Pretend magically that the problem is fixed with a band-aid;
- Treat the symptoms rather than the causes;
- Use diversionary tactics.

First, denial is actually helpful at times in order to endure overwhelming tragedy, fear or threat. To comfort a panicky child, how many parents have not told a child frightened by a terrifying nightmares that the scary characters are not real? Both parents and child benefit by denying the deep anxieties that are crashing into the vulnerable child's awareness.

The second approach for dealing with crises involves a rush to escape the tensions of conflict. Many persons take a tranquilizer or drug in order to get through stress. The proverbial advice, "take two aspirin and call me in the morning," or the latest anti-anxiety sedative is widely prevalent. Quick relief is the theme of many commercials for reducing pain. Alcohol and drugs can anesthetize people to temporarily bear the stresses of real conflict.

Thirdly, children like to feel that magical approaches permanently transform their painful "ouchy" when they miraculously announce – "It's all better." Naturally, from a child's perspective, any relief merits recognition that this superhuman solution is the final answer. Cultures are fascinated by enchanting magical displays that save them from threatening evils. However, domestic and international conflicts rarely lend themselves to such naive solutions.

Fourthly, relief of symptoms is much more appealing than wrestling with underlying causes of conflict. When causal factors are examined in depth, threatening questions arise for the *status quo.* Who wants to admit that we are part of the problem? Deeper problems can hide their basic causes from awareness such as complicated structural violence that is insidiously invisible to immediate observation. Contributing factors may be socially accepted as part of cultural practices. In many developing nations, poverty is understood to be fatalistically explainable. In American culture, military weapons are readily considered necessary rather than a compounding factor in domestic and global violence. As a consequence of such rationalizations, structural violence in the society is easily overlooked as a causal contributor to major calamities.

A fifth protective measure involves diversionary tactics employed by many deceptive international leaders and family tyrants. Crafty diversion may occur whenever enormous energy and attention are given to a particular problem. Diversionary tactics excuse failures to address problems hidden from awareness. Family and national leaders quickly divert from internal problems to external enemies rather than focus on pressing right problems at hand. Blaming someone else conveniently excuses accountability.

These five tactics do not resolve intransigent human problems that persist. There are complicated conflicts so deeply entrenched that they defy a single solution. These difficult conflicts are not solved with simple "either-or" thinking but need to be managed with "both/and" approaches. Polarities are unavoidable but are unsolvable issues confronted regularly. The best choice is to manage polarities well or to mismanage them poorly.

Temporary fixes often polarize people into extreme positions that are inherently conflicting. Both ends of polarized issues contain a degree of truth that requires consideration to arrive at reputable strategic policies. Paradoxically there is partial but incomplete truth in both polarities that seems contradictory on the surface. The truths within these polar opposites cannot be continuously ignored without unfortunate consequences. One-sided solutions too readily discredit the valid claims of the opposition that need to be included. The next section clarifies the nature of insoluble polarities that need to be managed.

**CLARIFYING POLARITIES:**

Imagine a baffling problem that is beyond denial, diversion or impervious to drug treatment. Assume also that this problem is so cantankerous that it is defiantly unsolvable. How could such an insoluble problem be confronted? For example, in a domestic crisis, someone in the family must acknowledge that there is a domestic emergency. Chronic alcoholics can ingeniously deflect away from their addiction. They can be so ingratiating that other family members are caught up in the alcoholic's web enabling them from facing their addiction. Another example in domestic violence depicts how abusive husbands can rationalize their violent actions. Often these men base their reasoning upon traditional ideas of religious authority, conventional discipline, and culturally endorsed punishment.

In order to address such problems, someone has to go beyond the blame game in order to identify "the monster" in the family. Children are easily blamed as the designated problem. Most experienced family therapists unpeel many layers of blame and denial that protect other family members who have nominated this particular child as the cause of their problems. These family leaders may send their nominee to therapeutic treatment secretly hoping that the rest of the family will be off the hook.

Clarifying these self-protective positions requires diagnostic insight to see these distortions. Helping members of the family search for the actual causes of problems is difficult. Even more challenging is the professional processes that help a troubled family recognize that they are contributing to their problems. Until this recognition occurs, family members may not take some ownership of the problem. As a result, families frequently polarize into camps with contentious arguments. These disputes may be husband against wife, children against parents, or all against the family member nominated as the problem. Blaming external causes can be distractions like an economic, political, or religious evil that provide reasons to deny their own problems.

Diversion is a very clever game when people do not want to face up to the ominous storm brewing around them. National leadership can be very astute in invoking an enemy. When a leader evokes an external enemy, they often divert from domestic problems they do not want to address. It is understandable that leaders prefer to identify problems for which they already have a solution. If they identify problems that they cannot solve, they may commit political suicide. The public is more comfortable with manageable outside problems than internal threats that are unmanageable. Mass media can also be manipulated to cleverly divert public attention from real causes of troubles. In international clashes and domestic crucibles, many volatile polarities ferment.

International misperceptions are widespread due to narrow ethnocentrism and skillfully promoted images in information technology. People in other cultures view many television programs and sordid movies. In developing nations, the rich and powerful in developed societies are seen to be consuming resources in opulent life styles. These visual images provide impressions that lavish consumption is the selfish motif of people in control. In contrast, media images about developing nations selectively cover violently dysfunctional tragedies while rarely providing comprehensive coverage. Distorted perceptions run rampant as if these portrayals are balanced accounts.

Stereotypes dominate ethnocentric attitudes. Long-standing animosities narrow tunnel vision for seeing what people prefer to notice. Revenge on the evil infidel and decadent pagans can easily be conjured up in the public minds of contending cultures. Polarities are fed with the simplifications of good and evil, us vs. them or friend vs. foe. International misperceptions by both leaders and citizens are rampant with these inaccurate biases. It may take an honest international broker or a detached analyst to help people accept ownership of their own problems rather than placing blame. Moving from "that's your problem" to "this is our problem" is a transforming step for the human family. Global crises are subject to hegemonic agendas as nations advance their own national interests. Realizing that all humanity is caught in quandaries is a major hurdle in discovering new paradigms of creative problem solving.

**Addressing Unsolvable Problems:**

Strategies of conflict management primarily address insoluble rather than problems that have a definitive remedy. For example, a country is faced with a problem of how to finance education so that children can achieve an expected level of schooling. Within the range of available resources, this problem can be solved. After deliberations, a legislature can eventually arrive at a decision by passing legislation, increasing taxation, or reforming education. Another example of a soluble problem involves governmental decisions whether to produce their own military weapons or purchase them from another source. With research and political will, this problem can be solved.

First, polarity management[3] involves identifying the key polar opposites inherent in unsolvable dilemmas like those that have been identified by example in the previous chapters. The second step involves analyzing the benefits of both polar interests while avoiding their downsides. An elementary illustration from human physiology clarifies the nature of polarities on a personal level. Figure 7-1 outlines the steps involved in managing the necessary processes of breathing in order to survive. The circles with arrows indicate an infinity sign ∞ showing how the positive inhaling and exhaling repeat in the breathing cycle while avoiding the negative downsides. Moreover, the infinity symbol recognizes that the breathing cycle throughout life that cross-over between inhaling and exhaling that goes on continuously during life.

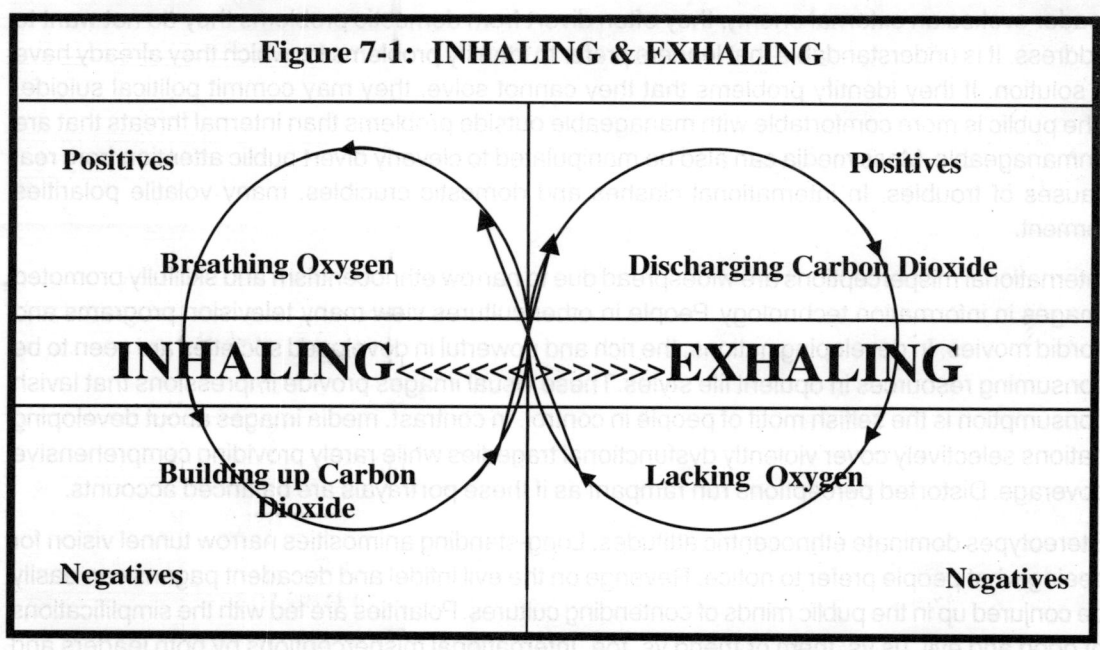

In order to stay alive both inhaling and exhaling are essential. Without exhaling or inhaling, the organism dies quickly. Hyperventilation may give short-term pleasure, but within seconds a person feels the panic of needing to inhale fresh oxygen. Fortunately, nature provides breathing organisms a brain that automatically monitors the rhythm of inhaling and exhaling. Otherwise the organism does not survive. While this simple breathing illustration is readily grasped, the complexities of human social interactions both domestically and internationally are much more complicated. There is not a family or global brain to automatically manage critical social polarities that monitor biological breathing.

Johnson[4] explains crucial steps for addressing insoluble problems involved in identifying oppositional polarities. Additional examples in numerous issues confronting international relations include:

- Rights vs. responsibilities.
- Free market vs. external regulations.
- Unilateral vs. multi-lateral relations.

Such issues defy permanent solution because any one-sided decision will certainly ignore the validity of opposing forces that eventually will reappear. The weaknesses of unbalanced solutions arise because such one-sided decisions neglect the valid truth held by the opposition. Consequently, there is not a durable solution that only advocates for one side because of the credible position of the polar opposite. These polarized positions must be managed effectively, efficiently and equitably with both polarities included in the policy decisions. If such balance is not pursued, the opposition will soon advance a credible case for re-balancing the policy.

Conflict management provides effective applications to both complicated domestic and international problems that defy immediate solution. An important strategy in conflict management is to have opposing viewpoints represented in the complexities of interpersonal practice and policy decisions. Moreover, it is important to include procedures to evaluate achievement of goals in an appropriate time frame in order to be accountable. Then necessary corrections can be made so that the negative downsides are avoided to prevent disastrous outcomes[5]. The next section identifies a series of issues equitably addressed by polarity management.

## POLARIZED ISSUES

To avoid blindness to opposing positions, it is essential to identify polarized issues for addressing insoluble domestic and international problems. This requires analyzing problems conflicting issues that penetrate behind symptoms into complicated causes that are not immediately apparent on the surface. Polarity management is an essential step for constructing the approaches for bridges between fear and peace.

## PSYCHO-SOCIAL POLARITIES:

### *RIGHTS vs. RESPONSIBILITIES*

How can human rights be expressed without interfering with the rights of others? This is a pivotal question for understanding domestic and international relations. Stated briefly, this issue of "I vs. We" is at the heart of numerous conflicts between individuals and the broader community. For each right there is a concomitant responsibility just as each freedom has a commensurate duty. For example, freedom of speech inherently presumes an obligation to use free speech responsibly. Moreover, each responsibility has a counterpart in a right. It is unfair to demand that a person be held responsible for a project without authorizing them with appropriate rights to complete the assignment.

This issue of rights vs. responsibilities is often difficult to balance equitably. There are two levels to express this issue – individually and socially:

- Expressing individual rights without interfering with the rights of other persons is a major challenge. Family members have difficulty managing these individual rights. The challenge increases exponentially in globally protecting human rights.

- Cultures disagree on the relative value of the individual in relation to the social rights. Individual rights readily clash with social rights when societies try to live harmoniously.

Personal responsibilities and social responsibilities crimp the individualistic style of liberated people. This issue needs conscientious management so that both the person and the community are protected while citizens express their autonomy. Age, gender, race, education and socio-economic variables further complicate polarized issues. Figure 7-2 analyzes the conflicts between personal rights vs. social responsibilities. The two circles are like an infinity sign ∞ with arrows indicating the cyclical nature of including the positive strengths of each polarity while avoiding the down sides. The infinity symbol suggests that polarity conflicts must be managed indefinitely since there is truth in both poles of individual rights <> social responsibilities.

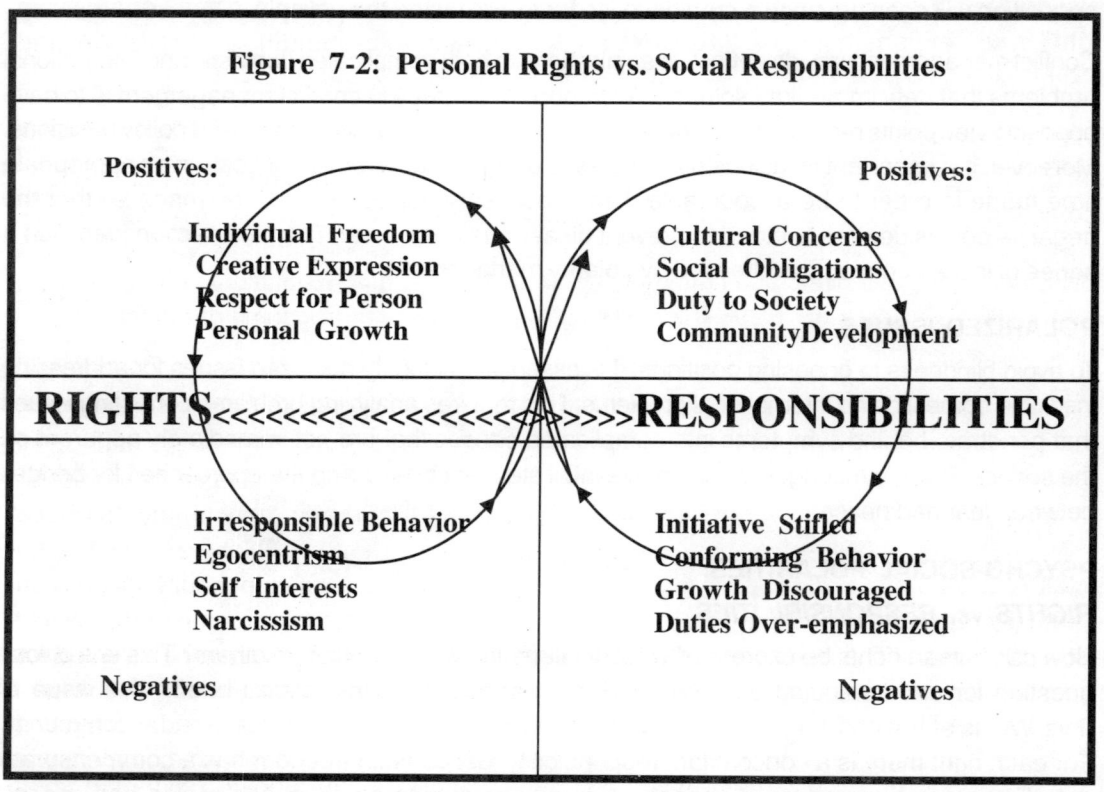

In social interaction, people can exercise their personal rights insofar as they refrain from interfering with the rights of others. Responsible exercise of rights involves respecting the rights of other persons. In many societies, the exercise of individual rights conflicts with fellow citizens who are also trying to act responsibly. Individualism is valued highly in many western cultures. However, there is a tendency for individual rights to be self-centered. Narcissism in young children and adolescents is understandable but becomes intolerably testy in adults. The worldview of youth is naturally confined to their immediate peer relations, family ties, along with their limited perceptions of the world beyond their immediate experience.

Children do have rights in many cultures with limited protections provided by governments in recent decades. In earlier decades, children had few legally protected rights even in enlightened cultures. In fact, until about 1860, children were protected in the United States by laws to protect animals from abuse. Humane treatment of animals was legislated before child labor laws were enacted for the humane treatment of children!

Nations and families have similar challenges but with much broader ramifications. National sovereignty is valued in much of the world since the eighteenth century. Glaring exceptions continue when one nation interferes with the national sovereignty of another. Major conflicts, global tensions and terrorism erupt when the ethnocentric rights of one nation aggressively ignores the rights of other nations. Interference with the sovereign rights of targeted nation may differ widely from the perceptions of the instigator since violations of rights strain relationships. Who can determine which nations are evil? How people differ in perceiving rights and responsibilities profoundly multiplies misunderstandings, retaliation and violent wars.

## *Freedom vs. Control*

Revolutions are inspired when oppressed people rally to fight for human values of freedom, liberty and equality. Liberation movements overthrow colonial powers, religious anachronisms, and economically unviable societies that are intolerably corrupt and oppressive. The birth of a new order eventually overcomes attempts to suppress emerging revolutions. Military action, law, tradition or religion often fails to control the human quest for freedoms of thought, press, religion and speech.

The human brain creatively adapts over eons to the natural environment and to human authorities who try to control human freedom. The human brain creates ingenious strategies to unravel rigid regulations. Efforts to use mind control counters the psychological value of promoting human freedom. Conformity, compliance, persuasion, guilt and fear-arousal have all been researched in psychological experiments and field studies.[6] History is replete with reactionary dictators and human institutions that fail to evolve as rapidly as human ingenuity. Opposition eventually retaliates against autocrats like Hitler who tried to establish an empire that would last a 1000 years. The ash heaps of history bury passé patterns of governance invented for earlier periods of history. Military power rarely liberates human institutions to function with self-government.

This line of thinking is not pessimistic but rather builds on the innovative human spirit to create institutions that progressively evolve socially, politically, economically and ethically. Dynamic public institutions are needed in education, the family, the justice systems and non-governmental organizations. Efforts to adapt to new technology provide better possibilities for improving social orders that meet the challenges of contemporary societies.

Democracy with built-in balances of powers are designed to provide adaptability for addressing new challenges.

Human beings discover that it is important to balance "liberty and security" for optimal social functioning. When one pole dominates, conditions for conflict automatically develop since there are valued truths in both liberty and security, or the parallel of freedom and control. This issue is central in the Patriotic Act in the United States that was legislated after 9/11. Managing polar opposites promotes possibilities for equilibrium in world order and security necessary for sustainable peace and enduring justice. Box 7-1 demonstrates that one person's freedom may become other people's burden as the poles of freedom and security are paradoxically intertwined.

---

**Box 7-1: Operation Enduring Freedom: Verb or Adjective?**

**While analyzing freedom, there is also an opportunity to evaluate a major conflict of this century. With the attack on the World Trade Center and Pentagon, a new wave of terroristic violence was experienced in the world. The response of a coalition of nations was named "Operation Enduring Freedom." This title reflects the values of this coalition and their determination to protect freedom militarily. Naturally there are divergent views about the nature and scope of this military operation to ferret out terroristic violence.[7]**

**A legitimate question arises whether the term "enduring" is a verb or an adjective. As an adjective, the word "enduring" suggests that freedom needs protection during development. As a verb, "enduring" freedom is the way some nations may feel who have been victims of military actions in "War on Terrorism." These nations have heard similar war slogans for protecting freedom, free trade, globalization, humanitarian and democratic values. Victims may rightfully wonder how much longer they can endure freedom that is protected by military force. There is evidence that Iraqi people have similar concerns about "Operation Iraqi Freedom" delivered by military force.**

**Freedom without constraints can make unwitting slaves of this prized human quality. Freedom and control are intricately related in a paradox. Both St. Augustine and Martin Luther perceptively understood this paradoxical issue. Luther succinctly stated an aphorism that expresses the inherent contradictions of freedom that needs to be balanced with obligations and duties. He poignantly stated in essence that true freedom allows a person to be servant of all,[8] and concomitantly held that freedom obligates human beings to responsibly serve others in social relationships.**

---

*Young Radicals vs. the Status Quo*

In both family and global concerns, a dynamic conflict is between youth and elders in human development. Young people represent fresh enthusiasm and new approaches energized with creative imaginations. Elders possess tested experience, powerful control of resources, institutions, and hopefully established wisdom. The inherent tensions generated in the conflicts between the young and the elderly can be resolved either constructively or destructively.

Few cultures over-value children. Elders retain power while youth often rebel against being considered property of their parents. Medieval views considered children to be miniature adults as reflected in paintings. Cultures may profess the importance of their next generation, but few take positive action to protect them with civil rights. Traditional societies want youth to demonstrate social responsibilities before gaining privileges. Women's rights still are not commensurate with men in both traditional and liberated societies. Rights of women to fair wages commensurate with men still await accomplishment. Civil, legal, financial, and voting rights are of very recent vintage.

When the conflict of youth vs. elderly is resolved constructively the best of both is blended into remarkable endeavors. Young and the old are innately linked although neither readily admits this truth. Stubborn control by the elderly can, however, stymie progressive movements. When the gray-headed wield control, they can deftly stifle youth with power plays. Elderly possess experience, powerful wealth and influential institutions that hold down youth who want to fly with their new approaches. But the weight of old inertia may drag youth down to earth like the heavy weight of gravitas. Box 7-2 presents dynamics repeatedly faced by persons who are adapting to changes in the family.

---

**Box 7-2: Old Traditionalists vs. Young Reformers**

**In polarity management there are creative tensions between promoting traditions and innovating change. Reformers envision future scenarios that change old practices into radically different patterns. They may reject the present and be ambivalent about the past since they focus on future changes. They may over-idealize aspects of the past while omitting repulsive recollections.**

**Both traditionalists and reformers need to appreciate valuable legacies of cultural accomplishments. At a minimum, culture survived to the present. However, there may be unexamined customs that are no longer beneficial. Intercultural exchanges stimulate changes that need current attention for reform.**

**When reformers and traditionalists respectfully mine rich treasures of the past, the future evolves more constructively. When traditionalists and reformers destroy treasures, they may defeat a creative dynamic. Young ideas and old institutions need each other just as reformers and traditionalists benefit from exchanges.**

---

When the elderly employ their wise experience and economic resources to under gird the enthusiasm of youth, together there are few limits to their joint creativeness. This can happen naturally in families and domestic concerns. Both the young and the elderly need each other for optimal outcomes of human development, personal growth and social progress. If one side prevails, the other side may suffer. The combination of youth and elderly together optimizes young radical ideas and old conservative approaches.

On an international level, the younger nations and the established nations can despise each other or respectfully enhance each other for the common good of humanity. The old powers may be threatened by upstart nations who have radical agendas. Empires have come and gone on the face of the earth as recorded in historical accounts. The challenges of two contemporary authors provide provocative insights that need consideration in contemporary geopolitical conflicts. One view by an Indian author is entitled Confronting Empires,[9] and the other is entitled The End of the American Era.[10]

Civilizations and empires have made enormous efforts to perpetuate themselves as human creations. Their longevity has varied widely. The realities of history report that each civilization has initially emerged, progressively expanded, experienced decline and eventually expired. Like human beings who have imagined that they are immortal empires and civilizations are deceived by imaginations of their own immortality. Reality reports that mortality prevails. Like all human cultures, there are survival instincts that deny mortality to prolong their terminal life. However, human denial does not control the eventual forces of cultural entropy and demise.

### Ethics vs. Expendiency

Expediency has a powerful influence upon ethical behavior. When threats of survival are dreadfully ominous, human behavior becomes more regressively primitive. When economic pressures bear upon parties in a transaction, ethical constraints are tested for whether profits or ethics will prevail. Individual behavior at times can stand up to moral dilemmas more consistently than social behavior.[11] Under other conditions of stress, group support can have a positive or negative effect in insular thinking. Experiments in social analysis and organizational case studies repeatedly uncover unethical behavior under adverse economic or political pressures. The temptations to fudge, cheat or neglect can overwhelm sound judgment and ethical practices. Ethical conduct is optimally learned in formative years.[12] Family life is the crucible where children traditionally learn personal morality and credible social behavior.

The experiments in social psychology that Milgram[13] conducted on obedience to authority continue to haunt human morality. Yielding to pressure and authority has been seen among not only corporate executives and employees, but also among military personnel and most organized social behavior. Pressure to yield and conform often overrides individual morality when the pressure of expediency outweighs the application of ethical conduct. When conflicts of interests impinge upon decisions, ethical standards are often compromised in professional and personal behavior. Moreover, corporate and political corruption has very negative impact upon public trust and confidence.

Political influence has historically been curried throughout organizations, empires and nations. Expediencies of economic influence and political pressure directly sway government officials. A continuum of response is depicted as follows:

**Voting – Supporting – Accessing – Influencing – Intimidating – Cheating – Corrupting–Bribing**

Where unethical behavior arises along this continuum is debatable. Momentary expediencies, the issues, the alternatives, the circumstances, and power are all variables that sway ethical behavior individually and in social behavior. Cultural values vary about criminal, unethical, illegal, immoral, fraudulent or corrupt. Consequently, these issues cannot be settled once and for all by any culture. In a global society, universal principles of ethical behavior that apply to decisions in all situations are notoriously few. Different cultural values have understandable conflicts when they are applied to specific situations. Credibility and understanding are essential in cultivating mutual relationships. The choices are more complex than often realized in international relations especially when one culture imposes its values upon other cultures.

## Genetics vs. Environment

In scientific paradigms, human behavior is typically explained by two phenomena plus a provision for unpredictability. Genetics is a key factor for explaining human behavior while the environment is the other major influence. Human development in the contemporary scientific paradigm is theoretically explained by genetic or environmental factors plus complicated interactions in various permutations.

In the past century, chaos theory from physics has challenged this elegant paradigm. Research in chaos theory concludes that nature inherently is unpredictable in ways that the traditional Newtonian paradigm of physics cannot readily explain. Consequently, the awareness of unpredictable factors further complicates classical scientific theory with the realization that chaos in human development and behavior is not clearly understood. Biology takes account of the phenomenon of mutations that contribute to biodiversity as well as unpredictability.

There have been periods in science when genetics were given greater attention than environmental factors, and vice versa. In the middle of the last century, behavioral sciences emphasized the social environment, learning, conditioning and education. With the contemporary genome project, genetics are given major attention in biological research. Lively debate centers around whether violence is primarily genetically-based or environmentally learned. Goldstein and Segall[14] and their associates support the social learning approach while stating the innate contributors are not scientifically supported.

In brain research, Pinker[15] concludes that parts of the brain are predisposed toward aggressive behavior. He drew upon studies that 80 percent of men and 60 percent of women have thought about killing someone but few carry through with the act. The frontal lobes of the brain that develops slowly help in inhibiting aggressive dispositions with self-control. These self-regulatory abilities are impaired when drugs, alcohol, and medications are consumed particularly when judgments and decisions are made[16]. During normal life processes, pre-frontal brain lobes slowly develop until late teenage years and deteriorate gradually in aging in elderly persons.

Neither genetics nor environmental factors alone are enough to explain all dimensions of human behavior.[17] Consequently, both need to be given consideration together in complex interactions. A child is not solely a product of the their genes, nor the product entirely of his/her environment and social learning[17]. At this stage of scientific knowledge, anyone who ignores either genetics or environmental factors has imbalanced explanations. As a result, the contribution of both needs attention so that emphases upon one determinant does not neglect the other components.

There is a continuous need to balance the polarity of genetic and environmental contributors in understanding human behavior. The conflict is not adequately resolved by over-emphasizing one pole over its polar opposite. When violent behavior is analyzed, both genetic and environmental factors are crucial facets of the clarification. Explanations for cultivating peaceful behavior require that careful consideration be given to both biological and social factors. Self-regulation depends on the mature development of pre-frontal brain lobes along with social institutions for managing global security.

## Cultural Diversity vs. Monoculture

In migratory interactions, collisions occur between cultural patterns of people including languages and tribal traditions. There are also complex factors of different religions, education institutions, diverse ecologies, economic values, political variance, social customs, and racial attitudes. There are unique moral values, medical and therapeutic practices, occupational specialties, artistic expressions, costumes, holidays, clothing, and housing arrangements for families. Additional social enrichments are entertainment and leisure interests, prized legacies and heritages, courting and marriage customs plus sexual and family practices.

Any one of these factors could cause misunderstandings when people interact from diverse backgrounds. In the cross-cultural metaphors of "rainbow," "mixed salad" or "patch-work quilt" there is profound enrichment from different traditions, tastes and preferences. Efforts to respectfully tolerate each other's differences are paramount to appreciate the benefits of this rich variety. Most cultures have considerable diversity within their bounds of influence. Fortunately, many of the differences are beneficial including different genes, special expertise, and artistic talent. Distinctive legacies, adaptive approaches, different philosophical, religious and educational approaches are expressed in ethnic traditions, food preferences and technologies important for survival.

Historical pressures to live peaceably together are not equal to contemporary stresses involved in mobility, migration, global communication and travel. Governance and economics are hard pressed by the complexities of modern science, technology and weapons. Hegemony imposes the values of the dominant culture. How minorities adapt to a majority culture has been one of the immense challenges of mobility. Four different strategies for minority cultures include integration, separation, marginalization and assimilation into the dominant culture.[18,19] Genocide poses additional problems in discovering peaceable arrangements for living together.

As these tense inter-cultural conflicts are worked through, potential for violence becomes staggering. The unusual term of ethnic cleansing describes the perverted justification for exterminating groups that challenge a monoculture. Major ethnic wars have been fought in the Balkans, Timor, Sri Lanka, Middle East, and many sectors of North and South Americas, Africa, Asia, Australia, and Europe. Antagonisms inherited from earlier generations fuel the hostile memories repeatedly acted out with violent revenge. Cultural diversity contributes contentious issues in ethnic conflicts. The strategies of conflict management provide nonviolent alternatives to address these tensions instead of perpetuating historical violence. The processes of polarity management are not able to cope with all variations of conflicts, but it is an important option that offers pragmatic strategies for policy makers forming legislation, and for family members who feel trapped in domestic abuse.

## POLITICAL ECONOMY ISSUES

Attention to pressing issues of political economy is needed in international conflicts that build upon the psycho-social-cultural issues previously analyzed. These issues have wide implications in the conflicts that influence governance and economics in international affairs.

### *Self-Regulation vs. Chaos*

Individual and collective rights are discernible in human behavior. Self-regulation is expected of a mature person. If another party is perceived as being out of control, efforts are made to regulate or restrain them. These controlling efforts may be covert or overt constraints to overcome the fear in chaotic behavior expressed in terrorism, suicide and anarchy. Chaos can be so threatening to people that major efforts are made to provide predictable order to limit human freedoms. Chaos and order are conflicting poles that human institutions confront in constraining unacceptable behavior. Conformity may be valued so highly that human creativity is corralled as if creativeness has to be penned up like a wild beast. Constitutions are respected social contracts that govern how citizens can live together with a semblance of social justice, peace and harmony.

Self-regulation always involves tensions that societies need to balance equitably. Over-constraining individual initiative can suffocate innovation and enterprising initiatives. Conformity to a narrow mold may assure tranquility, but it can also constrain personal creativeness so harshly that divergent views are not tolerated. There are understandable tensions that result from internal controls and external regulations.

Major power struggles occur over deciding who has authority to set the normative standards. There are professionals who think that they can regulate themselves because a recognized profession provides ethical codes that define capacities meriting public confidence in specialized services that can be trusted by the public. Among these are psychologists, physicians, clergy, lawyers, counselors, accountants, stockbrokers, health professionals, and other licensed professionals. An insight by Coffee provides insight for business professionals that should not be ignored when he stated: "Self-regulation is an oxymoron on Wall Street."[19] Box 7-3 provides several illustrations of organizations that have pushed the limits of deregulation.

The inherent conflicts of regulation vs. deregulation are obvious issues that can be addressed by procedures in polarity management. These methods discover valid truths in both regulation and deregulation that balance one-sided solutions. The insight of Akerlof[20] confirms the need for careful balance of polarities. He draws upon a toddler analogy stating that if you let toddlers out of their playpen, you need to watch them more.[20] Analogously, when deregulation allows free action by executives, employees and youth, it must be accompanied by increased regulatory oversight.

Constitutions establish checks and balances for different branches of government in recognition of individual and collective limitations for self-regulation. Governments that survive over many centuries discover the necessity for balancing powers among the executive, legislative and judicial branches.

---

**Box 7-3: Free Market vs. Regulation**

There are common themes in corporate scandals over the past decades that have erupted in bankruptcies, investigations or foreclosures. Violations were uncovered in companies like Enron, Arthur Anderson, WorldCom, Tyco, Adelphia, Health South, Prudential Securities, Columbia/HCA, Martha Stewart and Wall Street brokerage firms plus other corporations that used creative accounting. The details are now available after investigations and legal actions protect the public, employees and investors. Fraudulent adventures include corporations with broad business and political influence that flagrantly lack accountability.[21] Shocking revelations portray a pattern of both unethical and illegal wrongdoing with consequent financial damage running into billions of dollars.

Basic issues involve behavior by executives who positioned themselves and their corporations beyond the pale of regulators or public accountability. Their actions represented the excesses of rampant free market ventures. Under their leadership, corporations were led into dubious financial exploits that top management thought were outside the range of self-regulation, trusting financial clients, vulnerable patients, or uninformed government regulators. Their exploits were apparently fed by ambitious greed, unconstrained freedom, and lack of external regulation. Some were influenced by theoretical ideas about deregulation. Government regulations and professional standards were criticized for limiting managers. Economic rationales advocated ever-expanding free-markets both domestically and globally.

Over the past several decades, legislation deregulated energy markets, health care practices, air transportation and financial safeguards that intentionally controlled the excesses of irresponsible entrepreneurs. Political pressures were placed upon elected officials and regulators with free market slogans to craftily remove controls. Major profits were reported by corporate executives who also awarded themselves large salaries, incentives, and stock options. The public was not protected from these excesses.

Deceptive accounting procedures adversely ripped off stockholders, customers, employees, patients and clients. WorldCom's bankruptcy adversely impacted the entire telecommunications industry and the American stock market. The impact was felt internationally in the case of Enron's exploits in energy businesses in India and South America. With little accountability and regulation, Enron set back international investment ventures in India while leaving South American countries staggering economically. Many Indian citizens felt exploited prompting the Indian government to take additional protective precautions.

Assumptions that a constitution has permanently settled these polarized issues may be blindsided by the creativity in new generations of young untested thinkers. Without experience about the limits of human nature, radical crusaders may assume that they can be trusted to act upon their unproven convictions. In their eager enthusiasm to pursue self-interests, they may even assume that no external regulations or public accountability for their actions are necessary.

## *Short-Term vs. Long-Term Goals*

Business and government organizations confront tensions between short and long-term considerations in achieving objectives. Corporate timelines increasingly are short-term such as the next stockholders' meeting or the next quarterly earnings report. Stockholders' expectations and management's incentives dictate dividends and stock prices. Informed management is cognizant of these short-term pressures in order to keep their positions secure. Political timelines also have shortened to no longer than the next election since voters are easily influenced by popularity polls about elected officials.

With the acceleration of information technology, data instantly become the benchmark in domestic, corporate and international mentality. Attention span to one television commercial conditions contemporary viewers to expect quick satisfaction or else switch channels. Loyalty is only one consideration in such fast paced relationships. These rapid transitions describe fragile impersonal, business, and global interactions.

Immediate gratification places enormous pressure upon institutions that require long-term investments of human ingenuity, energy, and resources. Instant satisfaction places stressors upon the long-term processes of building cultures, lasting family bonds, and protecting environments. Globalization thrives on these powerful dynamics. According to the socio-biologist, E.O. Wilson from Harvard University[22], the great dilemmas in sound reasoning about the environment stems from the conflict between short-term and long-term values. He suggests that future life is challenged by the conflicting visions of short-term gain and long-term considerations in creating environmental ethics.[22]

The psychological time frame of the immediate "here and now" dominates modern decision-making. Except in legal matters, historical precedence is rarely considered in conflicting issues except for selective memories of love and resentments. How a person feels right now is pre-eminent in emotional decision-making. Current generations focus on present economic and political developments displaying limited concern for posterity and their environment.

Variations of short-term vs. long-term perspectives result from balancing thoughtfulness for the full range of past, the present and the future. Historical perspectives appreciate the lessons of past generations whose crystallized wisdom can inform contemporary minds. History provides awareness of rich customs for gleaning deeper understanding about today's conflicts. The multi-polar chronology of past-present-future competes with the *kairos* moment that dominates people's thinking. Maslow[23] suggests that people who self-actualize focus predominantly on the here and now. They apply their attention and energy to the present problems during a high percentage of their waking hours. While people who self-actualize appreciate the past and recognize that the future is significant, their primary efforts are addressed to the problems they presently face.

Marriages are also impacted by short term rather than lifetime commitments. These stresses prompt the question: Should marriages have annual reports to weigh utilitarian benefits against costs? Short liaisons influence many domestic as well as international relations. Futurists are concerned with long-term dimensions. They focus their imagination on the unknown realizing that predictions are easily visualized but rarely accurate. Without considering the future, the linear flow of history is cut off from imagination and idealism. Time advances from the then and there to the here and now, and proceeds beyond to ideal imagination. Balancing all three timelines – past, present and future – is essential for creative planning by families and nations.

## Macro vs. Micro Overview

The big picture vs. small details provides another polar issue that needs to be managed in dealing with conflicts. Highly specialized research scientists investigate specific variables in great depth while paying secondary attention to the larger context. The analytical methods of science differentiate complex phenomena into basic elements. Reductionism to biochemical elements places distance between people when the small picture becomes the focus of human interactions. Many persons are overwhelmed with the immediate conflicts so that there are few people who appreciate the macro picture.

Consequently, people are unable to holistically appreciate other people in the world. Finding common ground is a major challenge in dealing with the conflicts that inherently arise when people have only limited understanding of each other. Science has analyzed phenomena into minute parts so that integration of these highly specialized factors is a major challenge. In contemporary life, this emphasis on specialization can alienate both domestic and international affairs.

The global picture is so vast that no one possesses a complete macro overview. Approximating a bigger picture is a gargantuan challenge in the array of many specialized parts. Developing holistic approaches is a challenge to develop multi-disciplinary approaches. Optimizing the benefits of conflicting polarities is the domestic and global challenge of the current generations. Polarity management provides methods to gain the best of approaches from the traditional past and the strengths of modern innovations. Innovators who wish to introduce new reforms benefit from mastering these methods. Then both the assets of conventional approaches and the beneficial discoveries of specialized technology are optimized.[24]

## Entrepreneurial Politics and Divine Appointment:

Enterprising initiative has merits in commercial business, organizational problem-solving and community involvements. How appropriate entrepreneurial initiatives are in family, religious or political involvements is being continuously tested in modern cultures. The results for evaluating enterprising approaches need further research in family, domestic, religious and political activities.

Many dictatorships and military *coups* have occurred in the past when self-appointed leaders gained power with coercive force. However, in democratic nations, self-nominated candidates have taken personal initiative to promote themselves for elected offices. In recent decades as the influence of political parties declines, more entrepreneurial candidates enter public life. Rather than being selected through the proven ranks of political parties or public service, these enterprising candidates take initiative themselves to seek office. A number of these self-announced candidates are successful in business or professional endeavors so that they generate interests and resources to launch major political campaigns. They assume they can readily apply business methods in government offices.

Behind these candidates can be financially wealthy powerbrokers who utilize financial support plus personal contributions in kind, time and influence. People with shared ideologies often use their influence in political election and lobbying activities. An important related issue involves conflicting economics interests. Political observers see entrepreneurial candidates, who if they are not already wealthy, become wealthy in government service. Another sequence occurs when former public officials become even wealthier as lobbyists for special interest groups. Instrumental use of government influence promotes financially lucrative enterprises that need careful investigation.

On the other hand, there are political candidates who give the impression they are destined to exercise power by divine appointment or dynastic inheritance. Their worldviews can be highly eschatological in nature about the future destiny of humanity. Some of these persons possess a conviction of being divinely chosen to address global concerns and eschatological developments. Naturally motifs can be a mixture of religious destiny and self-interests. Often their language is religiously tinged thereby covering both their conscious and unconscious quest for power and authority. They may even engage in nepotism to perpetuate their family dynasty.

Common to both entrepreneurial candidates and religiously anointed leaders is the quest for power in order to exercise even greater control. Once people are intoxicated by powerful influence, it is very difficult for them to relinquish it. Powerbrokers try to perpetuate their own interests. They wield major influence not only nationally but also internationally. Phillips[25] has very critically analyzed the Bush dynasty in American politics.

This revolving cycle of government and private interests is illustrated in a corporation involved in military industry, oil, investments and insider political influence. The Board of the Carlyle Group discloses a number of the most powerful former government officials and elected officials of recent generations. Their influence upon foreign governments and global trade illustrates the power of international political economy along with other global organizations.

When powerful people apply these needs to their family life, it is not unusual for them to metaphorically see their family and possessions as their own personal kingdom. Such a royal family has extensive economic wealth alongside social needs considered essential for the well being of each member. Inheritance laws are traditionally designed to perpetuate wealth into following generations. Traditional and romantic marriages are like corporate mergers among qualified families. When the parents select the mate of their children, economic factors are prominently considered. Religious justification is expressed in "success theologies" in the Christian, Jewish, Islamic and Hindu traditions. These approaches assume divine intentions to design initiatives for power.

The motif of manifest destiny is applied by enterprising activities. This quest for more wealth, more power, more control and more possessions all coalesce in the intense dynamics of domestic family relations. "More" is a motif that children learn very early. Two words that children master quickly in early language development are "no" and "more." The human motivations behind both of these words include human appetites, control and power. When families list their goals, the acquisition of more material possessions, bigger houses, larger cars, and more power, and more prestigious status symbols are prominent. Many family therapists begin to wonder when people find satisfaction for what they have without needing to acquire more earthly symbols.

Acquiring more and more power and influence has been a quest in both Eastern and Western societies historically. In his analysis of <u>What Went Wrong? Western and Middle Eastern Response,</u> Lewis[26] entitled an entire chapter on "The Quest for Wealth and Power." Both within societies domestically and also among societies inter-culturally there have been enormous efforts made to control power and materialistic wealth.

Based upon cross-cultural research, the author has observed that many cultures have an unofficial religion that might be entitled the worship of the god who could be called "ACQ." ACQ is my abbreviation for the propensity to worship the ACQuisition of ACQuiring power, influence and wealth ACQuisitively. Historically and currently, humanity continues to be motivated for ACQuiring more. From philosophical perspectives, Harris sees this as "the desire to have more than others, without which no more amount of moreness is sufficient to avert misery."[27] Psychologist Barry Schwartz identifies the paradox that occurs when more choices can become profoundly stressful in affluent societies.[28]

Human beings often seem to be obsessed with becoming divine and god-like in an almost insatiable appetite to ACQuire more control and more possessions. Public and private enterprises, corporate control, and family empires all could be symptoms of these obsessions. Either by divine appointment or entrepreneurial initiatives the quests for more power, control and possession persists throughout human history. The old adage wisely cautions people involved in both international affairs and domestic conflicts: "Power corrupts…absolute power corrupts absolutely."[29]

**Concluding Comments:**

This chapter analyzes critical issues confronted domestically and internationally in human interactions. The necessity of managing insoluble conflicts is outlined along with the methods of polarity management to address these difficult problems. Naturally the chapter is not exhaustive of all possible issues that are encountered in human conflicts. Instead the approach offers methods to address difficult problems in a more effective fashion than imposing violent one-sided solutions.

Multi-polar issues can ignite major conflicts in the domestic family and international relations since many are insoluble and therefore need constant management. These issues are enmeshed in cultural values so that the causes of structural violence must be managed. Due consideration must be given to the truths of conflicting multipolarities in these issues. One-sided solutions eventually contribute to conflicts that feed problems of structural violence of injustice precluding sustaining peace. Quick-fix approaches do not endure while simultaneously creating problems for future generations to address again.

Power is apparently addictive in nature for human beings because the more power they have, the more they want. When addicts start to lose their power, they readily resort to tactics to regain power even by resorting to violence. People yearn for peace and tranquility that can be discovered nonviolently and justly.

# Endnotes

[1] Quoted in <u>UNESCO and a Culture of Peace: Promoting a Global Movement,</u> UNESCO Publishing, Cultures of Peace Series.

[2] Bergen P., (March 21, 2004) National Public Radio.

[3] Conflict resolution as another approach will be addressed in chapters eight, nine and ten.

[4] Johnson L., (1992) <u>Polarity Management: Identifying and Managing Unsolvable Problems,</u> HRD Press.

[5] When several issues are inherent in problems, balancing multiple polarities becomes even more complex. Decisions optimize advantages and minimize disadvantages of the action plan. The successes and failures of the implemented policy require periodic evaluation and corrective revision.

[6] Zimbardo P., (2002) "Mind Control: Psychological Reality or Mindless Rhetoric?" <u>Monitor on Psychology</u>, Vol. 33, No. 10, November, 2002.

[7] Middents G., (2001) <u>Crises in Violence and Peace</u>, Manipal Press, has indicated reluctance to use the term "terrorism" due to definitional problems and instead used the term "terroristic violence."

[8] Luther M., (1970) <u>Three Treatise</u>, Fortress Press.

[9] Roy A., (2001) <u>Power Politics</u>, South End Press, and her essay "Confronting Empires," Medical Consulting Group, Brazil, January 28, 2003.

[10] Kupchan C., (2002) <u>The End of the American Era: U.S. Foreign Policy and the Geopolitics of the Twentieth Century</u>, Alfred A. Knopf Publishers.

[11] Niebuhr R., (1960) <u>Moral Man in Immoral Society</u>, Scribner's Books.

[12] Middents G., "When is Ethical Decision-making Optimally Learned?" seminar conducted at Southwestern Medical School, University of Texas Health Care System, Dallas, TX, October 18, 2002.

[13] Milgram S., (1983) <u>Obedience to Authority</u>, Harper Torchbooks.

[14] Goldstein A. and Segall M., editors, (1983) <u>Aggression in Global Perspective</u>, Pergamon Press.

[15] Pinker S., (2002) <u>The Blank Slate: The Modern Denial of Human Nature</u>, Viking Press; also cited by Deborah Smith in "Dissolving Myths about Human Nature," <u>Monitor on Psychology</u>, November, Vol. 33, No. 10, November, 2002.

[16] Volkow N., (March 19, 2004) "Imaging the Addicted Brain," Lecture at University of Texas Southwestern Medical Center, Dallas, Texas. Dr. Volkow is Director of the National Institute on Drug Abuse, National Department of Health and Human Services of United States Government.

[17] Hillman J., (1997) in his book <u>The Soul's Code: In Search of Character and Calling</u>, Warner Books, raises provocative questions whether additional factors along with genetics and environment merit consideration such as character and calling for understanding human behavior.

[18] Middents G., (2001) Conflict of ethnic groups, minorities, and the impact on human development," chapter in <u>Crisis in Violence and Peace</u>, Manipal Press.

[19] Coffee J., (May 13, 2002) "Guarding the Gatekeepers," <u>The New York Times.</u>

[20] Akerlof G., quoted in an article by Louis Uchitelle, "Looking for Ways to Make Deregulation Keep Its Promises," <u>The New York Times</u>, July 28, 2002.

[21] Eichenwald K., (March 2, 2002) "White-Collar Defense Stance," <u>The New York Times.</u>

[22] Wilson E.O., (2002) <u>The Future of Life</u>, New York: Alfred A Knopf Publishers

[23] Maslow A., (1993) <u>The Further Reaches of Human Nature</u>, Penguin Books.

[24] Johnson L., <u>op.cit.</u>

[25] Phillips K., (2004) <u>American Dynasty: Aristocracy, Fortune and Policies of Deceit in the House of Bush,</u> New York: Viking Press.

[26] Lewis B., (2002) <u>What Went Wrong? Western Impact and Middle Eastern Response</u>, New York: Oxford University Press.

[27] Harris L., (2003), <u>Civilization and Its Enemies: The Next Stage of History</u>, New York: Free Press.

[28] Schwartz B., (2004), <u>The Paradox of Choice: Why More is Less</u>, New York: Harper Collins.

[29] Lord Acton (1988) <u>Essays in Religion, Politics and Morality</u>, Liberty Fund, Incorporated.

# Part III:
# RESOLVING CONFLICT

In Part III, attention is placed on resolving problems amenable to peaceful solutions. Because circumstances change, most previous solutions need to be reviewed for improvements since they are not indefinitely valid. Policies developed at one juncture of history may become problems for future policymakers or in need of updating. Consequently, it is wise to periodically evaluate earlier strategies to determine whether to revise or to discard them.

"Bullies or Heroic Figures?" – this is a question that addresses domestic and international aggressors as they try to induce fear in victims, gain control and achieve notoriety. Heroic figures can be equally aggressive as bullies but for different motives. They also have different targets and are recognized by different constituencies. A key question: Can bullies transform into heroic figures?

Heroes and heroines throughout history have solved gigantic problems. In Indian mythology, Krishna persuades Arjuna, a warrior, to battle not out of hatred or for personal gain but out of selfless duty even though his relatives and friends are his opponents. In Hebrew Scriptures, David was known as a hero who slew Goliath with stones from his slingshot. Heroic figures use violence to save their culture. But how can bullies transform their aggression into heroic venture rather than dubious actions against vulnerable victims? Chapter Eight explores this question cautiously. On their heroic journey, tribulations are encountered by potentially heroic "wannabes" who are tested for patience, courage and savvy.

Chapter Nine describes "special arrows" that would-be heroic figures have in their quiver. Long-term perspectives are described rather than silver bullets. Crafty opponents deceive heroic figures who need secret knowledge to fulfill their destiny in this chapter on "Alternative Dispute Resolution." Throughout history poets dramatize the risks that courageous heroes/heroines take not knowing whether they will survive the tests they must face. Symbolically, they deal with tricky witches, evil spirits, and their own internal demons as well as with threatening enemies. Heroic figures also have their own internal demons that tempt them to run away from terrorizing fear.

Chapter Ten encourages heroic figures to dig deeply into their courage, their wits, and their determination. This chapter is concerned with skills in mediation, negotiation and new approaches in collaboration for resolving conflicts. Heroic figures are tested to the very core of their character in order to save their people as they experience the treachery of "the deep night sea journey." They need fortitude, driving motivation and fine moral values discovered deep in their character.

# Chapter Eight

# Reframing Transformation

### Why do nations re-fight past wars?

Rival nations can contend like jealous family siblings. Placing a child into rivalries with superior opponents can be cruel if not devastating. Children cannot appropriately compete with powerful adults in many activities. When a child is introduced to a new skill, the wise parent, teacher, or coach starts with elementary facets of the activity. As the child gains confidence in their newly acquired skills, they need rewards and recognition appropriate for their level of learning. Children can easily be discouraged from further involvement in inappropriate activities when their physical, mental and emotional development is not ready for competitive relationships.

When parents are unduly controlling, a child's rights may be violated. In a contested divorce, a child may be expected to choose allegiance to only one parent. Loyalty to one parent may be subsequently rewarded or punished so that the child is caught in unfair competition between sparring parents. Likewise older siblings may control younger siblings by intimidation or bribery for taking sides in family rivalries.

In domestic conflict, immature members of the family can be unfairly treated with devastating consequences. Incest is a dramatic example when an older family member engages a child into sexual activity for the older person's gratification. A child can be victim of a powerful figure trusted to protect the child's basic interests. Young children usually do not know that sexual involvement within the family or a trusted adult is a criminal behavior in many cultures. Children may be enticed into experiences that an older person may justify as mutually gratifying and beneficial.

In international relations, smaller nations are jerked into and out of coalitions like pawns in a global chess game. During the Cold War, the Warsaw Block nations were buffers protecting the former Soviet Union. A number of Western European countries serve in counterpart fashion as buffers dependently bought out by the North Atlantic Treaty Organization. Economic and military support serves the interests of powers to protect them.

Vulnerable nations may be willing to prostitute themselves for monetary aid or protective security. Examples include the "Alliance of the Willing" who aligned with the United States, Great Britain and Spain plus others in the War in Iraq. Even more crass has been the subtle use of food and humanitarian aid as "Weapons of Mass Destruction" in foreign relations. During the Cold War, the United States and the former Soviet Union vied for allegiance from satellite countries in Europe while also playing this competitive strategy in Asia, Africa, Central and South America. Manipulating trade, sanctions, aid, and military weapons is devastating to innocent populations trying to survive under starvation conditions. In a divided world, non-aligned nations use cost-benefit analysis to determine how they might suffer less or gain the most benefit.

No wonder that much of the world consider a superpower as a bully with a hegemonic agenda in the world. Bullies choose their victims who are selected for optimal gain for the bully's reputation and interests. Victims usually involve people of vulnerable nations who are suffering from economic deprivations and social injustices involving violations of human rights. Other nations are bystanders to these displays of military might by bellicose superpowers. A number of nations consider the United States as a bullying superpower in its military interventions in Asia, Europe, and Africa.[1]

Aggressors gain short-term advantages by regressing into rigidly obtrusive actions. Not only can families be deadlocked into old contentions, but ethnic and international conflicts are also re-fought between ancient rivalries. The repeated conflicts in the Balkans manifest these rigid rivalries concerned with animosities harbored over centuries. International conflicts can become rigidly cantankerous with traditional labels and explanations. Ethnic groups frequently rekindle old hatred. Contending nations perpetuate frictions that become locked into self-justifying atrocities. Changes may be problematical because emotional investments satisfy inherited tensions. Even young people can be acculturated with rigid thinking as described in Box 8-1.

---

**Box 8-1: The "Friendly Villain's" Problem**

**An example from India clarifies how thought patterns become rigid from insidious past rivalries. Captain Raju, a movie star, and I were invited to speak at the inauguration of the Cultural Festival at the Toc H School in Kerala. Nearly 1000 teenagers waited for the start of artistic performances.**

**Captain Raju was obviously well known from many of his movies as a famous star in Malayalam cinemas. I asked him what roles he played and he replied: "A Friendly Villain." He immediately indicated that he would also like to play other roles as a leading man, a hero or a comedian.**

**But he was type-cast by his fans who did not want him to change. They loved him as a "Friendly Villain." In this role, Captain Raju was a villain destined to lose in the end. His teenage fans cheered for him because he brought them pleasure. They did not want him to change because emotionally they preferred him as their "Friendly Villain."**

---

The older the rivalries, the more rigid they can become. There are tremendously powerful forces locking up symbiotic relationships. Can roles be changed? As Captain Raju discovered – "my fans won't let me change." Aspiring heroes and heroines need villains in order to perform their heroic roles. The "friendly villain" and archenemies may be universal archetypes in the violent human dramas. Unfortunately hostile relationships are perpetuated in international conflicts reflected in the Gulf War and the Wars on Terrorism conducted in Afghanistan and Iraq.

Operation Desert Storm was one of the shorter wars lasting less than one week preceded by over six weeks of bombing. International frictions brewed before Iraq's leader, Sadaam Hussein, invaded Kuwait. Armed forces from the United States with a large coalition were deployed after weeks of air strikes that were televised around the world from Baghdad. Broadcast networks provided coverage into millions of homes around the world. Hussein's military forces were partially annihilated in the desert of southern Iraq. Within one week, victory was swiftly declared by the United States, troops were soon withdrawn, and military heroes were recognized.

Did war solve this international problem? Economic sanctions were immediately imposed on Iraq. Air space was narrowly defined and constantly patrolled by American planes. According to inconsistent intelligence reports, Iraq's production of weapons of mass destruction continued thereby defying numerous resolutions passed by the United Nations. Iraq was monitored for weapons of mass destruction by international inspectors until 1998 when they were ejected. Inspections were resumed in late 2002, but were arrested again on March 20, 2003 when another war against Iraq was launched by the United States, Great Britain and Spain along with a limited international coalition. Twelve years after Operation Desert Storm the War against Iraq continued the cycle of re-fighting a past war.

Are these wars providing contemporary evidence of antagonistic leaders who are caught up in mythical battles between cosmic good and evil? These recurrent historical patterns prompt grave concerns about perpetuating future terroristic attacks and subsequent war. Obviously defensive concerns, deception, delays and stalling are tactics used by aggressive nations in perceiving wickedness and evil.

**Deception & Delay:**

A typical human response to difficult problems is to delay dealing with the intimidating conflicts if deception and denial are not possible. Often national leaders and family members hope that the threatening problems will go away if ignored. People handle the stresses of prolonged conflicts that become oppressive with a range of collective patterns. In many cultures, people develop cosmic stories about future hope that oppressed people hold to as they wait patiently for a better world. Mythical stories celebrate heroic figures who valiantly cope with challenging threats. Box 8-2 describes a myth widely known around the world when fears preoccupy and control people.

> **Box 8-2: We're Not in Kansas Anymore, Toto[2]**
>
> In "The Wizard of Oz," Dorothy, the heroine, lives with her uncle and aunt in oppressive conditions on their farm in Kansas. She is swept away by a violent tornado along with her little dog, Toto, to a fairytale "Land of the Munchkins." They encounter three allegorical characters who join together on a long odyssey into the strange land of Oz. Dorothy finds Magic Silver Shoes that belong to the Wicked Witch of the East who is killed when the tornado deposited Dorothy's house in the Land of the Munchkins.
>
> Dorothy's three companions had previously been oppressed by social and economic circumstances. Each companion developed symbolic limitations waiting patiently for change. Tin Woodman has no brain. Mr. Lion has no courage. Mr. Scarecrow has no heart. Together their limited capacities are tested. The Wicked Witch of the West uses her evil cunning to trick them. However, Dorothy saves her vulnerable companions from disaster with her Magic Silver Shoes. She has now conquered two wicked witches that she could not slay back home in Kansas.
>
> Dorothy and her companions also have to negotiate with the over-rated Wizard of Oz who is actually a bluff, a buffoon and a humbug.[3] Dorothy and her companions who are easily overwhelmed do not know whether they can survive these tests. Once the deception of this inflated threat of the Wizard is uncovered, they all want to recover their full identity. They craftily deal with even more trials before they are restored. But Dorothy and her dog, Toto, have a deep desire to find their way back home to their family in Kansas.
>
> Testing each character adds to the drama of this winsome story. But delays provide Dorothy and her three companions with time to help them overcome their handicaps as they each become proudly successful as heroic figures. They liberate the oppressed inhabitants from their enslaving enemy to become free and happy. In their persistence for solving problems, Dorothy and her transformed companions discover patience, courage, intelligence and compassion. Naturally, children and adults in difficult relationships around the world find this magical story immensely appealing as they perceive bewildering wickedness.

In the "The Wizard of Oz", there are heroic accounts about coping with wicked witches, oppressive circumstances and natural disaster. Heroic figures mythically confront threatening forces in frustrating battles for freedom and control. This allegory portrays struggles between perceptions of cosmic good and evil. These classic dynamics of villains and heroic figures are vividly depicted in different cultural mythologies. There are seemingly irresolvable conflicts with evil forces. Heroic figures experience many defensive denials and frustrating delays as they make strategic plans to solve incorrigible problems with resourcefulness, technology and ingenuity.

Carefully assessing developments is preferable instead of blind reactions. The deep-rooted causes of conflicts may not be readily definable. In the Gulf War in 1991, Saddam Hussein was clearly defined as the bluffing wicked enemy.[4] The reaction of the American war machine along with allied support was swift. On hindsight, the solution was temporary. These outcomes were unforeseen by decision-makers so that peace was not sustained. A decade later, problems were not clearly defined in the War against Iraq. There were many options other than preventive war or a pre-emptive strike that requires infallible intelligence to be credible. Alternatives to war include thoroughgoing inspections for weapons of mass destruction, negotiations, sanctions, external pressures for disarmament, strategic delays, internal changes in Iraq, Hussein's exile or capture, further containment, or other nonviolent alternatives.

The Middle East is not Kansas or Texas or South Asia. Defining the causes of the threat is essential so that alternative solutions are effectively developed rather than making pre-determined military solutions to fit the definition of the problem. Unwise actions can actually compound problems beyond the purview of workable solutions.

Delays can have merit in order to preclude hasty reactions that are unseasoned with reflection. In both hostile domestic and international confrontations, violent retaliation can vent raging anger, emotional revenge, and irrational hostility. Cobble[5] uses the bluster of the Wizard of Oz as a metaphor to describe the ranting bravado of the National Rifle Association (NRA) in the United States. As a formidable bully, the NRA intimidates government officials, candidates for elections, and court officials in the United States. It denies the accidental violence wrought in homes and the intentional use of handguns and assault weapons by criminals and family members in society. It attempts to stall legislation designed to protect citizens with gun control while denying its vigilante approaches to criminal justice.

Delay tactics can have an opposite effect by permitting an aggressive cancer to metastasize and become life threatening before appropriate treatment. While delaying may be unconsciously unintentional, stalling is usually an intentionally deliberate response. Heroic figures are tested for their fortitude, their determination and their commitment to win against all odds. Human-made disasters such as environmental violence, structural violence and social injustice have tested humanity throughout history. In contrast, urgent challenges that confront families, schools, and crime areas need immediate attention before they fester out of control.

Intentionally stalling about domestic problems in a family can have contradictory consequences. Occasionally a family problem "works itself out." By waiting patiently, the possible backfiring of a hasty but unwise solution does not come back to haunt the family. Spontaneous remission[6] can actually happen. For example, young children and immature youth may have emotional symptoms that can heal quickly if problems are primarily interpersonal or socially developmental in nature. However, the risks of unwarranted delays can permit problems to enlarge, quickly expand and even take on a life of their own. Dangerous viruses and childhood diseases can be deadly if they are not treated. Stalling is not advisable when the virulent problems are not diagnosed for potential future dangers along with timely treatment and careful prognosis for recovery.

International conflicts can be short term although they have longer timelines than family conflicts. International tensions build up over generations and centuries. For example, conflicts in the Middle East have festered for not only decades and centuries, but deeper roots are traceable to several millennia. Attempts to address problems with hasty solutions are temporarily fragile at best. Future generations may be adversely affected beyond the effective lifetime of national leaders who may only be in office for limited terms.

Often people cannot make quick decisions especially when the consequences are unknown or when the objectives are poorly defined. Leaders and their advisors may be insulated in groupthink[7] if leaders dominate advisors so that they cannot readily provide objective advice. Leaders may cajole advisors into providing advice and biased intelligence that the leader subjectively favors. Loyal followers are beholden to their leader for their positions, their professional future, and for sharing political power. Under such compromising circumstances, delaying tactics can actually be wisely discrete. Often the threat of a disaster cannot be immediately assessed for possible damage while the causes of potential catastrophe may not be clearly known.

On an international level, quick reactions are risky without calculating the capacities of the threatening enemy to retaliate violently. The range of available options may be unpredictably violent or even possibly nonviolent. When war is a possibility, it is difficult to estimate the eventual costs of starting a deadly war let alone being able to sustain a war that prolongs endlessly for years. In democratic cultures, public support is enormously important particularly when adverse reports about the progress of the war come back to the public or when the body count takes its toll in war casualties. Consequently, democracies have been reluctant to engage in preventive war that Barber considers contradictory to democracy.[8]

In past history, cavalier actions have had disastrous consequences for nations. Germany is an example of a nation that failed to calculate either the costs or the consequences of what resulted in the conflagration of World War II. German leaders did not carefully assess the determination of allied forces against them in both World Wars. Japan also entered World War II without assessing their ability to sustain a long war against major powers. Japan's quick victories over nearby neighbors, including victories in China, inflated Japan's own sense of becoming a global power. Insular perspectives of groupthink compound miscalculations that occur to governmental leaders when they are particularly under stress to act decisively.[9]

Deliberately stalling has potential merit in order to circumspectly calculate the costs, the unpredictable consequences, and the capacities to carry out alternative actions. Bullies and buffons intuitively manage risks carefully to limit over-extending themselves in embarrassing defeat. Aspiring heroic figures are careful in their exploits because at times they find themselves driven by needs to act decisively. When their goals are highly motivating for a righteous cause, they can mobilize even more of their untested energy and courageous actions. Their immediate goals may blind them from their vulnerable dark shadow that unconsciously seeks more powerful control. People resist changing because of the fear and inertia that entraps them.

**Structural Inertia:**

Social sciences conduct research on cultural institutions such as education, family, government, education, justice, health, law enforcement, social services, commerce, religions, and other behavioral sciences. In long-standing cultures, institutional structures are remarkably stable but vary widely in their capacities to adapt to new challenges. Rigid institutions are very sluggish while others have limited resilience in responding to unpredictable stresses.

## Ineffective Justice:

Political, legal, social and economic structures are critical for responding to domestic and international violence. If a violent husband or father repeatedly threatens his wife and children, law enforcement is essential to protect vulnerable family members. If police do not respond effectively, there may be disastrous consequences for victims without other ways to protect themselves. Police responses can make the difference between life and death, maiming or surviving. Box 8-3 describes the failure of professions and institutions in constructively dealing with domestic violence when justice is delayed, services are unavailable and protection is not provided.

---

**Box 8-3: "One of Those Son-of-a-Bitches!"**

**Medical, religious, social and helping services are critical in times of emergency. The author has never forgotten the wake-up call from the founder of the first Emergency Shelters in London for abused women and children. Erin Pizzey was the keynote speaker at a workshop in the United States on domestic abuse and neglect. A small group of professionals had lunch with Erin. As we gathered, she asked us to identify our responsibilities.**

**Immediately upon hearing that I was a professor, a psychologist and a clergy, Erin retorted – "One of those son-of-a-bitches!" Erin instantly had my attention and that of colleagues. Her blistering charge convinced us as she explained how health, religious and law enforcement professionals typically misunderstood and compounded problems for abused women and children. She recounted how professionals quickly provide ineffective solutions without realizing the depth of their problems with abusive men.**

---

Social institutions are often ineffective because they under-staffed, poorly trained and under-funded. Victims may not gain access to the legal protections they need when vital social services are not delivered in a timely fashion. Protection may be unavailable in the most dangerous moments of a victim's life. Abusive men who forcefully control their families can be very vicious to wives and children.

Traditional helping professionals are often unsuccessful in responding to victims of domestic violence. Clergy often try to ameliorate the conflicts by advising victims to keep the family in tact. Psychologists and therapists are generally ineffective in solving public problems because they identify with the established power structures. Physicians and nurses often under-estimate emotional damage to victims. Police are notoriously hesitant to intervene in family conflicts because perpetrators frequently turn upon them. The court system often delays restraining orders that are unproductive or too late. Social services are overburdened with endless *administrivia*. Structural violence proceeds when these trusted professionals delay inefficiently in delivering secure safety to victims.

Another serious revelation of delay and denial is unveiled in the sexual abuse of children and youth by Roman Catholic priests for over the past 50 years. Two studies reveal that over 10,500 children were victimized by nearly 4400 priests between 1950 and 2002 in the United States.

For decades, these issues were denied by the hierarchy of this Christian Church while also failing to recognize that sexual abuse of children is a crime. Moreover, there are indications in these reports that these are conservatively low statistics due to under-reporting of this offense.[10]

Realistically there is very limited access to effective justice for the powerless, the defeated and the vulnerable masses of humanity. Structural violence is further compounded by social, economic and international injustice that does not protect human rights that ideally should be protected for all people. Freedom is not really freedom unless it is available for all human beings. If freedom is only available to protected people, it is freedom for the privileged who inordinately benefit from protection of their rights by established power structures.

Box 8-4 provides disturbing data that depict how rampant structural violence is against women and children in the world. These data are shocking particularly since they are chronically the result of structural violence. Women and girls are being violently destroyed by oppressive powers that control their existence and livelihood. Gender injustice needs to be addressed in this century by civilizing efforts to reduce domestic abuse and international violence.

---

**Box 8-4: Structural Violence in Gender Oppression & Injustice[11]**

100,000,000 women and girls worldwide are "missing" because either they are:
- Denied adequate food or medical care.
- Aborted during pregnancy.
- Killed at birth because they are female.

500,000 women die each year in pregnancy or childbirth.

60 per cent of the children kept out of elementary school are girls.

130,000,000 girls have undergone genital mutilation.

Between one to two million girls and women are trafficked into prostitution annually.

---

As Fatima Abdullazade from Azerbaijan aptly stated: "Underestimation of the role of women in society is fraught with danger of dehumanization of society at large."[12] Resistance to transformation and change persists. Oppressive conditions for women and children present a great challenge to achieving global justice. Increasingly people around the world are becoming aware of gender violence that destroys women and girls.

International conflicts are accented when there are major disparities between the privileged and unprivileged. People around the world are increasingly aware of economics disparities between the rich and the poor plus the social gaps between the wealthy and the impoverished. Kennedy and Kaplan consider the disparities between nations of the North and South as fault lines in pending global conflicts.[13a] There are flagrant contrasts between access to fairer distribution of resources, economic opportunity, gender justice, legal protection, economic security and political freedoms. Intolerable disparities are the predicate for major conflict, war, revolution and violence. Ruby Sharma has warned: "Women are the canary in the mine. Where their rights are limited, the rights of the rest of the society are in danger."[13]

These economic and social disparities are often culturally embedded without conscious awareness that these are brazen violations of human and civil rights. Many people tolerate unintended accidents and natural risk factors. In my teaching, I identify these disparities in cultures as "socially tolerated violence." However, as people become conscious of these discrepancies, most do not endorse oppression that exploits people. Socially oppressed and economically impoverished people need justice to rectify unfair conditions. They eventually learn that justice delayed is justice denied.

Structural violence is among the least understood problems in international conflicts. Economic injustice in developing nations happens both at the hands of oppressive governments and dictatorial leadership. Free market globalization assumes that market forces distribute resources impersonally and efficiently. The laws of supply and demand often are favorable for the economically and politically powerful. Furthermore, some economic theorists naively subscribe to the pseudo-theology that the market is divinely guided by what Adam Smith labeled as "the invisible Hand of God." Disrobed of this dubious theological justification, these impersonal forces are devastating to ignorant, powerless and impoverished people with little bargaining power.

**Pejorative Insinuations and Innuendoes:**
People become increasingly resentful toward people when they are victims of bullies who are perceived rightly or wrongly as their oppressors. Subjugated people hope to be delivered from tyrannical suffering and undeserved injustice. To feel like victims is one thing, but to accuse them as if they were the problem is blatantly unjust. Blaming the victim is a frequent accusation to explain poverty, unemployment and welfare. Mentally ill persons are also frequently accused of possessing limited willpower to control emotions that overwhelm them. Likewise homeless people may be blamed for not having secure places to live. Insinuations are frequently made that poor people are not working hard enough. Through parallel innuendo, women who are raped may become victimized again by accusing them of seducing their rapist or for presumably engaging in consensual sex with him.

Citizens of impoverished countries experience depreciating insinuations when they are considered deficient rather than culturally different. The inference is that they are inferior rather than uniquely distinctive. Through humiliating innuendo, they are seen as causing their own problems rather than haplessly born into a poor culture. It is so tempting for powerful people to blame the victim for conditions over which they have no choice! Then false accusations can be foisted upon them that they deserve what they have experienced because they did not work hard enough. These deceptions occur when people from developed nations take a stance of superiority while making insinuating accusations of helpless people in developing countries.

Pejorative terms can become devastating labels. Such terms as "homeless," "losers," "welfare bums," and "unemployed," are all used with negative connotations in many setting western countries. In India the negative terms may be "backwards," "tribals," and "communals." In international communication, the terms such as "third world," "undeveloped nations," and "deficient in technology" are degrading terms used to put-down struggling nations. People from industrialized, powerful and hi-tech societies use such condescendingly insensitive terms. Arrogant hubris describes the judgmental attitude for this haughtiness as viewed by people in much of the world.

Unjust innuendoes can forestall comprehending basic causes of problems. Symptom analysis is only one aspect of problem solving processes. Penetrating behind symptoms is crucial to discover underlying causes. Aggressive insinuations often become barriers because these accusations involve placing blame that is assumed to provide an explanation of causal factors. Within families, excuses are easily raised from past problems in the family that have been unfairly handled. Most family members have been guilty of small and large transgressions known to the whole family. Old gossip can coerce concessions to withdraw complaints. Children can lay a guilt trip upon older siblings and parents. In turn, the young are vulnerable to control by either shame or guilt.

Accusations misdirect the energy necessary for constructive problem solving. Finger pointing delays action by playing upon wrongdoing that has little to do with the current conflict. Husbands and wives resurrect past indiscretions as blackmail. Unresolved injustices fester as barriers to moving ahead toward productive solutions. Ignorance as well as innuendoes conceals threats that families and nations do not want to change or transform.

Productive solutions are also precluded by ignorance about the global threat of rampant diseases. Colin Powell calls the HIV/AIDS pandemic "a catastrophe worse than terrorism."[14] More people die from HIV/AIDS, malaria and tuberculosis (TB) each year than from terrorism or any war. Malaria and TB kill more than three million people each year and AIDS kills another three million. Moreover, in 2001, for every person who died due to violence in war, seven people died from these three diseases. Nearly all of them were children and young adults. Horrifyingly, the worst is still to come. The presidents of Botswana and Malawi have predicted the pending demise of their countries if rescue efforts are not made. Moreover, the Bush administration has watered down its commitment to provide funds to treat HIV-AIDS while diverting funds away from treating other devastating diseases. India and China will have half of all HIV-positive people in the world in the near future according to this report because these countries are currently denying the problems according to Feacham.[15] He cites a Central Intelligence Agency (CIA) report that AIDS/HIV infections rates for India will kill more people than would a full-scale war with Pakistan.

Much of the world's population is ignorant of these devastating disasters since old animosities dominate global conflicts. In the Middle East, Palestinians and the Israelis are astute at resurrecting past provocations that are countered by retaliations. Even very tentative solutions by either side are blasted with counter inferences of deceptive motives. Both sides have experienced a painful history of intrusions upon each other's human rights and territorial integrity. Terroristic violence practiced for centuries provide memories for counter accusations.

In tensions between Pakistan and India, when one side initiates an overture, the other side immediately questions the motivations of the initiator. The slimmest doubts about pure motives quickly resurface. These insidious accusations cast doubts upon many past initiatives. Pakistanis and Indians are cunning opponents who know each other so well that they have difficulty trusting any efforts for reconciliation. Paranoid suspicions are fed from adverse past experiences when promises were made but not implemented. Pejorative internal projections are flung as allegations against the traditional opponents.

The Pakistani-India and the Palestinian-Israeli disputes have common features. These cultures have been close neighbors for so long that they craftily anticipate the next move of their contenders. Conspiracy theory runs so rampant that they are locked into each other's deadly embrace almost assuring mutual destruction. One side can do massive damage to their opponent. Jealous animosities feed suspicions like hostile neighbors carefully watching each other's slightest move. "What are they up to now?" Defenses are protectively raised even before friendly initiatives are tendered or hostile provocations are threatened. Like contentious couples who continuously fight with each other, India-Pakistan and Israeli-Palestinian conflicts have developed symbioses that seem formidable.

Sparring is the name given to athletic practice between two fighters in the same boxing ring. Punch and counterpunch, fancy footwork, bluffing, crafty faking, dipping head movements and dodging knockout blows are all part of this violent game. They know how to counter deceptive ploys of their adversary. India and Pakistan much like Palestinians and Israelis have difficulty recognizing that there are other major enemies hiding internally within their domestic affairs. These old fighters contend with each other for survival while neglecting to address unjust structural violence rooted in cultural patterns. Old skirmishes are simpler to re-fight than incorrigible battles. Beating a dead horse is easier than addressing the gathering storms on the horizon because people resist changing their ethnocentric patterns of aggressive competition with old enemies.

## Can Enemies Transform ?

Can a bully change into a heroic figure? Bullies need victims, and likewise victims cannot carry out their roles without bullies. Bullies are caught up in an archetypal drama of self-aggrandizement that is unfulfilled without pummeling victims. Paradoxically, there are victims who gravitate toward volunteering to become victims needed by vicious predators. The specialized study of victimology in the social sciences investigates the symbiotic relationship between victims and violent bullies. To what degree are the predator and the victim locked into an unbreakable deadlock?

Functional analyses of enemy relations are explained in other publications.[16] In summary, it is very difficult for ingrained enemies to let go of each other once their symbiotic relationship fulfills addictive cravings. Both hostile parties need each other to carry out insidious purposes as mutual enemies. There are political, sociological and psychological functions that enemies serve for each other. Moreover, powerful functions are economic, religious and media-driven.[17] When bully nations possess military power, decision-makers over-rely upon war as the preferred military policy and philosophical methods of solving problems.[18] They are deceived into searching for enemies upon which to display their military prowess. Concerns about empire-building are being raised around the world about the hegemonic agenda of America particularly under the Bush administration with it doctrine of pre-emptive and preventive war.[19]

The addictive functions of enemy-making suggests that enemies cannot get along with each other peacefully, but can they let go of each other and still function? There are historical accounts of enemy nations becoming friendly allies. Some bully nations have historically transformed into more civil international relations. European, American, and Asian nations shifted their relationships after World War II and the Cold War. African, Asian and American nations changed their relationship from enemies to respected neighbors after wars of independence from colonial powers.

There are also limited accounts of abusive fathers and husbands who reform their violent behavior. With treatment and maturity, some amenable criminals can be rehabilitated. There are accounts of gang leaders transforming into more productive citizens particularly as they mature. Their personal transformation occurs when these former bullies become change agents attempting to reduce gangland conflicts among young people. Similarly, addicts also can change from their destructive behavior into therapeutic counselors who help unreformed addicts. However, these transformations of maladaptive behavior and national violence reports are optimistic. The puzzling question persists – can bullies in fact transform into heroic figures on behalf of global society?

Over the past half-century, there are other examples of military people transforming into peacemakers. Many veteran soldiers have returned to civilian life to become responsible husbands, fathers and productive people. A noticeable number of retired high-ranking officers and enlisted personnel have become advocates for peace and justice. In fact, remarkable numbers of soldiers have transformed into leaders for peace efforts domestically and internationally. Evidence from the Veterans for Peace[20] provides extensive data of former military personnel transforming into peace builders. They discover that war is not the goal of their life so they go on to find meaning and fulfillment in building peace. Veterans for Peace is a coalition including myself have joined in order to advance peace and justice. The mission statement of this group states:

> "We, having dutifully served our nation, do hereby affirm our greater responsibility to serve the cause of world peace by applying the concept of engaging conflict peacefully, without violence."[21]

These veterans disagree with Hedge[22] who was initially satisfied with temporary states of meaning that people find in war. He does not account for the millions of victims of war who have lost their lives while cultures have been destroyed. In contrast, fulfillment is found in the meaning people find in building peace. People discover enduring significance for their lives while pursuing strategies of sustainable peace and justice for their communities and global society.

It has been encouraging to see former military and defense department people make constructive changes into civilian efforts toward peace. Former military personnel and government officials are highly recruited by companies that produce weapons and lucrative defense contracts. These people know the inside operations and procurement procedures of governments that make them attractive contract negotiators for defense industry corporations. It is also encouraging to see a number of these highly trained administrators, pilots, engineers, scientists, and technicians channel their energy and talents into education, teaching, science, research, the justice system, social services and nonviolent activities. Major transformations necessitate the recognition of nonviolent methods as a "force more powerful" that provides meaning in life more compelling than war. Major research could appropriately be focused upon the processes involved that assist people and nations in transforming from enemies to friends.

Can aggressive hawks transform into wisely balanced owls? There is encouraging evidence that as people mature in social consciousness, many redirect their creativity into roles and careers that directly advance social and economic justice in the cause of building peace. The wisdom of owls is a very appropriate metaphor for this transformation process from the former role of being aggressive hawks. The balance of seasoned maturity helps people effectively channel their professional careers as expressions of their ethical concerns into causes of peace, economic and social justice. Communicating this wisdom to young people is a major challenge of education, culture and religion.

Major obstacles need to be overcome to develop these transformative changes. Rigid role-casting of identities becomes difficult to change. In addition, procrastination, delays, and stalling discourage transformation processes. When aggressive people commit to peace building, they may be accused of forsaking their earlier hawkish pursuits. In conflict resolution, these tensions are solvable challenges that require vision, persistence, determination and heroic courage. Future heroic figures benefit from the models they have seen who are already channeling major efforts into correcting structural injustice and intercultural understanding.

Resolving conflict with short-term solutions diverts away from changing basic infrastructures that permanently transform structural violence. To sustain change, it is essential to restructure entrapped institutions, attitudes and resource allocation. To change the basic economic and political direction of the humongous ship of state, a powerful helmsman is needed who charts the course toward lasting justice and peace. In order to turn cumbersome crafts, there are needs for long-term policy planning, steady navigating and reliable monitoring systems. Many people develop static inertia when the establishment institutions allow their energy to be dissipated by institutional captivity that absorbs all their identity, energy, commitment and motivation.

To re-direct soldiers into peacemakers is a major challenge for traditional military training. When soldiers are trained to use major weapons to kill enemies, it is very difficult to transform them into peacekeeping forces. Duties as peacekeepers involve sensitive measures of policing, nation rebuilding, relating to civilians, and preventing further violence. The reward system in peace making is not to destroy enemies but to promote human development that prevents violent conflict. Prevention of conflict is an entirely different strategy that differs from "preventive war" that involves violent retaliation against enemies. The War on Iraq signifies a change in foreign policy for the United States. In contrast, conflict prevention is a humane, nonviolent strategy. Using an analogy from medical care, Box 8-5 describes analogous prevention measures from health care strategies.

> **Box 8-5: Prevention Strategies**
>
> **Prevention of violence has parallels in issues of prevention vs. treatment in health care. Traditionally, cultures have given great value to the dramatic interventions of surgeons who invasively operated on the body. This approach rewards dramatically reactive intervention to do heroic surgery.**
>
> **Greater contributions to overall health are less dramatic preventive measures such as providing clean water, sanitation and vaccinations. The costs of preventive measures are a fraction of the expensive surgical interventions.**
>
> **Prevention by public health has been under-valued compared to emergency surgery. Both surgical interventions and preventive measures are needed in high quality health care. Low cost vaccinations are much more cost effective than expensive treatment of tragic illnesses. Each culture varies in the relative value placed upon treatment and prevention.[23] The shift toward preventive measures is a major transformation rewarded with better overall health, quality of life, cost effectiveness, and longevity.**

In the world of small-scale engagements rather than huge armies, intelligent soldiers need versatility, precision, and high technology. Transforming expensive military forces into preventive peacekeeping forces is much less dramatic than the role of heroic warriors. The image of truly heroic figures also needs basic transformation. What is highly valued by societies is emulated by heroic figures. Traditional military soldiers have been recognized for killing and destroying. Future peacekeepers will be recognized for preventing, managing, and resolving conflicts as they build democratic practices.

**Concluding Comments:**

This chapter purposely analyzes resistance to transformation and change. It explored the limits of short-term approaches for resolving obstinate conflicts that defy quick fixes. Avoidant defenses are explained such as delaying, stalling, inaccessible justice, and rigid aggression. Dubious measures are examined including provocative accusations, unfair competition, insinuations and innuendoes. Resolving conflicts encounter an array of diversionary tactics that avoid durable attempts at nonviolent solutions. These deceptive shortcuts need careful examination to proceed on the rough road toward enduring peace and justice.

Peacemaking challenges transform traditional military and domestic violence into nonviolent approaches. Transforming bullies into heroes, soldiers into peacekeepers, and expensive interventions into low-cost prevention was assessed. The difficulties encountered are apparent as barriers in establishing durable peace. Transformational strategies are essential to move from violent coercion toward long-term commitments that overcome structural violence. This chapter is a transition toward comprehensive conflict resolution in the next chapter that provides nonviolent strategies in addressing family and international dilemmas.

# Endnotes

[1] Goldfarb J., (August 20, 2002) "Losing Our Best Allies in the War on Terrorism, The New York Times.

[2] Baum L.F., (2002) The Wizard of Oz., Border Press.

[3] Baum, the author of the "Wizard of Oz" illustrates the bluffing nature of the bully analyzed politically and philosophically by Lee Harris (2003) in Civilization and Its Enemies: The Next Stage of History, New York: Free Press.

[4] Ibid.

[5] Cobble S., (2002) "Hiding Behind a Curtain: The NRA Plays the Wizard of Oz," TomPaine.common sense: A Public Interest Journal, The Florence Fund.

[6] Spontaneous remission describes remission of negative symptoms without professional interventions.

[7] Janis I., (1972) Victims of Group Think, Boston: Houghton-Mifflin.

[8] Barber B., (2003) Fear's Empire: War, Terrorism, and Democracy, New York: W. W. Norton & Company.

[9] Ibid.

[10] Goodstein L., (Feb. 27, 2004) "Two Studies Cite Child Sex Abuse by 4 Percent of Priest," The New York Times.

[11] Kristof N., "The Key Issues of the New Century," The New York Times, August 16, 2002.

[12] Abdullazade, Fatima, (2002) Service, Elkart, Indiana: Church World Service Publication.

[13a] Kaplan R., (2000) The Coming Anarchy: Shattering the Dreams of Post Cold War, New York: Random House.

[13] Sharma, Rita, (2002) Service Elkart, Indiana: Church World Service Publication.

[14] Quoted in an article by Feachem R., "The Real Enemy," The Washington Post Weekly Edition, January 20-26, 2003.

[15] Ibid.

[16] Middents G., (2001), "Enemy-making and Peacemaking," Chapter One in Crises in Violence and Peace, Manipal Press; Middents G., "Psychological Perspectives on Enemy-making," Organization Development Journal, May, 1990 also published in Psychology: An International Journal, Vol. 27, No. 4, 1990.

[17] These dynamics of enemy-making are also briefly described in Chapter Two of this book.

[18] Harris L., (2003), Civilizations and Its Enemies: The Next Stage of History, New York: Free Press.

[19] Barber B., op.cit.

[20] Website of Veterans for Peace provides extensive data at www.veteransforpeace.org

[21] Ibid.

[22] Hedge C., (2002) War is the Force That Gives Us Meaning, Public Affairs.

[23] Dugger C., (March 25, 2004) "Deserted by Doctors, India's Poor Turn to Quacks," The New York Times.

# Chapter Nine

# Navigating A Course

**Peace is not realized
until it is shared.**

This book includes major strategies to advance beyond horrendous violence toward goals of sustainable peace and justice in family abuse and international conflicts. Metaphors can help in pursuing these goals such as sailboat reeling in treacherous waters. No straight course can be plotted to sail through terrifying storms of violent war toward the destination of just peace. Without lighthouses, the crew fights abrupt directional changes due to rough waves. Unpredictable gales whip the rudder and bend the masts. The frightened crew is at the mercy of ferocious waves they cannot control. Without a secure anchor, they feel at the mercy of the rough sea with no one to rescue them.

This heroic voyage toward just peace has numerous storms and capsizing waves through which to navigate. In unpredictable headwinds, there is a need to steer with scores of zigzagging maneuvers. At the rudder, the helmsman sets a course that his crew, his ship and its equipment can hopefully withstand. The chapter title suggests navigating alternate courses that can be charted in the direction toward peace and justice.

**Promoting Democracy & Freedom:**

One of the encouraging facts of modern history is that democratic nations tend not to engage in war with other democratic nations.[1] Democracies have been involved in devastating wars with authoritarian adversaries. Barash stated paradoxically that democracies fight very energetically once they are provoked into war, but democratic people prefer to be peaceful. Furthermore, Barber holds that preventive war and democracy are actually contradictory.[2]

Kupchan recognizes that Great Britain and America engaged in the War of 1812 at early stages of democracy and that Americans also fought a Civil War.[3] There are three constraints why democracies avoid war according to Kupchan: 1) Popular opposition to incurring the costs of conflicts; 2) Tendencies to produce centrist and moderate policies; and 3) Democratic states that respect the rule of law at home are likely to abide by established norms of democracy in foreign policy.

The logic of Fukuyama goes further in advocating democratic governance. He holds that as democracy becomes more universal, states regard other democracies as equals thereby fulfilling irrational needs to seek superiority. As democracies become more universal they may accord one another recognition and dignity, thereby eradicating war. Fukuyama predicts that the ability of democracy to pacify politics within the state will also apply to politics between states. He concludes, therefore, that liberal democracy will lead to the disappearance of traditional geopolitical competition that will bring history to an end.[4] Fukuyama's hypothesis is criticized by Kupchan's[5] who claims that the international system is not itself democratic and equalitarian.

Moreover, Harris perceptively evaluates Fukuyama views about the end of history by offering his own ideas of "the next stage of history."[6]

These analysts evaluate the promise of democracy in national and international affairs. Because democracies tend to avoid war with each other, it is logical to promote democratic governments, institutions, citizenship and social practices. Fortunately, there has been major progress in fostering democracies in the world in modern history. A century ago there were only 22 democratic countries. By 2001 there were about 120 democratic countries or 63 percent of the world's people governed by some form of democratic rule according to Koh.[7]

Many educated people in Asia, Africa and Europe accuse the United States of being aggressive but also failing to promote democratic principles after the Cold War. Fostering democracy unfortunately has had a secondary role in the geopolitical policies of the United States in recent decades.[8] But major attention to building democracy is a special focus after the preemptive War on Iraq with hopes that this effort will influence other nations in the Middle East toward democratic practices. However, the results are not available at this time since these claims for the expansion of democracy in the Middle East is an uncertain empirical question that is currently being tested.

Researchers who study political systems along with international travelers discover that concepts about democracy are not uniform. There are different shapes and features of democratic governments around the world. One essential feature of a democratic society is freedom for citizens to vote for their leaders without coercive threats, along with having a choice between different candidates from multiple political parties. Free elections are a key feature of democracy provided by a variety of constitutions in nations ruled by law rather than at the caprice of rulers. Civil, political, social, economic and human rights are generally protected by constitutions in democracies.

Ferguson[9] cautions that there is something paradoxical and counter-productive about "imposing" democracy and freedom on another country. People in a democracy have to freely exercise their civic responsibilities that extend far beyond sham voting in contrived elections. An important hallmark of a vigorous democracy involves responsible citizenship in public affairs. Democracies are subject to being captured by economic interests or political ideologies. Globalization may be a captive of free market capitalism. Economic captivity of democracy is compounded by disengagement in civic affairs by citizens who express an attitude of "leave-us-alone."[10] Disengaged citizens easily turn democracy over to unelected experts, special economic interests and business leaders rather than elected officials.

Turning to micro family relations, there are convincing reasons to advance democratic and equalitarian patterns. Since democracies have an impressive track record of peaceful relations with other democracies, important challenges arise about fostering democratic processes in family affairs. But how could democratic practices be incorporated into domestic family relations? Traditionally authoritarian control by males is the cultural norm for many families around the world. This patriarchal dominance aggravates violent family abuse. So how can families be more equalitarian rather than authoritarian?

Patriarchal practices dominate the wellbeing of women and children when cultural and religious traditions are exploited to control family practices. As a result, economic rights and legal codes are employed to influence inheritance and property rights. These major legal, religious and social institutions are not easily transformed by modern challenges to these customs. Shared decision-making would certainly promote more equalitarian marriages. Expressing individual rights within the family would be essential while respecting the rights of others.

Another hallmark of a democratic family is that personal choices be commensurate with demonstrated capacities for responsibility. Both children's and parental rights need to be properly balanced with responsibilities appropriate to each person's maturity. Violations of the rights of grandparents and relatives have become essential concerns in marital separations and divorces. When parents divorce there are serious implications for relatives. Grandparents are still grandparents even when parents of their grandchildren divorce. Relatives continue to be relatives even in cases where there are very strained family relationships. Attention to the rights of relatives and friends warrants careful attention rather than excluding them.

Empirical studies and research are needed to transform violent conflicts into equalitarian practices that are democratic in modern families. It is also important to recognize free choices simultaneously bring greater existential anxiety and fears that produce many psychological tensions.[11] Freedom does not automatically result in peaceful tranquility in either intra-personal or interpersonal relations. Accountable responsibility is essential in exercising rights and freedoms individually and collectively. With changing definitions of the "family," there are increasingly complex issues affecting marriage, family and children.

**Flexible Positions**

Obtrusive rigidity is a major barrier in resolving human problems. When parties take frozen positions, there is limited hope for negotiated compromises or mediated agreements that are mutually satisfactory. When contending parties inflexibly protect unbending positions, they interfere with efforts for arriving at agreements. Elasticity is a very desirable quality in family conflicts and international disputes. Protecting particular opinions can become impenetrable walls around national or personal fortresses. Hostile comments, psychological damage or physical abuse all are types of domestic violence suffered in dysfunctional families. When disputing contenders deadlock, their unyielding positions quickly become apparent.

Inequalities in power positions are frequently entrenched deeply into people's psyches. Strong convictions are commendable when considered in their proper context. However, there are very few absolute positions that are universal in my experience. Is not the frequent use of the term "ABSOLUTELY" in contemporary media parlance a possible symptom of stubbornness in human discourse? Intolerant people believe that their personal assertions are absolute positions that should remain unchallenged. If another person expresses reservations, the suppleness of their relationship reduces sharply.

Absolute monarchies are a vestige of past history associated with the ignominious divine right of kings. Monarchs who assumed that it was their distinctive destiny to rule by divine right disillusioned themselves about the ultimate bases of authority. For periods of history, their subjects were duped into becoming vassals locked into medieval feudalism that still continues in regions of the world. Nepal is a country where royalty still continue a delusional fantasy while their parliament tries to establish shared authority.[12] Dictatorial leaders, who misinterpret a one-time referendum as a mandate of the people, perpetuate their own need for power. Even democratically elected leaders wisely recognize the tentativeness of their term in office.

Refusal to bring personal suppleness to the bargaining table is characteristic of arrogant authoritarian leaders in international relations. Inflexible foreign policies reflect the agendas of authoritarian leaders who simplify complex issues. Naturally conflicting parties have interests and values to protect, but announcements of non-negotiable positions contribute to fossilizing global relations.

Rigid positions prompt accusations of arrogance, inflexibility, unilateralism, and defiance of global realities in international and domestic affairs. Porous positions are more penetrable in providing greater hope for mutual agreements among both nations and family members. Discovering joint interests and shared values provides greater likelihood for progress toward peaceful relations without all the baggage of ideologically-driven human worldviews. Both families and international relations benefit from democratic decision-making for building peace, justice and global goodwill.

**Active Listening:**
I have difficulty hearing due to nerve ending damage in my inner ear that was aggravated by exposure to engines of loud military aircraft and heavy equipment. Both by personal inclination and in professional training, I make deliberate efforts to listen carefully to what other people communicate verbally as well as careful observation of their nonverbal behavior. It is a major challenge to listen actively plus tuning in with a third ear. This involves listening both to what is said while simultaneously noticing the nuances of how it is stated and reasoned.

Emotional meanings are also extremely important in psychologically understanding people. Deliberate concentration is continuously needed to hear what is cognitively stated and emotionally expressed while focusing on shades of non-verbal communications. Both content and feelings are critically important in interpersonal conversation.[13] Box 9-1 provides several examples of "hearing with a fourth ear" to illustrate the capacity to observe what is not stated or not yet mastered by teenagers, close-minded adults and national leaders.

> **Box 9-1: What's Missing?**
>
> Several examples clarify the function of fourth ear listening. A teenager in trouble with an authority figure like a teacher, a policeman or a parent may graphically describe problems other people cause. Due to their adolescent egocentrism, teenagers have limited sense of their own responsibility for conflicts. Teenagers[14] notoriously blame external sources for their problems without recognizing their own complicity.
>
> In domestic conflicts, adult family members may also blame someone else for their problems. Many blame the "goberment," the neighborhood, the schools or the economy. They also have major difficulties hearing each other. With limited listening skills, family conversations quickly deteriorate into verbal battles of defending themselves while accusing others for their difficulties. Although the blame game cannot be entirely solved by the fourth ear, active listening can ameliorate many problems.
>
> Accusations and counter-accusations in international affairs become even more complicated with limited understanding of diverse cultural worldviews. While diplomats are trained to develop special listening skills, heads of government often have notoriously narrow perspectives in understanding each other. Self-preservation is promoted at the expense of understanding deep cultural chasms. Unilateral pronouncements and monologues are tossed out like weapons into the morass of misperceptions. At times it is surprising there are not more wars and conflicts.

This "fourth ear" senses what is not stated verbally plus noticing what is incongruent non-verbally in interpersonal communications. These skills deduce omissions by another person in their efforts to communicate. Blunders can be made unconsciously, or can be completely outside the person's conscious awareness. Experienced therapists note what is verbally omitted, misstated, or unexpressed emotionally. Sensing the relevant omissions requires the understanding of complex theoretical frameworks about personality and cultural values in order to comprehend what is missing in communications. The insights of psychology help sensitize people to nuances about what is left out. These subtle clues help identify what is neglected by people that substantially contributes to understanding the roots of conflicts in depth.

### Commercial & Professional Transactions:

Business people have long known that negotiations for commercial transactions are much more likely to arrive at workable agreements when both parties sense that they have each been understood by the other party. This fact has promising contributions for addressing conflicts that need resolution in geopolitical affairs and economic globalization. Intercultural challenges in languages and customs make these transactions even more crucial as illustrated in Box 9-2 confirmed in my four trips to South Asia.

> **Box 9-2: India and Pakistani Rotarians**
>
> **More than 24,000 people from over 120 countries participated in the 2001 International Rotary Convention. Among these Rotarians were over 1000 registrants from India and Pakistan. One of their common bonds was their commitment to advancing Rotary International goals of peace and world understanding.**
>
> **Many delegates from India and Pakistan also have extensive business relationships and professional exchanges. They quickly exchange viewpoints and mutual interests even though their respective governments have policy differences and violent skirmishes. Their mutual understanding during nearly 60 years of conflict has promising implications for promoting peaceful relations.**

The leaders of the governments of Pakistan and India have major difficulty arranging meetings let alone arriving at peaceful agreements. Exchanges early in 2004 between leaders of these two nations hopefully may become constructive negotiations. These meetings can build on the experience between business people and professionals from these conflicting countries who have positive ties through trade and commerce.

Two recent sources confirm this constructive influence of commercial ties and professional exchanges in ameliorating tensions between India and Pakistan. Nafisa Hoodbhoy reports how women from Pakistan and India conducted constructive exchanges on peace, gender violence and justice. These women overcame differences officially advocated by the leaders of their governments. In fact, these women recognized "how governments on each side had hijacked discourse to portray the other as the 'enemy,'" according to Hoodbhoy.[15]

A second analysis reports how major commercial ties influenced reduction of India-Pakistani tensions. According to Friedman, India's huge software and growing information technology industry "essentially told the nationalist Indian government to cool it,"[16] referring to potential war with Pakistan. Representatives for these industries warned their national leaders that if war broke out, commercial transactions with India and western information technology would detrimentally impaired in crucial commercial business.

In many region of the world, reducing international tensions serves commercial interests. Rival nations generally benefit from business transactions, commercial trade, and professional exchanges. It is important that these interactions occur between people from different cultures who have basically equal status.[17] Kupchan[18] challenges the durability of commercial interdependence for bolstering peace based upon his historical analysis of broken trade relationships over the past several centuries. He also sees the entanglements of Friedman's "golden jacket" globalization as very temporary when political alliances shift into hostile relations.

Naturally, not all international conflicts can be ameliorated through regular commercial and professional relations. But interdependence of global markets does under gird vital understanding rather than threaten hostilities. The North American trade agreements exemplify peaceful relations among Canada, Mexico and the United States. China's role in international trade provides another case of increasingly strong economic relations conducive to international cooperation.

In domestic relations, problems experienced by families are better served when professionals from public and private family services are coordinated. Social, legal and health services complement each other with cooperation rather than competitive turfism and ultra compartmentalization.[19] The efficient coordination of public and private services is notoriously lacking in public health services and private social agencies. Many intra-governments and private agencies have limited interaction to coordinate social, housing, educational, legal protective and health service so that families may not discover access. Falling between the cracks between agencies often occurs without intentional cooperation among agencies for the ultimate benefit of families instead of the narrow benefit of specialized departments. There are parallel needs for cooperation in governmental and non-governmental humanitarian services.

**Scheduled Discourse:**

Dispute resolution involves bringing conflicting parties together to consider alternative approaches. Professional third parties interested in promoting peace and justice provide appropriate forums and meetings for discourse. Both diplomatic and organization officials are among the best experts in bringing people together to explore mutual concerns. These experts are more effective when they are free of vested economic interests in the outcomes.

Brokering peaceful negotiations is among the most challenging functions of world leaders at the international level. But where are the world leaders who have sufficient stature and credible experience to bring conflicting parties together for dialogue on sustainable peace? Few current world leaders are known for promoting peace processes except when they are making public statements. It is fortunate if international leaders are on "speaking terms" through effective diplomatic relations when they have conflicting agendas. Modern transportation, media and technology provide increasing means to know each other firsthand in face-to-face meetings. Miscommunications can be reduced when leaders and citizens are experienced in intercultural relations.

International crises provide unexpected opportunities for engaging in many interactions. By the time nations are polarized during emergencies, the chances for developing personal acquaintance with other leaders may have already become testy. Continuous working relationships are very essential for reducing disasters. Precautionary measures in global understanding are critical to avert misunderstandings and "preemptive wars" that can quickly elevate to global crises. The processes of conflict management are much more effective than the reactive methods of crises management in reducing tensions and securing peaceful agreements.

Delicate relations would be beneficial for more international leaders to cultivate. The difficult middle ground between benign neglect and intrusive intervention applies to family therapy and international conflicts. There is a common sense guideline that often works in threading the narrow road. This guideline suggests a middle ground between "showing interest and showing too much interest." Highly reliable intelligence is essential is arriving at decisions that include confrontations. Conflicting parties quickly see outside interventions as aggressive impositions on their sovereign turf. National leaders guard their own national sovereignty by quickly labeling outside interference as meddling in their internal affairs.

However, the leverage of world opinion has a powerful wedge upon most governments to amend their involvement or neglect in threatening situations. The role of the United Nations is uniquely valuable in providing a forum for world discussions about potential violent outbreaks. As globalization increases, the need for effective international institutions increases. International courts, laws and legal procedures are essential in a world that has numerous unresolved conflicts.

There are only a limited number of roles woven into the fabric of societies that provide preventive services for families and individuals. Among them are humanitarian efforts, community organizations, and charitable philanthropists to build trusting relations with destitute families. In Europe and Japan, educators traditionally are expected to provide parents with guidance about their child's progress. In law enforcement in many countries, police primarily react to complaints with criminal investigations. New models of preventive services expect police officers to take a proactive role to protect their community by anticipating crime and violence. This proactive model of peacekeeping takes deliberate training and recognition different from traditional methods of patrolling the streets. Police effectively organize community meetings in which forums provide expert educational and preventive approaches to address problems. Box 9-3 outlines concrete approaches for improving discourse in domestic and international relations.

> **Box 9-3: Advancing Human Discourse**
>
> ♦ **Culturally:**
>   - Cultivating respect for diversity.
>   - Communicating in common language.
>   - Discourse at family tables.
>   - Religious rituals, teachings, meditation and prayer.
>   - Appreciating visual and performing arts.
>
> ♦ **Educationally:**
>   - Researching substantive historical issues.
>   - Training facilitators, mediators and negotiators.
>   - Integrating disciplines and knowledge.
>   - Developing skills in creative problem solving.
>   - Encouraging multi-disciplinary studies.
>
> ♦ **Organizationally:**
>   - Sharing power and control.
>   - Flattening organizational structures.
>   - Fostering collaborative teamwork.
>   - Reducing differentiated specializations.
>   - Experiential training.
>
> ♦ **Communications:**
>   - Utilizing interactive communication.
>   - Cultivating skills in listening, writing, speaking, & dialogue.
>   - Reinforcing objective accuracy.
>   - Sharing information technology.
>
> ♦ **Political Economy:**
>   - Democratizing decision-making.
>   - Analyzing public issues in depth.
>   - Participating in civic affairs.
>   - Fostering equalities rather than disparities.
>
> ♦ **Internationally:**
>   - Partnership exchanges.
>   - United Nations forums.
>   - World security and order organizations.
>   - Trade and commercial relations.
>
> ♦ **Justice:**
>   - International Law and Courts.
>   - Alternatives to violence.
>   - Legal contracts.
>   - Global citizenship.

Many hospitals try to provide preventive programs and health education about new approaches to illnesses, attacks and accidents. Proactive educational institutions have possibilities along with the public service roles of print, broadcast and internet media. Judicial and educational leaders increasingly cooperate in truancy prevention and juvenile crime abatement. In all of these approaches, the educational role of media provides immense potential for public awareness, crime prevention, and community forums. Educational exchanges provide promising long-term benefits in which people of different cultures learn from each other. As a major benefit, participants learn to respectfully appreciate people from different traditions. Even more important is what participants learn about themselves because international education can be a transformative experience.

In order to engage in productive discussion, preliminary efforts are needed to initiate discussions among disputing parties. Stalemating can impede progress toward resolving conflicts by people who are notorious conversation stoppers. They make unfounded accusations about remote conflicts of interests, insinuations about subjectivity, and speculations about consequences. A favorite tactic of passive aggressive people is to be silent which has a double edge in conversations. Productive silences are useful when parties are giving careful consideration to their next comment by thinking through the implications of the exchange. Then there are silences when "nothing is verbally said" that are productive although many words may be used. Empty chatter and white noise are illustrations of unproductive silences. Nothing useful is contributed with such verbal emptiness. As a contrast, there are chronic jabberers who fill the silence with nothing but meaningless jargon. Then there are destructive silences. These negative silences express nonverbal disdain and provocative insinuations along with despicable comments and inflammatory innuendo.

Trained facilitators have experience in advancing constructive discourse even when the conversation is difficult. One approach involves reframing the discourse to new perspectives productive for conflicting parties to consider. Another facilitating approach evokes creative humor and lightness in the middle of tension. At very tense moments of stalemating, ingenious mediators can inject inoffensive humor that lubricates the friction between disputing parties. When innocuous humor fails to re-engage discussion, another tactic involves declaring time out when people can privately reduce their own tensions.

Parties may even constructively reflect on what is happening in the exchanges with tailored guidance from an effective mediator. Many of these approaches intentionally employ psychological techniques of counter conditioning during a tense silence. For example, negative attitudes and maladaptive behaviors often improve when food and beverages are introduced into tense conflicts. These tactics have direct applications to domestic family conflicts as well as international negotiations. Careful attention to time constraints are needed so that productive time is not squandered. Setting a timetable early in the process that is mutually agreeable provides important ownership by all parties to processes of negotiation.

**Improving the Quality of Living:**
Improvements in the standard of living make special progress in resolving problems that have feasible solutions. Improving the quality of living conditions of participants involves more than increasing the quantity of consumer activity when limited resources are available. If people's standard of living is limited, the challenge involves discovering more ingenious strategies to improve the quality of living. This section describes inexpensive changes that encourage people to negotiate settlements of their difficult differences.

- **Civility:**

Efforts to effect nonviolent changes from a sterile environment to a more congenial atmosphere can benefit negotiations. A neutral place to meet can positively facilitate further dialogue. People have understandable discomfort on an opponent's turf. Leaving the home turfs provides a more trustworthy setting. A favorable environment is conducive to better discussion with less acrimony and reservation. International negotiations include expectations of prestige and auspicious displays of power. Impressive buildings with lavish accommodations may be conducive to traditional practices in high-level negotiations. Neutral countries can provide impressive settings although formal arrangements do not guarantee that fruitful negotiations will ensue. Creative break-throughs can occur equally well in informal settings.[20]

Educational settings are inherently designed for learning. While not auspicious, the sterile atmosphere of an educational institution may be even more conducive than other distracting places, crowded people traffic, or busy offices with telephones, radios and televisions. Educational settings immediately suggest that the parties are there to learn rather than fight. Resources may also be available that are appropriate for learning more about the contentious issues between the parties. Investigative research can constructively breaks through deadlock and solvable problems.

Civility is a hallmark in improving the quality of living essential for working toward settling disputes. When people are accustomed to constant fighting, the atmosphere of civil discussion itself can be a positive contrast. According to Carter,[21] societies increasingly lack basic civility in human relations. People are often inconsiderate of each other in depersonalized commercial relations with strangers. Commercial customers and service people have roles that are typically politely short, curt and inconsiderate. In fact, many discourteous interactions are not acceptable in fostering civil relationships. That is why many relationships are temporary because brazen behavior is displayed even among acquaintances, family and friends. These audacious practices are not limited to America but are evident many places around the world.

When people experience cordial relations, a positive cycle of polite behavior is advanced. Giving a compliment is so inexpensive that it is often unintentionally overlooked. A simple "thank you" improves interpersonal relationships. Small gestures among people who have major differences can add a dimension of humanness to negotiations. All people have personal feelings that can be acknowledged even by disagreeable people. Understanding someone's feelings does not mean agreement.

In India, I have repeatedly been intrigued how effective "felicitations" are in fostering cordial civility. While many occasions are started with lighting a "Lamp of Enlightenment," the concluding felicitations are typically ingratiating experiences. Gratitude is lavishly expressed on behalf of the entire gathering. These gracious comments provide recognition of people who made special contributions to the occasion. The dividends for saying thank you far exceed the costs. Felicitations set a tone that conditions people to generously appreciate each other.

- **Women's Development:**

A number of communities around the world have programs that encourage the economic independence of people with limited opportunities. Self-development is an effective model for productively employing women. The benefits involve learning new skills and gaining greater economic independence. Training programs are incorporated along with assistance for persons needing rehabilitation. Investments into the skills of youth and women provide promise for improved wellbeing of families. Box 9-4 describes successful experiments beneficial to women and families.

---

**Box 9-4: Property Rights for Women**

Bangladesh established basic property rights for women where traditionally men hold title to real estate and financial property. Over the past decade, an experiment has benefited women and their families. The Grameen Bank of Jobra in Bangladesh made small loans to women to start home-based businesses with remarkably positive economic results. This bank also offered small loans without interest to women for home ownership with the condition that she received title to a plot of land for the house. Males in the family may have had title to the land. However, the woman could not get the loan for the lot and home unless she was given title. Males in the family hesitated to object because the whole family benefited.

Such transactions precluded granting the loan to a male in the family who would more likely spend the funds on non-essentials like a watch or scooter. A mother typically provided a home for her children and whole family. She also joined a small group of women to learn about health care, education, and small business processes. These support groups encouraged women to repay loans. With 99% loan repayment, this bank circulated the equivalent of over $4,000,000,000 of loans to women.[22]

Noreen Mirza[23] from Pakistan reported about an Islamabad bank owned by women. She is the past President of the Rotary Club of Rawalpindi. As a professional woman, she endorsed the validity of loans to women who advance the financial security of their family. Consequently, it is possible to address the longstanding dilemma of women with limited property rights. Financial institutions in Pakistan, Bangladesh and other countries have been able to find approaches that resolve traditional economic barriers that mutually benefit families, children, men and women.

---

In many cultures, women traditionally do not have legal rights to own property. While women have major family responsibilities, they often have limited rights concerning inheritance and finances. Efforts to introduce micro-credit, financial cooperatives, credit unions and self-development strategies have had noteworthy success in liberating women from these restraints. In developing countries, women have remarkable success in launching small businesses that provide hope for the security of their families.

Employing people who have had limited opportunities to work has multiplies favorable outcomes. Disadvantaged people, who have a disproportionate share of deprivations and violent conflicts, learn how to function more productively. Persons from very high unemployment find greater independence that breaks through walls of hopelessness, radical actions and potential crime. These constructive efforts for improving economic conditions directly address problems of structural violence, economic injustice and social oppression particularly for women and children.

Attention to advancing the civil and legal rights of women in Afghanistan and Iraq is a major challenge since cultural practices have confined their improvement. Educational opportunities for females multiply not only their personal and professional development, but also the future health, education and well-being of their children. Moreover, education of women and children reduces birthrates and population growth.

- **Social Exchanges and Volunteering:**

When people are trapped in domestic or international conflicts, they are restricted in meeting people from other cultures. Their perspectives are narrowed down to their immediate adversaries without realizing they live in a much bigger world. Meeting children who have never known a person from another country has been an enriching experience for both these children and myself in rural schools in India.

Diverse people provide additional viewpoints beyond the walls of a home in battle or a country in conflict. An example of a special effort involved a constructive experiment utilized by peacemaking parties in longstanding conflicts in Northern Ireland. This social experiment with teenagers illustrates a new approach designed to counter limited awareness of persons who geographically live nearby. Young people from these opposing communities in Belfast become personally acquainted at a neutral location in this experiment. Volunteer families in neutral countries host young people so that they can experience living together in their homes. These youth learn to help each other and cooperate with others. They experience nonviolent living not consistently provided by their own cultures. This experiment in peaceful living provides these young people memorable experiences in new interpersonal skills.

There are also much less expensive programs with produce similar outcomes. Volunteers become part of these social experiments for living peacefully together. Intercultural exchanges provide alternative approaches to constant hostile enmity between adversarial cultures. These nonviolent alternatives take the investment of energy and resources rather than investing in violent weapons of destruction and militaristic expenditures that perpetuate endless hostilities.

Volunteer service is not widely practiced around the world because many people expend most of their energy attempting to survive. On the other hand, some cultures foster attitudes that volunteering is inappropriate for their social standing. For people with such traditional attitudes, volunteer work is not practiced since it is considered a role for people in lower status. Volunteering produces rewards beyond what non-volunteers imagine. The Peace Corps is composed of international volunteers for service in developing nations. Vista in the United States serves domestic areas in need of social service.

A number of international non-governmental organizations (INGO's) and religious groups sponsor extensive volunteer service opportunities around the world. Volunteer services have long-term benefits for both volunteers and recipients. Broader cultural perspectives and narrow ethnocentrism are enlarged into regional and global understanding. Generally, with more intercultural exchanges, there is greater likelihood for peaceful coexistence for people in the world.

**Placating without Taking Action:**

The approaches outlined above may be considered skeptically if it is assumed that these measures are primarily initiated by "benevolent do-gooders." It is true that untested benevolence may not fully recognize cultural frictions inherent in violent sub-cultures. On the other hand, negative attitudes of cultural superiority may be conveyed that defeat the positive effects of these very initiatives. Resistance is created when people from outside try to introduce programs to cultures without explicit invitations.

Violent sub-cultures have defenses to deal with interlopers who have are not directly engaged in the culture they are attempting to assist with creative programs. While there may be appreciation of the structural violence of economic oppression or social injustice, the interlopers may have limited acceptance in the host culture. Without invitations from the grass roots, the potential effectiveness of external initiatives is severely limited. Without sensitivity to the needs of the host culture, little may be accomplished that is transferable into future action for peace and justice.

The people targeted to participate in social experiments may not necessarily be overtly resistant. Instead they may be agreeably acquiescent to proposals from outsiders at early stages. If they have not been involved from the beginning with a bottom-up approach, there can be resistance to top-down approaches of outside programs. Intended recipients can resist by passively placating efforts by aggressive outsiders. Early agreeableness may gradually change into placating the initiators with deferential indifference and passive aggression. Initial interest by recipients may deteriorate into non-action or non-participation so that proposed programs become wastefully ineffective. Since the ideas may be imposed from external sources, crucial inside ownership from the bottom-up may not be cultivated. Consequently, well-intended approaches can be passively undercut if not defeated.

In failed attempts, hopefully little overt harm is done and reflective learning occurs. Promising plans may be sabotaged without active engagement of participants in decision-making processes. These negative outcomes can amount to non-productive outcomes and mutual frustration. Deeply ingrained problems may remain unsolved. Placating can result in non-action while well-intended initiatives are neutralized without discovering potential benefits. The lessons of the adverse effects of colonialism provide innumerable illustrations of imposing values or proselyting with aggressive religious approaches that are resented. Consequently, it is important to recognize effective strategies for introducing constructive programs designed to address violence and conflict in sub-cultures.

**Transferable Skills:**

One of the key challenges for people learning new skills involves transferring the skills in solving new problems. Transferability from one problem to another new problem is critical in learning. Important ingredients in the transfer of learning to new situations include helping learners master not only the answers but also the crucial processes involved in new skills. Transferability from the social laboratory to the actual "back-home setting" is critical for new skills to be applied.

What are approaches that help facilitate future transfer of new knowledge? A highly preferred approach involves learning the sequences in creative problem-solving. These methods include both learning the immediate competencies and the problem-solving processes applied to different problems. Box 9-5 briefly explains essential ingredients in creative problem-solving concerned with addressing aggressive conflict and violence.

It is particularly important to note that the steps of developing solutions do not occur until major attention is devoted to investigating the problems inherent in the violent conflicts. Otherwise the favorite solutions get ahead of comprehending the problems. Only after there is significant effort made to gather evidence about the facts involved, can even tentative definitions of the problems be provisionally drafted. Many scientific investigators realize that defining the problem is more than half of the solution. From a parallel metaphor in medicine, careful diagnosis is essential before embarking on a course of treatment.

Generating alternative solutions become equally creative as defining the problems outlined in Box 9-5. It is important to create a wide range of possibilities for a full spectrum of solutions. Problem solvers need to be cognizant of the fact that no-action is itself a decision as one alternative to carefully consider. The ethical principle of non-maleficence, meaning "do no harm", should be carefully considered so that injurious damage is avoided. Anticipating ethical and social impacts is critical in problem solving because solutions may have mixtures of both beneficial and harmful consequences. At a minimum, the overall known benefits to be gained from the solution should outweigh the estimated costs that can be ethically acceptable and also financially managed.

| Box 9-5: Creative Problem-Solving Processes |
|---|

A. Identifying Symptoms of Aggressive Violence.
   i. Investigating factual data.
   ii. Analyzing cultural contributions.
   iii. Examining social environments.
   iv. Assessing international dimensions.
B. Analyzing Causes of Aggressive Violence.
   i. Economically and Financially.
   ii. Politically and Governmentally.
   iii. Socially, Ecologically and Environmentally.
   iv. Ethically and Morally.
   v. Culturally and Religiously.
C. Examining Characteristics of Aggressive Personalities.
   i. Environmental factors.
   ii. Genetic contributors.
   iii. Social dysfunctions.
   iv. Behavioral problems.
D. Defining the Problems of Violent Conflicts:
   i. Assessing multiple causations.
   ii. Identifying missing elements.
   iii. Refining operational definitions.
E. Developing Alternatives to Violence:
   i. Generating numerous corrective improvements.
   ii. Applying ethical criteria for effectiveness, efficiency, & feasibility of possible solutions.
   iii. Prioritizing the solutions.
   iv. Establishing steps toward implementation.
   v. Developing evaluation procedures.
F. Communicating Social Policy Recommendations.
   i. Formulating multiple levels of policy recommendations.
      a. Micro approaches for families.
      b. Macro recommendations for state & national policies.
      c. Global recommendations for international policies.
   ii. Pre-testing, revising & promoting recommendations.
   iii. Submitting recommendations for policymakers.
G. Decision-making by legislative bodies.
H. Implementing policies and programs.

When solutions are developed by families or by policy groups, blind spots can readily develop. Imbalanced enthusiasm about highly prized resolution may be a signal of one-sided approaches with unanticipated weaknesses. Anticipating adverse consequences of the recommendations is crucial. In cross-cultural and international policymaking, sensitivity to the different cultural impact is vital. These are very challenging processes when numerous cultures are involved in implementing the agreement.

Solutions cannot be effective until they are actually implemented by appropriate decision-makers and program administrators. On a micro scale of resolving domestic conflicts, families need to be involved in developing the solutions. Awareness of "the what," "how to" and "why" helps them implement, support and explain the approaches to people who are affected. When people comprehend the purpose, goals, benefits and costs of a program, their support and determination is increased to carry through to its conclusion. Considerations about the economic expenditures are highly important in the feasibility of implementation. On the macro level of national and international policy, not only the economic costs but also complex political considerations are very crucial for policymakers to evaluate. The levels of political, economic and social action vary from local, to state, to national to international scales of policy recommendations.

This brief coverage of creative problem-solving outlines the processes for effecting constructive changes that nonviolently result in solutions for domestic and international conflicts. In order to increase the transferability of these skills for solving a wide range of conflicts, it is important to comprehend and master these processes with practical applications.

**CONCLUDING COMMENTS:**

In order to chart a course, a mixture of positive and negative steps have been outlined that occur while attempting to sail the treacherous course from the storms of violent conflict toward the destination of sustainable peace with justice. En route, consideration was given to both micro domestic family conflicts and macro international conflicts. Problem-solving steps were outlined so that these skills can be applied to other conflicts.

Because the journey from violent conflict to just peace is stormy, it should not be surprising that difficult challenges persist. This difficult task faces many conflicts in using approaches of nonviolent problem-solving. Careful navigation is necessary to stay on course. Mid-course corrections described in this chapter are necessary in order to address the pervasive problems of structural violence. Naturally, problems of structural injustice are not readily solved en route. These frustrations are addressed in the next chapter concerned with extensive strategies toward mobilizing, negotiating, mediating and solving conflict.

# Endnotes

[1] Barash D., (1991) An Introduction to Peace Studies, Wadsworth Publishing Company.
[2] Barber B., (2003) Fear's Empire: War, Terrorism and Democracy, New York: W. W. Norton & Company.
[3] Kupchan C., (2002) The End of the American Era: U.S. Foreign Policy and the Geopolitics of the Twentieth-First Century, New York: Alfred A. Knopf.
[4] Fukuyama F., (1992) The End of History and the Last Man, New York: Free Press.
[5] Kupchan, op.cit.
[6] Harris L., (2004) Civilization and Its Enemies: The Next Stage of History, New York: Free Press.
[7] Koh H., (2001) "Preserving American Values: The Challenge at Home and Abroad," chapter in The Age of Terror, edited by Strobe Talbott and Nayan Chanda, Basic Books.

[8] Goldfarb J., (August 20, 2002) "Losing Our Best Allies in the War on Terrorism, The New York Times.

[9] Ferguson N., (2001) "Clashing Civilizations or Mad Mullah: The United States Between Formal and Formal Empire," chapter in The Age of Terror, edited by Strobe Talbott and Nayan Chanda, Basic Books.

[10] Morin R., (Feb. 3-9, 2003) "Leave-Us-Alone Democracy," The Washington Post National Weekly Edition.

[11] Schwartz B., (2003) The Paradox of Choice: Why More is Less.

[12] Shana Rishikesh, (1993) Politics in Nepal, New Delhi: Manohar Publishers and Distributors.

[13] Stone D., (2000) Difficult Conversations: How to Discuss What Matters Most, Penguin Books.

[14] These omissions are not confined to teenagers but are widely prevalent. Many parents blame school officials and teachers without recognizing their omissions in facing up to their own problems.

[15] Hoodbhoy P., (June 10, 2002 ) "What the People Want," The Washington Post National Weekly Edition.

[16] Friedman T., (August 11, 2002) "India, Pakistan and GE," The New York Times.

[17] Berry J., Poortinga Ype, Segall M. and Dasen P., (1992) Cross-cultural Pscyhology: Research and Applications, London: Cambridge University Press.

[18] Kupchan, op.cit.

[19] These were addressed in Box 2-3 "When Departments Become Compartments" in Chapter Two.

[20] Public places are inexpensive and often uplifting to people who feel they are down-trodden. Free public places that are readily accessible include libraries and courtrooms that can also be available for public use. The parties involved should mutually agree on the optimal environment for negotiations that are conducive to civility. Privacy is needed away from observation, interference and usual work responsibilities. Nearly every community has public places accessible for dialogue and discussion for addressing problems.

[21] Carter S., (1998) Civility, Basic Books.

[22] Ibid

[23] www.grameen-info.org

[24] Mirza N., personal communication, June, 2001.

## Chapter Ten

# Collaborating to Resolve Conflicts

> Men do not live only by fighting evils.
> They live by positive goals.[1]
>
> Isaiah Berlin

**Win-Win Strategies:**

In contrast to win-lose competition, win-win competition provides greater possibilities for solving conflicts. Win-win approaches offer options for both sides of a dispute to discover satisfactory resolution rather than losing as in zero sum conflicts.[2] In win-win approaches, there is a need for collaboration, imagination and patience to develop beneficial strategies for both sides, whereas traditional negotiations assume one-sided gains and the other side loses.

Win-win strategies require creative imagination to break out of the box of conventional patterns of settling disputes. Success in win-win competition excludes unfair gain by one party at the sacrifice of the other party. The potential benefits of win-win approaches soon become apparent when rival parties' discover that their interests are respected. In contrast, win-lose paradigms between unequal parties may not have constructive results because only winners are rewarded while losers are bitterly left with humiliating defeat.

Many bargainers do not possess the essential skills for discovering win-win possibilities. Patient creativeness is needed to discover agreements that provide them with a favorable gain that outweighs the relative costs for them. In many business transactions, a win-win agreement results when both parties realize their goals by arriving at a mutually beneficial deal. Successful commercial transactions result in gains for both the seller and the buyer. Poling[3] suggests that building on favorable past experiences of compromise can move people forward in learning how to negotiate win-win types in additional future agreements. Box 10-1 describes cases where win-win outcomes are likely to occur.

---

**Box 10-1: Win-Win Strategies**

**The old paradigm of how two people can divide a prized cake permits both to come out with fair treatment. The guideline is that each person gets a preference. One party cuts the cake while the other party has first choice of which piece they want.**

**In divorce cases, another win-win approach can be developed about the custody of children. Before either parent knows the judge's decision about who will have custody of children, they are expected to agree together about fair visitation procedures for the parent who does not receive custody. As a result of joint participation about visitation rights, many complaints about unfairness are reduced after custody has been decided.**

---

Both of these examples in Box 10-1, illustrate basic ideas of justice advocated by John Rawls.[4] He advances ethics based upon agreements made from what he calls an "original position." He theoretically postulates that ethical principles for protecting everyone, particularly the most vulnerable, be determined from this "original position" before the game of life begins. Before people know what their station in life will be, there is an agreement about what will be fair and just for the least privileged. So that the interests of the most vulnerable will be protected, everyone ideally agrees about what would be fair and just for the least privileged before knowing their actual life circumstances. Ethical preferences are ideally given to the least privileged consistent with Rawls' concepts outlined in his book, Theory of Justice.[5]

In practice, nations and families are challenged to take a perspective that is the fairest to all concerned. Compromise is the middle ground where both sides submit options in which degrees of mutual yielding are offered in order to reach a satisfactory agreement. Consideration must be given to ethical fairness so that the disputing parties approach have equal power in bargaining rather than acting under coercive duress or power differentials.

In international disputes, major challenges are confronted in arriving at win-win agreements between rival nations. Trade agreements provide important economic benefits to disputing nations that may be unfavorable if advantage is taken of the vulnerable weaknesses of either party. Nations naturally are very protective of their self-interests so that one-sided bargaining may result in less than optimal agreements. When favorable agreements are negotiated, countries benefit economically, politically and socially. Treaties that control nuclear weapons and materials present a survival challenge to global humanity. Until nations discover the benefits of win-win agreements, major issues such as environmental pollution and weapons of mass destruction continue to threaten peaceful co-existence.

Aristophanes, the Greek poet of 2500 years ago, provides humorous insight into ending war in his drama, *Lysistrata*. During the Peloponnesian War, *Lysistrata* protests the war by convincing all the female citizens of Athens to go on a sex strike for peace plus seize the treasury for good measure. In order to save mankind from man, she persuades her sisters to withhold all rights of sexual access and household entrance from every husband, lover or casual acquaintance. While this strategy expected sacrifice, it was an effective method of using human appetites by withdrawing sexual gratification in order to control behavior for the common good. Just practices in the interest of global well being can be enlightened by such win-win strategies that requires creative imagination in pursuit of fairness and irenic peace for global humanity.

**Accessibility:**

"Keeping in touch" is descriptive of an informal way for people to be available for each other in order to explore mutual concerns. In contrast to isolation, accessibility requires face-to-face intimacy at key stages. Availability requires attentiveness socially, intellectually and emotionally as well as physically. Hi-tech telecommunication can supplement direct contact with instantaneous verbal communication. Information technology is increasingly available for people to access each other. Diplomatic relations are necessary but not always sufficient when international disputes develop into crises proportion. Carefully arranged meetings by counterparts among disputing nations are essential on these occasions. Preliminary planning is critical for productive summits with prepared agendas, position papers, and analysis of differences in international relations. Accessibility increases the likelihood that the leaders will maximize their interactions.

While official interactions among national leaders are crucial, official government channels cannot resolve all differences. Official policies between governments may not accommodate the need for informal relationships among people from nations in conflict. Consequently, citizen diplomacy can have a constructive role in facilitating informal relationships among people whose countries are in tension. Many times people from disputing countries confuse the official policies of governments with the perspectives of the citizens that may not be identical. There are risks that informal diplomacy by citizens can complicate international relations. Nevertheless, positive impact on mutual understanding can be optimized with dual track diplomacy on a formal and informal level. Figure 10-1 provides a simple diagram contrasting these different levels of relationships that compound crossed communication.

Official relationships between governments A and B address formal policy and diplomatic affairs. Informal interactions are among citizens of country A and B. Crossed messages occur when citizens of one country assume that citizens of another country have the same perspectives as their government when in fact the citizens may have considerable variance with the official stance of their own government. Both levels of interaction are complementary. However, it is helpful for people from disputing countries to recognize the distinctions between official policy and informal relations. Then people of equal status who interact with each other in informal, business or educational levels can constructively foster mutual understanding and respect. While official government relations are essential, informal exchanges between peoples can multiply the effectiveness of official relations. Lubricating intercultural exchanges at many levels of mutual understanding can actually facilitate better formal relations. Dependable informal exchanges and regular official relations naturally promote greater probability of peace and world understanding.

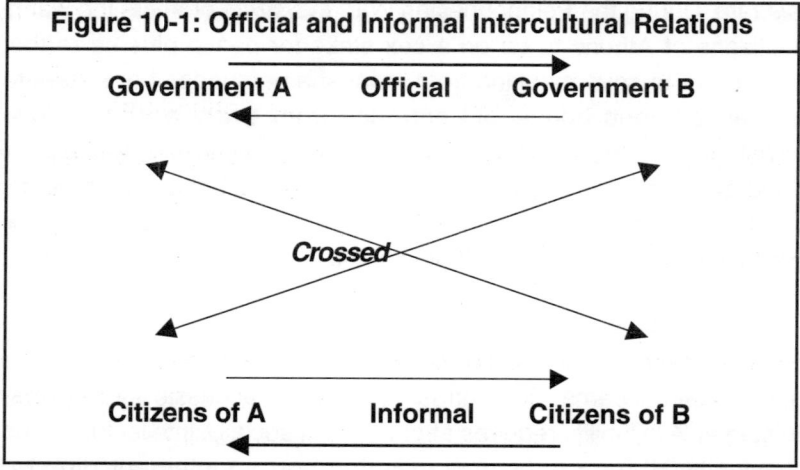

While nations have official diplomatic services, families may not have such tact built into their domestic relations. For families in precarious disputes, there are professional services available in a number of cultures that help families improve their communication. These resources assist people explore issues, clarify differences, improve mutual understanding, and develop skills in problem solving. Busy demands can be problems in maintaining face-to-face interactions. During tensions, personal overload may happen without noticing the extra distress. Abuse in the home is particularly prone to happen around these vulnerable times. If alcohol or drugs are consumed, the family members may arrive home in intoxicated state that worsens as the evening progresses.

Holidays can add even more stress plus unemployment, emergencies in health, financial binds and transportation problems. Too much time together may actually aggravate relationships when people lack patient skills for coping with chaotic interruptions.

The fast-paced schedules of modern working families with highly involved children complicate being physically and emotionally accessible to each other. Industrious people work longer and longer in order to support their families while advancing their own careers in competitive organizations. In many households, the period between 5.00-8.00 p.m. is the most volatile time to deal with each other rationally and peacefully. Children can be stressed from school, activities, teachers, and friends. Employed parents face the stresses of competing hassles involves in work and travel to provide for the economic needs of their family household.

It is more humane for everyone to find time when people are not stressed. Postponing discussions may increase the likelihood that problems will be handled more constructively. Intentionally scheduling a mutually workable time is a critical step in reconciling differences. Difficult as it may seem, "special family times" can be made for pressing concerns without distracting interruptions. Availability is more than physical proximity. It involves emotional understanding of interpersonal nuances along with careful listening to double-check communication for accuracy in pursuing reconciliation.

**Reconciliation & Confidence - Building:**

While many conflicts result in violent recriminations, conflict resolution strategies encourage efforts toward reconciliation among disputing parties. In reconciliation, attempts are made to restore relationships so that parties can live together in harmony without exploiting or destroying each other. Box 10-2 describes empowering criteria for achieving reconciliation among alienated parties.

---

**Box 10-2: Criteria that Facilitate Reconciliation**

**Mutuality** that discovers agreeable solutions to disputing parties.
**Parity of power** in the agreement so that coercion is minimized.
**Forgiveness** when wrong-doing has damaged trusted relationships.
**Sacrifice** by all parties to invest themselves in workable agreements.
**Respect** by all parties involved.
**Sustainable working relationships** for disputing parties.
**Implementation** of agreements for mutual benefit without exploitation.
**Feedback** from all parties regardless of power positions.
**Periodic re-evaluation** in a predetermined schedule of reviews.
**Consideration** of unforeseen circumstances after agreement.
**Expense sharing** consonant with the available resources of the parties.

---

One of the most difficult expectations of reconciliation involves forgiveness of both offensive wrongs from the past and violations of trust in the relationship. Often pride precludes readiness to reconcile differences, wrongs or disputes in moral behavior. Mutual forbearance is essential for the relationship to heal and move forward. Human forgiveness effectively comes after acknowledgement by offending parties that wrongdoing has occurred. Human forgiveness develops more effectively when there are joint efforts to re-establish trustful relationships.

A major challenge in reconciliation is to restore credibility after a relationship has been broken. Family members usually are vulnerable to each other because they expose themselves openly to each other. Married couples are naturally susceptible to each other as intimate love and bitter hate emerge at equally concomitant levels. Partners are capable of either building up or literally destroying their partner. When destructive dynamics occur, couples in the processes of reconciliation can expect that their future relationship will include understandable contradictions of both attraction and intimate avoidance.

All parties should expect to experience personal sacrifices essential for healing in reconciliation. Sacrifice and suffering are among the most formidable costs of a reconciled relationship. Arnold reflected the wisdom of numerous people throughout history when he stated: "…there is no lasting peace without struggle."[6] Without sacrificial suffering there is little likelihood that the emotional, spiritual and tangible investment will develop into a newly established relationship. Relationships that move onward to a renewed level of higher intimacy have potential for even stronger respect and mutual appreciation than when their love for each other remains untested.

Children and parents are capable of the most supportive, and at the same time, the most destructive behaviors in their close relationships. The family is where the crucible of conflict is basically experienced in parental-child and sibling relationships. Family dynamics are the most intimately volatile and simultaneously most inspirational. The family is a microcosm where people ideally learn how to relate to people outside the family including social, professional and international experiences.

Nations have even greater challenges to achieve reconciliation than families. History provides illustrations how warring nations arrive at reconciliation. In modern history, the warring nations of World Wars I and II emerged with scars but also with greater respect and mutual understanding. Many of these former enemies are now allies although not with complete agreement over all issues. The United States and England were enemies in the later part of the 18th and early 19th century. Since that time, they have been very close allies as repeated again in the War on Iraq.

The Ottoman Empire was in conflict with European powers and Eastern powers in Asia for centuries. At one time, Switzerland was composed of warring cantons that now are one unified nation. Sweden was a major warring power in Europe centuries ago, but now has peaceful relations with its neighbor and with nations of the world. Mexico and the United States have transformed from enemies into friendlier neighbors. African nations are showing progress in transforming into respected neighbors. China, Japan, United States and Vietnam have had bloody wars in their violent past while currently they are not in direct military conflict.[7]

Many nations have had civil wars within their own boundaries only to emerge as a unified nation. The possible outcomes of civil war include reconciliation after clearly determined defeat or cessation of hostilities. These outcomes developed after violent strife and division in which citizens killed many of their own fellow countrymen. Paths toward reconciliation have occurred frequently in human history. There are conflicts that have resulted in even greater strength for both sides after major destruction had occurred.

Can Israelis and Palestinians arrive at peaceful reconciliation after their horrendously destructive conflicts? When previous differences seem insurmountable, pessimism may develop that perhaps differences are irreconcilable. The people involved may consider the abyss between them is too great to bridge, the chasm too deep to forge, and the bitter animosity beyond any hope of repair. Pessimists are often not committed to peaceful negotiations or to serious efforts that promote reconciliation. Obviously, optimists are more likely to be effective in processes of negotiation than pessimists.

Can India and Pakistan discover peaceful reconciliation of differences after decades of bloody disputes, war and terrorist activities about Kashmir and Jammu? An overture by Prime Minister Vajpayee[8] provided hope particularly with the initial positive responses by leaders of Pakistan.[9] These initial responses to this "Third and Final" bid for peace signal optimism for discovering eventual resolution of these long-standing conflicts between India and Pakistan. These failed negotiations have been patiently followed by further attempts at negotiating settlement of difference in early 2004 that were being held during my visit to India. Optimists advance the promise of such official exchanges that are further scheduled for the future.

In contrast to pessimists, optimists keep open possibilities of a better future for parties entrenched in grave disputes. An important step toward peaceful relations has often been called confidence-building measures in international relations. These steps can also be adapted for alienated family members to gradually regain greater assurance in repairing fractured relationships. People who have been divided by disputes first need to take small steps toward resolving their differences. Suspicion needs to be balanced with manageable risks by exploring neutral ground where joint interests can be discovered. Many of the steps described in previous chapters contain small openings for further mutual benefit. These steps can be rightly called constructive engagements. They provide for confidence building that encourages disputing parties to take risks involved in another constructive measure. Building trust is a key objective for opening windows that bring parties together for resolving conflicts.

Fortunately, there are well-tested strategies for resolving conflicts in different cultures and disciplines. For people with imagination the following opening present themselves:

- To a Chinese, a crisis is an opportunity.
- To an educator, a crisis is a teachable moment while a problem is an occasion to discover new learning.
- To a scientist, a difficult problem can be formulated into a testable hypothesis.
- To a mathematician, a complex relationship can be expressed in a formula.
- To a policymaker, a conflict can be reframed into a "bridgeable fault line" of transitional differences.
- To a problem-solver, a dispute is a challenge in reconciling human relationships that are fractured but subject to repair.
- To a diplomat, a tense confrontation calls for exploring mutual interests between nations rather than emphasizing differences.

All of these divergent methodologies provide promising alternatives that the creative imagination can pursue as alternatives to violent war.

## Dispute Resolution Approaches:

Over the centuries, a number of approaches have been developed in conflict solving between disputing parties. Three formal approaches are outlined in this section. Each of these requires specialized education, training and practice in order to effectively deliver these professional services. Non-professionals may often approximate these techniques while being hampered by lack of experience, credentials and capacities to implement the favorable outcomes of these methods. Persons who possess effective interpersonal skills, patient objectivity, and capacities to establish trustful relationships are most helpful in approximating these roles between conflicting parties.

## Collaborative Law:

One approach that has received recent attention is known as "collaborative family law." This recently pioneered dispute resolution process provides for creative problem-solving in domestic conflicts with promise for applications in international disputes. This creative approach engages disputing parties and their representatives in patient peacemaking that emphasizes communications, emotional sensitivity, and legal procedures in which clients are in control rather than lawyers. Figure 10-2 portrays the paradigm that contrast litigation communication with collaborative law collaboration that will be elaborated in another section of this chapter.

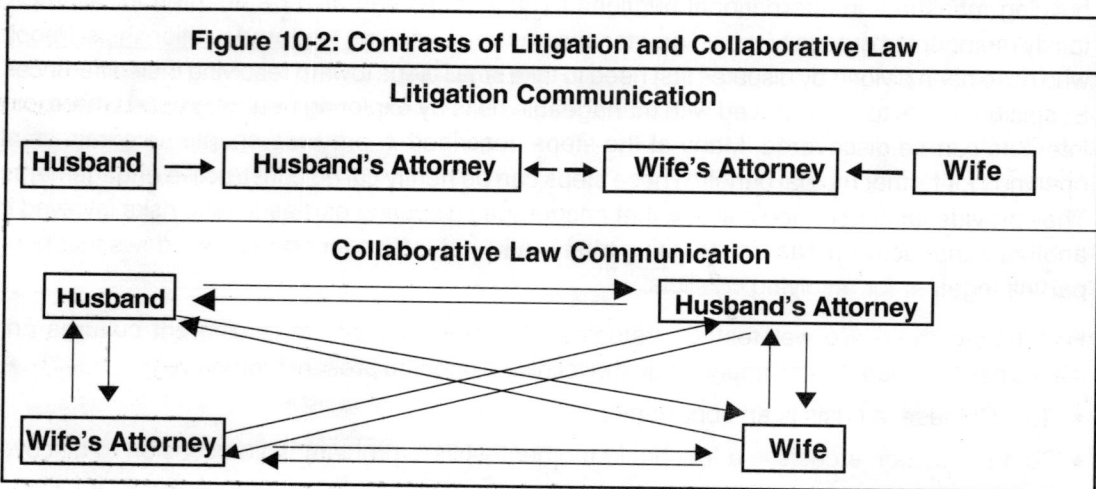

This multi-disciplinary process involves collaboration between parties toward reaching a mutually agreeable settlement in which attorneys provide services as counselors at law. Disputing parties control the process rather than turning over decisions to approaches of adversarial adjudication. Collaborative law communication has basic parallels to international relations. The mission statement of the Collaborative Law Institute is:

> "...to create and practice collaborative non-adversarial strategies to help clients in family law matters achieve agreement in a dignified and respectful manner."[10]

In collaborative law, divorce is achieved without contentious litigation that is expensive for both parties personally, emotionally as well as financially. Often divorce begins with a love story and ends in disappointment.[11] While litigation sets up a couple to engage in losing self-esteem and finances, collaborative law provides for much more likely possibilities for win-win settlements. This approach claims to be the most efficient and productive way to end a marriage that is beyond repair or reconciliation.

Originated by Stuart Webb, this approach removes control of the divorce process from judges, juries, and attorneys who typically manage controversial litigation. There are incentives to reach a peaceable agreement while minimizing destructive side effects. A particularly unusual feature of collaborative law is the requirement that attorneys for both sides to withdraw from a case rather than go to court if it cannot be resolved through collaborative law negotiations.

Collaborative law needs further empirical research by disciplines in the social sciences to refine its effectiveness. It may not be appropriate in cases of that involve domestic violence, substance abuse or mental disturbances although these uncertainties need further refinement and study. Brumley provides 10 keys to a collaborative law divorce in order to evaluate what cases of family dispute that it is optimally appropriate. It provides a promising alternative that is nonviolent while reducing damage to persons affected by settling conflicts. Brumley claims that President Theodore Roosevelt in the United States understood the value of using intellect and tact over violence settlements in international disputes.[12]

**Mediation:**
Mediation is another non-litigatious approach useful in many domestic conflicts when contrasted with adversarial judicial approaches. Mediation is less expensive emotionally and financially than legal adjudication of interpersonal disputes. The adversarial system in civil law that grew out of Common Law often has devastating effects on couples seeking dissolution of their marriage. This adversarial approach polarizes couples into battling opponents further compounded by attorneys who also tear down the opposing party. Any future hope of a workable relationship after one parent has custody of children results in high risks for unsatisfactory outcomes of additional problems for alienated couples.

Mediation is a process for reaching an agreement between the parties in conflict prior to adjudication procedures. People with disagreements are encouraged to settle their differences by voluntarily engaging in mediation. Professional mediators provide a context in which each party can express their views and interests. Through systematic procedures, each party has opportunities to voice their interests, positions and viewpoints. All parties committed to mediation can fairly and humanely express their case while hearing the case and responses of the other parties. Mediators objectively facilitate communication with effective techniques for arriving at mutually agreeable outcomes for the dispute. Research[13] results reveal that couples engaged in mediation have higher levels of satisfaction with the outcomes than persons who have decisions made through adjudication. Moreover, there is much higher satisfaction with their subsequent relationships. Box 10-3 provides further description of mediation approaches.

| Box 10-3: Mediation in Family Disputes |
|---|
| **Mediation differs from litigation and out-of-court negotiations in three important ways:**<br>**1. In mediation, communication takes place with a single professional.**<br>**2. Mediation is based on an assumption of cooperation rather than competition.**<br>**3. In mediation, the parties in dispute make their own decisions.**<br>**The goal of divorce mediation is not to reconcile combative spouses. Rather the goal is to help couples reach mutually satisfactory agreements on such emotionally charged issues about who raises the children, who keeps the house, and who pays whom and how much.**[14] |

This alternative in dispute resolution provides more options for divorcing couple to be less acrimonious in their custody and property settlements. Both the separating couple and their children benefit when the parties are more cooperative in terminating their marriage.[15]

A number of governments recognize the positive benefits of non-adversarial procedures in family law for domestic cases. In international disputes, applications of mediation approaches encounter more complexities than in domestic disputes. Questions of legitimate jurisdiction are often unclear unless the parties have relationships through global organizations such as the United Nations. Regional world organizations are also alternate possibilities for providing mediation services for disputing parties in their region. The role of a credible third party is essential for bringing the parties together for serious exploration of their differences. Nations like Sweden and Norway have been able to preserve their credibility as honest brokers in modern times while the United States has jeopardized this role in the post Cold War era.

There is a need for the professional services of mediators who do not have a financial conflict of interest in the outcomes of mediation. International non-governmental organizations (INGOs) and experienced world leaders may serve in vital mediation roles. The functions served by mediation are capable of nonviolently helping nations in conflict arrive at agreements without resorting to violence, neglect or non-resolution of international disputes. The establishment of world courts has become increasingly important in settling differences by encouraging parties in conflict to seek out mediation processes that are fair and credible.

**Negotiations:**

Negotiation processes are also effective strategies for resolving difficult conflicts. This nonviolent method requires great skill, patience and creativity among all parties particularly the negotiators. The benefits of compromise and win-win outcomes can be pursued with greater mutual satisfaction than resorting to violence. Negotiations follow procedures for discovering settlements that are more satisfactory than if one side dominates, as occurs in win-lose situations.

Over the past six decades, violence has not resulted in a peaceful or just solution to the Middle East conflict between the Palestinians and the Israelis. Disciplined approaches in nonviolence pioneered by Gandhi have not been persistently attempted in the Middle East. On the other hand, serious negotiation techniques have been attempted several times. The United Nations has persisted in endeavoring to arrive at settlements over a period of decades. Both negotiators from Norway and the United States have brought Palestinian and Israeli leaders together in repeated attempts. More recently, former Senator Mitchell's plan has been a thorough and common sense attempt. Negotiations continue to be the most viable option that could nonviolently move these disputing parties toward sustained peace with justice.

At some point in the future, a negotiated settlement may eventually become one of the most promising options available. Violent war is unlikely to result in a just or sustainable peace because even more problems are frequently created by the devastation incurred in war. With capable leadership, negotiated agreements have the greater promise for the most satisfactory overall outcome.

Domestic conflicts in families can negotiate amiable agreements that have higher levels of satisfaction than alternatives of violence or judicial decisions. The approaches developed by the Harvard Negotiation Project[16] have provided the most effective principles and techniques for negotiating conflicts that:

I. **Separate the People from the Problem.**
II. **Focus on Interests, not Positions.**
III. **Invent Options for Mutual Gain.**
IV. **Insist on Using Objective Criteria for Evaluating Outcomes.**

The most important facet of a negotiated agreement involves "GETTING to YES."[17] The discovery of a "yes-able" proposition is a key turning point in an agreeable solution of stubborn conflicts. Arriving at "yes" is an important high level agreement that has potential for further peace building. When both parties agree to a negotiated settlement they have progressed beyond the impasse of unresolved differences. In contrast, many parties make refusals or engage in further violence. These negative approaches forestall settlements while perpetuating the cycle of retaliation with the mutually destructive approach of "an eye for an eye, and a tooth for a tooth."

On an international level, leaders may protect narrowly defined positions that they consider absolutes in philosophical ideologies that they may use to control their people. Political abuse of power precludes innumerable disputes from nonviolent settlement. The propensities of leaders to expand control of their people and their opponents have been repeated historically as well as in contemporary international crises. Their obstinate obsession with addictive power bars achievement of peace and justice for much of humanity. Inhumane relationships cry out for leaders to arrive at "yes-able" compromises. Violence threatens humanity and entreats cultural leaders to pursue negotiated settlements that are nonviolent, peaceful and just. The obstinacy of parochial leaders perpetuates political control over their own people and wider humanity fearful of constant violence.

On a micro scale, negotiations may be gainfully pursued by cooperation between former enemies who discover they can become peaceful neighbors. It may involve offering and accepting an invitation to a hospitable event. It may be the positive response to a marriage proposal. "YES" is an affirmative response that empowers relationships, treaties, contracts, covenants and sacred vows often stated as "I DO!" or "I WILL!" Human social interaction thrives on "YES-ABLE!" affirmations.

**Bridging Walls:**

While walls divide people, bridges facilitate movement toward mutual understanding. Bridge-building challenges ethnocentrism that often dominates misunderstandings that develop from the narrow perspectives of the culture where a person spent their formative years. Amerocentric and Eurocentric thinking has preoccupied Western thought. Other cultures are not immune to parallel limitations. Historical xenophobia and isolation are being tested in modern global relations. People from many cultures ethnocentrically see their society as the center of the universe. These narrow worldviews limit constructive engagement in the global family of nations.

Howell[18] provides perspective about European cultures that have a perceptible advantage over America. Europeans know languages of their international neighbors whereas Americans frequently are monolingual. Europeans' multi-lingualism helps them appreciate cultural viewpoints of other societies. Europeans also read more challenging literature such as novels, dramas and poetry. In contrast, Americans read more pre-digested information that does not require the reader to take the perspective of people from different vantage points. People who primarily rely upon television for news and entertainment arrest cognitive challenges to their thinking. People are enriched by diverse sub-cultures for appreciating multiple perspectives.

There is no guarantee that people will immediately appreciate divergent views of diverse neighbors. International relations are replete with feuding nations who harbor old antagonisms. In order to overcome these inherited hostilities, people with fresh perspectives need to create unsullied agendas that bridge between alienated populations. People who build bridges that transcend old walls are essential in promoting exchanges and programs for discovering mutually beneficial interests. These bridge builders possess the creative talents essential for bringing people together to interact plan-fully and peacefully.

Intercultural communication can help bridge greater world understanding. These interactions expand the appreciation of people who have conflicting views about global issues. When there are regular exchanges with people from other cultures, there is additional hope for mutual respect about strongly held viewpoints. International relations are enhanced with regular opportunities to learn about how other cultures grasp emerging problems. In contrast, isolated people retreat into mono-cultural vision that inherently lacks depth perception and divergent attitudes. Analogously, depth perception in vision occurs when the brain fuses disparate images from two eyes. Likewise, blending different perspectives provides awareness of broader realities instead of mono-cultural perceptions dependent on only one viewpoint.

Domestic parallels provide deeper appreciation by family members who facilitate discussions on a regular basis. If only one dominant voice is heard, the other members of the family become passive if not resentful. "Finding their own voice" is phenomenally empowering for people to responsibly engage in discussions. Creative persons can build bridges of understanding between people with entrenched enmity. Communication requires careful listening along with actively voicing of one's own perspectives. Silence may be productive for brief periods of contemplation and reflection. However, regular contributions to social discourse are essential for productive dialogue.

Teenagers often sullenly "go silent" thereby baffling their friends, teachers, and parents. At times this silence is a tactic used by inexpressive teenagers to avoid responsibility while at other times their silence may involve adolescent immaturity. Developing mature relationships are essential for teenagers in order to develop adult responsibilities. Crises are typical because changes in the volatile growth of adolescents are characteristic of normative tensions and conflicts. Regular times designed to open up subjects with mature adults possessing mutual concerns have constructive influences on stimulating mature growth in young people.

Both families and nations can make improvements in volatile relations by anticipating crises around familiar tables. Peaceful relations are more likely to transpire when regular dialogues take place rather than resorting primarily to crisis management. When discussions anticipate problems, then unanticipated crises can then be dealt with more effectively because of practice in nonviolently talking out difficult conflicts.

**Educating for Peace & Justice:**

The purposes of education are widely disputed among professionals, students, citizens, families, and policymakers. Broad perspectives value education for humanizing a learner's perspectives culturally, globally, intellectually, spiritually and cognitively. Another purpose is designed to educate people as citizens to be civically responsible in democratic societies. A traditional purpose in all cultures involves socializing children through informal schooling and formal education. There is an economic viewpoint that education should serve an instrumental purpose preparing learners for employment, developing career skills, and advancing competencies in professional life. These economic functions of education are predominant in many areas of secondary schools as well as higher education. Additional purposes of education combine instrumental, cultural appreciation, socialization and civic contributions along with unique personal and political agendas. As a common core, all functions of education develop the brain for cognitive problem-solving.

Official purposes of education may also be contaminated with hidden agendas. Unannounced priorities may not be obviously apparent when education is subverted. Political agendas may involve promoting particular ideologies, inventing technology or developing military power. Advancing particular philosophical views or religious beliefs may also be intentionally promoted as functional purposes of education. Another diversion involves training athletes so that educational institutions become the farm system for the entertainment business. Moreover, education as a related form of "edu-tainment" is another diversion in a variety of cultural forms. Then there are practices that education implicitly is a "holding pattern" for persons who have not yet attained legal age for assuming independent living and marriage. Under these arrangements, education provides social interaction and contextual propinquity for finding a mate and a job. This latter function of education can serve on the unannounced of the families of young people. At the same time, these holding functions can become the hotbed for devious criminal activity and sexual promiscuity among youth.

Education has not consistently advanced the causes of peace and justice. However, educational experiments in this direction are emerging. Schools have always had a socialization function for children and youth. The social skills necessary for functioning in a society are very legitimate purposes alongside cultivating cultural values, intellectual and cognitive development that are hallmarks of educated people. Collaterally, learners can learn dispute mediation, respect for diversity, and conflict resolution skills applied to interpersonal problems inherent in school and social environments. Teaching humanistic tolerance is particularly important as an educational function in increasingly diverse societies that are no longer mono-cultural.

Schools are an ideal laboratory for developing the skills involved in expressing one's rights while refraining from interference with the rights of other people. Concomitantly, schools provide important complements to families in fostering responsible behavior to contribute constructively to the cultural microcosm that combines both families and schools. The immediate benefits to the global community occur when schools in all cultures prepare people to be responsible global citizens. Research in these areas bolsters responsible behavior in the midst of expanding diversity in many communities.[19]

Amartya Sen[20] made the case that basic education contributes not only to economic development, but that education also has intrinsic importance to the quality of peoples' lives. The ability to read and write can deeply influence one's participation in democratic opportunities. Literacy helps subjugated women and men to exercise their civil rights while enabling them to demand greater fairness in social justice. Female literacy in particular enhances the effectiveness of women's voices in family affairs. Education reduces gender inequalities in their domestic work and employed careers. Education in India, China and other cultures empowers women to reduce child mortality while decreasing fertility rates according to Sen. In addition, he cites the research of Murthi and Dreze[21] that female literacy along with their economic participation significantly advances the quality of life of both women and their families.

According to Varshney research about violence in India, the relationship between literacy and violence is not clearly linear but more complex. He discovered a curvilinear relationship between communal violence and levels of literacy. In his findings, the lowest communal violence in India was found in states that had the extremes of the lowest and the highest rates of literacy. The highest communal violence was discovered in states that had moderate levels of literacy such as in Gujarat and Maharashstra. Varshney concludes that for a variety of related reasons, India should continue to make efforts educationally to improve literacy.[22]

Specific curricula have also been developed in Peace Education for children at various levels of elementary schools. In addition, religious and community programs have also contributed to these crucial interpersonal and intra-personal skills. Reardon[23] and others have pioneered the basic educational philosophy and curriculum resources for incorporating peace and conflict resolution skills into school programs. Reardon proposed five values of world order that are essential to include in peace education. These include such commendable goals of economic equity, social justice, ecological balance, political participation and peace.[24]

Curricula in secondary and higher education address a number of societal needs from intellectual, physical, cultural arts, nutrition and health education to drug and sex education. At their best, extra-curricular programs serve an important function in leadership, teamwork and interpersonal skills. Earlier comments may have inferred negative views about athletics, cultural and social programs that would be an erroneous interpretation of the author's views. Athletics, cultural and social programs provide important options for cultivating interests, friendship and leadership skills.

Equally as important in contemporary society are the teamwork competencies that participants develop in these activities where people work effectively together for a common cause. While there may be imbalances in many co-curricular programs, these excesses should not be permitted to distract from the legitimate role that sports, music, drama, arts, debate, vocational, social and interests groups provide for young people. In addition, future problem-solving teams cultivate exciting skills in addressing challenges that the next generations will address. These teams learn to cooperate and compete together with each other for constructive goals. They learn to challenge and support each other in team and social endeavors. Many of these become lifetime involvements that, in contrast, are given limited attention in classical education focused on intellectual development.

At this point it is appropriate to introduce the concept of "beyonders.[25]" These beyonders are creative people who go beyond what traditional people ever expected these creative persons would ever be or become in the future. Teachers, parents, and community protectors often label persons' early years with a prediction about what they will become in the real world. These predictions are made by well-meaning people who are convinced what will be the future for a young person. There is a pretentious omniscience to be decisively all-knowing in these predictions. People who protect the *status quo* are particularly prone to make these predictions including traditional conservators of "our way of doing things." These prognosticators give a divine aura in casting molds that are predetermined by their prognosis. Fortunately, there are "beyonders" who make contributions far greater than the forecasts of gatekeepers.

Higher education has effectively provided the educational foundations for deeper understanding of the complex conflicts in the world. History, literature, language, and the arts enlarge perspectives particularly with multi-cultural dimensions. Mathematics, the natural and social sciences enrich the capabilities of participants along with computers and technologies. Professional education, policy studies, specialized and continuing education further expand human horizons with applications to living in community. Refresher education[26] keeps up with the new developments that emerge so rapidly that no one can incorporate all new knowledge simultaneously.

Education unfortunately can contribute to an erroneous mentality of giving answers. Many students, parents and voters assume that education is primarily about providing answers, or training for a job, or becoming immediately employable. Annual testing programs assume that answers are the primary measure of quality education. The testing industry serves an important quality assessment function for competitive and comparative purposes. However, to equate quality education with comparative test scores has become a weapon wielded by politically motivated policies that fail to understand the complex processes involved in teaching, learning and education. These testing approaches employed by governments place undue emphases on statistical results of test scores. As a result, many people are satisfied with quick testing measures without grasping the complicated nature of education. Many do not know how to evaluate statistical data. Others do not realize the limits of rote memory to repeat answers without understanding concepts, complex interactions and intangible qualities.

Questions naturally arise whether studies in sustainable peace and enduring justice are also legitimate purposes of education? Can nonviolent peace and justice be taught and learned educationally?  Correlated with the assumption that war is created in the minds of men, it is therefore logical to also assume that peace and justice are also learned through educational processes. Empirical research provides evidence that peaceful solutions are basically learned so that constructive strategies can be developed for international conflicts. These findings suggest that by helping young people understand peace to resist moral disengagement, it may be possible to inoculate them against war fever and other forms of mass violence. Moral engagement can be a valid tool for peace educators because it can help evaluate educational efforts to advance the causes of peace and justice.[27]

Fortunately there is increasing evidence that processes of peace and justice are being taught effectively on theoretical levels along with research studies that have applications to domestic and international problems. The fields of peace and conflict resolution studies are being established in different regions of the world at a variety of educational levels.[28]

**Concluding Comments:**

This chapter builds on basic presuppositions that conflict resolution can be taught, learned and practiced. The rationale for designing win-win approaches provides a launching point for resolving conflicts nonviolently. Global mutual interests help people discover measures toward reconciliation between disputing parties who are willing to make avail themselves to learn nonviolent resolution of differences.

Confidence building measures provide essential conditions for disputing parties to take risks for engaging in procedures of mediation and negotiation in order to discover mutually beneficial agreements. Building bridges through intercultural communication provides a framework for establishing future peaceful solutions for many family and international conflicts. Educating for peace and justice is based upon learning models that provide foundations for formulating educational curricula. Wide application to schooling in domestic affairs and international relations provides hope for a more peaceful and just world for humanity in the future.

## Endnotes

[1] Sen, Amartya, (May 27, 2002) "To Build a Country, Build a Schoolhouse," made this quote in a published in the op-ed section of The New York Times.

[2] The problems with zero sum strategies in win-lose models were evaluated in Chapter Five.

[3] Poling D., (2002) Pulse Point: Dealing with Conflict and Differences, Workshop on Transformation, Plano, Texas, April 12, 2002.

[4] Rawls J.,(1999)  The Theory of Justice, Harvard University Press.

[5] Ibid.

[6] Arnold J., (1998) Seeking Peace, The Plough Publishing House.

[7] Research during my trip to Vietnam in 2004 provided historical and current evidence for these observations.

[8] Waldman A., (May 2, 2003) "India to Make 'Third and Final' Bid for Peace with Pakistan, The New York Times, plus "India's Leader Gambles on Peace," The New York Times, May 5, 2003.

[9] MacDonald M. and Ikram T., (May 5, 2003) "Hopes for peace running high in South Asia," Reuters, India News.

[10] http://www.collaborativelaw.org

[11] Brumley J., (2004) Divorce Without Disaster: Collaborative Law in Texas, Dallas: PSG Books.

[12] Ibid.

[13] Wright S., (April 13, 2000) "Alternate Dispute Resolution," Austin College, Sherman, Texas.

[14] Wrightman L., Neitzel M. and Fortune W., (1998) Psychology and the Law, 4th edition, Brooks/Cole Publishing Company.

[15] For more information, a website is: www.collabgroup.com

[16] Fisher R. and Ury W., (1991) Getting to Yes: Negotiating Agreement Without Giving In, Penquin Books provides details plus additional professional resources for negotiators.

[17] Ibid.

[18] Howell P., (1990) Beyond Literacy: The Second Gutenberg Revolution, Saybrook Publishing Company, Inc.

[19] Middents G., unpublished paper based upon research in Texas helped to evolve these concepts during community diversity projects conducted in the mid-1990's.

[20] Sen A., op.cit.

[21] Ibid.

[22] Varshney A., (2002) Ethnic Conflict and Civic Life: Hindus and Muslims in India, London: Yale University Press.

[23] Reardon B., (2000) "Sexism and the War System,:" chapter in Approaches to Peace, edited by David Barash, New York: Oxford University Press. Another source is a youth program, "PeaceJam," www.teach-peace.us

[24] Ibid.

[25] Hebert T., Cramond B., Millar G., Silvian A., (2002) E. Paul Torrance: His Life, Accomplishments, and Legacy, Storrs.CT: The National Center on the Gifted and Talented, University of Connecticut. Torrance was the author's mentor and doctoral dissertation advisor.

[26] The term "Refresher Courses" is used in India for professional continuing education.

[27] Grussendorf J., McAlister A., Sandstrom P., Udd L., and Morrison T., (2002) "Resisting Moral Disengagement in Support for War: Use of the 'Peace Test' Scale Among Student Groups in 21 Nations," Peace and Conflict, Volume 8, Number 1.

[28] Middents G., (Oct. 9, 2001) "Peace Scholars," Concord, A Publication of the Rotary Club of Udupi-Manipal, India.

# Part IV:

# SUSTAINING PEACE by DOING JUSTICE
### Micah 6:8

Part IV is the culmination of this book for designing strategic steps that move away from making enemies toward building peace and justice. Part I was preoccupied on the devastating fears of making enemies in domestic family abuse and international conflicts. Part II focused on managing these conflicts in order to maintain tolerable degrees of order out of chaos. Then Part III moved toward resolving conflicts with nonviolent processes of mediation and negotiation.

Part IV offers strategic processes toward the goals of sustaining peace by doing justice. While previous chapters wrestled with pragmatic problems, these final chapters delineate future goals that idealistically project into future scenarios. Readers deserve to be engaged in both an analytic exercise, but also know the author's visionary perspectives and worldviews.

"Re-Marriage of Peace and Justice" is metaphorically explored in Chapter Eleven to strengthen this partnership with bonds of commitment. Gandhi's nonviolent concepts, methods and applications are outlined in order to counter the temptation to continue employing violence to settle disputes. The challenges of suffering are incorporated so that this re-marriage persists through plenty and want, sickness and health, for better or for worse. Ingredients of peace and justice are explored in this chapter from various languages and cultures. Essential conditions for sustaining this partnership are outlined.

Chapter Twelve, entitled "Traveling the Rough Road to Just Peace," explores the limits of peacekeeping and peacemaking in contrast to peace building. This chapter provides reminders of how thorny building peace becomes because people need to sacrifice in order to counteract economic interests and social injustice. Efforts are made to move beyond the negative definition of peace found in ending violent war by providing positive strategies. Essential components for creating cultures of peace are analyzed before synthesizing them into global peace and irenic justice.

Elaboration of challenges for building just peace and world security and order are addressed in Chapter Thirteen. Specific strategies are identified to jointly build peace in concert with equitable justice. Sustainable development is considered key in sustaining a peaceable world accompanied with specific examples. Themes are outlined to advance both domestic and international relations toward goals of building a better world.

"Shaping Tomorrow Together" is the thesis of the final chapter. Conflicting worldviews are evaluated in undertaking this long, rough road from making enemies to building peace. Intentional designs are outlined for conscious control in evolving a peaceful world in the future. This chapter culminates with overriding concerns for posterity who are dependent on how we as their forebears address the chaotic problems of structural violence and destructive war. Creating cultures that establish peace with justice provides the final focus for jointly shaping tomorrow together.

# Chapter Eleven

# Re-marriage of Peace and Justice

> **Peace is dynamic. Peace is a just and non-violent solution of conflicts.**
> *Source: Cultura de Paz*[1]
>
> **Non-violence leads to the highest ethics. Until we stop harming other living beings, we are still savages.**
> **Thomas Edison**

As one of the founders of a citizen's movement in the 1980's initially called the Alliance for Peace, I discovered very early the need to broaden its mission for action. Soon after organizing, we made an intensive analysis of underlying issues involved in the nuclear threats in the Cold War. A serious gap became apparent in the goals envisioned for this organization. Obvious social and economic injustices demanded that this grassroots organization incorporate issues of assertive justice. A new name wisely reflected this mission as the "Alliance for Peace and Justice." [2]

Peace and justice are essential soul mates in order to build an enduring peace capable of addressing the stubborn injustices involved in structural violence. Unfortunately, there has been a regrettable separation if not an actual divorce between global peace and justice. Consequently, this chapter makes a case that the goals of peace and justice need to be re-united. The covenant of marriage metaphor is a unifying theme of this chapter reflecting the fundamental need for a committed partnership. Like a couple contemplating marriage, it is helpful to face what the downside could become.

## NEGATIVE PEACE

When violence rages in domestic abuse and international conflict, there is a powerful desire to bring the viciousness of war to an end. In fact, abhorrence of violence may temporarily persuade people to think that when the battling ends, people will automatically experience peace and order. Ending violence may provide immediate relief for an interim period of quietude. However, termination of violence often results in what has long been recognized as "negative peace" or a longed for period of quietude.

Often people are satisfied with bringing violence to an end that in effect is a negative definition of peace. However, absence of violent war does not assure positive peace and assertive justice. It is true people no longer feel the painful anguish of violence when battles end. Reprieve from hostilities psychologically provides negative reinforcement to end violence since devastation is finally relieved. This respite stage does not assure that the necessary and sufficient conditions for building peace and justice are adequately established. If constructive measures are not pursued to correct the causes of conflict, ending violence may actually result in empty disappointment.

Rather than just a temporary cessation of hostilities, hopefully positive steps will be taken toward more enduring peace. It may not be possible to jump directly from the horrors of violent war to efforts in rehabilitation. There are major obstacles that must be challenged on the journey from making enemies to building positive harmony. A vivid illustration involved the transitional difficulties in restoring Iraq with civil governance while violent insurgency and civil war occurs. In actual peace building, stubborn conflicts need transparent strategies, patient conflict management, and positive resolution. Only then is there hope for lasting peace that re-unites with justice.

**Strategies of Positive Peace:**

Peacefulness is a counter-balance to the scourge of violence. Representative John Lewis, a civil rights activist and now a United States Congressman, literally called non-violence as "doing battle."[3] The struggles are fought with truth rather than with weapons of destruction. The goals of peaceful power is focused on efforts for:

- Ending oppression.
- Foiling invaders.
- Securing rights.
- Establishing democracy.[4]

Nonviolence was practiced by Gandhi to cope with injustice and structural violence in South Africa. When he retuned to his native land, India, he led a prolonged effort to achieve independence from the colonial domination of England. Gandhi believed that what distinguishes human beings from all other animals is our capacity to be nonviolent. He held that human greed is the root of all evil leading to structural violence in forms of economic oppression and social injustice.

Positive peace is much more than the absence of violence. The cessation of violence must be seen as only a preliminary step in defining farsighted strategies of nonviolence. Gandhi painstakingly understood that nonviolence is a way to vindicate the truth by the infliction of suffering not on one's opponent but on one's self. Consequently, positive peace not only metes out friendliness upon external enemies intended to exterminate them or bludgeon them into defeat. Instead nonviolence internalizes the battle within people. This readiness to experience self-suffering is one of the greatest challenges for being nonviolent in destructive conflicts.

Recent interpretations by veteran proponents discern nonviolence as the greatest force with which humanity is endowed. This positive understanding considers nonviolence a force more powerful than even the enormously destructive power of modern military weapons. Often aggressive people regard nonviolent people as passive and ineffectively dovish. Rather than dismissing passive resistance of powerless people, many modern historians document astounding evidence of wide applications of nonviolence around the globe. This powerful force has been applied hundreds of time around the world in the last 100 years with greater success than often realized. Dramatic videos provide accounts of nonviolence applied to extremely difficult international conflicts in A <u>Force More Powerful</u> edited by Peter Ackerman.[5] Additional evidence is documented by Deats and Wink about the global reach of active nonviolence for purposes of positive peace.[6]

**Concepts of Nonviolence:**

Drawing upon the lifetime work of Mohandas Gandhi, the modern pioneer of nonviolence, his basic concepts of nonviolence include:[7]

***SATYAGRAHA*** is composed of two concepts in the Hindu language. The first part is the term *satya* means holding forth the truth, while *agraha* contains the meaning of force. Combining these two concepts, the ideas of "truth force" or "soul force" are derived. Truth as the essence of nonviolence is further characterized:

- One cannot seek truth while participating in unjust violence.
- Nonviolence exposes injustice and violence.
- Nonviolence is the power of the powerless.
- When nonviolence is used, hatred dies as everything does from disuse.

***AHIMSA*** means non-injury in Hindu similar to the ethical concept of non-maleficence or do no harm. Gandhi's ideas of *ahimsa* included non-injury, nonviolence, and renunciation of the wish to kill plus abstention from hostile thoughts, words or actions.[8] Love serves as the means to truth in Gandhi's thinking. He was not a categorical pacifist illustrated by the fact that he would destroy poisonous snakes to protect his family and himself.

***SARVODAYA*** incorporates concern for the welfare of people in promoting the uplift of all. *Sarvodaya* involves humanitarian approaches that emphasize community building over individual ambition. This concept contains a profound sense of people's well being in their community. Gandhi's own ideas of positive peace are expressed in his words "There is no way to peace: peace is the way."

***TAPASYA*** involves willingness to undergo suffering that is not self-serving. Both Jesus and Gandhi experienced suffering in their lifetime. They were bullied and persecuted by violent leaders in political and religious power. Jesus was rejected, tried, brutalized and finally crucified. Gandhi was ridiculed, criticized, imprisoned, and eventually assassinated. They each demonstrated self-discipline, self-restraint, and self-denial in their suffering. Gandhi frequently drew upon the teachings of Jesus that real peace comes through suffering. Both Jesus and Gandhi held that there is no peace except through the sacrifice of peace.[9]

**Nonviolent Methods:**

Box 11-1 identifies methods of positive peace applied in numerous conflicts around the world to address structural violence.

> **Box 11-1: Nonviolent Methods**
>
> **Nonviolent Protests:**
> - Marches.
> - Picketing.
> - "Haunting" Officials.
> - Distributing protest literature.
> - Voluntary emigration.
> - Pilgrimages.
> - Vigils.
> - Public meetings.
> - Humorous pranks.
>
> **Non-cooperation:**
> - Strikes:
>   - General Strike.
>   - Sit-down Strike.
>   - Go-slow Strike.
>
> **Boycotts:**
> - Economic boycotts.
> - Consumer boycotts.
> - Trader boycotts.
> - Refusal to pay rent.
> - International economic embargo.
> - Social boycotts.
>
> **Political Non-cooperation:**
> - Boycott of elections.
> - Boycott of governmental employment.
> - Refusal to pay taxes and revenue.
> - Civil disobedience.
> - Mutiny.
>
> **Nonviolent Interventions:**
> - Sit-ins.
> - Reverse strike.
> - Nonviolent invasion.
> - Negotiations.
> - Fasting.
> - Nonviolent obstruction.
> - Parallel government.
> - Demonstrations.

Gandhi was also involved in "Experiments" that resulted in considerable suffering and personal sacrifice. Discipline and renunciation helped him suffer for the sake of justice. He possessed dedicated discipline to carry out nonviolent methods in the face of challenges from both supporters and opponents. Fasting was one of Gandhi's methods for expressing self-discipline to influence the subsequent behavior of other people. In national crises, when people in India became violent, he fasted until they stopped their violent actions. Gandhi derived his fasting discipline from both cultural and religious Hindu traditions found in the Ramayana[10] and The Bible.

Imprisonment became a badge of pride for Gandhi. In fact, he wrote an essay entitled "How to Enjoy Jail." His distinctive views about the dynamics of social change are best expressed in his own words:

**"You must be the change you wish to see in the world."**

Gandhi was a pioneer in practicing the disciplines of nonviolence. Expressed positively as "The Force More Powerful," nonviolence has been successfully applied to more than 100 global experiments. Over half of these applications resulted in overthrowing dictatorships without violence, reforming social and economic injustice.[11] Additional evidence of the effective employment of positive peace is expressed by Deats in his work, "The Global Spread of Active Nonviolence," and by Wink in his book entitled Peace is the Way.[12]

## Definitions of Peace:

Linguistically the term "peace" provides a valuable lesson for realizing both how rich and how impoverished languages are in understanding this word. Selected languages provide an illuminating commentary. In Greek, the primary word *eirene'* has double meaning including harmony as well as the absence of war.[13] From *eirene'* the academic discipline of "Irenology" has been recovered in the curriculum of educational institutions. This term provides a distinctive identity for fields related to peace studies in colleges and universities. Irenology is directly derived from the Greek goddess, Irene,[14] the symbolic archetype of irenic peace.[15]

Arabic and related languages where the Islamic tradition is practiced provide enlightenment about peace. Multi-faceted connotations are derived from Arabic words for peace. The term "Islam" itself is derived from an Arabic word for peace. The very term for Islam is *Al-islaam* which essentially means pacifying. Other variations in Arabic include *Assilm* which means peace in contrast with war. *As-salaam*, the most frequently used word in Arabic, connotes security. It is a greeting that may be accompanied by a raised hand along with different gestures used for nonverbal communication.[16] The Arabic, Aramaic and Semitic languages of the Middle East connect concepts of peace with justice in *The Torah*, the *Quran*, and *The Bible*.

There are long standing terms in Indian languages that express the profound dimensions of positive peace. *"Shanti,"* the Hindu word for peace, is a widely expressed term in India. By placing the prefix "su" to form "sushanti" one derived the meaning of "good peace" in the Hindu language. The same word "shanti" is the term for peace in both Sanskrit and Urdu that are basic languages in the multi-lingual cultures of India with over one hundred distinctive languages.

*Pax* in Latin essentially means peace frequently connected in history to the dominant military power of the period. *Pax Romana* refers to peace guaranteed by the Roman Empire that overpowered threatening invaders. Since the demise of the Roman Empire in the western world, there have been subsequent periods of hegemonic peace by other powers and empires. One such period is known historically as *Pax Britannica* for peaceful protection of the British Empire. In contemporary international relations, the role of the United States in global affairs is widely debated. History will eventually evaluate whether the United States provides the global peace that may be referred to as *Pax Americana*.

The Chinese language has three prominent terms for peace. *"An"* denotes a woman under a roof suggesting the need for domestic tranquility for peace to be experienced by families in the home. *"P'ing"* signifies equality so that no one dominates another person when *'p'ing"* prevails in their relationships. *"Ho"* is represented by a kernel of grain being placed in a person's mouth suggesting that there will not be peace until there is enough food for everyone to eat. Medard[17] uniquely combines two of these Chinese words, *"ho"* and *"p'ing"*, in the title of his book: Ho-ping: Food for Everyone. These Oriental ideas suggest that peace will not be experienced until everyone is nourished with food to eat. Global economic and social justice requires equality in human relationships plus equitable food distribution to feed all people.

The Japanese word for peace is *"hei-wa"* which curiously has a relatively brief history in etymology of the Japanese language. In daily living, *"hei-wa"* denotes a state of harmonious relations marked by unity and calm applied to one's thinking, family, community and nation. *"Hei-wa"* is never used as a greeting, but it is incorporated into the ringing slogan, "*Sikai kno hei-wa no tome ni wo shimashou,*" which can be translated into English as "Let us do it for world peace."

On my trip to Vietnam in 2004, I discovered that *"binh"* is the Vietnamese word for peace. This nation has a long history of wars with China, with other neighboring countries, plus war with the United States. In Vietnam, this later was is known as the American War rather than the Vietnam War as known in the West. "*Binh*" is a healing concept of positive peace that has special meaning to the Vietnamese who have had devastating civil wars in addition to invasions by outside nations. This experience raises a grave concern whether Iraq will experience ravaging civil wars fed by a combination of internal strife and external interference.

The Hebrew word "*shalom*" has multiple dimensions of peace with justice. Shalom is a greeting and salutation with profound meaning. *Shalom* incorporates the ideal state of existence of prosperity, health, justice and wishing another person their highest good, in essence their *summum bonum*. Physical, mental, spiritual, social and economic wellbeing are all incorporated into the profound meanings of *shalom* and terms derived from it. Consequently, *shalom* is one of the most complete terms for peace known to humankind. In its purest sense, *shalom* incorporates completeness, wholeness and justice. As a greeting, it wishes the greatest good physically, spiritually, socially and economically to another person and their posterity.

*Shalom,* is frequently used in Hebrew Scriptures[18] for the ultimate living condition that God wishes for people. It is intimately connected with justice as the intrinsic living conditions in the peaceable kingdom. Peace with justice is essential since peace requires justice as a condition for sustainable living. Peace and justice are two sides of the same coin as partners as in the covenant relationship of marriage. The contemporary re-marriage of peace and justice is essential for global humanity.[19] An immediate inference that can be from these various languages is that peace is impossible without justice. Justice is the concept woven throughout the diverse meanings of peace in many languages of the world. Box 11-2 provides concepts with greater depth and global appreciation.

> **Box 11-2: Dimensions of Peace**
>
> **Peace is a dynamic process, not a static condition.**
>
> - **Peace pursues non-violent and just solutions for structural injustices and violent conflicts.**
>
> - **It generates an equilibrium in social interactions, so that all of the members of human society can live in harmonious relations with each other.**
>
> **Peace is good for society:**
>
> - **Where there is violence there is no peace.**
>
> - **Where there is injustice and absence of liberty, there is no peace.**
>
> - **Without trust, working relationships beyond the tribal family preclude democracies, business organizations and sovereign governments**
>
> *Source: Cultura de Paz*[1]

Paradoxically, the name Jerusalem is composed of two words. "*Jeru*" means city and "*salem*" is derived from the words for peace. Jerusalem literally means "the city of peace." How ironical it is that Jerusalem has historically experienced a great deal of violence and war. Jerusalem has been built, destroyed and rebuilt on numerous occasions. For both historical reasons and contemporary violence in the Middle East, a common phrase prophetically states that "the road to peace is through Jerusalem."

Jerusalem is a religious seat of three of the world's religions – Jewish, Christian and Islam. Jerusalem has been divided, destroyed and desecrated – yet it continues to survive. The rough road to peace will obviously be a long journey in order to provide comprehensive peace in the world. Other cultures around the world also regard historical cities and communities as key to efforts in building peace and justice. People in India know that Delhi has been rebuilt seven times after violent wars and conflicts. Beirut has been rebuilt after the destructive violence in that city during a process that became known as "Lebanonization." Cities of the former Yugoslavia have been heavily damaged by war involving the violence known as the "Balkanization" of ethnic groups.

Building on this background about the linguistic meanings of peace from a number of languages and cultures, it is timely to fathom additional dimensions of irenic peace and assertive justice.

## Making Joint Plans:

Building on the metaphor of the marriage of peace and justice, joint planning is essential for this partnership to endure. Decision-making becomes crucial as well as implementing plans as partners. Teamwork is an important skill in the complexities of contemporary life, in the challenges of modern marriage, in the demands of technical employment, and certainly in international relations. In marriage, partners encounter powerful stresses faced in living together. Unilateralists quickly discover that marriage is a difficult duet for individuals to be a couple.

When they have offspring, teamwork is even more essential for families and global humanity to function effectively. Teamwork is vital for addressing these complex challenges. Even people in careers that once attracted independent practitioners have discovered their vital interconnections. Physicians, artists, farmers and scientific professionals, who at one time might have independently practiced their professions, now work jointly on projects with global teams. Nations that act unilaterally discover that they cannot function effectively without global partners. Problem-solving by teams requires trusting organizational relationships as a pre-requisite drawn for developmental stages beyond family and tribes.

However, many people and nations live in traditional cultures that have difficulty working together as partners. Without team trust levels, working relationships beyond the tribal family are preclude democracies, business organizations and sovereign governments. To the dismay of many private organizations and international leaders, major difficulties in collaborating occur because people lack teamwork capabilities. According to Harris, these dilemmas also show up in cultures of the Middle East and Balkan states.[20]

On the international scene, cultural differences and language barriers compound these dilemmas for working cooperatively. Even in the face of these challenges, there have been amazing success stories in worldwide teamwork. Imagine for a moment the complex problems addressed by technical space programs. Engineers, scientists and technicians working on international space projects discover that they can trust each other in working together on international joint projects. Colleagues in the Organization Development Institute who are professionals in human resource development describe how the National Air and Space Administration (NASA) facilitate the progress of space program projects. Engineers and technicians from different countries work effectively by utilizing information technology provided these professionals periodically meet face to face to develop trust in teamwork.

Professionals in both governmental and private organizations discover needs for regular joint meetings. At these periodic meetings, agendas can be set to address issues that affect disputing parties. Equally important are the opportunities for these professionals and leaders to become acquainted personally and professionally. Face-to-face meetings contribute to both current trust and future working relationships. Planning, analyzing, reporting and decision-making are all essential on a regular basis rather than unscheduled emergency meetings. While emergency meetings can be essential, regular meetings for joint planning ameliorate predictable tensions. National leaders find that international consultations are essential in economic, environmental and ecological issues. Global consultations are increasingly critical in international affairs in order to foster multi-lateral approaches to peace, justice and trade.

Modern marriages and international alliances need teamwork for planning. Within modern day families, the frantic schedules of each family member are centrifugal. Without deliberate efforts to share, support and plan together, families are torn apart. Setting aside a transitional period for recuperation from the day's demands helps to lower stress. Each person then has an opportunity to download the typical tensions of the day so that emotional dumping can be neutralized with understanding and mutual support. These suggestions lead directly into the next topic. Both modern families and international communities benefit when members jointly cooperate toward common goals and objectives. Nations absorbed in their own internal problems are easily diverted from their own internal domestic interests at the expense of other nations.

**Presence at the Planning Table:**

A planning table with regular meetings can address many joint concerns in both family conflicts and international problems. Periodic conferences reduce the need for "peace tables" which may arise because regular discussions are neglected, or not attended, or not even held. Proactive prevention is much more effective in solving problems than waiting until they begin to fester. Addressing problems in their early stages reduces the damage that occurs when problems are overlooked. Neglecting early symptoms of conflicts has consequences that lead to greater abuse or violence.

While periodic meetings to plan are valuable, they are effective only if the concerned parties are present physically and emotionally. Shear physical presence is necessary but often not sufficient for resolving difficult human problems. The parties must also be emotionally available to each other in order to understand feelings and nuances. These layers are not immediately transparent to listeners since powerful emotions are mysteriously expressed non-verbally and verbally. Face-to-face interaction is essential to comprehend these messages so that people can carefully observe each other's reactions. This may be puzzling to people who primarily hear verbal statements. Emotionally-loaded communications are couched within, between, above and around what is verbally expressed.

Intense communications cannot be exclusively conveyed by documents or messages. Opportunities to clarify, affirm, and disagree are crucial for bonding that assures deeper mutual understanding. Leaders of international governments and organizations discover how important informal and formal meetings can be for effective understanding and joint action. Most national leaders prize these experiences for addressing important issues for confidence-building measures essential in peaceful relations. While personal diplomacy cannot be an exclusive approach for international affairs, interpersonal familiarity can make the world safer, more secure and predictably peaceable. Experienced diplomats are critically needed for precluding violent reactions of retaliation and war. Culturally sensitive diplomats are worth their weight in gold when international tensions near explosion.

Joint meetings take enormous energy and valuable time. The most effective world leaders know it is essential to be available to each other. Many global leaders find these meetings to be essential not only for themselves but for global issues. If global leaders find these interactions critically important, the logical question arises: what about the necessity for family conferences? Couples who fail to provide time for each other may precipitate abrupt separation leading eventually to divorce. Emotional ties are frayed when family members are not available to each other.

The book title, <u>I Thought We'd Never Speak Again</u>, comes out of the experience of families who have had deeply rooted conflicts.[21] The author describes numerous case studies where fractured interpersonal relationships are unresolved when family members are unavailable during crises in their relationship. They leave old wounds fester into irreconcilable differences. Until people discover the need for mutual understanding, emotional reconciliation is almost impossible. Couples frequently do not talk with each other, they do not emotionally understand each other, and they are often unavailable to each other except to fight. Their children are caught in their parent's maelstrom of coolly calculated destruction. Many of these separated couples are emotionally crippled for the remainder of their lives with emotional wounds of resentments.

Is happiness an appropriate goal for marriage? Gugenbuhl-Craig[22] raises this question for professional therapists to contemplate these concerns with our clients. In his view, happiness and personal well-being as goals of marriage almost assures defeat for a couple. He recognizes that marriages inherently encounter periods of unhappy strife. When couples conclude that their marriage is not working because they are not happy, they may all too quickly conclude that the marriage is failing. However, when couples consider their personal growth and development as important criteria for the success of their marriage, there is greater assurance that their marriage will succeed. When both members of the relationship are committed to growth rather than subjective happiness, the chances of a satisfying and successful marriage remarkably increases.

Growth for couples cannot happen in a vacuum and neither can international relations. Both relationships require regular communication, candor about economic realities, emotional sensitivity and a commitment to joint planning. When international leaders emphasize national security and interests of their citizens, conflicts will continue with the vital concerns of other nations. Goals for a particular nation need to be correlated with the interests of people around the globe. Otherwise inherent conflicts threaten future generations in their efforts to resolve as inherited international conflicts. Global leadership inherently requires vision for future posterity that can be sustained with enduring justice and peace. Narrow self-interests and unilateral approaches quickly deteriorate into preoccupations with narrow agendas. Global leaders need to build bridges between national interests and the well-being of global humanity. Nations that value peace and justice recognize their important role in bringing conflicting powers to the negotiating table provided by agencies for world security such as the United Nations and other international teamwork.

**Transforming Processes:**

When specific arrangements were negotiated for my invitation to teach in India in 1998, my host advised me to be ready for a transforming experience. He invited me to teach psychology and consult with him in developing the curriculum for a masters degree in Clinical Psychology and Behavioral Medicine.[23] Professor Thomas John's frank advice was that if I were not prepared for a transformational experience, I might want to carefully reconsider my acceptance of his invitation. Fortunately, volunteering turned out to be transformative, but neither was it an imbalance on my part as an Indophile or Indophobe, nor as a Hinduphobe or Hinduphile, nor as a Islamophobe or Islamophile.[24] Rather these experiences of teaching and consulting provided an opportunity for building intercultural partnerships. Professor John's advice was invaluable for future developments.

Unexpectedly, an invitation came to fill the Peace Chair endowed by UNESCO at Manipal Academy of Higher Education in 2001. These experiences provided personal, professional and intercultural enrichment even greater than all of my previous international involvements. This happens when people engage in cross-cultural exchanges. We typically learn a great deal about the cultures visited, but we often discover even greater self-understanding. Multi-cultural experiences challenge participants to pursue enriching discoveries about people around the world. Consistent with social science research the question arises: How does a person develop openness to transformation? Box 11-3 suggests qualities essential for transformation.

Interacting with people in another culture challenges our inherent ethnocentrism. Openness to transformation is essential for these experiences to transpire. My counseling with many hundreds of students who are preparing to study abroad in international education, an interesting observation recurs. Parents want their son or daughter to have broadening cross-cultural experiences, but secretly parents may hope that their child remains unchanged. Rarely does a person remain untouched intellectually, emotionally and culturally when they interact with people in another culture. International education challenges the filters of narrow ethnocentrism in which the world is seen primarily through the eyes of our native cultural values. Intercultural experiences expand global horizons while challenging parochial perspectives.

> **Box 11-3: Transformational Processes**
>
> **Social Dynamics:**
> - Openness to confront the realitiy of change dynamics.
> - Empowerment of community organizations.
> - Collaboration in challenging power structures.
> - Awareness of historical causes of current problems.
> - Readiness to engage in coalitions for political action.
> - Discontent, dissatisfaction and unrest with the *status quo.*
> - Involvements in intercultural diversity.
> - Capacity to build supportive global networks.
> - Leadership in causes of peace and justice.
>
> **Political Economy Change:**
> - Conflicts with economic and political institutions.
> - Inquisitive curiosity for exploring the unknown.
> - Expectation to modify existing realities.
> - Sophistication in knowing public policy processes.
> - Access to engaging *status quo* power structures.
> - Resources to invest in modern innovation.
> - Advocacy of nonviolent change.
> - Consciousness as global citizens.
>
> **Creative Problem-solving Competencies:**
> - Skills in analysis, research, and big-picture synthesis.
> - Awareness of missing elements that cause problems.
> - Capacity to diagnose and define complex problems.
> - Envision alternative models of future developments.
> - Freedom to make untraditional decisions.
> - Capacities to take risks and make commitments.
> - Intercultural communication skills.
> - Celebration of transformative changes.
>
> **Personal Qualities:**
> - Capacities to trust oneself and others as partners.
> - Awareness of professional limitations and strengths.
> - Emotional strength to cope with distresses.
> - Spiritual sensitivities that provide anchors in reality.
> - Roots in ethical commitments and intercultural values.
> - Physical stamina, mental health and psychic resilience.
> - Fascination with learning, growing and development
> - Persistence, patience and perseverance.

These same transformative experiences are also present in marriages between two committed people as well as between people from nations who engage in international relationships. These qualities characterize willingness to go beyond the conventional borders of personal comfort. Persons who enter into their marriage relationship without readiness to adjust to changes are likely to have unanticipated difficulties. A secret for each party in a marriage is to be ready to adapt without hiding an intentional agenda to change their partner or their family.

One of the striking observations made by people who pursue noble causes is the discovery that important goals in life necessitate disciplined sacrifice and unsolicited suffering. Those who engage in inter-cultural experiences eventually discover unforeseen dynamics of positive and negative changes. These people learn to be resilient, to survive and eventually to discover growing development that is mutually beneficial. Along with others, Frankl[25] observed as a holocaust survivor, that people are able to withstand almost any oppressive circumstance if they understand why suffering occurs. As he succinctly stated, people can withstand almost any "what" if they know "why." As a consequence, the author offers the hypothesis for other to test that "human beings find meaning when they are important to people who are important to them."[26]

Gandhi and Martin Luther King, Jr., recognized necessary suffering when they advanced strategies of nonviolence as they experienced suffering at the hands of their opponents. When injustice, oppression and structural violence become intolerable, it is necessary to suffer for the causes of truth, peace and justice. Without readiness to pay the costs of nonviolence, worthy goals cannot be achieved.

Prophets like Moses, Jesus, Mohammed, Gandhi and King risked their own personal well-being. They were imprisoned or exiled as they stood up for their convictions for ethical justice. People persecuted them because of disagreements about their dedicated pursuits of human rights, truth, liberty, freedom and independence. They put their lives on the line to liberate their people rather than preoccupations with their own comfort and survival. They understood what is meant by commitment to risk their own lives and willingness to pay the ultimate price.

**Searching for Mutual Interests:**

A surprising discovery in international travel is to find that there are over-whelming similarities among diverse people. Human beings have a great deal more in common around the world than they have differences[27]. The strangeness of diversity is generally overridden by the commonalities that people mutually share together. While intercultural adventurers learn a great deal about their commonalities with people from other cultures, adventurers learn even more about themselves. Self-discovery becomes one of the unexpected byproducts of intercultural interactions. The parallel axiom is true in international relations.

Nations learn a great deal about their own collective identity when they engage in multilateral engagements. While there may be obvious differences between the official government positions and cultural misperceptions, there can be amazing similarities among people from different cultures. Discovering mutuality provides hope for sustainable peace and justice. When people look for common bonds, they are amazed how their relative differences are diminished by appreciation rather than tension. These human ties provide the glue that holds polarities together when international tensions tear people apart. Principled negotiation emphasizes the necessity of discovering "shared interests" between conflicting parties upon which to endorse agreements for their joint benefit. When common interests are identified, remarkable movement accelerates for the advantage of the parties involved.

Violent conflicts in the Middle East have historically persisted through wars, terrorism, suicidal bombings, cycles of retaliation, and oppressive reactions. The willingness of 30 activists from Europe in the midst of Prime Minister Sharon's siege of President Arafat baffled both the Israelis and the Palestinians. Observers were perplexed by the bold risk-taking of these volunteers.[28] In the middle of military efforts by the Israelis to counter suicide bombing, these young advocates of non-violence from Europe indicated readiness to place their lives on the line for the causes of peace and justice. They also made efforts to provide food and water for the survival of people they did not know personally but who were caught in the middle of a war zone.

Leaders of conflicting international parties may be reluctant to uncover mutual interests possessed by both their enemies and themselves. The tragic polarization of "us vs. them" becomes diametrically locked into the rigid thinking of conflicting leaders. Frequently leaders avoid exploring the mutual concerns that jointly encapsulate common bonds for both sides. People may become enamored with their own distinctiveness. This type of "exceptionalism" is descriptive of unilateral America foreign policy.[29]

Moving from polarized international tensions to domestic conflicts, even family members who know each other intimately are reluctant to explore mutually beneficial options. There are natural dynamics in sibling rivalry to pursue their own unique distinctiveness in order to stand out from the rest of the pack with special difference. Polarized rivals can lock themselves into vicious past enmities. In order to break self-defeating cycles of violence, both parties benefit by stepping back from their immediate hostilities. They benefit from reframing the destructive issues into strategies for discovering their mutual interests without becoming caught up in cloning others to conform to their own preconceived model.

**Promoting Human Growth & Creativity:**

Human development can be an implicit concern without actually being promoted in public policy. Advancing human growth goes beyond intellectual, political or emotional levels of polarized concerns. In order to move toward sustainable peace and justice, proactively promoting special talents and creative gifts is essential. Otherwise the agenda of peace with justice will remain a platform without being enacted.

Many dimensions of human development need to be advanced. Equality and freedom are both desirable conditions in human relationships. However, advancing equality may conflict with the freedoms of other people who also possess human rights. There can be conflicts between maximizing either peoples' freedom or equality. It may be necessary to pursue the optimal realization of both freedom and equality realizing that each quality can limit achieving the other ideal. More specifically, expressing one's freedom many interfere with another group's equal treatment. Conversely, equal treatment for one group may disrupt the freedoms of other people.

Economic justice is also essential in advancing human development. The resources of the earth cannot be consumed at the expense of global humanity as a whole. Developed nations must constrain themselves so that the developing populations may also have access to these finite resources. Excessive consumption patterns of developed cultures are not sustainable for all humanity to survive. Using water and oil resources illustrates imbalanced burning of nonrenewable resources without providing for future posterity. Such lavish consumption needs to be reduced as a balanced sacrifice for use by humanity as a whole.

Basic nutrition, potable water, clean air, physical safety, shelter, energy resources and health care are necessities for human development that need to be protected for even minimal survival needs. Without the fulfillment of these basic physiological needs, there are obvious risks threatening human survival. These basic necessities suggest minimal standards for human development. Basic safety and security needs are essential in order for human beings to subsist. Due to fears of violent terrorism, human beings may have only a primitive, inhumane existence of endless despair and hopelessness. Global humanity, not just the privileged, needs the security of home and work in order for children to thrive as human beings.

Building peace and justice requires even greater commitment than the efforts made by powerful forces that resort to violent war for controlling vulnerable people. Conventional guidelines provide limited help for building just and sustainable peace. Failed solutions from past history have very limited application for transforming the structural violence and ingrained conflicts now faced by humanity. Both international policymakers and family decision makers can benefit from cultivating processes of creative problem solving.

Creativity does not stop when solutions occur in the creator's mind or captured in the research reports of think tanks. Delivering solutions to legitimate decision-makers for action is essential because until solutions are communicated, decided, and implemented, the creative processes are incomplete. Solutions need to be endorsed, enacted and implemented. After a reasonable time of testing new public policies, subsequent evaluation processes are essential to make improvements. Evaluating the effectiveness of programs are subsequent steps in refining the solutions.

Families are often handicapped within their microcosm because of their limited originality. Without outside help, the family may smother in its own stifling ways of dealing with human conflicts. Professionals in marriage and family therapy can facilitate growth by providing safe environments and fresh ideas for revising old patterns of violent conflicts. On a macro scale, governments can also benefit from interventions that unfreeze the "group-think" of policymakers. Otherwise the narrow limits of old patterns and solutions devolve into stagnation. External sources for advice and research are essential for discovering creative strategies. Creative thinking and action are essential to address domestic family conflicts and international violence.

**The Re-marriage of Peace & Justice:**

The metaphor developed in this chapter is the re-marriage of peace and justice. Unfortunately, peace and justice are separated when tough conflicts are addressed with structural violence and devastating war. Trustful bonds are tragically broken by the injustice of abusive violence. This separation occurs when force is used to coerce opponents into compliant submission. Enemies forsake truth and justice during violent war between nations and abusive family relationships. Disorder and chaos breaks out during the tragedies of wartime and divorce proceedings.

Restoring peace requires that orderly justice be re-established with fair procedures, dependable security and trustful relationships. In approaching this re-marriage, a common mistake is to consider peace as a static living condition or to consider justice as the permanent cement holding trustful relationships together. Marriage produces growth rather than an unchanging prison where individuality is stifled and purposely broken down. Peace and justice are not primarily statically changeless. Both are the dynamic partners that need to be re-united as mates for the mutual enrichment that benefits global humanity.

In correcting additional misconceptions, it is helpful to realize that transformative processes have different dynamics for changing conditions. In human growth, persons experience the dynamics of observable change over time. While children develop rapidly, elderly people make gradual changes. Certainly marriages of couples also evolve through major transitions in the development. Likewise similar dynamics occur in re-uniting peace and justice. Both are enriched as they engage in fostering mutual growth.

As marriage is a trustful relationship, peace and justice are processes of building trust as a team with assurances and commitments. Peace and justice are not momentary events. Rather they are dynamic processes that evolve and devolve, grow and ebb, strengthen or weaken if not nurtured with care. Like marriage takes energy, time and commitment, peace and justice vitally need to be re-united in marriage into a dynamic partnership. When they are not mutually bonded together and carefully nurtured, the eventual deterioration of peace and justice can end in a painful divorce.

When peace and justice are publicly re-united, this dynamic couple can sustain many difficult conflicts that are inherent in living together. Through repeated public affirmations, justice and peace enrich each other as interdependent mates. Apart they cannot reproduce offspring for posterity. But when peace and justice are united as committed partners, they can produce offspring that are nurtured in the strength of their mutually beneficial covenant. Together they have the potential of creating the global family that hopefully will live in peaceful tranquility, mutual support and sustainable covenants. Box 11-4 provides further understanding required to re-unite peace and justice into a marriage covenant.

> **Box 11-4: Marriage Consummation & Termination**
>
> Marriage as a metaphor is helpful in understanding dynamic processes and transitions. From professional experience with families, it is obvious that weddings and divorce proceedings are very different but related experiences. In premarital counseling it is a common practice of mine to ask a couple: "When do you know you are married?" Typically they pause sensing that the question is designed to prompt reflection about marriage rather than think just about their wedding date. They may have difficulty answering this question because each uniquely experiences their relationship. While communicating their commitments to each other, they clearly realize that marriage is a growing process for better or worse.
>
> While the couple ponders their commitments, I am not hesitant to pose a hypothetical possibility to them: "When does a couple know that their marriage is dead?" By contemplating the nature of divorce, they clarify the nature of a marriage covenant. When asked how they would know that a marriage relationship is over, most begin to recognize that divorce is a painful process that distressingly occurs over time. Most couples are aware that divorce involves prolonged processes of breaking trust as their relationship slowly dissolves. A marriage does not end the day a judge officially signs the divorce decree because it ends long before that official divorce document is signed. The death of a marriage is not an event but a torturous process of estrangement and dissolution. Gradually a couple realizes that their marriage is over long before a judge signs the final divorce decree.
>
> As a result of pre-marital preparation, a couple is provoked into an awareness that their marriage partnership is a process of growing together over a period of courtship, trusting companionship and committed engagement. Their marriage does not precisely happen at a magical moment of official pronouncement at their wedding. They intentionally commit themselves to a trustful relationship. The officiant's signature on behalf of the state and the community publicly declares their marriage partnership.[30] Marriage does not happen just at the moment when the presiding official pronounces a couple to be husband and wife.

## PUBLIC CELEBRATION of SUSTAINABLE PEACE & ASSERTIVE JUSTICE:

A constructive step involves holding public observations that celebrate the re-marriage of peace and justice. This reuniting calls for celebrations like the International Day of Peace to observe the founding of the United Nations each September.[31] Governments at all levels and private organizations enhance the strength of mutual actions by commemorating the highest values of freedom, peace and justice. Nations around the world indicate how the United Nations is valued by how they celebrate the anniversary of its founding.

Many national and religious holidays inherently hold peace and justice among the highest of human values. Setting aside special days and events adds to the appreciation that children have of the significance of hard-won peace and freedom. The importance of universally recognized symbols enhances these observations. Creating additional powerful symbols is essential since many are confined to past cultural practices. When people do not recognize or understand a symbol, it has less powerful meaning to them. Examples include the olive branch, or the dove or the peace table. Few people are aware that these peace symbols are derived from various cultural accounts of a Great Flood. The rainbow is also connected to the promise that God would "never again" permit such a devastating deluge.

The sword as a sign of war is readily recognized throughout the world. In contrast, Box 11-5 describes an archetype symbolic of peace tables around the world.

---

### Box 11-5: The Great Peace Table

**My favorite symbol of peace is the table. At first a common table is seen as a domestic piece of furniture found in every home. But after contemplating its symbolism, this kitchen table has numinous power and universal understanding. The table is symbolic of hospitality for strangers and friends. Families eat at their table for sustenance and social support. The table symbolizes family unity, communication and conflict resolution.**

**In a deeper sense, the table is employed in international negotiations for peace treaties. The size and shape of the table has frequently been debated before negotiations take place. The Paris Peace Agreement between North Viet Nam and the United States was preceded by months of preliminary negotiation about its size and shape. Such haggling is typical in both family and international disputes.**

**It is highly important that disputing parties agree to come to a table in order to work out differences. In conflict resolution, the table is literally in the middle of a peaceful settlement. Professionals in law and justice realize the importance of a table for legal and jury deliberations.[32] The table is a central focus in processes of mediation, negotiations, and arbitration.**

**In religious symbolism, the depth of "The Great Peace Table," recognizes it's central in family meals in all cultures. People around the world see the table as a significant symbol of family, cultural and religious traditions. Peace is found in the Eucharist, the Holy Altar and the Communion Table. The Great Peace Table is concretely represented by the family table used for meals and conversations where domestic differences are resolved so that peace may prevail.**

**All ordinary tables are symbolic of peace as these deeper meanings are recognized. Boardroom tables, international peace tables, negotiations tables, dining tables, and mediation tables become deeply symbolic of the human quest for peace and justice. Families, friends and even enemies can gather around these tables. The most difficult disagreements of violence, war and strife can hopefully find peaceful resolution at The Great Peace Table.**

---

The universal symbol of the table is simplistically compelling. The table is present in the home where meals are served and eaten. A family meal is prepared in order to provide nourishment, hospitality and tranquil dialogue. Hopefully all members of the family will continue to gather regularly to share a common meal together face-to-face. The concerns and aspirations of each member can be brought to the family table for exchange, discussion, decision-making and support. There are many kinds of tables to gather around and for international leaders and for families to use for negotiations. There are very simple tables for informal conversations, and there are exquisite tables of various shapes around which international leaders negotiate agreements. Being present at the peace table is essential for resolving differences, common interests and conflicting positions. This formal table for peace talks has major symbolic value. It also has parallel symbolic value in religious observances and hospitality for strangers and enemies. From the common meal shared daily by families to the festive banquets of state dinners for honored guests, the table is the common symbol for re-uniting peace and justice fostered by public celebrations and mutual respect.

When these symbols are not adequately explained to successive generations, they lose their effectiveness in motivating people to protect and defend peace. Symbols of justice are equally important. The symbol of the balance scales held by the goddess of justice has profound meaning of fairness when it is understood. Contemporary cultures need to create original and powerful symbols depicting the long-awaited re-union of peace and justice.

One of the more widely accepted symbols of peace and justice is the bridge. Often oppressive injustice and structural violence result from walls, barriers and fault lines that become chasms between people in need of each other. In the face of high impervious walls, bridging the divisions becomes a creative action. Bridges typically must be built from both ends of the abyss reaching across chasms or treacherous waters. Building from both sides is symbolic of joint efforts to construct trustworthy connections and communications between people who have been previously separated. Bridge-building between nations is the great challenges of this century reflected in the title of this book.

**Concluding announcements:**

Marriage is a metaphor for re-uniting sustainable peace and assertive justice as partners. Throughout this chapter, invitations are extended to celebrate this re-marriage. The nature of peace is described and defined along with the nature and role of justice. These announcements about this re-marriage need to be made repeatedly with affirmation both by their families, by their communities, and also by cultures around the world.

Any marriage is threatened by interpersonal conflicts, by meddling from families and by the negative attitudes of society. Global society, cultural traditions and religious tensions can add further stresses to this fragile re-marriage. Repeated celebrations of anniversaries reaffirm commitment between justice and peace so that global humanity realizes how important this partnership is for posterity.

## Endnotes

[1] Published by the Peruvian Permanent National Commission for Peace Education, quoted in UNESCO and a Culture of Peace: Promoting a Global Movement, UNESCO Publishers, Culture of Peace Series.

[2] Founded in November, 1982, this group included citizens from Texas and Oklahoma known as the "Texoma Alliance for Peace and Justice."

[3] Ackerman P., (2000) quotes Lewis in the book, A Force More Power, St. Martin's Press.

[4] Many decades were involved in establishing democracy in India during the struggles before independence from the British colonial empire in 1947.

[5] Ackerman, op.cit.

[6] Deats R., (2000) "The Global Spread of Active Nonviolence," in Walter Wink (ed) Peace is the Way, New York: Orbis Books.

[7] Gandhi M., (2000) "*Ahimsa,* or the Way of Nonviolence," and G. Sharp's article "Civilian Resistance as a National Defense," both included in Approaches to Peace, edited by David Barash, New York: Oxford University Press.

[8] Emilsen W., (editor) Gandhi's Bible, Delhi: ISPCK Press, 2001.

[9] Gandhi M., "Speech at Bardoli Taluka Conference," 29 January 1922, Narajivan, cited by W.W. Emilsen, (editor) Gandhi's Bible, Delhi, ISPCK, 2001.

[10] Gandhi M., (2001), "Thinking Aloud," Harijan cited by W.W. Emilsen (editor), Gandhi's Bible Delhi, ISPCK.

[11] Ibid.

[12] Deats R., (2000) "The Global Spread of Active Nonviolence," a chapter in Walter Wink (ed) Peace is the Way, New York: Orbis Books.

[13] Arndt W. & Gingrich F., (1957) A Greek-English Lexicon, Chicago: The University of Chicago Press.

[14] Geyer A., (1982) The Idea of Disarmament: Thinking the Unthinkable, Elgin, IL: The Brethern Press.

[15] Irenic peace is used in various chapters of this book to express the Greek concept of Irenology.

[16] Murphy (1985) "Peace Around the World," The Christian Science Monitor, Boston.

[17] Medard G., (1979) Ho-ping: Food for Everyone, New York: Anchor Press.

[18] Kittel R., (1937) Biblia Hebraica, Privileg, Wurtt, Bibelsanstant, Stuttgart, Germany.

[19] Murphy, op.cit.

[20] Harris L., (2003) Civilization and Its Enemies: The Next Stage of History, New York: Free Press identifies the necessity of trust in teams as an essential predicate for organizational development beyond the authoritarian dynamics that dominate family and tribe relationships.

[21] Davis L., (2002) I Thought We'd Never Speak Again: The Road from Estrangement to Reconciliation, New York: Harper Collins.

[22] Gugenbuhl-Craig A., (1977) Marriage: Dead or Alive? Dallas: Spring Publishing Company.

[23] Professor Thomas is a Psychologist and Vicar in the Church of South India on the faculty of Union Christian College in Alwaye, Kerala in India. He has since served as Dean of the Faculty of this college that is affiliated with Mahatma Gandhi University in India.

[24] "Phobe" refers to phobic fear, and "phile" indicates brotherly love.

[25] Frankl V., (1959) Man's Search for Meaning, Boston: Beacon Press.

[26] Developed by the author in 1963 while developing a paper on "Our Search for Meaning."

[27] Collins F., (2006) The Language of God, New York: Free Press. Collins who headed the Genome Project team of 2000 scientist states that 0.01% of DNA differs from person to person & over 99% similar.

[28] Greenberg J., (April 4, 2002), "Peace Advocates in Arafat Compound Hope to Deter Israeli Troops," The New York Times.

[29] Daalder I. And Lindsay J., (2003) America Unbound: The Bush Revolution in Foreign Policy, Washington, D.C.: Brookings Institution Press.

[30] One exception may be in very traditional cultures when the couple may have their marriage arranged by parents. These couples may not actually consummate their marriage as a couple for some time after the marriage announcement, particularly when they are very young.

[31] Middents G., (2001) The Crisis in Violence and Peace, Manipal Press.

[32] Wrightman L., Neitzel M., and Fortune W., (1994) Psychology and the Legal System, 3$^{rd}$ edition, Belmont CA: Brooks/Cole Publishing Company.

# Chapter Twelve

# The Long, Rough Road to Peace

**If you want peace, educate for peace.[1]**
Maxim of the University for Peace,
Costa Rica, Chartered by the United Nations.

**If you want peace, you don't talk to your friends, you talk to your enemies.**
Moshe Dayan[2]

In earlier chapters, limited metaphors express inherent difficulties on the journey toward peace. This expedition is not a smooth highway, but rather a rocky road with many dangerous potholes, treacherous canyons and unexpected dead ends. There is increasing evidence that the road to peace must across uncharted territory, traverse fault lines, and maneuver diplomatic mazes through the United Nations. Symbolically, this pilgrimage takes humanity through Jerusalem[3] and revered holy sites for both historic and contemporary reasons. For enduring peace, pioneers must build strong bridges that cross over the great divides between fear to peace.[4]

This chapter is difficult because it recognizes that establishing peace and justice requires sacrifice. Whereas violence and war are costly in human deaths, valuable resources and the natural environment, there are people who assume that peace and justice is inexpensive. These erroneous ideas of painless peace and cheap justice are deceptively seductive as alternatives to costly war and violent struggle.

**Facing Hard Challenges:**

Security of the family home and native country has many appeals. At the same time, the cocoon of enculturation stifles further growth in both of these sanctuaries. But risking the loss of treasured comforts is essential to pursue these compelling treasures since human beings inherently avoid painful suffering. Consequently, there are powerful attractions to familiar surroundings thereby avoiding the fear of unknown stresses. In the struggles of building peace with justice, there are natural hesitations to take unknown hazards in leaving the familiar comforts of the homeland.

Gandhi was convinced that suffering is inherent in pursuing nonviolent peace. Without sacrifice, peace would not be possible according to Gandhi whose views were echoed by Martin Luther King, Jr., in his persistent pursuit of civil rights. They were incredibly disciplined leaders of this nonviolent force. Box 12-1 provides brief accounts of selected applications of nonviolence around the world.

> **Box 12-1: Successful Applications of Nonviolent Methods**
>
> Brief accounts of successful experiments recounted by Ackerman and his associates in a book entitled <u>A Force More Powerful:</u>[5]
>
> - Polish dissidents led by Lech Walesa and his co-workers nonviolently defied communist oppression. They won the right to organize labor unions, formed Solidarity and eventually help to bring an end to Communist domination in Poland.
> - Argentine Mothers outraged by the disappearance of their sons, started marching non-violently in Buenos Aires. They did not stop their protests until Argentina's military hunta was brought to justice.
> - Salvadoran students, doctors and merchants, fed up with fear and brutality, organized nonviolent strikes that ended a violent military dictatorship forcing the dictator into exile.
> - During World War II, citizens of Denmark nonviolently resisted the Nazi occupation of their country. They also inspired other Europeans to resist and frustrate the German Nazis.
> - Citizens of Chile mounted a series of nonviolent protests against the dictatorship of General Pinochet. Their persistent protests eventually helped defeat Pinochet so that democratic actions could be re-introduced.
> - President Marcos was removed from office as leader of the Philippines through nonviolent protests and actions that were carried out by citizens.
> - After the Berlin Wall fell, communist regimes were brought down nonviolently in Eastern European countries such as East Germany, Hungary, Estonia, Lithuania, Latvia, Bulgaria, and Czechoslovakia.

Gandhi and King both faced assassination by brutal opposition that could not withstand their relentless quests for truth and justice. They recognized that suffering was necessary for the sake of nonviolence that would be experienced not by one's opponents but by oneself. When the injustice, oppression and structural violence are intolerable, sacrifice for the causes of truth, peace and justice becomes necessary. Without readiness to pay the costs, worthy goals cannot be pursued, let alone achieved. Both Gandhi and King promoted human rights, liberty and freedom. Liberating people became much more important to them than their own security. There have been numerous efforts made in the past century to apply the principles of nonviolence to other crises globally.

Few people are willing to undergo pain for noble causes when they do not recognize that redemptive suffering is required to pursue important truths and compelling causes. Throughout history, many important human accomplishments have resulted from the sacrifice of committed persons. In pursuing the imperatives of peace and justice, the costs of these goals should not be underestimated. A striking discovery in pursuing noble causes is that important goals in life necessitate disciplined sacrifice in facing unsolicited suffering. Religions are distinguished into those that recognize redemptive suffering, and those who deny it while emphasizing blissful prosperity and comfortable pleasure. Religions that acknowledge the paradoxical polarities of human nature affirm faithful suffering in the pursuit of worthy causes.

**Sacrificing for Durable Peace & Irenic Justice:**

To have a passion for peace inherently incorporates positive motivation at a costly price. The Latin root for "passion" is lodged in the word suffering.[6] Peace and justice are possible but not without personal, social, and economic sacrifices. This type of uncomfortable worldview is not psychologically or politically popular. The author forthrightly acknowledges that this approach will be reluctantly endorsed by a number of readers.

There are many ominous symptoms of unresolved conflict in the world just as there are threatening symptoms in a person's body when grave illness occurs. In physical illness, a fever is a symptom that indicates that the body needs treatment and healing to recover better health. In a parallel way, violence is a symptom that the collective body is experiencing fearful "diseases." Painful fear is a perilous indication that major illnesses are rupturing international relations.

In the long term, effective treatment for collective conflicts can be very painful. Both grievances among nations and structural violence within countries need corrective measures that are expensive. Economic oppression, political strife and social injustice must all be remedied in order to establish durable peace and justice. Constructive measures are needed to address the losses of millions of civilians, social chaos, and decimated economies. Addressing ingrained structural violence and civil disorder with peaceful remedies is not cheap because peace building is incredibly expensive.

Parallel suffering has been the risk experienced by other champions of peace and justice besides Gandhi and King. Religious motivations have been essential for people who pursue peace and justice including Moses, Mohammed and Jesus. In recent history people in South Africa, under the leadership of Nelson Mandela, have paid heavy prices in order to overcome apartheid. International peace and justice obviously requires a heavy price of personal suffering on the part of committed people who are working for a better tomorrow together.

Such sacrifice does not inherently appeal to people who hope that peaceful tranquility can be established internally with a serene frame of mind. Sacrifice in marriage and family is widely accepted as a cost of living together peacefully. Wives and husbands sacrifice their personal independence, individual freedom, emotional energy and even their physical bodies. Marriages that endure involve sacrifice on the part of both partners to build healthy relationships. Persons unwilling to undergo sacrifice place conditions on the durability of their marriage when they narcissistically pursue their own individual agendas. In addition, parents sacrifice for the sake of their children's well being in families. Children typically cannot thrive unless parents are willing to give priority to their offspring.

On an international scale, societies must make sacrifices for the greater common good of global humanity so that collective peace and justice can prevail. While patriotism is commendable, fanatical allegiance to nationalism at the expense of the well being of global humanity immediately limits international peace. High consumption levels in developed nations ravage water, air, energy and environmental resources at the expense of protecting future generations. Developing nations also pollute air and water resources to dangerous levels of contamination for posterity. Equitable balances include concrete commitments to support the well being of the environment for future generations. Global interdependence and intergenerational ethics entail sharing burdens for the benefit of all humanity.

Insofar as selfish greed motivates people to be indifferent to others' well being, then peace and justice will be crippled. If personal suffering and collective sacrifice are left out of the equation, there is only remote hope for enduring peace with justice. But when contemporary people are willing to sacrifice for the welfare of others, there is hope for future posterity. We in the current generations need to willingly pay the price of unavoidable suffering and necessary sacrifice.

Fortunately, there are people with vision willing to accept painful costs involved in equitably distributing resources. People's readiness to make personal sacrifice will advance international peace that will bless humanity with a sustainable environment. Transformations toward peacemaking are very costly and demanding. There are no painless solutions to achieve enduring peace. The peddling of shallow slogans by unrealistic peaceniks, technological quick-fixers or hegemonic maniacs lacks trustworthiness in addressing the difficult changes in this nuclear age.

**Scape-Goating Arrested:**

"The Blame Game" is an informal term to describe psycho-theological scape-goating. In order to sustain peace and justice, scape-goating needs to be internally arrested. Because psychological scape-goating is deeply ingrained as a defense mechanism, its elimination is a major challenge on the rough road toward peace-building. When children have problems, they often blame someone or something. Scape-goating is a very effective way to externalize an excuse for problems that protects internal self-esteem. Cultures vary how they inculcate responsible behavior through emphasizing shame and guilt. In cultures where external shaming shapes behavior, external scape-goating is more naturally used even by mature people. In cultures where internalized guilt is inculcated, less scape-goating occurs.[7] Further explanation is necessary.

In family and international affairs, the problems of scape-goating can become rampant and self-serving. Shameful scape-goating is a widely known dynamic in child development such as the developmental tasks provided by Erikson.[8] A young child's normal development resolves the conflicts of initiative vs. shame and guilt. A child's curious initiatives to explore beyond boundaries are managed by either imposing external shame or experiencing internal guilt.[9]

Guilt develops when children gradually internalize guidelines from external sources to learn self-regulation in society beyond the family context. As children develop internal controls, they experience more guilt than children primarily controlled by shaming sanctions from external sources. Understandably shame and blame are closely related in development and behavior. In contrast, children who learn self-regulation through internalized guilt tend to become more independent of external blame sanctions so that they can function in their social environment. Children and youth have major conflicts as they learn to develop initiative during early childhood, industry during late childhood, identity during adolescence and intimacy during young adulthood. As mature adults, responsible people tend to rely more on internal morals and less on external blame according to Erikson.[10]

Immature persons who still use the blame game tend to rely upon scape-goating as a psychological defense rather than learning internalized responsibility to function as a mature adult who can be trusted in teamwork. People who do not learn self-control can expect external coercion in order to protect both family members and local and global neighbors from harm. Unfortunately, to constrain international and domestic conflicts, nations may resort to scape-goating that blames external enemies. International coercion and military actions are forceful controls for threats that are considered intolerably violent. Until nations and people learn to regulate themselves within parameters of civilized behavior, there will be severe limitations for sustaining peace and justice.

Cultures that emphasize shame more readily blame other nations for their problems. This convenient blame tactic is particularly apparent if national leaders appeal to primitive motives that regress to immature development. Since the populations of nations vary widely in their internal locus of control versus their external locus of control, international relations become unpredictably complex.[11] Through exercising their voting rights, citizens in a democracy to a degree can place limits on their elected leaders both politically and psychologically. Democracy is not something responsible citizens watch, but something citizens with trustful expectations do when they vote to decide who is their democratically elected leader. These elected officials are rightfully expected to be accountable to citizens. Ramanathan recommends that responsible voter "elect and engage" rather than "elect and forget."[12]

Authoritarian tyrants are less susceptible to control by their own people than in democracies. In fact, these authoritarian leaders may have major difficulty controlling their ambitions. Evil leaders and autocratic people have difficulty controlling their thirst for power, pride and control. In contrast, democratic nations may find that external sanctions, censure, elections, impeachment and recall are alternatives when elected leaders fail to exercise internal controls for acceptable behavior.

**Internalizing Unconscious Projections:**

While scape-goating is a conscious defense, psychologically there are unconscious defense mechanisms outside of conscious awareness. An extremely difficult step toward just peace involves transforming unconscious dynamics involved in making enemies and keeping them. The transformation of the individual and collective psyche is an exceptionally difficult challenge. In fathoming the causes of war, it is essential to recognize the powerful destructive dynamics of unconscious projection of the collective "national shadows" onto external enemies. Likewise, enemies viciously reciprocate by mutually projecting their evil shadow in return.

The shadow is defined as the direct opposite of the ideals held dearly by a person or nation. The shadow is obsessed with power and evil, plus destructive actions, thoughts and emotions.[13] Unless this shadow is owned, the shadow will possess the unconscious actions of a person or nation. For nations, these aggressive shadows are the unconscious side of each nation's collective psyche that is typically denied by leaders and disowned by society. In fact, the negative qualities of this national shadow may be unconsciously rejected by leaders and unacknowledged by citizens. Wars can occur when nations unconsciously project their own negative qualities onto enemy nations. Two warring nations reciprocally project their destructive shadows onto each other in threats, military warfare and propaganda. Enemy nations create negative images of their opponent in order to motivate their own populations to sacrifice in violent battles.

The shadow can be described metaphorically as the "enemy within." This internal enemy is unconsciously projected onto the adversary as if this enemy actually possesses the evil qualities that are unconsciously rejected as unacceptable by the projector onto a projectee. This dark, sinister side is unconsciously repressed so that it is psychologically denied and diverted from conscious awareness. The shadow is so unacceptable that it is projected onto the opponent as if the adversary possesses these evil qualities. It is so threatening for a nation to consciously recognize their destructive shadow that these negative qualities are externally attributed to the enemy. For example, during the Cold War both the United States and the Soviet Union saw each other to be aggressively threatening war. Each superpower perceived the other to be evil and sinister by projecting their own shadows onto their adversary.

The former Soviet Union apparently became somewhat aware of its shadow during its unsuccessful invasion of Afghanistan in the decade of the 1980's. Both superpowers at that time also produced propaganda about each other as hegemonic and materialistic in their attempts to control the world. In the post-Cold War era, nations are still possessed by a shadow archetype that creates enemies because they are functionally valuable to the nation. They insidiously seek enemies while having difficulties in letting go of old enemies who have permitted them to divert from their own internal problems. The United States partially confronted its shadow in the American War in Vietnam,[14] but continued to project its shadow onto enemies in Afghanistan and Iraq plus other nations invoked as the Axis of Evil.

The unconscious shadow may be briefly pushed out of awareness, but it soon becomes very dangerous in seeking powerful control collectively and individually. This shadow eventually emerges in unexpectedly destructive eruptions of power. In order to control this collective shadow, it must be consciously acknowledged before it can be respected for its insidious power and then deliberately managed. It is malignant and does not quit when it is denied or disowned. Rather, this destructive shadow searches for opportunities to viciously erupt with powerful determination to act out. Individual persons who do not deal with their shadow typically have their personal development arrested without growing into responsible maturity. Nations retard their maturation as responsible members of the international community when they fail to civilize their collective shadow by continuing to seek external enemies to blame.

Transformation of the shadow, known as the dangerous enemy within, initially begins with becoming aware of the collective shadow as an integral facet of the culture's identity. This conscious integration of the shadow is considered a moral problem that requires managed restraint.[15] If it is not controlled, its menacing power is likely to be unleashed upon targeted enemies and even upon innocent victims. The mutual projections of national shadows onto enemies need to be arrested by taking the battle internally within rather than externalizing it onto victims.

Bully societies find it extremely difficult to cope with their collective national shadows.[16] They continue to seek out external enemies to blame, attack and intimidate. These diversions into international conflicts permit them to divert from cantankerous domestic problems. Confrontation with the collective faults in a nation quickly provokes public reaction because internal pain is incurred. When unresolved issues are conveniently pushed into the garbage heap of forgetfulness,[17] these destructive powers unconsciously plot with deceitful denial.

Marie von Franz[18] points out that "...to a great extent all political dissensions and conflicts are exteriorizations of inner conflicts that should be resolved within..." In order to establish peace and justice, it is essential to gain control over hostile projections onto enemies. In addition, it is essential to refrain from projecting the conflicts of aggressive shadows onto external enemies. Withdrawing mutual projections of shadows by two antagonistic enemies calls upon each side to take ownership of their respective shadows by internalizing them within their culture. Internalizing these conflicts becomes a major psychological challenge in order for cultural hostility to terminate so that relational peace can prevail.[19]

Few people individually or nations collectively are willing to internalize the externally projected conflicts and cultural battles. This requires suffering, internal pain and collective sacrifice on behalf of humanity. For peace and justice to prevail, withdrawing externally projected shadows is essential both personally and collectively. Citizens and leaders are obliged to withdraw their personal, family and collective projections onto external enemies.

The paradoxical teaching of Jesus offers insight into this dilemma when he states "I have not come to bring peace, but a sword."[20] There are aggressive interpretations of this teaching to justify battle with external enemies. A compelling alternate understanding considers the context of this enigmatic teaching. Jesus was arguably speaking about the context of domestic strife advising each family member to resolve the battle inside the home. The temptation to draw the sword is redirected to peacefully keep it inside the sheath within the family rather than using the sword against external enemies in military wars. Then unconscious projections that are viciously destructive can be collectively withdrawn for the greater interest of international peace and justice.

For peace and justice to be sustained, external projections that result in war and violence need to be internally arrested. Naturally, it is easier to state these words than to terminate the cycles of repeated domestic and international violence. Deliberate establishment of justice must overcome the long-term devastation of structural violence. Enduring peace re-unites with assertive justice in contrast with negative peace that is defined as the absence of war and violence. Nonviolent alternatives go beyond the absence of violence. Ending war and violence is a necessary but not sufficient condition for sustaining peace and justice.

Terminating war and violence does not guarantee that persons will never experience domestic tension and conflict. It is essential that persons withdraw external projections onto other persons and family members with whom they have conflict. This challenge to withdraw destructive projections involves taking their externalized projections inside themselves. Consequently, persons who have enemies need to internalize their battles thereby managing their own conflicts rather than projecting them onto others. Realistically, these transformative processes my take many generations into hundreds of years. The dynamics of history are long-term developments that need to be sustained by successive generations who are easily tempted to seek a quick conquest, quick fix, or short-term solution by the next election.

In international violence, internalizing violent conflicts rather than externalizing them becomes even more difficult for leaders and citizens. Too often national leaders engage in international affairs when difficult domestic affairs are in turmoil. Invoking a threatening external enemy is a political function for making external enemies. Leaders often gain power and popularity when external enemies are identified and declared as dangerous. When unduly threatened, leaders heroically initiate military actions claiming to protect their people from imminent threats.

Extraordinary leadership over successive generations is required to reverse this powerful dynamic involved in aggressively pursuing external enemies. Instead of invoking external enemies, leaders need to address the domestic injustice within their nation and around the world. This type of uncommon leadership requires possession of unusually broad perspectives about the well being for their own citizens and for international harmony. Managing these internal conflicts within a nation demands both extraordinary leadership and enlightened citizens who possess the highest regard for sustaining peace and justice for global humanity.

**Demilitarizing:**

A major step on the rough road toward lasting peace involves demilitarization. There are powerful economic forces based on military weapons along with the investment of many professional careers. Major components of national budgets are designated for military weapons, equipment and personnel around the world. Few military leaders have the insight that former President Eisenhower of the United States wisely expressed about military expenditures. He recognized that every weapon made for purposes of military purposes and war diverted resources from those who are hungry, impoverished and unclothed as stated in this quotation:

> "Every gun that is made, every warship launched, every rocket fired signifies, in the final sense, a theft from those who hunger and not fed, those who are cold and not clothed. This world in arms is not spending money alone. It is spending the sweat of its laborers, the genius of its scientists and the hopes of its children. This is not a way of life all, in any true sense. Under the cloud of threatening war, it is humanity hanging from a cross of iron."
>
> President **Dwight D. Eisenhower**

Unfortunately, status symbols of political leaders are often measured by the size of their armies and their military prowess. This is not only true in leaders of wealthy nations, but also of impoverished developing nations. Internationally, there have been many military leaders who have become authoritarian dictators or else become part of oppressive regimes that dominate their nations while attempting to conquer others. Large proportions of national budgets of developing nations are expended for military weapons. Eisenhower knew that military weapons are expenditures rather than investments for human development. The military-industrial nations perpetuate many of these expenditures at the expense of the health of people, their education and social services for people. If we want peace, we must take steps to educate for peace so that crucial investments can be made in human development.

In the second half of their life, a number of military and civilian leaders make the transition to public service for the benefit of society. Fortunately there are many military leaders who have made transitions to nation building like Generals Washington, Marshall, and Eisenhower who are revered in world history. Innumerable veterans are also balancing their early aggression as young people have with even greater concern for peace and justice as reflected in the motto of Veterans for Peace. As veterans who dutifully served our nation during wartime affirms, we have even greater responsibility to serve the causes of world peace.[21] Psychologically, the second half of life is a natural development of maturation for both men and women to counterbalance their approaches of the first half of their lives during their later years.

On the domestic scene, many more young adults abuse their families than grandparents. Unfortunately, weapons in homes notoriously contribute to domestic violence. Many parents, particularly fathers, are stronger and also possess weapons in their homes. Some people acquire guns for hunting and sports. For others, there is the questionable belief that weapons will help them protect their home from outside intruders. The sorrowful fact is that numerous accidents occur in homes while someone inappropriately handles a weapon. Often the weapons are unattended with assumptions that they are unloaded and that ammunition is hidden. Children can quickly find both weapons and ammunition in their home even in the most secret places. When children find weapons, too often they mishandled as toys. These weapons frequently contribute to a fatal accident for a family member or an innocent visitor in the home.

While weapons may have been procured with the rationale of safety in mind, there is also a shocking discovery that these very weapons intended for protection of the home actually injure or kill the owner. If not intentionally used by the owner or accidentally misused by children, burglars readily search for such weapons. Sometimes burglars unexpectedly take them away from the owner in a confrontation who then becomes the victim. This finding is consistent with the known fact that when weapons are introduced into a hostile confrontation, the level of violence immediately heightens. Berkowitz[22] communicated this research in a provocative educational bulletin for the public entitled: "When the Trigger Pulls the Finger."

Weapons are invented for both defensive and offensive purposes. Most weapons are utilized for either intended or unintended purposes. Whenever a class of weapon has been invented, it has been developed, and eventually used. This is verified in the use of weapons of mass destruction including nuclear, biological and chemical weapons. The inventor, producer, distributor or owner may have never conceived of the eventual use or abuse of the weapon.

The presence of weapons in a national arsenal or in a home heightens the risks of catastrophic accidents. As weapons proliferate, unpredictable accidents are more likely to occur. These unintended accidents add to provocations for international war and domestic misuse. People often resort to using dangerous weapons when they are threatened. The probability increases that weapons will eventually be used for unexpected purposes when it was invented and produced or later purchased, deployed and ultimately used. The proliferation of the black markets for nuclear weapons illustrates these global problems where fanatical terrorists seek intimidating offensive weapons to terrorize foes, while nations seek weapons for both defensive and offensive purposes. Profits motivate desperate cultures and private parties to sell nuclear technology plus other weapons of mass destruction.

Consequently, there is a need for demilitarizing national arsenals of weapons as soon as possible. Demilitarizing is a logical outcome of disarmament that goes beyond arms control. Rational policymakers advocate disarmament of nations that possess weapons of mass destruction. Non-proliferation is not only crucial for the global peace, but also for domestic peace in family homes. Disarming a home is in the interest of the safety of family members is logically recommended. Accidents too readily happen while unnecessary military arsenals in a nation endanger the well being of citizens of the world. The former republics of the Soviet Union clearly illustrated countries that have enormous military arsenals. These weapons of mass destruction not only endanger their own citizens but also risk the lives of global humanity with the ominous danger on the black market, potential misuse or eventual accidents.

Box 12-2 provides contrasts of an unresolved issue in demilitarizing between the concepts of arms control vs. disarmament.

| Box 12-2: Arms Control vs. Disarmament |
|---|
| There are conflicting differences about how to address the overall issue of demilitarization. The following contrasts identify the different approaches of arms control and disarmament. |

| Arms Control | Disarmament |
|---|---|
| Assumes violent conflicts | Assumes nonviolence |
| Concerned with control | Concerned with autonomy |
| Identifies with weapons | Identifies with relationships |
| Images of war | Images of peace |
| Weapons of mass destruction | World without weapons |
| Traditional military strategy | "Thinking the unthinkable"[23] |
| *Realpolitik* position | Future model of security |
| Nation-state protection | Global law & order |

The United Nations advocates disarmament in order to prevent war, accidents and violence. In the United States there has been a government agency called the "Arms Control and Disarmament Agency." The title of this agency encapsulates a philosophical debate concerning issues related in demilitarization.

The contrasts in Box 12-2 represent different philosophical strategies toward realizing sustainable peace and enduring justice. It becomes apparent that the realists who identify with arms control have contrasting goals from idealistic advocates of disarmament. When there is one-sided emphasis on only one of these polarities, the other side is neglected. The policymakers who formed the Arms Control and Disarmament Agency incorporated the strengths of both ends of this polarity. This compromise of the wise founders represents contemporary tensions about the potential for sustainable peace and justice in the future of global humanity.

**Trusting but Veifying:**

Transparency is an increasingly important stance in international, domestic and even private affairs. In this age of interdependency, the dilemmas derived from cover-ups of vast pits of injustice and oppression. These concealments of structural violence that is flagrantly overlooked. The self-serving propensity to secretiveness fuels the potential for both domestic and international insecurity. Public and private organizations have painfully discovered the importance of transparent openness and accountability. As leaders of Great Britain and America painfully learned in the aftermath of war in Iraq, no intelligence measures are either totally reliable or accurately interpreted. Inspections and documented verification are absolutely essential to verify the unashamed violations of international justice, ethical codes and legal standards.

In addition, there are dangerous national tyrants and leaders of non-state terrorists. The problems with Saddam Hussein in Iraq illustrate the international need for disarming, inspecting and verifying disarmament. Sovereign nations challenge external observation because they do not want their own violations of human rights exposed to the world. On an international level, verifying the production and presence of nuclear, chemical and biological weapons is a contention that many closed nations would prefer to keep private. The enormous danger to humanity and the environment of deadly radiation and contamination has demanded that verification of treaties be carefully observed by external inspections.

Clandestine secrecy diminishes trustworthiness when nations conceal their intentions and capabilities for exercising destructive violence. In order to cope with secretiveness, transparent openness is one approach to counter concealment of dangerous weapons that potentially could result in devastating effects for human beings. Transparency in both policy and practice becomes essential for the human family in order to trust both neighbors and strangers. The viability of democracies is directly correlated with openness to citizens who are the ultimate policymakers in democratic nations.[24]

In domestic affairs, human beings are tempted to cover-up violations of legal and ethical codes. Sunshine laws, open meetings and full disclosure have facilitated trust and honesty in relationships. Flagrant domestic abuse can no longer be socially tolerated as an acceptable family matter that occurs privately behind closed doors. Families typically deny that they have problems of violence and abuse. Because of intensive research of the culture of India, it did not surprise the author that this denial was again clearly expressed by two Hindu leaders in an assembly of religious leaders.[25]

Domestic abuse is more rampant around the world than typically acknowledged in many parts of the world.[26] Physical abuse and neglect of children is increasingly considered a crime in enlightened societies including sexual abuse. Likewise emotional and spousal abuse should be seen as a criminal violation of civil legal codes. Governments in civilized countries are expected to openly address these abuses as crimes in order to protect the human rights of vulnerable children and adults.

**Economic Conversion & Transformation:**

When wartime concludes, reduction of military budgets among the warring nations may or may not occur. After World War I and World War II, there were major reductions in military procurement, personnel and expenditures in nations directly involved. During the last half of the twentieth century, the Cold War was fueled by high military expenditures by the superpowers who also supplied weapons to many other nations. The Warsaw Pact nations were heavily supplied by the military production of the Soviet Union. The United States, South Africa, Israel, Great Britain, France, Germany and Israel became major suppliers of military weapons to developing nations in Asia, Africa, Europe, South and Central America. The Cold War was militarized with dreadful weapons for nuclear delivery systems alongside of major arsenals of conventional military weapons. These high military expenditures risked global violence in civil and international wars. Accidents were overlooked as a normal risk of security.

When the Cold War concluded, expectations that there would be peace dividends were not realized. Military budgets were perpetuated with enormously high expenditures. Hawkish proponents of the military-industrial complex obviously have major difficulty making adaptations to lower military budgets. Politicians often perpetuate military expenditures, bases and contracts for constituents who are economically tied to their ideological positions for profits. It takes deliberate adjustments, particularly for scientists, engineers and technicians, to adapt to civil production. The aggressive mindsets of national leaders are addictively enamored with being commanders of vast military power.[27]

A limited number of economists and policymakers foresaw the benefits of demilitarization processes. Their approach known as economic conversion involves making orderly transitions from the production of military weapons and services to civilian products and services. Dumas[28] and colleagues[29] advocate systematic phases in economic conversion from military mobilization to economic conversion to peacetime civilian production:

- The main economic action lies in procurement and research and development expenditures, because these are outlays that draw engineers and scientists, industrial capital, and other productive economic resources into the military sector.
- Shrinking the military sector does nothing to repair the economic damage of the arms race unless the released resources are reconnected to contributive civilian activity.
- The successful conversion of these workers, especially of engineers and scientists, holds the key to the kind of industrial renewal that can and will brighten the economic prospects of the entire labor force.

Because the high technology in military equipment requires great precision in the specifications, professionals employed in this military-industrial sector develop meticulous skills to meet requirements set by defense departments. These specifications are known as "gold-plating" a military product. These same scientists, engineers and technicians often have limited skills that can be transferred to civilian products where market forces expect mass production with less precise specifications. These principles apply to western military powers as well as eastern military powers who continue to drain precious resources into military systems that are rarely justified for the economic productivity of a nation. Citizens are reminded that military prowess serves the power needs of national leaders more often than the security needs of the culture.

Economic conversion provides for retraining these high tech personnel so that they can adapt to the civilian employment. Financial provisions to implement economic conversion include a percentage in every contract for military weapons and equipment for the eventual transition of personnel and plants from military to civilian production. Many defense contractors seek to perpetuate lucrative economic benefits for their industries. As a consequence, there is a need to make financial provisions for this economic conversion when military contracts terminate. The overall health of an economy benefits directly when these processes of economic conversion are anticipated and eventually made in an orderly pattern during peacetime.

National economies overburdened with military expenditures benefit significantly when the production of weapons is converted into investments in education, school, human resources, infrastructure, research, cultural institutions, health and social services. This reallocation of resources to civilian production and services makes major contributions to addressing problems inherent in structural violence. These reallocated resources through economic conversion make a major difference in alleviating problems of human suffering caught in economic oppression and social injustices.

One argument to the contrary that is frequently voiced by national leaders is that investment in military defense increases jobs for employment. This position is only a minor truth when contractors hire engineers, scientists and technicians. There are much more effective ways to employ people than in the production of military weapons that are primarily expenditures for destruction, that drain resources, and that are not investments in future development. If comparable funds are invested in human services, infrastructure, civilian institutions, education and social programs, several times as many people gain employment as when expended for military purposes. The reason for investing in human development is realized due to at least the following reasons:

- Investments into human development actually improves cultures overall.
- Economic health is historically the key factor in the long-term defense of cultures.
- By a margin of three to four times, more people are productively employed in the lower wages for people in human services, education, cultural and social programs compared to high salaries of scientific and technically trained employees in military expenditures.
- Higher employment in civilian sectors has a multiplier effect that bolsters the overall economic health of a nation rather than employment in military production or service.

This multiplier effect is clearly evident in the investment of the "G.I. Bill" in the United States that assisted millions of military veterans in pursuing education for civilian fields. Educating a workforce in civilian peacetime employment increases the productivity of economies. If a culture wants peace, then it is necessary to invest in human resource development, health care, and education.

**Transitions toward Peacebuilding:**

There are additional steps in converting segments of the military-industrial complex to peacetime civilian production. This contemporary role is found during post-war transitions in the Balkans, Afghanistan and Iraq. Soldiers trained to for wartime fighting are not equipped in functions of peacekeeping, domestic security and nation building when the war concludes. Even before the war in Iraq, it was known that peacekeeping involves very different skills than fighting in combat. Building democracies involve close interactions with civilians in the defeated nations moving from the conflicts of wartime to the challenges of peacetime. Democracy building typically requires decades, generations if not centuries of cultural development. The flexibility needed to accomplish peacekeeping is difficult for traditional soldiers trained in destructive operations against defeating enemies. Transforming the military sector of both the animosities between the conquered and the conqueror is a major challenge so that grievances instigated by the war will not be perpetuated into future cycles of violence.

Contemporary war involves fighting violent battles with the latest technical weapons that require specialized training and equipment on land, sea and air. In contrast, national re-building involves very complex skills in human relations, cultural understanding, language and the construction of social, political and economic structures. In order to contain insurgency, it is necessary to repair infrastructures and renew broken institutions. These institutions require long-term investments, vast experiences and humane commitments. Democratic institutions protecting human rights cannot be quickly established quickly. Generations of people who survive wartime hostilities have to make gigantic transitions in order to be self-governing, self-supporting and independent. The Marshall Plan that restored a number of European countries after the destruction of World War II continues to be an unique humanitarian model for rebuilding the institutions and infrastructures necessary for demolished nations and cultures to function. Persuasive reasons question whether the Marshall Plan has analogous applications to transitions after contemporary conflicts in the Middle East.

There are important distinctions between restoring peace, peacemaking and peacekeeping. Restoring peace involves re-establishing workable governance that provides basic law and order out of chaos after a violent conflict has halted. Restoring peace includes efforts in reconciliation between conflicting parties as advocated by Abu-Nimer.[30] Post-conflict reconciliation can provide important healing processes for lasting peace and stability. In family disputes, children and their parents may be able to restore conditions for their benefit and society. Coexistence after conflict benefits from efforts to reconcile fractured relationships. External sanctions by law enforcement or religious forgiveness can have constructive effects on restoring peace.

Restoring order after war rarely recognizes adequate provisions for addressing the original causes of war or conflict that corrects structural violence or promotes economic justice. Restoring peace as a strategy goes beyond negative peace that is satisfied with ending violence and war. When tensions persist, it may be essential to provide peacekeeping efforts that combine restoring peace and reconciliation. There have been attempts to employ police or military troops to monitor areas that have persistent tensions and violent conflicts such as in the Balkans, Middle East, Central Africa and North Ireland. Military forces are poorly equipped to be effective peacekeepers. The traditional training of soldiers to kill and destroy makes it very difficult for them to provide policing actions that monitor volatile civilian populations in the midst of chaotic conditions.

Beyond peacekeeping functions, peacemaking involves proactive steps toward advancing civilian order and harmony. However, the achievement of civil tranquility needs long-term perspectives that promote lasting peace and doing justice. Peacemaking is often a holding action in addressing the causal contributions to structural violence in a society. Consequently, peacemaking primarily focuses on establishing temporary conditions of tranquility without violence, but by itself does not address causal factors of violent war. For example, transcendental meditation, while commendable for individuals, does not address the need of just laws for living together in society. Beyond peacemaking there is a long-term strategy conceptualized as peace building. This strategy addresses problems of structural violence in economic and social injustices. Measures of peace building are designed to establish longer-term sustainable peace with enduring institutions of justice. In order to understand peace building in more depth, Box 12-3 contrasts peacemaking and peace building.

Strategies of peace building inherently include threat to the existing power structures that represent the *status quo* contrasted in the last point of Box 12-3. The militaristic interests within both democratic and non-democratic nations are threatened by strategies of peace building.

There are numerous reasons why peace building is actively resisted by traditional power structures, international leaders and people who control family affairs. They gain control by violence to preserve their positions with coercive power. In contrast, peace building advocates are not as manageable as violent approaches that assume that coercive force are methods for controlling other people in families or nations.

Nation-states rarely promoted peace building because they jealously protect their own sovereign interests and borders. In contrast, the controversial agenda of the United Nations and related

| Box 12-3: Contrasts between Peacemaking & Peace Building[31] | |
|---|---|
| PEACEMAKING | PEACE BUILDING |
| Reduces Direct Violence | Resolves Structural Violence |
| Emphasizes Nonviolent Methods | Emphasizes Socially Just Ends |
| Reactive | Proactive |
| Focus on Current Conflicts | Focus on Conditions for Future Peace |
| Preserves Economic & Political Structures | Challenges Economic & Political Structures |
| Prevents Violent Episodes | Promotes Social Justice |
| Interest in *Status Quo* | Threatens *Status Quo* |

global organizations reflect peace building agendas more than the self-serving policies of individual nations. Consequently, organizations that intentionally advance themes of peace building are often the target of intensive criticism, skeptical blame and scape-goating. There is no reason to believe that the road to peace building is smooth, easy or inexpensive.

**Concluding Comments:**

Positive peace and enduring justice does not happen without suffering and sacrifice. Positive peace and assertive justice are costly for both leaders and citizens. The challenge is staggering, but hopefully the promise is even stronger for humanity to discover a better world tomorrow. Demilitarizing, disarming, and economic conversion are essential for lasting peace.

In domestic affairs, violence and abuse needs to be arrested in order for families to experience irenic tranquility. Peace building goes beyond restoring peace, reconciliation, peacekeeping or peacemaking. In international affairs, violent wars and conflicts need to come to an end in order for global humanity to live in sustainable peace and enduring justice. The long, treacherous road to durable peace and justice is rocky, rough and bumpy.

# Endnotes

[1] Barash D., (1991) Introduction to Peace Studies, Belmont CA: Wadsworth Publishing Company.

[2] Dayan Moshe, (Dec. 23, 2003) The Times of India.

[3] Adapted from Bill Keller's claim that the road to Baghdad goes through Jerusalem made also in his article "The Loyal Opposition," The New York Times, August 24, 2002.

[4] The author appreciates important aspects involved in the divine-human paradox that peace can be understood theologically as God's gift of grace while also simultaneously attempting to grapple with human contributions concerned with building peace temporally.

[5] Ackerman P. (2000), (editor), A Force More Powerful, St. Martin's Press.

[6] Safire W., (March 1, 2004) editorial, The New York Times.

[7] Harris L., (2004), Civilization and Its Enemies: The Next Stage of History, New York: Free Press provides a historically and philosophically sophisticated analysis of parallel explanations. However, Harris' approach is largely confined to western concepts without providing in depth psychological analysis or understanding of eastern political thought, philosophy, history or contemporary scientific psychology. He offers a provocative explanation about civilizations that help to channel the inherent aggression of young men into productive employment. What psychologists call sublimation of aggression into socially constructive roles, permits a civilized society to be productive for the benefit of families and society so that this aggression is diverted from abusive violence, crime and military violence.

[8] Erikson E., (1993) Childhood and Society, W.W. Norton and Company.

[9] Shame involves external sanctions from an authority like a parent who sets boundaries when a child ventures outside of acceptable activity.

[10] Erikson, op.cit.

[11] Harris, op.cit, offers parallel historical assertions and philosophical explanations that are worthy of careful consideration without providing scientifically tested empirical data to support his views.

[12] Ramesh Ramanathan cited by T. Friedman (March 21, 2004) "Software of Democracy," The New York Times.

[13] Odajynk V., (1976) Jung and Politics, Harper Colophon Books; Guggenbuhl-Craig A., (1979) Power in the Helping Professions, Spring Publications, Nuemann E., The Origin and History of Consciousness, and Depth Psychology and a New Ethic, translated by E. Rolfe, New York: Harper Torchbooks, 1969.

[14] The documentary film, "The Fog of War," provides the agonizing accounts of Robert McNamara who was the American Secretary of Defense during the Kennedy and Johnson Administrations during the Vietnam (American War) that has also been labeled as "McNamarara's War."

[15] Hillman J. (1967) In Search: Psychology and Religion, Spring Publications.

[16] Contemporary examples include the painful national awareness in the United States that it aggressively projected its American collective shadow onto enemies in the Vietnam War (called the American War by people of Vietnam. Likewise, the Soviet Union eventually confronted its aggressive shadow in its demoralizing defeat in Afghanistan during the 1980's. History will determine whether the war in Iraq will eventually be labeled as an American War.

[17] Harris, op.cit., Forgetfulness is a generational problem that Harris elaborates with incisive clarity.

[18] Von Franz M., (1976) foreward to Jung and Politics, by V. Ondajynk, Harper Colophon Books.

[19] Middents G., (1984) "The Psychology of Enemy-making and Peacemaking in the Nuclear Age," Unpublished manuscript.

[20] The Gospel According to Mathew 10: 34, The Holy Bible Containing the Old and New Testaments, new revised standard edition, Iowa Falls: World Bible Publishers, Inc.

[21] This statement expresses the motto of Veterans for Peace in the United States, www.veteransforpeace.org

[22] Berkowitz L., "When the Trigger Pulls the Finger," American Psychological Association publication.

[23] Geyer A., (1982) The Idea of Disarmament:Thinking the Unthinkable, Elgin, Ill: The Brethern Press.

[24] Middents G., (1994) "Public Education and Accountability," The Canadian Health Care System: Lessons for the United States, S.B. Eve, B. Havens, and S. Ingram (editors) University of North Texas Press, republished by University Press of America, 1995.

[25] Hindu representatives stated that there was no domestic abuse in India except in the lower socio-economic classes at the a conference of the Interfaith Coalition of Dallas, Texas, Jan. 28, 2004.

[26] Goldstein A. and Segall M., editors, (1983) Aggression in Global Perspective, New York; Pergamon Press.

[27] Hedges C., (2003) War is the Power that Gives Us Meaning, New York: Anchor Book.

[28] Dumas L., (1986) The Overburdened Society: The Causes of Chronic Unemployment, Inflation and National Decline, University of California Press; plus Dumas L., (1989) Making Peace Possible: The Promise of Economic Conversion, Pergamon Press; and Dumas L., (1995) "Finding the Future: The Role of Economic Conversion in Shaping the Twenty-First Century," in Approaches to Peace, edited by David Barash, New York: Oxford University Press.

[29] Dumas L., editor, (1995) The Socioeconomics of Conversion from War to Peace, New York: M.E. Sharpe.

[30] Abu-Nimer M., (2001) Reconciliation, Justice and Coexistence: Theory and Practice, Lanham, MD: Lexington Publications.

[31] Christie D. J., Wagner R. D., and Winter V. V., (2000) (eds) Peace, Violence and Conflict: Peace Psychology for the 21$^{st}$ Century, Prentice-Hall.

# Chapter Thirteen

# Challenges in Building Peace

**When justice is done, it brings joy to the righteous, but terror to the evildoer.**[1]

**If we have no peace, it is because we have Forgotten that we belong to each other.**
　　　　　　　　　　　　　　　　　Mother Teresa[2]

When peace discussions take place, people envision different levels of harmony and concord. Two common misunderstandings occur when one person is thinking of a personal state of internal serenity while others think of global peace. Consequently, there is a need to re-examine these distinctive perspectives that frame references different people contemplate about individual and community peace.

This book primarily addresses social dimensions of peace but does not overlook subjective states of personal serenity. Internal and external harmony is held in tandem while emphasizing social dimensions. Dual attention is also given to family conflicts and tranquility while addressing international conflict and global peace. Both domestic and international conflicts have many similarities and obvious differences in scale for dealing with nonviolent strategies. This chapter bridges "internal-external states" plus the "domestic-international dynamics" of violence and mutual agreement.

Peace can be considered a by-product that occurs in the quest for justice. Peace may be intangibly subjective whereas justice is more tangibly observable. Parallel to happiness, personal serenity is a reflective condition whereas justice is intentionally established with decisive actions in society. Box 13-1 contrasts internal and the external states of concord.[3]

| Box 13-1: Internal & External States of Concord | | |
|---|---|---|
| **INTERNAL STATES of SERENE PEACE** | vs. | **EXTERNAL STATES of SOCIAL PEACE** |
| **Intra-personal:** | | **Inter-personal:** |
| Subjective | <> | Objective |
| Individual | <> | Relational |
| Implicit | <> | Explicit |
| **Intangible:** | | **Tangible:** |
| Invisible | <> | Observable |
| Nonverbal | <> | Documented |
| Moral | <> | Legal |
| Religious | <> | Secular |
| Spiritual | <> | Ethical |
| Serenity | <> | Order |
| **Intrinsic:** | | **Extrinsic:** |
| Mental | <> | Societal |
| Tranquil | <> | Economic Justice |
| Contentment | <> | Social Justice |
| Treasured Gift | <> | Intentionally Built |

It is important to acknowledge that conflict persists in both internal and external states of peace. To be alive means to inherently experience conflicts. Social interactions immediately have dimensions of conflict between people with differing subjective perspectives. These normative conflicts can be managed peacefully in social relations since people are motivated to satisfy deficiencies for biological homeostasis while seeking stimulation for social needs. Without conflict, life ceases to exist. Creativity would be non-existent and curiosity would become flat brain waves signifying death.

Conflict and life innately occur together, but must be managed personally, socially and internationally. Problems that have a solution are repeatedly handled in the course of normal living. Problems without permanent solutions must be managed. In order to sustain peace, it is essential to pursue equitable justice while at the same time recognizing that harmony is a treasured gift of great price.

**Expressing Constructive attributions:**

Enduring peace flourishes when genuine compliments are given to other people in contrast to withdrawing negative projections. People are up-lifted by supportive comments that are authentically complimentary. People respond much more constructively when they are built up rather than "put-down" during competitive rivalries. Positive attributions produce dividends that bolster people's best qualities while guarding that these commendations are authentically verifiable. Critical evaluations assess ideas and policies. So what is constructive about degrading criticisms that tear down people in global relationships?

Positive attributions need to be truthfully accurate to establish credibility. Truth is best tempered with special kindness rather than with vitriolic aspersions. Discovering both what to say and how to state it becomes the diplomatic art of wholesome human relationships. These include the highest concepts of goodwill that are found in such terms for peace as Aramaic, Arabic and Hebraic terms *assaalam, Islam, and shalom.* The connotations of these genuinely wish another person their highest good, health, and prosperity. *Sushanti* in Hindu and *Binh* in Vietnamese are positive statements that build up "good peace" rather than tear down. Every language possesses positive attributions that humanize people with positive qualities.

What has happened to human civility in contemporary international discourse and domestic relations? A sincere "thank you" is more often than not appropriate for relationships that include the performance of services that are of mutual benefit. In fact, expressions of gratitude provide a lubricant of cordiality that far exceeds the costs. People remember expressions that radiate appreciation. Metaphorically, even the most evil person alive might be minutely transformed by genuine respect for another human being. Who knows? – they could even have a lapse in their constant evil-doing and pathological violence.[4]

Of course, optimism psychologically motivates these suggestions. Hopefulness is essential to balance the pessimism generated in sacrificial suffering for a peaceful world. Positive approaches are often neglected among people in family conflicts and in tense international relations. Fighting families cling to memories of vicious disputes that blind them to positive qualities emerging in a young child, a volatile sibling, or a stubborn parent. Hostile put-downs unload bitter revenge whereas human kindness interrupts depressing cycles of violence. Constructive attributions require carefully praising even the most infinitesimal slip in evil-doing. These transformative changes can reverse violent cycles into upward spirals where small kindnesses are reciprocated.

In international tensions, intangible qualities are easily overlooked in ameliorating hostile confrontations. Consider these contrasts between western and eastern cultures. Western thought emphasizes linear time in contrast to cultures that value special moments. Western science emphasizes quantitative data in contrast to qualitative features. Consequently, western cultures take aggressive initiatives to achieve tangible gains while undervaluing symbolic gifts that are intangible. As a result, western approaches to peace accentuate proactive measures rather than allowing these peaceful conditions to emerge as unmerited gifts to receive.

Box 13-2 describes attributions of intangible qualities that are given rather than earned as achievements. The concept of gifts infers the need for acceptance rather than earned as an aggressive accomplishment. Without receiving the gifts graciously with appreciation, the true nature of giving is unfulfilled. These suggestions include concrete expressions for illustrative purposes.

> **Box 13-2: Intangible Attributions of Peace**
>
> - Gift of Concord that replaces violence and war.
> - Gift of Love that abolishes hate.
> - Gift of Grace that is undeserved acceptance.
> - Gift of Time in order to deactivate weapons of mass destruction.
>
> - Gift of Justice that equitably addresses:
>   - Violations of human rights.
>   - Racism and prejudice.
>   - Gender injustice and sexism.
>   - Poverty, famine and starvation.
>
> - Gift of Law & Order to justly cope with:
>   - Chaotic fears.
>   - Anarchy and anxiety.
>   - Disorder and insecurity.
>   - Ecological degradation.

Spiritual contemplation is common among people of eastern cultures like India and South Asia particularly in contrast with the action-oriented cultures. Assertive people attempt to correct social injustice that directly addresses problems in their societies. In contrast, there are understandable reasons why people conditioned by contemplative cultures naturally consider harmony as an inward state of mind. Serene tranquility is more descriptive of intra-personal peace. Intangible gifts are identified in Box 13-2 in order to recognize that tranquility incorporates supernatural qualities that are often beyond human accomplishments. These gifts can then be seen as more than human endeavors in order to acknowledge both the natural and mystical attributed to divine sources of peace.

Constructive inter-cultural relations deal with issues of deficiencies versus differences. Whereas violence, war and conflict result in negative images of evil, positive attributions discover beneficial differences. From ethnocentric perspectives, people in developed nations tend to see deficiencies in developing nations.[5] Their technology may be backward, their education inadequate, and their health, food and nutrition noticeably deficient. As mutual understanding builds, these negative assessments are seen as qualitative differences rather than quantitative deficiencies. Cultures have different approaches to living on this planet. Some cultures waste resources, while others are resourceful. Everyone learns when observable differences are recognized as potentially beneficial rather than as negative evaluations of deficiencies.

**Multi-logues in Multi-Versities:**

If you want peace, talk with your enemies. This advice counters the tendency to narrow discourse to people who agree with us. We may confine our interactions with people in our own family or culture who share our own worldview. As a consequence, people in conflict engage in "narrowcasting" with friends rather than broadcasting with the wider audience of diverse perspectives. In threatening conflict, anxiety creates fear, fear leads to anger, anger breeds violence, and violence becomes more deadly as weapons of mass destruction are employed. As aptly stated, "… the greatest single antidote to violence is *conversation,* speaking our fear, listening to the fears of others, and in that sharing of vulnerabilities discovering a genesis of hope."[6]

Intercultural understanding is increasingly essential in travel, communication and global understanding. Thereupon narrow perspectives are balanced with more accurate appreciations of people with strange languages, traditions and values. Inaccurate stereotypes are challenged with personal exchanges and cross-cultural partnerships. Global friendships challenge previous misconceptions. The mutual benefits of different viewpoints and diverse gifts multiply into outcomes previously inconceivable.

Monologues are direct contrasts with dialogues, trialogues, and then multi-logues. Multi-logues are an inclusive model for communication in comparison to formal lectures, broadcast messages, and official pronouncements. Informal forums encourage voicing divergent views. Multi-logues help people find their voice to express their views and to defend their rights. "Voice" is used metaphorically because many people need help in discovering their voice in forums heard by the larger community. "Finding our ethical voice" about social and economic justice issues is critical in re-uniting peace and justice. Disenfranchised populations need opportunities to directly voice their concerns through democratically elected representatives. Ideally, preference is that everyone has opportunities to express their democratic voice and be heard.

One of the finest human qualities is that of listening carefully to the views voiced by other people. While some people have hearing problems, many more have deficiencies in listening. Oppressed people often state with remorse that no one listens. This is a condemnation of the monologues that dominate one-sided talking. Communication via the internet initiates further possibilities of highly complex messages. Modern information technology offers potential for multi-channel delivery systems in global communications. Even with expanding populations, technology has the capacity to solicit great input so that many opinions and viewpoints plus values of individuals, representative groups and cultural values are voiced and heard. These inputs simultaneously offer ownership of the eventual outputs when the components of the social equation are considered.

Multiple dialogues between people at many levels both in official government roles and between citizens are necessary for sustaining peace. Researchers and activists encourage multi-logues with increasing levels of sophistication. Saunders[7] provides a five-stage process for representative persons gathered into small groups to address conflict peacefully:

- Deciding that the *status quo* is actually more harmful than engaging in dialogue to move toward resolution of conflict.
- Identifying issues and prioritizing problems to address.
- Probing problem relationships, framing and weighing choices, and setting a direction.
- Experiencing a change in their relationships and working together to generate new paths toward ameliorating conflicts.
- Implementing transformations of relationships by applying ideas that have occurred in the smaller group to a larger community.

Saunders applies these stages for sustaining peaceful settlements in both domestic and international problems of conflict and violence. The strategies in this book along with Saunders' five stages involve long-term processes. These strategies require commitment to peace building in order to effectively participate in conflict resolution, implement agreements, and persist in re-connecting peace with justice.

**Sustaining Development:**

The theory and research in sustainable development provides significant strategies for advancing peace. Behind these concerns are two assumptions: One is that the human race on earth will continue to evolve over the foreseeable future; and the other assumption is that human beings have responsibility in influencing future development. Every century of human history has had religious or fanatical persons who have predicted the end of the world with varying degrees of apocalyptic images. The common factor among all of these prophets is that they have all been false prophets in their predictions because the end of the world has not happened.

The growing human population of this planet challenges the earth's ecosystem. Fortunately, there is evidence that the pessimistic forecasts of the twentieth century are being challenged by current demographic data. Birth rates in developing nations are radically reducing while European countries have negative growth according to United Nations demographers.[8] While the world's population continues to grow, current birth rates predict a leveling off by 2050.

The concept of sustainability necessitates balancing competing consumption of limited resources.[9] Unless current consuming patterns are constrained, future generations will become increasingly impaired. A working hypothesis for investigating sustainable development combines human welfare and ecosystem health.[10] Dimensions of human wellbeing include health, population, wealth, knowledge, culture, community and equity. The dimensions of the ecosystem's health include land, water, air, space, energy, oil, laws of nature, resource use, species, and their populations.

Sustainability involves discovering equilibrium between three basic factor namely environment, economy and society. Each one of these concepts is of critical importance for sustainable development in order to advance peace and justice. This section provides basic understanding of sustainability with concrete illustrations in two Indian states. It has been my privilege to become familiar with these two cultures that approach sustainable development during four trips to India. In 1998 and 2001 I lived in these states along the southwestern Malabar Coast. In the course of teaching and consulting, I came to appreciate the people Karnataka and Kerala that are often overlooked in international research.

**Economics and Employment:**

Geographically, Kerala is an elongated state on the lower southwest coast of India covering almost 39,000 square kilometers along the Arabian Sea. Kerala includes only 1.18% of India's land. However, its population of over 31 million is about 3.4% of India's population. While overall India's population is now over 1.1 billion people, Kerala's birthrate is lower than many western societies. On the other hand, Karnataka is a larger state located above Kerala bordering the state of Tamil Nadu on the east and the Arabian Sea on the west coast. Karnataka's population over 53 million people with about 66% in rural areas and 34% in urban cities composes about 5.8% of India's overall population.[11]

The economies of Kerala and Karnataka have traditionally been based upon agriculture, fisheries, education, health care and social services. They have limited heavy industry that includes processing coconut products and coir. Kerala produces over 90% of India's rubber, 70% of its coconut, and 60% of its tapioca. It is also a large producer of bananas, ginger, tea and coffee plus cashews and bamboo. Food products include spices, fruits and vegetables. However, shortages continue in food grains including rice. In contrast, Karnataka is more industrial than Kerala. Karnataka possesses minerals including iron ore, manganese and produces 84% of India's gold. Both states have lush natural environments that have a number of rivers that flow with fresh water from the mountains called the Western Ghatts. Pollution increasingly contaminates the water supply that is abundant during the monsoon season but scarce during the dry month. Kerala actually possesses more water resources with wide inlet waterways that are also tourist attractions.

Information technology industries are providing economic growth over the past two decades. Bangalore, capital of Karnataka, has high tech industry of computer software as a city of over five million inhabitants located on a high plateau. Bangalore has numerous transnational computer plants that attract many international business people and visitors. Hundreds of thousands of educated young people in India are employed by the information technology companies from around the world. Saritha Rai identifies the opportunities and challenges that young educated women encounter in living in Bangalore and other computer centers.[12]

Cochin in Kerala currently has one of the largest international airport in India providing transportation that stimulates potential for a growing tourist industry. Because there has not been major capital investment in industry in Kerala, employment opportunities are lower than in Karnataka. Both states have large rural regions that provide major employment in agriculture. A fact that astounds many people is that the populations in these states are able to approach basic sustainability on annual per capita incomes of less than $500 when converted into dollars.

Many people from Kerala and Karnataka have skills in professions so that they can find employment as Non-Resident Indians (NRI's) in other economies around the world. Many are employed in Western Europe, the Arab Gulf states, the Pacific Rim, and the United States. Their professional skills include engineering, science, management, and technology, plus health care, education and social services. Others contribute to the world's arts, literature, religion, philosophy, and performing arts.

**Education and Health Care:**

People from these states along the Malabar Coast possess skills sought in many countries in the world. Technology in health care is approaching the levels in developed nations particularly in medical, dental, and mental health care. Commendable attention is also given to preventive measures of public health with credible results. Alternative health care, traditionally called *Ayurveda*, has been pioneered in these states. Longevity in Kerala has reached 71.3 years in the 1990's, while Karnataka's longevity is slightly lower. Basic health care is available for most people at a nominal cost compared to expensive health care in the United States.

An initial invitation was extended to teach and consult in 1998 at Union Christian College in Aluva which is a pace-setting college affiliated with Mahatma Gandhi University. This invitation involved serving as a Visiting Professor of Interdisciplinary Studies teaching psychology, conducting seminars in human development and counseling, plus offering workshops and lectures in the Departments of Economics, Physics, Botany, Zoology plus religious programs. The Department of Psychology wanted to develop a graduate curriculum for a Masters Degree in Clinical Psychology and Behavioural Medicine. This curriculum was carefully planned into a two-year program with internships. This involved planning the two-year curriculum for this degree, and more amazingly gaining approval by the Ministry of Education. Graduates are now completing degrees that lead to roles in psychological health services and educational roles in India and internationally.

Basic education of people in Kerala features their outstanding literacy level. This state has achieved over 95% level of literacy of its population. Among adults the level of literacy is 90% while among young people the level is well over 97%. This is a credit to the deliberate educational emphases in Kerala and volunteer efforts to teach basic literacy to those who are not in school. The implication for this amazing level of literacy results from its multiplier effect in the quality of life. The higher levels of literacy and education, result in higher professional competencies of the graduates. Moreover, educated young people delay early marriage. At the same time, couples have fewer children. In recent decades, the birth rate of Kerala has been less than the United States.

The ratio of 1036 females to 1000 males is the highest of any state in India. In view of the cultural preference for male children, this ratio is particularly noteworthy.[13] Infant mortality in the 1990's was 16 per 1000 births. On the other hand, Karnataka that is predominantly Hindu has a ratio of 964 females to 1000 males. At the same census, Karnataka's literacy rate was overall 67% with men higher than women. The traditional language of Karnataka is Kannada whereas in Kerala the cultural language is Malayalam plus Hindi that is the official language in India. Young people communicate in their native language while many are fluent in English in secondary schools.

These levels of education and literacy also have positive influences on the quality of life in both Kerala and Karnataka. The professional skills of people from these states have become increasingly known in health care, medicine, education, science and computer technology along with other professions requiring advanced education.

**Social Service and Peace Studies:**

Manipal Academy of Higher Education extended an invitation to teach in Karnataka to fill the Peace Chair in 2001. This unique Peace Chair, endowed by UNESCO, is designed to broaden the inter-disciplinary education of students enrolled at this deemed university composed of 11 colleges plus 42 related institutions. It includes two medical schools; two dental schools; a large institute of technology, science and engineering; pharmacy school; nursing school; institute of communications; management school; allied health school; and hotel management school.

This large international university has a highly qualified faculty that attracts students from different nations in Asia and beyond like England and Africa. Its graduates are found not only throughout India and South Asia, but also at universities and professional roles in Europe and the United States. This university's vision for advancing peace studies is increasingly important in international conflicts as well as domestic and regional affairs. Manipal University published my 2001 lectures and program in a previous book entitled: Crisis in Violence and Peace.[14]

When the adjoining state of Kerala became a state in India in the 1950's, intentional decisions were made by Kerala's government to invest in social services as well as health care and education. This emphasis in human resource development provided basic investment in people as their most important resource. While there is room for considerable development in further human resources, the social service dimension is commendable for a culture that has budget limits.

Naturally, social problems persist in both of these Indian sub-cultures. While caste problems continue, Roy addressed problems of gender issues, caste injustices, and domestic abuse.[15] Problems remain in social and economic injustice among the Dalits[16] and also among the people in social castes although denial is the cultural stance. Land reform problems continue to exist in these socially conservative cultures. Welfare problems persist in the Public Distribution System of Kerala.[17] In Karnataka, a special case study of sustainable development is clearly reported by Najam in a research assessment of the Daudi Gram Panchayat.[18]

The Indian sub-cultures of Kerala and Karnataka possess many social, economic and environment problems that make these dynamic societies valuable for understanding sustainability. Sociologists and anthropologists consider the Indian society as a whole to be a vast laboratory for research, analysis and study about social issues and theory. Both states illustrate major contrasts with other developed and developing countries concerned with pursuing the rough roads to sustainable peace and irenic justice. Domestic challenges within families and international conflicts of globalization are dramatically expressed in these cultures. Domestic conflicts, ethnic and religious violence is present in these states of South India, but not to the degree of major violence in northern states like Gujarat and Bihar. Varshney's research[19] contrasts the characteristics of peaceful cities in South India that have sustained peaceful relations while other cities in India have experienced major violence.

A recent regional development is noteworthy for a negotiated peace settlement in Sri Lanka that is adjacent to the east coast of South India. The island nation of Sri Lanka has been the site of violent civil war over decades. Sri Lanka and the Tamil Tigers recently arrived at a commitment to peace after 19 years of strife and 65,000 deaths as well as the displacement of 1.6 million people.[20] This civil war parallels the prolonged violence in Northern Ireland. This peaceful settlement in Sri Lanka confirms the validity of persistent negotiations that advocate nonviolent measures to address what had seemed incorrigible to many observers.

**Transparency:**
Transparency in human relations counters secretive approaches of covering up what people want to avoid. Openness counteracts efforts to hide repulsive maladaptive emotional, behavioural conflicts while providing a positive atmosphere in which human relations can grow. People in both family and international relations often hid disagreeable developments so that the proverbial "closet" may be crowded with skeletons. They become public where the actual damage to offended people may be devastating when they are no longer hidden.

Problems in open policymaking are well illustrated in the United States in the approach the Clinton Administration took in health care planning in 1993-94. The secrecy of the committee of 500 citizens was a major flaw in gaining essential consensus for the Health Care Security

Act. President Clinton appointed his wife, Hillary, to co-chair this committee that took more than a year to research the problems and develop legislative proposals. There had not been a confluence[21] of politics, social problems and policy-making dynamics in the previous 20 years. However, secrecy has been identified in the autopsy of what went wrong because of the lack of public transparency displayed by this committee.[22]

In the past century, secretiveness has been justified by nations in the encapsulating concept called national security. With due respect for caution,[23] there is excessive usage of the term "national defense" in the United States. Attempts are made to justify many budget items under the rubric of national security. More recently the term homeland security has been adopted in the United States for conducting the so-called War on Terrorism. This secrecy becomes a critical problem when administrations like the President Bush is reluctant to permit his National Security Advisor, Condoleezza Rice, to testify about developments preceding 9/11/01. While there has been reason to provide national and homeland defense, there are also excessive efforts to remove military, intelligence and government operations from public awareness. Public transparency is necessary because excessive secretiveness contributes to unnecessary suspicion, national paranoia and unjustified controls on civil liberties, plus constraints of human rights.

Openness is essential for the functioning of democratic societies. Transparency is also one of those practices widely appreciated in India, European and North American democratic states. The case must be made repeatedly that transparency is essential for a democracy to be a free society. Openness in turn also holds the public accountable to be responsible citizens. Irenic justice is conditioned by transparent openness as the oxygen for a viable democracy. In pursuing independence and democracy in India, Gandhi exchanged his ideas and thoughts with his own people, their oppressors and for the world to understand. Box 13-3 provides selected insights that Gandhi openly made about nonviolence in the face of formidable challenges, resistance and eventual assassination. These quotations are applicable to both family and international relations.

Public awareness is essential for the exercise of responsible citizenship with a great need for unambiguous transparency. When public officials resort to closed meetings, they indicate distrust of the voting public. Judge Damon Keith succinctly states the necessity for openness in democratic societies in his opinion: "Democracies die behind closed doors."[24] Secret officials forget their accountability to the citizens who are constitutionally responsible for democratic government of the people, by the people and for the people. Otherwise free democracy may be perverted to serve the pragmatic interests of powerful elites or political ideologies so that democratic processes are impaired from functioning effectively.

Authoritarian states are frequently involved in internal civil wars and external wars internationally. Dictators too easily control the media and the education of the public much to the detriment of their society. Even though a free society is vulnerable to irresponsible actions, it is the nature of freedom that the public can act responsibly when the citizens have open access to accurate data, information and news. A free press counters the temptation of public and private organizations to gain control of the media to promote special interests while limiting full disclosure and vital public information.

> **Box 13-3: A Force More Powerful – Positive Nonviolence**
>
> The following statements were made by Gandhi[25] during his lifetime as he openly expressed his ideas of positive nonviolence in these succinct quotes:
>
> "Nonviolence is the greatest force at the disposal of mankind. It is mightier than the mightiest weapon of destruction devised by the ingenuity of man."
> <u>Harijan</u>, July 2, 1931
>
> "Just as one must learn the art of killing in the training for violence, so one must learn the art of dying in the training of nonviolence."
> <u>Harijan</u>, September 1, 1940
>
> "It is not nonviolence if we merely love those that love us. It is nonviolence only when we love those that hate us."    Letter of December 31, 1941
>
> "Nonviolence is a universal principle and its operation is not limited by a hostile environment. Indeed, its efficacy can be tested only when it acts in the midst of and in spite of opposition."    <u>Harijan</u>, November 12, 1938
>
> "Everyone admits that sacrifice of self is infinitely superior to sacrifice of others."
> <u>Indian Home Rule</u>, 1909
>
> "Suffering is the law of human beings; war is the law of the jungle. But suffering is infinitely more powerful than the law of the jungle for converting the opponent and opening his ears which are otherwise shut, to the voice of reason."
> <u>Young India</u>, November 4, 1931
>
> "Nonviolence is a power which can be wielded equally by all – children, young men and women or grown-up people – provided they have a living faith in God of Love and have therefore equal love for all mankind."
> <u>Harijan</u>, September 5, 1936
>
> "The policy of retaliation has never succeeded."
> <u>Young India</u>, December 15, 1927
>
> "I am not a visionary. I claim to be a practical idealist...I have ventured to place before India the ancient law of self-sacrifice."
> <u>Mahatma, II, Young India</u>, August 11, 1920

**Cooperation & Collaboration:**

Teamwork is essential for public and private organizations as well as for families to thrive. To function effectively together as a team, careful collaboration is required among the individual members. Without teamwork, families are in danger of becoming dysfunctional due to their lack of trustful cooperation and cohesion. When families pull together as functioning teams, individual strength is beneficially multiplied both socially and psychologically. Similar dynamics occur when nations jointly cooperate.[26]

Peace cannot effectively function in private isolation, but instead is social and political in scope. Peace is not only an internal quality of serene personal tranquility, but it is also reaches into domestic and international affairs. The social dimensions of cooperative living are basic for peace to be globally experienced. This book attempts to make the case for re-uniting peace with justice that is also a vital relational concept. Justice is primarily experienced in social relations with other among cooperating countries and cultures. Justice cannot be experienced in isolation by itself. Justice is an integrative process of living together in collaborative harmony, legal fairness and social cooperation. Justice is best imputed on the bases of established law rather than the individual whims of temporal leaders. Justice is served as the expression of fair, equitable and consistent relationships.

One of my most intriguing personal experiences involves a close relation in my community with a person known as "The Justice of the Peace." I often reflect on this title while my son has served in this elected office in the justice system for over 12 years. The role entitled "The Justice of the Peace," is briefly known by the acronym, the "JP." The JP daily encounters problems in the community with jurisdiction over criminal proceedings, civil court trials, and officiates over numerous legal proceedings. The position includes conducting marriage ceremonies, authorizing protective orders in domestic abuse, certifying unnatural deaths in the community including murders, suicides and family killings.[27] The JP also authorizes commitments to mental hospitals, search warrants for probable cause, criminal arrangements plus determines bond for accused criminals. The JP has responsibilities for adjudicating juvenile truants charged with violating state laws for failing to attend school. All of these responsibilities make it very apparent that "The Justice of the Peace" is an appropriate title concretely connecting the processes of justice for advancing peace.

As a judge who is an elected official, the role of the JP inherently requires cooperative teamwork and collaborative involvement with many other professionals and agencies in the community. In the social community, judges and police are known as peace officers who serve the causes of justice. The new field of collaborative law already has produced favorable results in divorce and domestic conflicts.[28] One of my professional roles involves consulting with a number of judges about judicial cases and proceedings, plus providing professional education for law enforcement officers. Jurists have repeatedly assisted me in teaching courses on "Law and Psychology" that I have taught in courtrooms for two institutions for over 20 years. These professionals have extensive responsibilities to collaborate in providing law and order that counters crime and social chaos. Peace officers, as vital members of the justice system, have a noble history in civilized societies around the world.[29]

In order for justice and peace to permeate international relations, nations need to cooperate together for the well being of humanity. Leaders of nations need to be held accountable for collaborating to promote peace and justice. Collaboration is obviously essential for international intelligence gathering agencies as vividly revealed in the problems in obtaining, integrating, and interpreting intelligence data by British and American governments leading up to the decision to initiate the preemptive war with Iraq. They need to be cognizant that war and weapons do not assure either lasting peace or justice. Wars are fought with weapons used as instruments of coercive force and control. The termination of violent war is no assurance that peace and justice will prevail in war torn societies that are victims of violence. Cessation of violence is only one condition but not a sufficient condition for re-uniting peace and justice as partners for the social benefit of posterity.

International tribunals with jurisdiction to enforce international laws are progressively more essential for applying principles of law and justice to violent conflicts and chaotic anarchy. As people from diverse culture interact, civilized humanity requires institutions of legal justice empowered with authority to enforce decisions. Then world organizations can experience irenic harmony, security and order. Cooperation in social and legal justice plus economic and political competition promotes the aspirations of global civilizations.

Competition and cooperation are complementary polarities that can be balanced with the dynamics of conflict management. The remarriage of justice and peace thrives when the strengths of collaboration are managed while curtailing their negative components. When nations and family members compete about who is the most cooperative, humanity finds optimal harmony. As people live peacefully together, they synergize both internal peace and irenic justice in the global environment. The vision of the charter of the United Nations establishes a world institution for nations to collaborate in working out the issues involving rivalries, competition and cooperation.

**Consensus-Building:**

Humanity continues to develop political structures that incorporate universal participation in team building,[30] collaborative planning and democratic decision-making. Authoritarian decision-making in public and private organizations obviously falls short of involving responsible citizens to help determine the future of even small societies let alone the intricacies of global developments. Even the most refined methods of democratic decision-making still have serious limitations in universal election of representatives and voting on referendums, let alone extensive consensus building among citizens.

Increasingly, the discoveries in information technology are within the reach of more and more people. Information technology contributes both positively to human communication while it also is subject to economic exploitation for the benefit of special interests. The technological tools are rapidly emerging for much broader participation of citizens around the globe. However, the political, educational, economic and social structures still have not discovered effective methods for interactive consensus building for joint decision-making. Voting technology still needs to develop trustworthy recording of votes. The modern corporation rarely balances democratic consensus and executive who are traditionally authoritarian. Autocratic management ironically counters democratic processes, consensus building and democratic decision-making. Even with these limitations, there are goals toward which humanity can strive. Box 13-4 provides strategies for establishing cultures that re-unite peace with justice in effective consensus building.

> **Box 13-4: Peacebuilding Themes[31]**
> - **Challenges Prevailing Structures of Injustice Economically, Politically, Socially, Culturally.**
> - **Honors Multiple Voices of Social Change from Diverse Sectors.**
> - **Engages Democratically in Problem-Solving, Public Policy and Transparent Decision-making.**
> - **Empowers Individual and Group Efforts that are Socially Inclusive.**
> - **Addresses Basic Human Needs with Sustainable Development.**
> - **Practices Global Human Rights and Intergenerational Justice.**

With growing inter-cultural interactions, the globe has very few isolated pockets of humanity for whom meaningful exchanges are unavailable. Technological discoveries provide greater likelihood that historic impasses can be surmounted. There are promising potentials for global consensus building with further cooperation rather than violent competition and with greater collaboration devoid of domination. The peaceful future of global humanity involves visionary leadership collaborating with vitally concerned global citizens.

Peace-building themes in Box 13-4 are designed for global citizens and leaders to pursue comprehensive agendas for durable justice. These goals provide constructive strategies for advancing nonviolence settlement of conflicts. Peace-building parallels the concerns addressed by enlightened models for future action.[32] These themes challenge prevailing power structures of economic, political and social injustice. Cultural structures and radical religious ideologies are challenged by these transformations. Moreover, educational, scientific and technological institutions need to re-evaluate their contributions to constructive goals of concord rather than destructive ends.

Building peace and justice challenges advocates of social change from diverse sectors of society. Obviously, no single discipline possesses the wisdom necessary for addressing all the problems encountered in structural violence. Consequently, multi-disciplinary approaches and broad-based coalitions are essential in public and private organizations. No particular culture has all the insights or the means to address the global challenges in economics injustice and social oppression. The strategies of creative problem solving are essential in issues of domestic and international public policy.

**Establishing Partnerships:**

As an outgrowth of teamwork, collaboration and consensus building, human beings establish global partnerships upon which peace and justice can be sustained. Mutually beneficial partnerships are viable on both a domestic and international level. In considering the metaphor of the human relationship of marriage, a solid partnership between wife and husband is cemented with interpersonal trust, mutual commitment and open transparency. Essential ingredients also include fidelity to each other grounded in mutual commitment, love and trust. Companionship that is expressed by trusted partners provides models for quality relationships. Such a marital partnership can withstand unexpected times apart, plus sickness and health, plenty and want along with solemn vows for better or for worse. In strong relationships, partners benefit from the each other's strengths and assets while also being legally liable for the partner's debts and legal encumbrances.

Children can more likely thrive when their parent's partnership is sufficiently strong to eagerly include each child who comes into this family. In this nurturing atmosphere, the optimal development of children thrives into maturity. The family provides the incubator for optimal development in which joys and conflicts are jointly shared. Moreover, optimal learning takes place when children are fairly disciplined, challenged to risk new experiences, and supported when setbacks occur.

The concept of partnership in domestic relations is analogous to alliances between nations with mutual interests. There are coalitions that develop out of varying degrees of coercion or necessity. These alliances exist for specific goals over limited periods of time. Mutuality may be achieved to only a limited degree as members protect their national sovereignty and interests. The United Nations has functioned for six decades as the vital forum for the global family of nations where rivalries are explored, differences resolved, and sanctions imposed. Member nations need to provide additional under girding for the United Nations to pursue its goals of peace-building in the world. Transformational developments are essential for advancing the effective functioning of global organizations.

Partnerships have a significant role in promoting comprehensive world security and sustainable peace. Inherent in partnership are expectations of mutuality, reciprocity and good faith efforts in resolving conflicts. Collaborative teams help to establish strategies for addressing future disputes and differences. Nonviolent methods including negotiation, mediation, collaboration, and arbitration can displace destructive wars for violently settling conflicts.

International law is essential to base justice upon recognized law rather than upon the capricious whims of autocrats or violent force. As deadly duels were used to settle interpersonal disputes of honor in the past, war could eventually be relegated to the annals of history. In due course, reference would be made to war as the notoriously violent history when military weapons were utilized to settle conflicts that incurred tremendous bloodshed and the costly loss of resources. As human sacrifice was once practiced in earlier cultural religions, values that respect human life hopefully will emerge when peace endures and justice is sustained as re-united partners. The living condition for humanity will then become partnerships that advance the goals of peace-building and the values inherent in justice.

**Concluding Comments:**

The concept of partnership inherently includes collaborative efforts among people with mutual concerns and aspirations. The strategies involved in establishing partnerships are in direct opposition to the hopelessly violent practice of making enemies. In family relationships, partnership is integral to the marriage covenant between mates who become committed partners. In international relations, the strategies of partnerships are inherently involved in challenges of peace-building for nations that consolidate mutual interests for global security.

Building peace in concert with justice is a future strategy for human families and nation-states in order to live in harmony for their mutual benefit. As the African aphorism states, it takes a whole village to raise a child. Likewise, it takes the global village of nations to engage in lasting peace, sustaining justice and building democracies. Major challenges for global order are in need of being addressed by the United Nations. This current chapter envisions peaceful co-existence in the world. The final chapter provides the future stratagems for shaping tomorrow together for global humanity.

## Endnotes

[1] Proverbs 21:15, The Bible, New International Version, Grand Rapids, MI: Zondervan Publishing House, 1991.

[2] Mother Teresa, (2003) "War and Peace," Service, A publication of Church World Service, Spring, 2003.

[3] Parallel terms for internal and external peace are psychologically expressed in intra-personal and inter-personal relationships plus concepts of internal locus of control vs. external locus of control.

[4] Readers may presume that the author is an unreconstructed optimist whose ideas are untested. It is appropriate to remind readers that the author has honorably served in the military: has been employed in the communications industry: has had decades of experience as a psychotherapist: international organization consultant; resource to judges, clergy, physicians, ethicists, and researcher in social sciences; professor at major universities; colleague of skeptics, cynics, and empirical scientists; and traveled to countries in all continent except Australia and Antartica.

[5] Segall M., (1994, 2nd ed.), Cross-cultural Psychology: Human Behavior in Global Perspective, Monterey, CA: Brooks/Cole.

[6] Sacks J., (2003) The Dignity of Difference: How to Avoid the Clash of Civilizations, United Kingdom.

[7] Saunders H., (1999) A Public Peace Process: Sustained Dialogue to Transform Racial and Ethnic Conflicts, New York: St. Martin's Press.

[8] Wattenberg B., (March, 3, 2003), "It Will Be a Smaller World After All," The New York Times.

[9] Sacks, op.cit.

[10] Najam A., "Community Level Sustainability Assessment," www.iucn.org

[11] Ibid.

[12] Rai Saritha, (Feb. 22, 2004) "US Payroll Change Lives in Bangalore," The New York Times.

Friedman in his op-ed article in the same edition, "Meet the Zippies," identifies the newly prosperous who are financially supporting both themselves and their families while replacing the yuppies who had promising employment in America until out-sourcing relocated the employment overseas largely in India.

[13] In several northern states of India, these ratios have noticeably favored male children so that future problems are likely to occur in these states.

[14] Middents G., (2001) Crisis in Violence and Peace, Manipal, Karnataka: Manipal Press.

[15] Roy A., (2001) The God of Small Things, Cambridge MA: South End Press.

[16] Dalits are the untouchables outside the caste system. They traditionally have had few civil rights except for voting rights. There are estimated to be over 150,000,000 Dalits in India.

[17] Omvedt R., "Disturbing Aspects of Kerala Society," Bulletin of Concerned Asian Scholars.

[18] Najam, op.cit.

[19] Varshney A., (2002) Ethnic Conflict and Civic Life: Hindus and Muslims in India, New Haven: Yale University Press.

[20] Associated Press report (December 6, 2002), "Sri Lanka, Minority Rebels reach, "Commitment to Peace," The Dallas Morning News.

[21] Longest B., (1998) Health Care Policymaking, Health Administration Press.

[22] Middents G., (1995) "Public Education and Accountability," The Canadian Health Care System: Lessons for the United States, S.B. Eve, et.al, editors, University Press of America.

[23] The author has been responsible for the security of highly classified military documents and materials. He was as a former Top Secret Military Officer cleared to the Atomic Energy Commission with a "Q" Clearance during a period when Nuclear Tests were conducted in the Pacific and in Nevada by the Air Research and Development Command in which he served as Assistant Adjutant in the United States Air Force in the mid 1950's.

[24] Judge Keith was cited by Bob Herbert in his article "Secrecy is Our Enemy," in the Op-Ed section of The New York Times, September 2, 2002.

[25] Gandhi M., "Ahimsa, or the Way of Nonviolence," chapter in Approaches to Peace, edited by David Barash, (2000) Oxford University Press.

[26] Sacks, op.cit.

[27] These responsibilities include certifying deaths that include tragic multiple murders, suicides and automobile fatalities are as horrendously gruesome as battlefield casualties in combat at the hands of enemies. In domestic murder cases, the tragedies are perpetrated by a member of the family with whom the victims previously experienced trust, love and intimate experiences.

[28] Collaborative law as a field is described in Chapter Ten.

[29] For 12 years, Judge Gregory Middents has served as Justice of the Peace. There have been numerous occasions to consult with him as my son along with dozens of other federal, state and county judges.

[30] Harris L., (2003) Civilization and Its Enemies: The Next Stage of History, New York: Free Press.

[31] UNESCO and the Culture of Peace: Promoting a Global Movement, Cultures of Peace Series, UNESCO Publishing, Paris, 1995.

[32] Middents G., op.cit. Crisis in Violence and Peace.

# Chapter Fourteen

# Shaping Tomorrow Together

**Not everything that can be counted counts,
And not everything that counts can be counted.**
                                        Sign in Albert Einstein's Office

**Creative Tensions:**

Conflicts are inherent in the dynamic relationship between justice and peace. In this re-marriage metaphor of marriage, peace and justice do not experience tranquil happiness forever after. Instead their marital relation has many productive conflicts that result from creative tensions between this interdependent pair. They need each other in order to realize their joint potentials as dynamic partners. Justice provides processes for establishing fairness, equality and equity in their interactions and in the social context. Concord provides ideal goals for a trusting partnership with their natural environment. However, the need for social order may be disturbed by testy pursuits of justice that constrain freedoms that are inconsistent with the interests of the common good of humanity.

Box 14-1 provides reasons that making more enemies may thwart strategies of building just peace. For example, nations do not want their sovereignty challenged by charges of human rights violations. Pursing concordant goals places demands upon the processes of justice to counteract structural violence in the form of social oppression and economic injustice. Enforcement of safety regulations upsets businesses that consistently violate codes designed to protect employees from injury in the workplace. The economic interests of corporations can conflict with the legal protections of employees who are forced to work in unsafe environments. Similarly, a violent husband who prides himself in giving a peaceful impression in the community may secretly abuse his family. He may feel mistreated by restraints by police or court orders that curtail his criminal abuse.

> **Box 14-1: Making Enemies or Building Just Peace?**
>
> The peace building strategies advanced in this book will likely take decades before they are seriously undertaken by people prone to violence. The following reasons explain why delays may occur in order to temper expectations of immediate results:
>
> **Counter-forces:**
> - Stubborn persistence of evil that resists peace and justice.
> - Coercive violence rewarded by gains in control, influence and power.
> - Patriarchy that perpetuates over women, children and vulnerables.
> - Economic interests and military power that manipulate democracies.
> - Nations protecting their vested interests rather than global humanity.
> - Structural violence linked with traditional power structures.
>
> **Impairing Processes:**
> - Short-term goals that stifle commitments to long-range strategies.
> - Competition in domestic-international relations impairing cooperation.
> - Enemy-making that serves functions difficult to terminate or transform.
> - Violent force that commands obedience and conformity by victims.
> - Instrumental education that is predominantly entrepreneurial.
> - The *status quo* that resists transformative changes.
>
> **Conflicting Outcomes:**
> - Aggressive violence that gains instant coverage by media.
> - Intangible results in building peace & justice unattractive to media.
> - Weapons designed for war that are economically profitable.
> - Peace & justice strategies that are typically unprofitable.
> - Acquisitive needs prompting use of coercion to protect possessions.

Peace and justice can also frequently clash with international conflicts. A supposedly peaceful nation may want a threatening nation to curtail the production and sale of dangerous weapons because the sales would upset the equilibrium in the current international balance of military power. Or nations pursuing concordant relations may engage in unfair trade practices that negatively impact the economic development of the uncooperative nations. Peace between nations for fair trade might directly conflict so that neither nation could establish commerce without changing the disputed practices of both nations. For example, North and South Korea, while seeking harmonious relations, may engage in selling weapons to other nations.

Other examples of creative tension can be found in war torn nations of Afghanistan and Iraq. The Clinton Administration possessed intelligence of Al Qaeda plotters for attacks, but was apparently indecisive in deciding upon action except for one attack in the mountains of Afghanistan.[1] In addition, valid attempts to investigate violations of war atrocities cannot always be pursued immediately. Witnesses to crimes may be threatened by alleged perpetrators of atrocities who want to quiet them. Consequently, in order to achieve some semblance of fair justice, the interests of peace may need to be disturbed by delaying trials until witnesses could be adequately protected.

The partnership of peace and justice has inherent conflicts so that neither one can be maximized to pursue its highest goals. In their dynamic re-marriage, this harmonious couple needs each other as anchors in reality. When separated, they lose their equilibrium and moorings that mutually contribute to each of their growth as partners. In a strongly committed relationship, each party provides realistic feedback and courageous support for the optimal development ultimately of both. Couples who have deeply-rooted commitments of mutual trust can make healthy demands on the other partner that are reciprocated for the benefit of their marriage. Should death or divorce separate this couple, they lose mutual support plus the stimulation for creative conflict so that each can grow. Figuratively, if peace and justice are divorced, neither can function optimally for their joint benefit, for their family, or for their community. They function together at their best when they jointly serve as committed partners while each is vitally involved in the world around them.

Conversely, as trusted partners, neither party has a right to coercively control their partner. For such an important relationship to thrive, both peace and justice need to respect each other as valued partners. Domination by either one is counter-productive when one coerces the other into submission with threats of duress. With mutual respect, this concordant partnership creates cultures that shape the future of global humanity.

**Creating Families & Cultures of Just Peace:**

Innumerable factors influence how equitable harmony is expressed in the microcosm of family affairs and the broader macrocosm of international affairs. The worldviews of people are very significant in domestic and foreign relations by influencing how people implement their strategies in times of conflict. Worldviews also have enormous impact upon how people contemplate future scenarios for global humanity. Gallagher[2] provides a succinct analysis of divergent global images that could result from managing nuclear weapons and other means of mass destruction. A brief description of these divergent perspectives provides a helpful frame of reference for this final chapter concerned with shaping a better tomorrow together.

Unilateralism is a worldview held by aggressive hawks as labeled by Gallagher. She characterizes unilateralists as intellectual descendents of Thomas Hobbes, the 17th century British philosopher, who maintained that life in an anarchic world is nasty, brutish, and short. Unilateralists see human beings and nations as inherently self-interested and competitive. Furthermore, life is fundamentally filled with conflict in a zero sum game between "us" vs. "them" or between "good" vs. "evil." In this perspective, all relationships are dominated by the use of coercive power so that arms control of dangerous weapons is basically an illusion. According to Gallagher, periods of peace are considered by unilateralists as only temporary interludes that provide additional time to rearm for the next assault, battle or violent war.

A second worldview is described as "cautious cooperators" who are considered intellectual descendents of Hugo Grotius, a 17th century thinker considered the father of international law. Cautious cooperators in Gallagher's view are human beings and states that have a mixture of common and conflicting interests. They want to avoid destructive violence in their relationships. This hesitancy prompts them to need weapons primarily for purposes of defense rather than initiating aggression. Their approach to interpersonal and international relations prompts cautious cooperators to rely upon the strategy known as deterrence. But deterrence can result in an unwanted and a costly arms race according to cautious cooperators due to the presumption of defensive necessity directly derived from this worldview.

Globalists are people who possess another worldview in Gallagher's analysis. They are philosophical descendents of Immanuel Kant known for his 18th century book entitled <u>Perpetual Peace.</u> Globalists hold that economic interdependence and other mutually beneficial interactions signify that people have far more interest that they jointly hold in common rather than in antagonistic conflict. For globalists, the world functions as a universal community in which states are important players. Geopolitical experts, business leaders, and scientists plus other non-governmental organizations also have important roles to play. In this worldview, military power is considered not only costly, but also ineffective. Military power may even be counter-productive in the pursuit of world peace. Consequently, arms control is primarily useful in order to stabilize deterrence, and to transform political relationships toward more cooperative directions.[3]

Because worldviews are crucially important in determining overt actions, it is critically important to understand the implications of various worldviews. The hawkish strategies of unilateralists rely primarily on controlling others by means of violent force, power and weapons. Globalists tend to advocate optimistic approaches that assume humanity can live together nonviolently. In contrast to hawkish approaches, people who are aggressive unilateralists tend to see globalists as wimps who in turn see unilateralists as belligerent warmongers.

The European Union is persuaded that its newly found coexistence is a model for a more peaceful world according to Bronner.[4] Europeans consider American worldviews as more Hobbesian unilateralists, whereas the European Union cultivates a civilizing mission in their coexistence. As the only superpower since the end of the Cold War, America is searching for its leadership role in global relations. Kupchan suggests that America needs to balance its propensity toward unilateralism with strategic restraint in order to develop multi-lateral policies.[5]

Another alternative to the polarized worldviews of unilateralists or globalists originates on a different plane. This approach is clearly a distinctive alternative that differs from a strategy of intermediate compromise at the middle ground that might typically be proposed by cautious cooperators. This non-traditional alternative reframes conflicting relationships into perspectives not addressed by the three traditional worldviews described above. This alternative option is neither pessimistically aggressive nor romantically passive. The author advocates this alternative that instead calls for recasting traditional analyses for resolving difficult conflicts by reframing another totally different dimension. Box 14-2 outlines key issues that require the wisdom of creative problem-solvers in shaping a better world for both the present and the future.

> **Box 14-2: Building Families & Cultures of Just Peace**
>
> A number of international organizations are concerned with cultivating long-term strategies toward peace and justice. The following are ten findings recommended for moving towards "Cultures of Peace:"[6]
> - **Revisit history to discover how people contributed to their cultures.**
> - **Research non-military actors and make them models to be emulated.**
> - **Advocate for women's role in the development of their societies, and the causes and consequences of violence against women.**
> - **Promote peace goals as the dominant factor in all forms of art.**
> - **Teach the need to be aware of, and take responsibility for, the consequences that scientific discovery can have for society as a whole.**
> - **Promote responsibility for the wellbeing of the local and global community, including protection of the natural environment.**
> - **Promote gender-specific analyses that encourage women to organize themselves to make an impact on decisions that affect society.**
> - **Teach approaches of co-operation as well as competition, solidarity for mutual support, and appreciation for the rich diversity of multicultural societies.**
> - **Combat racism and discrimination while teaching respect for human rights, for human life and the dignity of the person.**
> - **Advance economic, social, cultural, civil and political rights to create conditions for disarmament and peaceful conflict resolution.**

This preferred strategy calls for mutual respect based upon intellectual wisdom that is within the grasp of human creativity. Drawing upon intercultural worldviews, this approach toward just peace synthesizes strategies of creative problem solving derived from research from intercultural insights. Rather than the regressive pessimism of unilateralists or the untested optimism of globalists, this alternative combines anchors in pragmatism synthesized with visions of idealism. This judicious alternative is symbolically characterized by the perceptive realism of the wise owl who penetrates into vast darkness while reflectively probing its surroundings with nearly 360-degrees perception. The key components of this strategy visualize peace and justice as realistically anchored in domestic and international conflicts that envision irenic future for humanity.

The future challenge for shaping cultures embracing both peace and justice places enormous demands upon these proverbial "wise owls" to interact judiciously between divergent global cultures. Cultures embracing concord already challenge their own aggressive agendas for moving away from unfortunate blunders of making enemies toward the higher goals of intercultural peace building. While political psychologists frequently make these clinical observations with domestic and international clients, the reflective wisdom of individual persons and cultures occurs in later years.

The contrast between precocious intelligence and seasoned wisdom is dramatically evident in the film "The Fog of War" that depicts the remorse of Robert McNamara, Secretary of Defense for the United States, during the war in Vietnam. His reflective confessions provide lessons learned from the failures of wars. He gained insights that his highly touted intelligence did not fathom during the tragedies incurred in deaths and damage. He was a young officer in World War II who disparaged the incendiary bombing of Japanese cities to near annihilation. He carried out massive attacks of Vietnamese as a powerful government official in charge of the American military in what the Vietnamese called the American War.[7] Two to three million Vietnamese were exterminated in these horrendous raids while over 58,000 American and Allied soldiers were killed. Hundreds of thousands of veterans were traumatized with many continuing to suffer from Post Traumatic Stress Syndrome known as PSTD.

It is apparent that perceptive wisdom did not occur to McNamara until after his younger and middle years when later he was President of the World Bank. If insights of this depth ever occur, such life corrections appear in seasoned years of reflective insights in contrast with the aggressive agenda of youth and young adulthood. Several adult development frameworks help to fathom the life correcting dynamics between younger and older adulthood in how seasoned judgment, decision-making and wisdom emerge in psychological, physical and cognitive maturity.[8]

As humanity learns from past mistakes, collective wisdom gradually develops peace and justice for the whole global village. Nation-states are slowly maturing beyond aggressive youthful stages toward experienced seasoning that provides opportunities for wise insights. The parallel occurs with youthful brains that have yet to mature toward more reliable judgment, risk management, and decision-making. Sociopaths, bullies and tyrants often do not learn from past mistakes but are motivated by immediate gratification. Mature people typically benefit from correcting mistakes whereas sociopaths often have difficulty learning from errors.

On a global level, the United Nations is the embryonic form of the rule of law in the world. In its first century, it is naturally distressed from managing the conflicting rivalries of immature nations. It is evolving toward a accomplishing reliable and trustworthy international concord. The United Nations is a modern expression that approximates Kant's solution of the world federation of nation-states. In his book, <u>Perpetual Peace,</u> Kant realized that the Hobbesian solution was a dangerous approach of military domination of the state of nature seen as "solitary, poor, nasty, brutish and short." In the Kantian village, there is a strong police force backed up by the authority of law and the courts for shaping just peace.[9]

**Rationale for Conscious Control:**

This book recognizes the intense need of human beings to exert control over their environment. This propensity of human beings to exert power extends over other people, the natural environment as well as self-control. Controllers resort to coercive force to dominate controllees as subjects at their best or victims at their worst. This human need for control extends not only to contemporary developments, but also extrapolates forward into the future toward exerting influence over unfolding, but yet unknown tomorrows.

When consideration is given to alternatives for evolving futures, there is, of course, an interplay of totally divergent worldviews. Understandably there are passive people who think that human beings were never designed to control future evolution. These persons may even believe that it is presumptuous to influence evolution and may actually try to prohibit such human interventions.

Other people have serious reservations whether human beings are capable of designing the future of global humanity and the natural environment. This latter group often identifies the chaotic conditions of the present world as evidence of human limits. On the other hand, equally sophisticated observers are fascinated with the scientific order, natural laws, artistic form and aesthetic beauty of the cosmos.

While respecting both views that humans are forbidden to shape their future or the presumption that they have exclusive responsibility for their future, the author continues to address these conflicting challenges.[10] Human beings and other living organisms are shaped by complex combinations of their biological genes and the natural environment. Simultaneously, they are also shaped by humanly invented memes.[11] Memes are considered "any permanent pattern of matter or information produced by human intentionality."[12] Memes include any human invention from the simple brick and tool all the way to computers, religions, and Mozart's Requiem. Memes also include all institutions and organizations that are composed of people and their cultures. Memes include human knowledge, science, invented technology, weapons, information systems, plus all cultural artifacts.

While human beings create memes, they are also threatened by the propensity of memes to selfishly reproduce themselves by consuming energy similar to genes. Blackmore[13] has concluded that the memetic drive to replicate is expressed by the human capacity to imitate. In the process of replication, memes typically consume more energy than they return to the environment. Memes like genes try to reproduce themselves consuming resources in the process of reproductive survival in which memes, like genes, take on a life of their own in order to perpetuate their own self-interests. Memes develop further complex systems that evolve themselves to the edge of chaos.[14]

For example, consider the seductive promise of nuclear power whose destructive by-products like enriched uranium need careful management in order to conscientiously control possessors of nuclear weapons. With the challenge of nuclear memes, a number of questions naturally arise:

- Are human beings the actual controllers or the potential victims of human discoveries that are themselves cultural memes?
- How can human beings foresee whether technology as a form of meme will actually benefit us, seduce us, eventually control us, or possibly even rape the ecosystem?
- How do genes and memes control humanity or is controlled by them?
- How does information technology as a meme simultaneously provide both immeasurable human benefits while overloading people with conflicting data and internet spam?

Both genes and memes take on a life of their own if they are not carefully managed. If humanity does not control them, the most ominous challenges indicate that they will control humanity along with the social and natural environment. Consequently, the following questions are offered for further consideration:

1. **Will evolution be consciously managed or be controlled by genes and memes rather than humans becoming their future masters ?**

2. **How can the enticing potentials of memes and genes be optimized for future development while avoiding disasters to the ecosystems?**

Peaceful co-existence expects even more of human beings in order to nonviolently control the future without employing means of coercive force, weapons or violence. The common good of irenic concord will become the high ground for just social policies of governance.[15]

In order for these constructive strategies to take place, intentional design becomes essential for assuring the nonviolent future for humanity. Direct human involvement in designing the future of the world becomes increasingly essential. The question is not whether these changes will evolve, but the key question becomes – how will these transformations take place? How will these transformations be intentionally be controlled by human beings who possess constructive worldviews for evolving peaceably?

Strategies for intentionally designing the future of humanity and the environment is consistent with the assumption that an ultimate purpose of human life is to meaningfully contribute to the creation of human and cosmic consciousness.[16] Ornstein confirms this challenging perspective with his conclusion that there will be no future evolution without conscious evolution.[17] A major challenge for peace building is that these transformations transpire nonviolently. Consequently, the following section provides deliberate strategies to influence the future of humanity toward nonviolence, sustaining peace and doing justice. Box 14-3 provides strategies for implementing peaceful and just futures.

---

**Box 14-3: Transformations for Peaceful Existence**

Merry[18] suggests several major shifts necessary in human awareness as to address transformative challenges. These shifts in cognitive processes include such stressfully demanding challenges as:

- **Evolving consciousness in which humanity guides its own evolution.**
- **Functioning on the creative edge of chaos and complexity.**
- **Learning to shape evolution by cooperation, altruism, and ecological ethics.**
- **Re-inventing ourselves in order to be co-creators in a multi-verse.**
- **Enhancing creativity as human brains cope with chaos.**

Merry also suggests necessary transformations in human values. She characterizes these transformations by identifying the following changes in human relationships:[19]

- **From competitiveness to collaborative cooperation.**
- **From linear thinking of unidirectional causality to nonlinear chaos and creativity.**
- **From narrow specializations to multi-disciplinary sciences of learning.**
- **From dominator male models of governance to co-creative sharing by both sexes of roles and responsibilities.**
- **From economic indifference about the environment to ecological consideration of intentional efforts to evolve the future.**
- **From people serving as functions of work toward forming responsible and caring relationships for each other.**

## Threefold Bridging Fear And Peace:

The rough road to peace and justice involves coping with threats that can paralyze constructive action. Fear is hampering humanity in dealing with violent terrorism and war. There is dread of suicide bombings and potential chaos that challenges order and security. Fears are polarized with fault lines across from their opposites in peaceful existence in both domestic and international relations. Even freedom can be dreaded in open democratic societies so that controlling procedures are introduced to constrict civil liberties in the name of national and homeland security. These conflicts produce both specific fears that feed basic psychological anxieties that people experience in families and in global relations.

Figure 14-1 provides a crude visual design for identifying fault lines with bridges across fears on the right and peace on the left.[20]

The reader is advised to refrain from over-interpreting this model beyond its rudimentary bounds since the author realizes its limitations. It could very well be wrong, too narrow, too idealistic, and be too limited in worldviews. With these cautions, it is offered to provoke thinking, responses, and dialogue that hopefully will lead to improvements. As a guide, it is preferable to follow the model through the six Roman numerals as phases of fears identified in early chapters first along the right hand side depicting fear. Then come full circle across the imaginary bridge over the middle fault lines toward world order and security upward to global peace, justice and family health.

Families and tribes inherently foster trust, inclusiveness and control[21] that permit these units to develop working relationships. Loving nurture and mutual affection foster intense loyalty and identification with the welfare and health of family members. Degrees of autonomy, freedom, language, socialization, and personal identity are grounded in immediate families. Families provide for survival needs, comforts and social status. These positive qualities of trust are counter-balanced on the dark side with family abuse, punishment and neglect as suggested in Number I.

Usually families gather together into larger groups for mutual support, protection, production and survival. The ties of blood relationships influence mating and marriage partners. Marital preferences can emphasize selecting mates from outside the immediate tribe. No. II in Figure 14-1 depicts how tribal loyalties are developed. Positive trust in the community of these extended families has blind shadows of hidden domestic violence, abuse and neglect. Abusively violent fathers (and vicious mothers to a lesser degree) can hold family members hostage with psychological terror, authoritarian control, and physical abuse that literally threatens life and death. Unfortunately, there are tragic cases in which children are killed by their own parents as well as children engaging in Oedipal tragedies of patricide and matricide.

As an extension of sexual abuse, inbreeding in tribes is a corollary to incest in the nuclear family instigated by power figures. Provincial values generate from singular worldviews taught within the tribe. Ideological values and parochial religious views generate out of insular thinking and isolation from different perspectives that threaten the group. Religious cults may even justify dishonorable rationales for authoritarian leaders to engage in sexual intercourse with any member of the cult that he chooses. Internal discipline is readily enforced with emotional and physical violence, while weapons are often used to resist external threats from invading tribes.

Much of the world's population continues to live in tribal communities. These tribes may have harmonious relationships that permit peaceful co-existence that depends on the authoritarian leaders who may be benevolent or a tyrannical autocrat who holds life and death decisions over subjects. Controlling members of the tribe with threats, rewards and incentives is crucial for preserving the tribe. The leader is the one who has freedom to make decisions of life and death, mandate taxation, or coerce members to sacrifice for the defense of the tribe or for conquest of targeted possessions.[22]

Another level of organization is essential for nations to formulate into identified sub cultures beyond bonds of family trust and tribal loyalties. Numbers III and IV in Figure 14-1, identify the nation-state that has dominated western governance for several hundred years. Trust has been developed by professions that assure competent delivery of complex services as illustrated by licensed physicians. Doctors have gained the confidence of societies to deliver medical, surgical and healing services that gain the trust of patients. Physicians are trusted to place the needs of their patients ahead of their own economic interests in order to deliver vital health care services.

Politicians have a mixture of trust from their constituents due to the corruption of financial influences in elections. Democracy and economic interests have formed insidious coalitions in American politics and other democracies. Major corporate accomplishments have developed through science and technology, economic globalization, military power, collectivism, and cultural achievements. The dark side of these achievements may become corrupted by structural violence, social and economic injustice, racism, xenophobia, civil and world wars. Major segments of society have not been able to compete due to destructive competition, national patriotism, and violations of civil social contract. In addition, greedy exploitation by unethical individuals and corporate management occur when regulations are weaker than unbridled aggression.

Harris[23] suggests that the capacities to functions as a trusted team member who possesses self-control are essential for collective action so that coercive violence threatening death is unnecessary for gaining joint effort. To be trusted, a person needs a personal conscience generated out of guilt rather than external sources of shame for managing them. Persons governed by guilt possess self-control that permits them to protect the interest of customers over their own economic greed. Professionalism is possible when non-tribal members can trust a person to perform services that protect the interests of a client exemplified by physician's care for patients. In contrast, persons controlled by shame may take advantage of another's weakness that serves their own greedy interests unless external shaming sanctions prohibit them. Persons reared in guilt cultures develop self-regulation whereas shame cultures rear people who require external sanctioning control. Harris goes on to make a number of provocative assertions in political theory, philosophical analysis, history and economics about sovereigns, tyrants, violence, democracy, capitalism and ethics.

In order for global peace to emerge, the interests held in common by nations must become primary for international justice, global social ethics, world order and security. The United Nations Declaration of Human Rights illustrates one of the highest expressions of the human family. While endorsed by many nations, regrettably it has not been officially ratified by the United States. On the downside of the highest achievements of humanity, there continues a series of developments that retard the development of No. V for World Security and Order including in Figure 14-1:

- The sovereignty of the primary powers on the Security Council of the United Nations who protect their own national rather than global interests.
- The limited agendas of smaller nations when major issues are confronted.
- The lack of established international law and justice systems that together address the problems of humanity.
- The historical rivalries of nations, cultures, and narrow ethnocentrism.
- Development of major weapons systems of mass destruction without enforceable treaties for arms control and disarmament.
- Lack of mutual trust between conflicting cultural, political, religious, scientific, and economic ideologies of governance for global humanity.
- Unwillingness to suffer and sacrifice for the greater good of humanity.

Phases VI in Figure 14-1 of global peace and justice requires a vision partially emerging among peoples with a passion for shaping a better world tomorrow. It figuratively goes off the page into future evolvement that combines interaction of human genes and social memes. Hopefully a break in the cycle of violence will lead to a orbital future that provides for irenic concord.

1. **Bridging Intrapersonal Rifts:**

A constructive bridge of intrapersonal rifts is visualized in Box 14-4. These conflicts need management by leaders who comprehend polarities struggling for resolution. Rifts on the left side need to cross over the bridge to goals on the right side of this Box. The following outline provides agendas that facilitate crossing by managing past conflicts moving toward the outcomes of just peace:

- Respect the dignity of differences among diverse cultures.[24]
- Appreciate the divergent paths toward unified truth.
- Comprehend that humanity's health and genetic pool can jointly thrive on planet earth.
- Realize that the fragile environment is sustainable by trusting team efforts, scientific research, and personal stewardship.
- Construct bridges across fault lines that divide humanity into enclaves of special interest motivated primarily by self-preservation.
- Honor multiple identities by individuals and nations for global citizenship right alongside local loyalties and national loyalty.
- Discernment that humans gain wisdom only by suffering.[25]

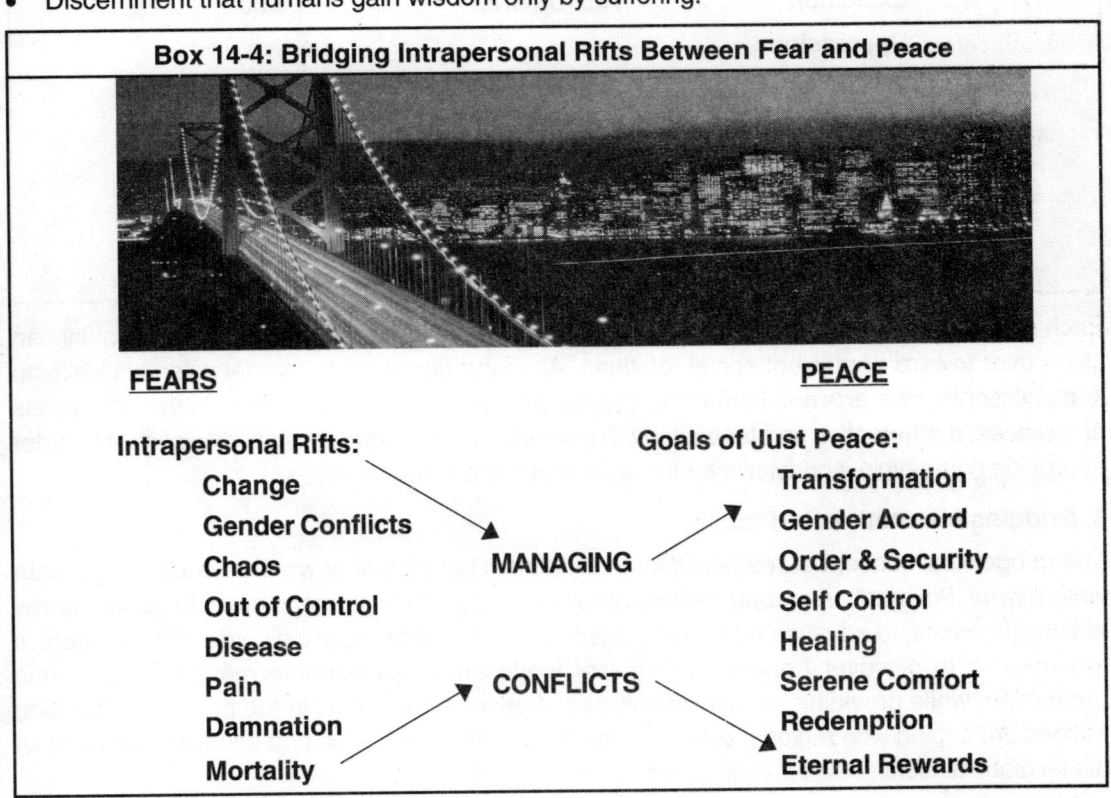

Box 14-4: Bridging Intrapersonal Rifts Between Fear and Peace

**FEARS**

Intrapersonal Rifts:
- Change
- Gender Conflicts
- Chaos
- Out of Control
- Disease
- Pain
- Damnation
- Mortality

MANAGING

CONFLICTS

**PEACE**

Goals of Just Peace:
- Transformation
- Gender Accord
- Order & Security
- Self Control
- Healing
- Serene Comfort
- Redemption
- Eternal Rewards

## 2. Bridging Social Rifts:

The social barriers outlined in Box 14-5 between fears and peace are represented by deep fault lines in need of bridging. These chasms are not exhaustive but suggestive in moving across the bridge from left toward the goals of just peace.

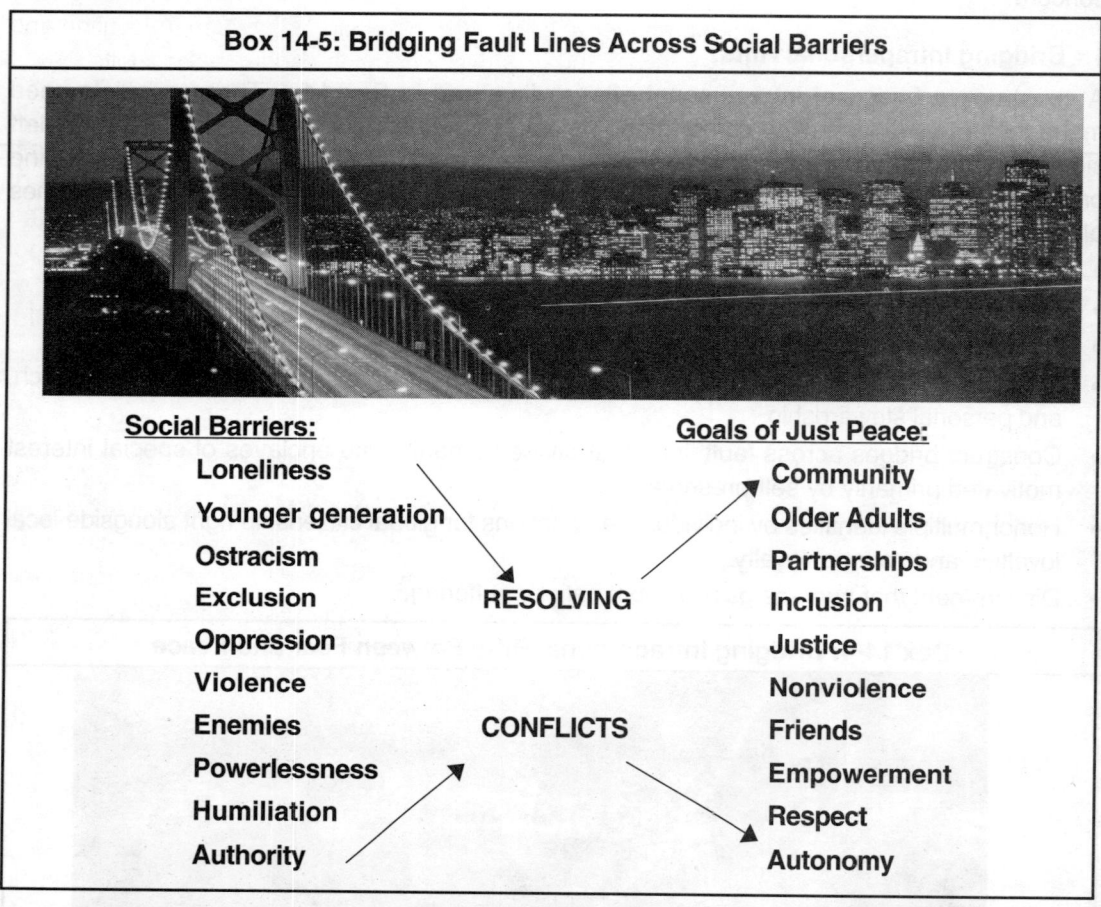

**Box 14-5: Bridging Fault Lines Across Social Barriers**

| Social Barriers: | | Goals of Just Peace: |
|---|---|---|
| Loneliness | | Community |
| Younger generation | | Older Adults |
| Ostracism | | Partnerships |
| Exclusion | RESOLVING | Inclusion |
| Oppression | | Justice |
| Violence | | Nonviolence |
| Enemies | CONFLICTS | Friends |
| Powerlessness | | Empowerment |
| Humiliation | | Respect |
| Authority | | Autonomy |

Each of the barriers on the left of Box 14-5 demands thorough resolution so that humanity can cross over toward nonviolent social relations. All of the disciplines of social sciences, religion and philosophy, plus arts and humanities can contribute to life together alongside the discoveries of sciences, mathematics and technology. These efforts are inherently multi-disciplinary in order to provide compatible worldviews for living on earth and in the universe.

## 3. Bridging International Rifts:

The geopolitical concept of *realpolitik* for international balance of power has been fraught with violent wars. Polarization among nations results in threats to violence in order to serve narrow national interests, to advance hegemonic agendas, and control chaotic disorder. New strategies are needed to discover nonviolent forms of world order, sustainable means of economic production, while providing security in cultures of peace and justice. In the post-Cold War era, nations are coping with regional conflicts, one dominant superpower, and economic stresses of digital globalization.

Deep fault lines depict Huntington's clash between major world civilizations,[26] Kennedy's concepts of the West vs. the Rest,[27] Kaplan's analysis of the prosperous North vs. impoverished South,[28] Fukuyama's description of democratic vs. non-democratic societies,[29] and Friedman's identification of the fast digital world vs. slow globalization.[30] Nye poses the contrast between nations who use hard vs. soft approaches to resolving disputed differences. Psychologically there are also fault lines that need creative bridging such as tensions between masculine and feminine plus the ongoing conflicts between the younger generation and the older adults.[31]

In Kupchan's terminology,[32] the historical means of production, governance, and community identity have cultivated violent means for authoritarian control enforced with threats of domination over more than 10,000 years. To understand his integration of these three factors (means of production, governance, and community identity,) imagine a three-legged stool holding up the world. Each of the three legs represents economics, politics or religion. This metaphorical stool draws upon Kupchan's parallel ideas for the means of production, dominant institutions of governance, and institutions of communal identity that need to be balanced for peaceful coexistence. When anyone of these legs gains dominance or is shortened, the stool becomes unstable and tipsy. As these three legs undergo transformations in the digital age, each leg experiences stresses. These conflicts result in disequilibrium that can precipitate local violence and global war. The world can become very volatile when any of the three legs is altered.

Global rifts are symptoms that reflect the need for better strategies for managing and resolving conflicts. Box 14-6 bridges international fault lines with rifts outlined on the left contrasted with the other side that outlines goals of just peace identified on the right. For global concord, the rifts must be addressed with constructive actions in order to cross the bridge toward building nonviolent international relations.

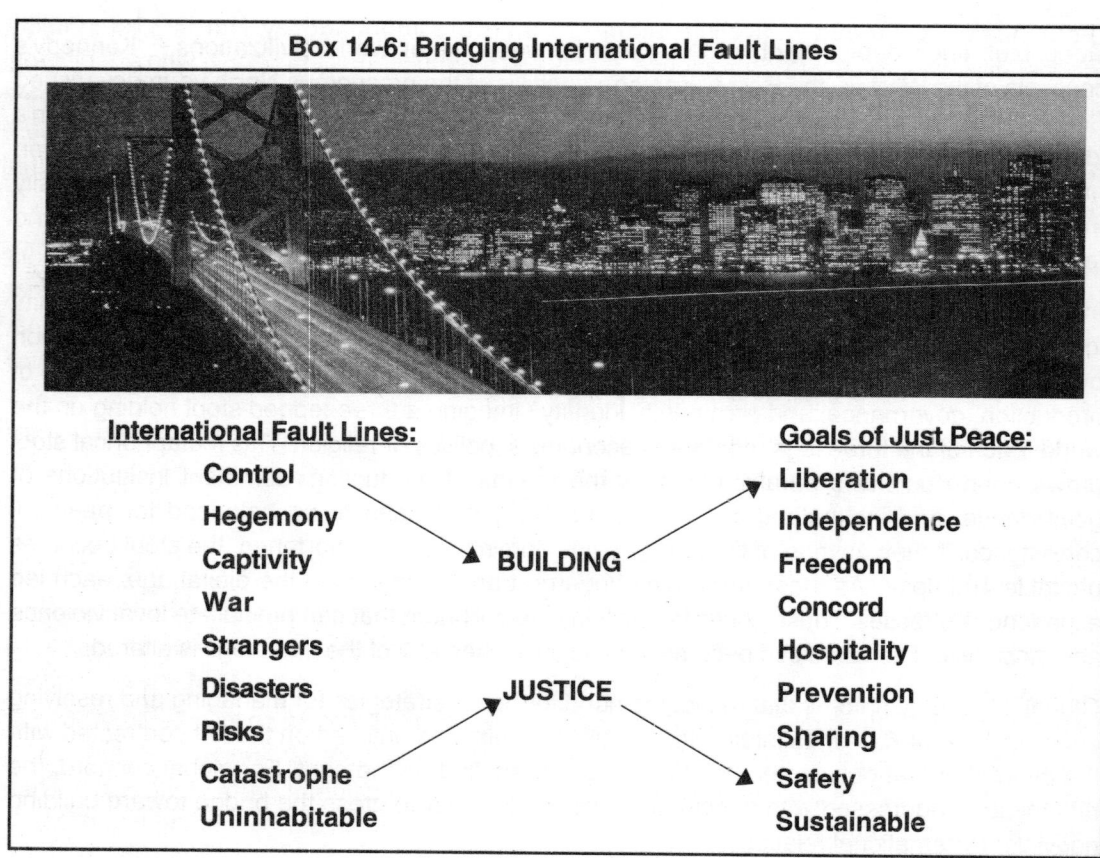

In view of these challenges, what strategies can shape a better world tomorrow? Geyer's[33] vision provides promise for overall equilibrium with his perspectives of a "convivial world." He imagines a new world that envisions living together as a human family in peace. This convivial world needs stable bridges that stabilize the three vital legs of the mode of production, national and international governance, and institutions of communal identity. Justice, truth and knowledge are critical components for constructing bridges between fears in a violent world to reach toward a peaceful, nonviolent world.

Conflicting issues in the modern struggles of the digital era are emerging that require nonviolent resolution. In the realm of biological genetics and social environment, there are basic struggle between more intelligent brains that conflict with primitive approaches of violent brawn that use violent force to settle differences. The fault lines between war and peace are being polarized between military powers and nonviolent approaches advocated by the United Nations. The issue of population explosion and sustainable development are being played out by current generations who influence posterity. The issue of younger and older civilizations needs to face challenges of cosmic space beyond earthly boundaries. When tyrannical control conflicts with autonomous freedom, struggles occur in family and international conflicts between the younger and older generations that can be creatively bridged. Liberating bridges can be built to free victims and enemies as well as controlling bullies, tyrants and empire builders from their narcissistic worldviews.[34]

Four historical factors that civilizations develop are identified by Harris[35] as stability, cooperativeness, refusal to use violence, and social tolerance. Trusting people who are different in their worldviews as well as trusting the "dignity of diversity"[36] are risks in bridging divergent cultures in order to avoid the destructive clash of civilizations. Major efforts to transcend traditional barriers is essential in building bridges across old walls, fault lines and chasms that divide people into opposing camps.

The bridges built between fears and peace challenge humanity to guide future transformations toward a convivial world. Skills in managing conflicts are essential for addressing intrapersonal, social and environment problems. Competencies in negotiation also apply to intrapersonal, interpersonal and global tensions that grow beyond the need for controlling other people's destinies. Economic, legal and social justice is essential for bridging problems that are encountered in personal, domestic and international conflicts. The processes of conflict management, conflict resolution, and justice are nonviolent methods for transforming anxieties into irenic conditions that advance global living.

**Bold Experiments in Peace Building:**

Governmental and private organizations have pioneered experiments that address the peace building for the long term. The United Nations provides nonviolent approaches for managing and resolving international conflicts. It continues to struggle with global fault lines in restless world conflicts. Naturally, the United Nations has many critics as well as an increasing consensus that it is a forerunner of world order and security. Its constituent components involve peace restoring and peacemaking in a variety of violent conflicts in different parts of the world. There is tremendous need to train millions of people to serve as peacekeepers and peace-builders in roles that traditional soldiers cannot be expected to fulfill.

International institutes have been created in visionary cultures that deliberately invest in strategies for peace rather than squandering resources unnecessarily into military systems that heighten rather than resolve tensions. Creating peace communities have been projects undertaken in Australia, India and Japan. For decades Sweden and Norway have pioneered institutes for peace research and education that include concrete negotiating services offered to cultures that have experienced entrenched violence. South Africa is involved in providing leadership for resolving conflicts in Africa and in the broader world. Costa Rica provides a non-military model for nations in North and South America. The Organization Development Institute composed of international consultants includes constituent units designed to facilitate nonviolent changes in large cultures. The Carnegie Institute for International Peace likewise contributes expertise and financial support toward peace efforts in global problems.

Similar to other international service programs, the Peace Corps has involved 168,000 volunteers in a wide range of community development, educational, social and health programs in 70 developing countries. The Americorps has involved over 150,000 persons in service to people who experience social and economic stresses. In addition, the United States Peace Institute was formulated in the past two decades with advanced education, peace and conflict resolution research, fellowships and internships. It also publishes studies and provides expert consultations for both private and public agencies vitally concerned with advancing the causes of peace.

Fortunately, educational institutions are teaching skills in resolving conflicts for children, adolescents and adults. These programs make constructive impact for long-term contributions to peace and justice. A number of world-class universities have developed academic departments that offer both undergraduate and graduate degrees in fields directly related to peace studies, conflict resolution, negotiation, mediation, public policy, justice systems and sustainable development. Governmental organizations (GO's), non-governmental organizations (NGO's) and international non-governmental organizations (INGO's) are increasingly involved in concerns for peace and justice. These efforts have multiplied concrete programs that address structural violence to alleviate economic poverty plus advance social injustice and human rights. Religious groups from around the world are making major efforts to advance peacemaking and justice. Religions also provide unheralded charities, volunteer opportunities and internships for people with global concerns.[37]

Another pioneering and innovative experiment merits additional special attention. After more than five years of careful planning, The Rotary Foundation has launched the program for educating Peace Scholars. This experiment is a long-term investment in creating highly educated leaders for international peace building. Rotary International is building on recognized contributions of 100 years to international education, cultural exchanges, humanitarian, health and social service programs. Over 33,000 Ambassadorial Scholars have engaged in educational programs for studying in various countries in the world. The Rotary International health program called Polio Plus currently engages in partnerships to eradicate polio by vaccinating over 1,500,000,000 children around the world.[38]

Building on these accomplishments, Rotary International is underwriting through its Rotary Foundation investment in advanced graduate studies for 350 outstanding young Peace Scholars.[39] These scholars commit major facets of their professional careers to efforts in peace building and conflict resolution. After careful selection processes, these Peace Scholars enroll in one of seven universities around the world that have recognized track records of graduate programs in peace and conflict resolution. These universities include: University of Queensland in Australia, International Christian University in Japan, University of Bradford in England, Sciences Po in France, *Universidad del Salvador* in Argentina, University of California in Berkeley, USA, and the joint program jointly sponsored by Duke University and University of North Carolina, USA. These Peace Scholars enroll in one of these universities outside of their native country to foster international and intercultural competencies in conflict resolution. It is obvious that Asia needs additional educational centers for peace scholars since as a continent it is a laboratory for strategic studies, domestic abuse, international war and terrorism. Governments and leading universities could fill a crucial gap in constructively dealing with conflicts with preventive and intervention measures.

These universities provide quality faculty, educational experiences, internships and research resources with demonstrated capabilities to provide significant components of interdisciplinary studies. No traditional discipline has a monopoly for addressing the challenges encountered in domestic and international conflicts. Consequently, these Peace Scholars are prepared for careers by investigating a wide range of educational and experiential programs that incorporate the following fields:

- **Mediation, Conflict and Peace where there is War.**
- **Understanding where there is Disharmony.**

- **Food Security where there is Hunger.**
- **Health Care where there is Disease.**
- **Education where there is Illiteracy.**
- **Conservation where there is Environmental Degradation.**
- **Sustainable Economic Development where there is Poverty.**

While many people around the world have vital interest in peace building, realistically many aspiring people can be described as predominantly peace hopers and peace talkers. With encouragement, these people are becoming peace doers and peace builders for the future of global humanity in their family relations and in their international relations. Many people have ethereal ideas about peace. These ideals are often reflected in having a "mentally soft" concept of peace. This is characterized by limited ideas of peace as primarily a mental state of serenity that experiences cognitive tranquility on an individual level.

Peace must be pursued actively and sacrificially in physical actions and social practices. Peace building is done together with partners rather than internally as individuals. If individual peace is the total scope of concern, then future social interactions has limited possibilities. Individual peace focuses on isolated private affairs without concern for neighbors. Holistic peace is principally expressed in social relations. Conflicts arise predominantly in social relationships as well as within personal perceptions of problems. People are socially engaged with their neighbors and most poignantly with their enemies.

Scientific experiments are conducted by psychologists for understanding how to extinguish and conquer fear. This research uses de-conditioning and de-programming approaches based upon "unlearning fear responses" that have been conditioned by terrifying experiences. Learning a fear response may take exposure to a long series of negative stimuli or a one-time terrorizing trauma. However, extinction and conquering these phobic fears and panic attacks may occur under special short treatment approaches. The feared stimuli are presented by flooding or massing bursts of negative cues that are surprisingly efficient in animal experiments and has promise for possible applications for reducing and conquering human fears.[40]

The thrust of various concerns for reducing fear while advancing peace and justice is that people cannot possess peace exclusively for themselves. Peace involves dimensions of freedom, justice, love and truth that are profoundly social in nature. Precisely because interactions with enemies are threatening, violent retaliation perpetuates conflicts rather than resolves them. Peace involves relationships with our friends as well as with our enemies. Peace is costly to personal serenity, personal vulnerability and social hospitality. Realistically, there are negative dimensions to acknowledge:

- **Peace is not about humiliating our opponent.**
- **Peace is not about criticizing faults in our neighbors.**
- **Peace is not limited to human beings but includes creation.**
- **Peace is not accomplished by dominating other people.**
- **Peace does not rely on military weapons and violent force.**
- **Peace is not cheap or painless.**
- **Peace is not a spectator activity.**
- **Peace in not about building walls, barriers or fault lines.**

In contrast, the positive challenge calls people to directly interact with enemies and neighbors for peace-building that:

- **Demands passionate commitment.**
- **Requires cooperative collaboration.**
- **Constructs bridges across divisions, fault lines and walls.**
- **Engrosses transforming self, society and the *status quo*.**
- **Includes protection of a sustainable natural environment.**
- **Becomes a vocational calling to public service.**
- **Involves reconciling with our enemies.**
- **Requires sacrificing and suffering.**

People who engage in peace building need to challenge old ways of thinking, feeling and acting. Unless there is social involvement domestically and internationally for peace and justice, preoccupations with peace are spiritually private and individualistic. Existing power structures prefer to co-opt peace builders in order to appease and control them. Vested interests in structural violence naturally prefer peace agents with limited savvy whom they can control. Power structures do not want the existing *status quo* threatened. Younger nations observe what happens to nations just as young people succeed their forbearers. The insight of Asad Latif aptly observes from history that "America, too, will grow old one day."[41]

Challenging questions confront people aspiring to peace that invite further investigation:
- **Are there other alternatives that provide greater challenges or more tangible rewards?**
- **Is there any greater adventure than to become involved in experiments for peace?**
- **What more heroic involvement contributes more to the peace and hope of global humanity?**
- **Grandchildren will likely ask important questions addressed to us as their forebears:**
  - **What did we do to make the world a better place for peace, justice, hope and the well being of the future?**
  - **What answers will we give them?**

# Epilogue: Bridging to Future Generations

**Pursue Peace with Everyone.**
Hebrews 12: 14[42]

**Call to Public Service:**

The task of peace builders is a call to public service in the world of apprehensive fear. Among the highest callings is willingness to make the necessary sacrifices including unknown personal and professional risks. At the juncture where the pressing needs of human society match our personal passions and gifts, there are compelling calls to public service. This vocational calling involves significant exciting careers and voluntary service absorbed with advancing peace for humanity now and the future.

These claims are substantiated by the experience of people who unselfishly engage in serving health, educational and social needs of people. People possessed with a passion for peace recognize that the Latin term for "passion" is rooted in the capacity to sacrifice personal agendas and suffer on behalf of a better future for children, families and nations. These involvements contribute vitally to spiritual, economic, artistic, scientific and humanitarian needs of domestic and global neighbors along with thriving in physical and psychological development.

Humanity worldwide desperately needs peaceful approaches for solving human problems both within families and among nations in conflict. The previous chapters repeatedly identify unfulfilled needs that violate human rights, economic and social injustice. Moreover, family conflicts, structural violence, international violence, terroristic and criminal violence have been analyzed. The focus now involves understanding the problems of making enemies and keeping them so that efforts are made to transform them into friends to build peace.

Concerned people need to address these urgent problems by providing visionary leadership in nonviolent solutions. Human needs call for new competencies in conflict management, conflict resolution, plus public policies that address economic, political and social disparities. These crises in violence and war are issues inherently involved in building concordant relations. The needs are overwhelming and the challenges are global in nature. Old worn-out alternatives of war cyclically perpetuate more violence, despair and hopelessness. These violent approaches are obviously inadequate as long-term solutions to the urgent problems of global humanity.

Young people and adults around the world are challenged to invest their intelligence, energies, creativity and enthusiasm into building peace and resolving conflict. Children, youth and adults from diverse cultures possess the gifts essential to transform the world from enemies to friends. Rather than having young people conscripted into military service, universal humanitarian service holds promise for nonviolently transforming domestic and international conflicts. This universal service would be invested in human development, food production and fair distribution. In addition, there are challenges in providing health care, education, conflict resolution, governance, science, technology, social ethics, plus civil and human rights along with social and economic justice. Intercultural experiences of these young people that confront global problems of humanity have enormous possibilities for creating global peace cultures.

The highest values, ideals and commitments of people hold the potential for impacting cultures to build peace and do justice. Humanitarian efforts call for a range of one to three years of universal service. The challenge calls for nations to invest financial resources adequate to cover expenses for subsistence and training in peace-building. Within a few generations, many cultures in the world could transform violence by channeling their energy into nonviolent resolution of conflicts inherent in human living. The multiplier effect could reach billions of people within 25 years if each learner teaches one other learner per year.[43] Young people possess interests in challenging adventures and new experiences that impact human destiny. They are motivated to make a difference in their generation by tackling problems that confront humanity. Children, youth and adults can create cultures of peace while discovering direction for their future and the lives of future generations around the world.

Challenges to engage in universal service need to be identified by global leaders who formulate agendas that address the domestic and international problems. World leaders with visions of a better world endorse parallel involvements for people globally. Channeling the passions, talents and energies of young people makes an immeasurable impact upon cultural development as well as upon the future careers of young persons. The call to public service multiplies the causes of building peace and justice to address the domestic problems and international conflicts of global humanity.

**Toward Building Just Peace:**
This book charts a course designed to advance humanity beyond making destructive enemies toward the destination of building peace in partnership with justice. Charting this course is based upon pragmatic optimism of hopefulness for a nonviolent future rather than reliance on destructive force that violently controls other people. Naturally, these goals involve a stretch for both family life and international relations. On the other hand, a chronic pessimist is inclined to take a dim view of charting peaceful directions for humanity. An immediate skeptic would claim that these nonviolent strategies are not practical either domestically or internationally. A constructive response to this cynicism realizes that ideals by definition are not immediately workable in the short run. Rather peace built with irenic justice are long-term goals for which creative imagination is necessary to develop strategies that require thinking outside the confines of the traditional box.

Global consciousness is at the threshold of a major leap toward much wider involvement of people across many cultures of the world. Technologies are now available so that differences in languages can be overcome for efficient communication. Modern transportation already provides for extensive global travel. Hi-tech messages are conveyed in instantly. Legal procedures for justice are gradually emerging with wide international acceptance. However, vested political, religious, social and economic interests possess turf loyalties and narrow ethnocentrism. Intercultural education provides growth experiences that overcome the parochial provincialism. It is vital to embark upon creative transformations away from destructive violence in aspiring for a peaceful and just future. In order to envision a better world tomorrow, Box 14-7 provides synergistic strategies for establishing cultures that re-unite peace with justice.

> **Box 14-7: General Conclusions from the
> First International Forum on the Culture of Peace**[44]
>
> - **The objective of a culture of peace ensures that the conflicts inherent in human relationships be resolved non-violently.**
> - **Peace and human rights are indivisible concerns of everyone.**
> - **The construction of a culture of peace is a multidimensional task requiring the participation of people at all levels of society.**
> - **Cultures of peace contribute to enhancing the strengths of democratic processes and institutions.**
> - **Implementing cultures of peace requires a thorough mobilization of all means of education plus all forms of communication.**
> - **Cultures of peace expect learning new techniques for the peaceful management and nonviolent resolution of conflicts.**
> - **Cultures of peace should be elaborated within the process of sustainable, endogenous, equitable human development because it cannot be imposed from the outside.**

With unprecedented cultural interaction, the globe has very few isolated pockets of humanity where meaningful exchange cannot effectively transpire. There are enormous potentials for greater global consensus building for cooperation rather than violence, collaboration rather than condescending domination, and transparent communication. The future of humanity calls for inclusive visions and constructive imaginations that are exercised by global leadership and responsible citizenship.

## Who is Responsible for Tomorrow?

There are at least four perspectives to consider in shaping a better world tomorrow. A primary perspective for people of faith acknowledges that God as Creator is the ultimate source of life and the future. Many religious views consider Divine Providence to be continuously engaged in sustaining creation. Providence transeuntly sustains life in the universe not only as the first cause in ordering chaos, but also working through second causes and permutations beyond. This perspective addresses the propensity for presumptuous human egos to become inflated and over-reaching in their individual and collective influence.

A second perspective is that of past generations of humanity who represent our genetic forbearers. Without question, our worldwide ancestors are essential to the very existence of contemporary humanity. Our forbearers passed the gift of life onward to us as their offspring. Our own spark of life came directly from these vital progenitors. Without them we would not be alive nor have our story to share. They risked their lives in childbirth, they expended their energy to nurture us, and they placed their hopes in their descendents. Even with their mistakes that have become our lessons for today, they collectively transmitted their precious heritage to us. This heritage embraces not only the gift of life, but it also includes our cultures, our institutions, and our aspirations.

The third group that needs a voice about a better future includes the children of the world. Children directly depend on us to establish a better world for their wellbeing. The degree to which our children experience irenic justice is highly dependent on their parents plus other adults alive today. With immediate concern for the world's children, it is important to remember that global cultures, human institutions and the natural environment are always very fragile. Democracies are vulnerable to extinction unless it is diligently practiced by successive generations. Unless global citizenship is conscientiously exercised, the future security of the children in the world is unpredictably precarious. Human destiny is directly dependent upon our investments in civilized culture, education, political freedom, effective structures of justice, health care and social institutions designed to nonviolently resolve conflicts.

The fourth group equally as important as our children is inclusively known as our human posterity. Their very existence is imperiled without our concerns for the care of the natural environment, ecosystem and cultures, plus the conscientious stewardship of our genes, health, and human inventions. Future posterity is dependent upon the current living generations for their future viability. However, this vulnerable posterity is readily overlooked and even treated with disdainful indifference. This ignorant lack of concern for posterity is reflected in the crass statements that were addressed to me by an extremely narcissistic person who explosively questioned: "Why should I be concerned with posterity? What has posterity ever done for me?"

These egocentric questions arrogantly pose this final point. Unborn posterity has never done anything for us in the current generations or for our progenitors from the past. Nor can posterity do anything constructive until they are actually born and nurtured into maturity with loving care. Future posterity is undeniably dependent on how current generations responsibly handle the sacred gifts of life, the natural environment plus the hopes and aspirations passed on to them for a better world.

The expectations of this book are for shaping a better world tomorrow by advancing cultures of peace together with justice and nonviolent management of conflicts. The key ingredients are democratic processes, social ethics, humanitarian services, intercultural sensitivities, Divine guidance, science and economic justice in order to transmit sustainable peace with equity for the global thriving of future generations.

## Endnotes

[1] Risen J. and Lichtblau E., (Feb. 24, 2004), "C.I.A. Was Given Data on Hijacker Long Before 9/11," The New York Times.

[2] Gallagher N., (2002) "Nuclear Weapons and New Security Challenges," Shalom Papers, published by the Churches Center for Theology and Public Policy, Washington, D.C., Vol. 4, No. 1.

[3] Ibid.

[4] Bronner E., (Jan. 3, 2003), "Why Today's Europeans Object to America's Worldview," The New York Times.

[5] Kupchan C., (2002) The End of the American Era: U.S. Foreign Policy and the Geopolitics of the Twenty-first Century. New York: Alfred A. Knopf. Kupchan's book is a provocative analysis of contemporary developments understood in the context of history and cultures with an multi-disciplinary approach.

[6] Quoted from April, 1995 International Peace Update, newsletter of Women's International League for Peace and Freedom in UNESCO and a Culture of Peace: Promoting a Global Movement, UNESCO Publishers, Culture of Peace Series.

[7] The label of American War is used by Vietnamese people in referring to what Americans label as the Vietnamese

War. This insight was discovered while traveling to Vietnam in January, 2004, on a humanitarian project representing American Rotarians.

[8] Levinson D., (1986) The Seasons of Man's Life, Ballantine Books; Stein M., (1998) Transformation: Emergence of the Self, Texas A & M University Press.

[9] Glover J., (Feb. 5, 2003) "Can We Justify Killing the Children of Iraq?" The Guardian.

[10] Middents G., "For Better or for Worse? Intentional and Conscious Evolution," paper presented at the 15th World Congress of the Organization Development Institute, Kathmandu, Nepal, July, 1995.

[11] Dawkins R., (1976) The Selfish Gene, University of Oxford Press.

[12] Csikszentmihaly M., (1993) The Evolving Self: A Psychology for the Third Millennnium, New York: Harper Collins Publishers.

[13] Blackmore S., (2000) "The Power of Memes," Scientific American, October, 2000.

[14] Merry U., (1995) Coping with Uncertainty: Insights from the New Sciences of Chaos, Self-Organization, and Complexity, Westport, CT: Praeger.

[15] Bellah R.,(1991) The Good Society, New York: Vintage Books.

[16] Edinger E., (1984) The Creation of Consciousness, Toronto, CA: Inner City Books.

[17] Ornstein R., (1991) The Evolution of Consciousness, New York: Prentice-Hall Press.

[18] Ibid.

[19] Ibid.

[20] The author acknowledges limitations that models and metaphors inherently carry in the minds of readers. I am aware that mistakes are an important process in learning. Mistakes are made and will be made. As my educational philosophy holds, mistakes are encouraged when we are learning. Therefore, it is important to make our mistakes fast enough, learn from them, correct them and build of these improvements in order to shape better tomorrows. In the learning laboratory we should make all the mistakes that will be encountered in actual life decisions when it really counts.

[21] Schutz W., (1969) Joy, First Evergreen Black Cat Edition; (1989) Joy: 20 Years Later: Expanding Human Awareness, Ten Speed Press Schutz identified the dynamics of family and group formation with the sequential dynamics of inclusion, affection and control inter-generationally. As a continuation of family dynamics extended into tribes, similar dynamics occur depending upon the levels of trust vs. mistrust learned in the nuclear families.

[22] In western societies, the appropriate term is mafia relationships in which the godfather determined the destiny of members.

[23] Harris L., (2003) Civilization and Its Enemies: The Next Stage of History, New York: Free Press. Harris' propositions are not supported with empirical data like Huntington provides for his hypotheses for testing. There is a need for Harris to provide testable hypotheses, psychological theory and supportive empirical data to test his assertions for validity and verification. In addition, his theoretical propositions are in need of cross-cultural validation as most of his claims are relevant to western cultures without in-depth analysis of eastern cultures. Without further empirical support, his claims remain provocative theoretical statements that attempt to defend American capitalism and superpower status.

[24] Sacks J., (2003) The Dignity of Diversity: How to Avoid the Clash of Civilizations, United Kingdom.

[25] Harris, op.cit who quoted this insight from the Greek poet, Aeschylus.

[26] Huntington S., (1993) "The Clash of Civilizations," Foreign Affairs Vol. 72, No. 3, Summer 1993.

[27] Kennedy P., (1994) "Must It Be The Rest Against the West," Atlantic Monthly, Vol. 274, No. 6, December, 1994.

[28] Kaplan R., (1994) "The Coming Anarchy," Atlantic Monthly, Vol. 273, No. 2, February, 1994.

[29] Fukuyama F., (1992) The End of History and the Last Man, New York: Free Press.

[30] Friedman T., (1999) The Lexus and the Olive Tree, New York: Farrar, Straus and Giroux.

[31] These fault lines were introduced in Chapter Four.

[32] Kupchan, op.cit.

[33] Geyer A., (1997) Ideology in America, Louisville KY: Westminster John Knox Press.

[34] Goodman E., (Feb. 3, 2004) "Echoes of Vietnam," Boston Globe, quotes Henry Stimson, Secretary of Defense during World War II in the Franklin Roosevelt and Harry Truman administrations when he was asked "How do you bring peace to the world?" Stimson replied: "You begin by bringing to Washington a small handful of men who believe that the achievement of peace is possible. You work them to the bone until they no longer believe it is possible. And then you throw them out – and you bring in a new bunch that believe it is possible."

[35] Harris, op.cit.

[36] Sacks J., op.cit. Sacks also includes chapters on "Conservation," "Creativity," and "Cooperation" in his perceptive prescriptions for harmony, justice and peace.

[37] Many religious organizations have educational, social service, humanitarian, medical and volunteers programs with information on their websites about opportunities in global activities.

[38] In January, 2004, Rotary volunteers from India and the United States including myself were involved in a "final push" to eradicate polio from a resistant pocket in North India. As volunteers, we inoculated over 30,000,000 children under five years of age with oral polio vaccine plus three other childhood diseases. Additional Rotary volunteers inoculated children in nations of Central Africa in Feb. 2004 for this final assault on polio.

[39] Additional information, qualifications and applications for becoming Peace Scholars can be obtained at the website for Rotary Foundation: www.rotary.org

[40] Adelson R., (2003) "Conquering Fear," Monitor in Psychology, Vol. 34, No. 11, based upon research by Steve Marin, Mark Bard, Gregory Quirk, Michael Davis, Mitchell Schare, and Edna Foe whose research studies are reported in the Journal of Experimental Psychology: Animal Behavior Processes, Vol. 29, No. 4, October, 2003.

[41] Latif Asad, (Jan. 16, 2004) "America, Too, Will Grow Old One day," The Straits Times.

[42] Hebrews 12: 14, (1989) The Holy Bible: New Revised Standard Version, Iowa Falls: World Publishing.

[43] Middents G., (2001) The Crisis in Violence and Peace, Manipal Press.

[44] Quote from UNESCO and a Culture of Peace: Promoting a Global Movement, UNESCO Publishing, Cultures of Peace Series.